THE STORY OF AMERICAN GOLF

VOLUME ONE 1888-1941

THE CALLAWAY GOLFER

CALLAWAY EDITIONS

64 Bedford Street New York, NY 10014

Printed in Hong Kong by Palace Press International

First Edition

10 9 8 7 6 5 4 3 2 1

Library of Congress Catalog Card Information Available

ISBN 0-935112-52-9

A Note on the Type: The text is set in Hoefler Text, designed by Jonathan Hoefler from the Hoefler Type Foundry.
Cover titling and the sans serif through the book is Griffith Gothic, a revival of C. H. Griffith's 1937 Bell Gothic
Mergenthaler original, redrawn by Tobias Frere-Jones in 1997. Chapter titles are set in Ziggurat,
designed by Jonathan Hoefler.

Editor-in-Chief: Nicholas Callaway   Editor, The Callaway Golfer: Edward Brash
Associate Publisher: Paula Litzky   Director of Production: True Sims
Art Director & Designer: Jennifer Wagner   Assistant Editor: Christopher Steighner
Art and Research Assistants: Marlene Goeke, Alston Neal

Also available from The Callaway Golfer:

Breaking 90 with Johnny Miller
Golf Rules Illustrated

Visit Callaway Editions at www.Callaway.com

THE STORY OF AMERICAN GOLF

VOLUME ONE 1888-1941

HERBERT WARREN WIND

CALLAWAY EDITIONS

New York
2000

PART ONE

SOWING THE SEEDS 1888-1913

PART TWO

THE DILIGENT DECADE 1913-1923

PART THREE

THE AGE OF BOBBY JONES 1923-1930

PART FOUR

THE CHANGING OF THE GUARD 1930-1941

FOREWORD

After serving with the Army Air Corps in China during World War II and with General MacArthur's Occupation Army in Japan for a year, Herbert Warren Wind settled in New York City toward the end of 1946. He wanted to make his living as a writer—ideally a writer for *The New Yorker*, which was then a classy, humorous, literary magazine with a liberal social conscience.

Herb had the good fortune to meet Amy Loveman, a doyenne of the New York literary scene and one of the selectors for the Book of the Month Club. They agreed that the best move for his career would be to write a book. *The New Yorker* already had a golf writer, a Harvard man, who was planning to retire to California to grow lettuces and tomatoes but who was, perhaps understandably, procrastinating. Herb wanted to write about sports and he knew much more about golf than any other sport. He felt that a complete history of golf in America was needed and would be welcome. Amy told him to prepare a three- or four-page outline of his idea and to submit it to the publisher Farrar, Strauss and Company. Herb's proposal was accepted, and he was paid the princely advance of $350.

No one has ever researched a golf book, or possibly any sports book, as thoroughly and meticulously as Herb did *The Story of American Golf*. He uncovered layers of golfing incidents, trends, and personalities that no one had paid attention to. He, more than anyone, grasped how profoundly British golf had shaped the game in America.

During his research, Herb was unable to find any detailed description of the famous play-off for the 1913 United States Open championship between the twenty-year-old American amateur and former

caddie Francis Ouimet and the two great English professional champions Ted Ray and Harry Vardon. This was, historically speaking, the most important 18-hole match in the history of American golf, and Herb wanted to present it in full detail. He called Francis Ouimet who suggested that they meet at The Country Club in Brookline, Massachusetts, and walk the 18 holes over which the match had been contested. When Herb arrived, Francis asked, "Did you bring a notebook and pencils?" Francis remembered not only every shot he had hit and every putt, but also everything that Ray and Vardon had done. He was able to show Herb the exact position of all three balls during each hole of the play-off, and he described as well his state of mind. In the hands of as fine a writer as Herb, Ouimet's reconstruction allowed him to report the event as if he had been an eyewitness to it. Herb drops the reader right into the midst of the action, the muddy ground, the mist, the swirling crowds.

Just before completing *The Story of American Golf*, during the early part of 1948, William Shawn, the editor of *The New Yorker*, offered Herb a job. In the Idea Department. Herb would feed ideas to those writing short pieces for "The Talk of the Town" section that opened the magazine. By 1950, Herb was a staff writer doing "Profiles", a particular *New Yorker* invention—extended biographical essays on subjects who would be unfamiliar to most of its readers. Herb's first contribution to "Profiles", in 1951, was on the prolific golf-course designer Robert Trent Jones.

When Herb was approached with the idea of bringing out *The Story of American Golf* in a new edition, he said, "I hope they do it in two volumes." And so they are. The first volume covers the origins of golf in Scotland, its beginnings in America, and follows the game to the beginning of World War II. Both volumes will be newly illustrated. Great ingenuity and research has gone into the development of a succession of photographs and illustrations that not only complement what is discussed in the text but also convey the atmosphere and spirit of golf at the time.

As you would expect, not a single word has been changed.

—ROBERT S. MACDONALD, FOUNDER OF *THE CLASSICS OF GOLF* AND PUBLISHER OF *FLAGSTICK BOOKS*

PART ONE
SOWING THE SEEDS

Sowing
The Seeds

1888—1913

The Apple Tree Gang

TODAY, just about wherever you travel, golf courses with their green fairways, greener greens, and pristine white bunkers have become an intrinsic part of the face of America. The game has also penetrated deep into the American consciousness. Nearly fourteen million people, from every class of society, now play at least a couple of rounds a year. Most Saturdays and Sundays, from January to October, one or another of our national television networks carries that week's professional tournament, a segment of the series of tournaments that fills up almost the entire year and is currently close to the ten-million-dol-

lar mark in total prize money. Attendance at the big, well-established events has reached the point where tickets for the Masters, which takes place in April, are completely sold out months before, and where the United States Open, which takes place in June, must annually set a limitation on attendance, depending on the maximum number of daily spectators that each particular course can comfortably accommodate. Presently there are over seven thousand registered professionals in our country—and about sixty thousand unregistered pros, the fellows you run into at every club who, if you will just ripple through a few swings for them, will be delighted to tell you what you are doing wrong, gratis.

This rampant golf-consciousness is rather remarkable, considering that the game has been played in our country for less than a hundred years. While the first permanent Canadian golf club celebrated its centennial in 1973, the first permanent American club, St. Andrew's, in Ardsley, New York, will not reach that milestone until 1988, which is still quite a few years away. In 1888 the United States was, generally speaking, a sports-minded nation, but not to the extent it was to become later. The big game was baseball, which, in mid-century, had evolved from a number of regional variations into a standardized national pastime. The first professional league, the National League, was established in 1876, and all America followed it with tremendous interest. It would be decades before there would be another professional team sport to challenge baseball's monopoly of the public's devotion. There was professional horse racing, of course—the Travers Stakes at Saratoga was first run in 1864 and the Kentucky Derby in 1875—but that was not the same thing. Neither was professional boxing, though it should be noted that when one of the big heavyweight fights was looming, people talked of little else for weeks and weeks. The adoption of the Marquis of Queensberry rules, which supplanted bare-knuckles fisticuffs in 1885, had something to do with boxing's increased popularity, as did the arrival of John L. Sullivan of North Abington, Massachusetts, as world heavyweight champion (and last of the bare-knuckles champions) in 1882.

What else was there? Well, among the amateur sports, college football was at the top. It had been since 1869, when it was introduced in rudimentary form by Princeton and Rutgers. There was some sailing, but the America's Cup involved a comparatively small section of the country. There was some tennis, the national championships having been instituted at the Newport Casino in 1881. Basketball wasn't invented until 1891, when Dr. James Naismith had the janitor nail up that historic pair of peach baskets in the gymnasium at Springfield College. Some running and jumping competitions existed, but enthusiasm for track and field sports was laggard until the first modern Olympic Games were organized in 1896 by Baron Pierre de Cou-

The Clubhouse of The Apple Tree Gang" 1888

AN APPLE TREE IN AN ORCHARD IN YONKERS, NEW YORK, ABOVE, MARKS THE SPOT WHERE JOHN REID AND OTHER MEMBERS OF THE ST. ANDREW'S GOLF CLUB PLAYED THEIR GOLF IN 1892. REID ACTUALLY FOUNDED ST. ANDREW'S, THE FIRST PERMANENT GOLF CLUB IN THE UNITED STATES, IN NOVEMBER 1888.

bertin. If golf caught on rapidly in America, it was partially because there was room for another new game and partially because it was such a good game.

Golf started off with a great advantage over many other sports: you did not have to be a young, fast, beautifully coordinated athlete to play it acceptably. As a result, it found ready converts among the two sexes and people of all ages. They soon discovered that once golf gets you in its grip, it never lets you go. On the one hand, there was Andrew Carnegie declaring thoughtfully that golf was "an indispensable adjunct of high civilization," and, on the other, there was the story of the Scotsman who threw his clubs into the ocean after a

bad round and nearly drowned trying to rescue them. Both statements added up to about the same thing.

In 1888 there was no Ouimet, Hagen, Sarazen, Jones, Nelson, Snead, Hogan, Palmer, Nicklaus, or Trevino, but the game had been played in Scotland for many centuries and had from the beginning produced many attractive and skillful players. Looking back from today's perspective, perhaps the greatest of the early golfers was Young Tom Morris, the son of Old Tom, who had won the second, third, fifth, and eighth British Opens in 1861, 1862, 1864, and 1867. Young Tom also won the British Open four times—in 1868, 1869, 1870, and then, after a one-year hiatus in which no

Scottish seaside courses called links, where the first golf champions played, were characterized by sandy terrain. Both sand and champion are present in the 1890s photograph, opposite, of Prestwick's celebrated course. Old Tom Morris, a four-time British Open winner, is the bearded figure highest up the dune watching a player's attempt to escape a sandy lie.

championship was held, again in 1872. He would have undoubtedly gone on to win it many more times, but he died in 1875 of heartbreak soon after the death of his wife and their newborn child. He was only twenty-four at the time.

Young Tom's finest achievement took place in the 1870 Open, which was held at Prestwick, on the west coast of Scotland, as were all the early Opens. Prestwick was then a twelve-hole course, and each entrant played three rounds. Young Tom's total

26.—TOM MORRIS, JNR.

for the thirty-six holes was 149, the equivalent of a 74 and a 75. An idea of how amazing a performance this was can be gained from the fact that no one had previously scored below 160 in the championship. Young Tom's 149, for that matter, was never beaten or even approached through 1891, after which the championship was changed to a 72-hole event. Undoubtedly the most effective way to bring out the quality of Young Tom's golf in the 1870 Open is to chart his progress hole by hole:

HOLE	LENGTH	1ST ROUND	2ND ROUND	3RD ROUND
1	578 YARDS, 1 FOOT, 9 INCHES	3	5	5
2	385 YARDS	5	5	5
3	167 YARDS, 7 INCHES	3	2	3
4	448 YARDS, 2 FEET, 5 INCHES	5	5	7
5	440 YARDS, 1 FOOT, 4 INCHES	6	6	4
6	314 YARDS, 1 FOOT, 9 INCHES	3	5	5
7	144 YARDS, 1 FOOT, 7 INCHES	3	3	3
8	166 YARDS, 4 INCHES	3	4	3
9	395 YARDS, 1 FOOT	4	5	5
10	213 YARDS, 1 FOOT, 2 INCHES	3	3	4
11	132 YARDS	4	4	3
12	417 YARDS, 2 FEET, 1 INCH	5	4	4
		47	51	51

It is not going too far to say that Young Tom Morris' three rounds in the 1870 British Open, made with the old gutta-percha ball, were the first glimmer of modern golf, the game we know today. (Imagine a 35 for the first nine way back then!) Young Tom's scoring in an important competition certainly bears comparison with the celebrated 36-hole bursts of later years, such as Bobby Jones' 66-68—134 at Sunningdale in 1926, Gene Sarazen's 70-66—136 at Fresh Meadow in 1932, Ben Hogan's 71-67—138 at Oakland Hills in 1951, Cary Middlecoff's 68-68—136 at Inverness in 1957 (which didn't win for him), Mickey Wright's 69-72—141 at Baltusrol in 1961, Arnold Palmer's 67-69—136 at Troon in 1962, and Jack Nicklaus' 66-68—134 at St. Andrews in 1964 (which didn't win for him either).

17.—THE TEE SHOT.

Over the last hundred years, golf has changed in many ways. It is difficult to picture Bernard Darwin careening down a fairway at the wheel of a golf cart, or Walter Travis fluffing out the sleeves of an alpaca sweater, or Harry Vardon in the press tent patiently running down his round hole by hole ("On the fifth, driver, brassie, two putts. On the sixth, drive, brassie to four feet, one putt for the birdie . . ."), but, essentially, golf has remained the same strange, elusive, maddening, beckoning, wonderful game it has always been.

Considering that it has been a part of the American scene for less than ninety years, golf's expansion has been incredible. In 1888 there were less than a dozen golfers in this country. Today, as we noted, there are over fourteen million. To take care of this multitude, there are more than eleven thousand courses, a major part of a capital investment that now surpasses $3,500,000,000. Each year, by the way, American golfers spend close to half a billion dollars for golf balls, clubs, shoes, gloves, bags, tees, hats, and what have you. The number of American golfers expert enough to play in the national tournaments is rather astounding too. In 1971, a record-breaking year, 2,329 golfers entered the United States Amateur Championship, 4,174 entered the United States Public Links Championship, and 4,279 entered the United States Open Championship—quite a jump from the combined total of 43 who entered the first official Amateur and Open. The course laid out by John Reid, "the father of American golf," consisted of three abbreviated holes in a cow pasture. American golfers today miss their first shots cold and hit their practice shots unerringly on courses where the turf has been scientifically bred for the 3-wood and the putter, the holes designed and redesigned to punish the weekend golfer and the professional in correct proportion. Some of our modern golf

courses have been blasted from the wild forest and pushed through swamplands and, occasionally, dredged from the sea. There are courses that stretch to 7,400 yards and courses where each par 3 is built in duplicate to alleviate the Sunday driving. The clubhouses at these layouts are a far cry from the tent that served John Reid and his cronies as their headquarters. A good number of the contemporary clubhouses have cost over half a million dollars, and they offer all the accommodations of a metropolitan hotel, and sometimes the unreal stare of a Euro-pean castle transported half-timber by half-timber across the Atlantic.

Every year more and more young Americans set their sights on making golf their profession. It is easy to understand. Today a successful tournament golfer can make over $300,000 a year in prize money alone. If a pro who wins a major title is moderately photogenic and articulate, he can scoop up, additionally, several hundred thousand dollars in advertising sorties and related ventures. He can retire to a spreading ranch in Texas, like Byron Nelson, with

A MILD FEBRUARY 22, 1888 SAW ONE OF THE EARLIEST ROUNDS OF GOLF PLAYED IN THE UNITED STATES. JOHN REID, SHOWN LEANING ON HIS CLUB AT RIGHT, ABOVE, IMPROVISED A THREE-HOLE LAYOUT OVER A FIELD THAT SERVED AS HIS COW PASTURE. REID, HIS OPPONENT THAT DAY, JOHN B. UPHAM, AND THREE OTHER MEN, LATER FORMED THE ST. ANDREW'S GOLF CLUB.

periodic returns to the outside world to serve as an announcer on national telecasts; he can, like those two other Texans, Jimmy Demaret and Jack Burke, Jr., establish the Champions Golf Club outside Houston and develop it into one of the region's finest golf plants; or like still another Texan, Ben Hogan, he can manufacture his own line of golf clubs and golf balls. It is impossible, of course, to keep up with Arnold Palmer's and Jack Nicklaus' myriad global activities, they are so farflung and diverse.

American attitudes toward golf have changed as America has changed, but the game itself has remained fundamentally the same frappé of pleasure and pain it was for Reid and his Apple Tree Gang, and for the Scots and the English before them.

There is a fascination in golf that every player at one time or another has tried to define, but no one as yet has been able to put his finger on. He and the fourteen million other American golfers, all of whom have given up the game at one time or another, will be out on the fairways the next sunny afternoon, cheerfully enslaved again. There is apparently no release. Of course, someday, shortly after everyone knows what the Mona Lisa and Sphinx are thinking about, golf's secret will out and the Man-on-the-Tee will understand perfectly why golf has become the most successful game in the world.

John Reid, the father of American golf, was a transplanted Scot who lived in Yonkers, New York. As a young man, Reid

had emigrated from Dunfermline at about the same time as his fellow-townsman, Andrew Carnegie. While Reid had carved no empire for himself in America, he had risen to a top executive position with the J. L. Mott Iron Works in Mott Haven and by 1880 had attained that degree of prosperity which allows a man to devote a good share of his energy to his recreation.

At first John Reid was content to pass his weekends away from the plant hunting and shooting. In a nation of good shots he stood out as a very good shot, and yet field sports left Reid curiously dissatisfied. As a boy in Scotland he had observed the first big boom of the cult of games, and though he had not then had the time to take up golf, rackets, or cricket, Reid was a games-player at heart. In Yonkers he first tried his hand at tennis, converting a part of his front lawn into a court where his friends could gather on weekends and on which he could unleash some of that tremendous vitality exclusive to self-made men. A few years after this, Reid and his friends decided there was everything to be gained in importing the equipment for golf, a game that was winning an amazing number of converts in England and was, as Reid reminded himself, certain to be a remarkable sport since it was a Scottish sport. Robert Lockhart, another lad from Dun-

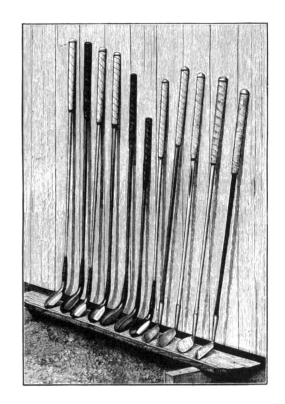

fermline who had made good in the new country, was returning to Britain in 1887 on a business trip, and Reid asked him to purchase a good set of golf clubs and some golf balls for him.

Lockhart did not spare himself in executing his commission properly. To make sure he got the best, he went to St. Andrews, the old gray town by the North Sea revered as the cradle of the game. There, in the shop of Old Tom Morris, the most celebrated professional of the day, Lockhart purchased two dozen gutta-percha balls and a set of clubs: three woods—

IN THE LATE NINETEENTH CENTURY, GOLF CLUBS WERE HICKORY-SHAFTED LIKE THE WOODS AND IRONS SHOWN IN THE ILLUSTRATION ABOVE, FROM HORACE HUTCHINSON'S 1890 VOLUME ON GOLF. CLUBS WERE MADE BY PROFESSIONALS LIKE OLD TOM MORRIS OF ST. ANDREWS, SCOTLAND, SHOWN IN THE PASSENGER SEAT OF THE TOWN'S FIRST MOTOR CAR, OPPOSITE.

driver, brassie, and spoon; three irons— cleek, sand-iron, and putter. He arranged for the box to be shipped to his home in New York and went on his way, quite unmindful that his morning had been in the least historic or that the box from St. Andrews, in the minds of millions of Americans in later years, would be esteemed the surest antitoxin ever devised by man to combat the evils set loose from an earlier box, Pandora's.

When the clubs and balls arrived in New York, Lockhart tried them out on an open stretch near Seventy-second Street and the Hudson and, finding nothing amiss, turned them over to his friend Reid.

Washington's Birthday, 1888, was a wondrously mild day. Reid had originally planned to wait until late March or April before trying the clubs himself, but that twenty-second of February was the kind of a day that makes a man want to hurry the spring, and John Reid could wait no longer. He got in touch with his old sports crowd, and buoyed with the sense of adventure, they crossed to the field that Reid used as his cow pasture. Three short holes each about a hundred yards long were laid out over the hilly ground, and "cups" were scooped out of the earth with the head of a cleek. There weren't enough clubs for everyone to play, so John B. Upham was selected to oppose Reid in this, the first game of golf

to be played by the men who later formed the St. Andrew's Golf Club, the first permanent golf club in the United States. No scores were kept that morning, fortunately, and the two players and the spectators were in full agreement that golf was great fun, a game with a very bright future. Scotland could well be proud of itself.

Immediately following this first exhibition, other sets of clubs were ordered by the members of Reid's circle. Future rounds, however, had to be delayed for a while, for winter returned in earnest: on the twelfth of March the most severe blizzard in the history of New York paralyzed the entire area. When warm weather finally came, the men, dressed in old derbies or slouch hats and their loosest-fitting jackets, drove the cows off their three holes and played their rude version of golf. In April they decided they needed a larger course and moved to a cow pasture at the northeast corner of Broadway and Shonnard Place, an expanse of some thirty acres owned by the local butcher. Here they proceeded to lay out six rough holes.

This new course, apart from the increased length of the holes, was hardly closer to the standards of the Scottish links than the original three-hole field. The greens were circles about twelve feet in diameter, slightly less bumpy than the rest of the turf, and responded with equal infidelity to the putter or the midiron. But Reid, Upham, and the other regulars— Harry Holbrook, Kingman, H. Putnam, and haberdashing young Henry Tallmadge—were entirely pleased with their new home. The pioneers played through the heat of summer, supported by the first 19th hole, an improvised table presided over by a servant of Reid's who handled the ice and water.

The St. Andrew's Golf Club was officially founded at a dinner at John Reid's house on November 14, 1888, sort of an informal celebration of the golf group's successful first year. With dinner out of the way, the ebullient Reid, with little coaxing, rose and cut loose with his renowned rendition of *Scots Wa Hae* and other Scottish ballads. Then he got down to business. The real purpose of this dinner, he reminded his friends, was to devise the best ways and means for continuing their enjoyable outings on the golf course. Reid felt that it was time now to set up some form of organization—not that there was anything wrong with the informal way they had gone about things in 1888, but there were undeniable advantages to an organization. For one thing, expenses were bound to be higher the coming year, and a club could handle financial matters much more effectively than men acting as individuals. For another thing, it probably would not be long before other members of the community would want to join them, and there again they needed the machinery of a club. The four regulars present—Messrs. Upham, Holbrook, Putnam, and Tallmadge—did not have to be sold. They were all for founding a club, and moved to get on with the election of officers. Reid was unan-

imously elected president, Upham was elected secretary-treasurer, and the other three original members were to make up the board of governors of the St. Andrew's Golf Club. That was the name they all wanted. St. Andrews in Scotland had been the cradle of golf, and who knew, perhaps this new St. Andrew's would assume the same role on the American continent? Robert Lockhart, the man who had made all this possible, was named the first active member of the St. Andrew's Golf Club. A few toasts in that other great importation from Scotland, and the first meeting of the St. Andrew's Golf Club was adjourned. The men walked to their homes with the good glow that they had accomplished a lot that evening—and they had.

The next few seasons of the first American golf club were relatively uneventful. In March 1889, in the first mixed-foursome played on the six-hole course, John Reid and Miss Carrie Low defeated the team of Mrs. Reid and Henry Upham in a very close match. The membership rose to thirteen. Occasionally one of the group would suggest that the six-hole course was becoming too confining and that the club should find a larger piece of land. No action, however, was taken in this direction, and the expansion might have been delayed a few more years had the City of Yonkers not decided to extend Palisade Avenue farther north, right through the heart of the course. So once again, in April 1892, the players gathered their clubs and the tent that

THE ST. ANDREW'S GOLF CLUB MOVED TO ITS FINAL LOCATION AT MT. HOPE (IN HASTINGS-ON-HUDSON), NEW YORK, IN 1897, WHEN THIS PHOTOGRAPH WAS TAKEN. HORSE-DRAWN CARRIAGES BROUGHT NEW YORK CITY GOLFERS FROM THE NEARBY TRAIN STATION TO A SHINGLE CLUBHOUSE THAT HAS BEEN IN CONTINUAL USE SINCE THEN.

served as a clubhouse and headed north. This time they settled on an apple orchard on the Weston estate, about a quarter of a mile up the road from their old course. They spent a happy day exploring the thirty-four acres of their new home and laying out six holes amidst the apple trees. The tent was pitched beside the land marked for the first tee, and the superb apple tree bending low behind the home green became the new 19th hole. During shirtsleeve weather, the players tossed their coats into the crotch of the tree, and a basket of sandwiches and a wicker decanter were hung on a low bough. Life was pleasant in the shade of the old apple tree.

The Apple Tree Gang, as the golfers of Yonkers were now called, and much to their delight, were more than willing to overlook the fact that the orchard's unique hazards were developing a breed of golfers who played two-thirds of their shots with the niblick or the lofter. When seven new members were admitted, however, the first serious rift within the club was precipitated. Now, when a simple majority of the members were out playing, the six holes were acutely overcrowded. A number of the younger men, such as Harry Tallmadge, were all for moving to a larger tract. The conservatives, older members like Reid, were staunchly in opposition. As they saw it,

the primary purpose of the club was to promote good fellowship and there was the danger of losing this if St. Andrew's expanded. The younger members argued that the apple orchard was hardly a golf course in comparison with the nine holes Newport had built or the fine seaside course that Willie Dunn had laid out for the Shinnecock Hills Golf Club on Long Island. Shinnecock had seventy-five members and a wonderful clubhouse designed by Stanford White—they were doing things right down there. St. Andrew's had been started well before those clubs, the expansionists continued, and their club should have been *the* leader in the growth of golf rather than an also-ran. Now take Chicago—way out there in the West. Already there were two eighteen-hole courses on the outskirts of that city, and judging from the number of prominent Chicagoans who were joining the clubs, good golf and good fellowship hadn't proved to be incompatible.

It took time but gradually the sincerity of the younger element wore down all opposition to their campaign for an up-to-date course. St. Andrew's was on the move again, for the third time in six years. A committee selected to study possible sites for a new course reported that an ideal one had been found in the Odell Farm at Grey

THE PAINTING ABOVE SHOWS JOHN REID IN THE GOLFING ATTIRE FAVORED BY ST. ANDREW'S MEMBERS.

Oaks, three miles north on the Sawmill River Road. Nine holes, of respectable length, were laid out over the sharply rising ground. It took two or three days before this layout was completed, but, as Harry Tallmadge commented, it was worth all the trouble. On May 11, 1894, the St. Andrew's Club, twenty strong, the conservatives as jubilant as the youngsters, moved to their new course at Grey Oaks and went to work transforming the Odell farmhouse into their first real clubhouse and locker room.

The cradle of American golf had proved to be a very portable one. Some three years later, in August 1897, the St. Andrew's Golf Club moved again, this time to its present location at Mt. Hope, where there was room for eighteen good holes. However, it was during the years the club was situated at Grey Oaks that St. Andrew's found itself. The membership began to climb rapidly. The new course was nicely accessible by train from New York, and up from the city came the tired businessmen seeking relaxation along with gentlemen-sportsmen eager for a new merit badge. Andrew Carnegie joined the club and Sir Arthur Conan Doyle was a frequent visitor. St. Andrew's guarded itself against becoming too social by barring ladies from membership, but it did succumb to the fad for fancy clothes promoted by Shinnecock Hills and Newport. In addition to the required red coat with brass buttons, the well-dressed St. Andrew's man wore a blue checked cap, a winged collar, a blue checked waistcoat, gray knickers, plaid stockings, and gray gaiters.

What is more to the credit of its members, the club became a forerunner in the spread of golf. The first United States Amateur Championship at match play was held at Grey Oaks in 1894, and St. Andrew's players participated in the first team match between American golf clubs. St. Andrew's was instrumental in the formation of the United States Golf Association, and in arranging the American tour of Willie Park, Jr., the famous British Open Champion, who incidentally took the Grey Oaks course apart with a brilliant 81, although handicapped by a giant boil on his neck.

John Reid stepped down from the presidency after nine years, but he remained the leader of the descendants of the Apple Tree Gang and a vigorous force for many years in American golf. He was extremely pleased when his son John, a student at Yale, won the Intercollegiate Golf Championship in 1898. He was not so pleased when another son, Archie, was defeated one year in the United States Amateur. Reid read about this in the morning paper at breakfast, and said gruffly to his wife, "I see where your son has lost a golf match."

Before and After
St. Andrew's

SOME four-hundred-odd years before John Reid's gang invaded their first cow pasture, golf was a flourishing game in Scotland, and in the minds of not a few historians, most of them of Dutch extraction, a flourishing game in The Netherlands as well. The age-old controversy as to who originated the game of golf, the Scots or the Dutch, has never been settled to the complete satisfaction of the contending parties, and there are some antiquarians who propose that both nations climbed aboard a bandwagon that had been rolling for centuries. The difficulty in establishing once

and for all the birthplace of golf arises from the fact that striking a ball with a stick toward a certain object is a very natural movement, notwithstanding the impression to the contrary one receives on Saturday afternoons watching his brethren coiling and uncoiling off the first tee. No one has ever tried to pin down the person who first writhed to a drumbeat and became the world's first dancer, and yet striking a ball with a club is an action hardly more involved than moving one's body to a certain rhythm.

If you follow the theories of the romantic historians, then the first golfer was a shepherd—place him on a hillside in Greece, Palestine, or Scotland, as suits your taste—who was bored with his work. He started to swing his crook at stones, just to give himself something to do, and then, purely by accident, one of the stones disappeared into a hole and a strange tingling sensation raced up and down the shepherd's spine. He tried hitting a few more stones as close to the hole as he could, and when he had mastered the shot, called over to a colleague and invited him to match his skill at the sport. They became the first twosome and had the right-of-way all over the hillside.

Even when we step from legend into recorded history, it is difficult to fix upon the first emergence of the sport because of the number of ancient games that bear some resemblance to golf. The Romans at the time of Caesar, for example, went in for the game of *paganica,* in which the opposing teams, armed with club-shaped branches, tried to bat a feather-stuffed ball against their rival's goal, a post planted several hundred yards down the street from the one they were defending. A few centuries later the French *seigneurs* were going in strong for a less shinny-like game called *jeu de mail.* The courses this time were the old national highways with their borders of heavy hedges, and the players swung at peach-sized spheres carved from boxwood with clubs shaped like croquet mallets. The goal was a raised pole down the highway. Bypassing such other stick-and-ball games as *chole* and *cambuco*, the trail then leads to Holland, and it is here that the mystery of the origins of the game begins in earnest.

The scholars who favor Holland as the home of golf can make out a fairly provocative case. They can point out that in the middle of the fifteenth century the town of Naarden issued an ordinance forbidding the playing of a game called *het kolven* within the sacred precincts of the church. For pictorial proof that Dutchmen played a game called *kolf* on their frozen canals, they can refer to the illustrations in the *Book of Hours* (1500-1520) and to later Delft tiles depicting children and men preoccupied with a sport that looks very much like the real thing. These scholars find it harder to explain away *kolf's* development into an indoor game played on a hard floor

ALTHOUGH THE ORIGINS OF GOLF ARE UNKNOWN, THIS DETAIL FROM A 16TH CENTURY FLEMISH MISSAL SUGGESTS THAT A GOLF-LIKE GAME WAS PLAYED IN EUROPE DURING THE MIDDLE AGES.

THE ROYAL AND ANCIENT GOLF CLUB OF ST. ANDREWS, SCOTLAND, AS PERSONIFIED BY ITS STARTER AND
HIS PORTABLE HUT IN THIS 1905 PHOTOGRAPH, HAS BEEN CONSIDERED THE RULING BODY AND INTERNA-
TIONAL SHRINE OF THE GAME FOR CENTURIES. ITS SEASIDE COURSE HAS BEEN PLAYED OVER SINCE AT LEAST
THE 15TH CENTURY AND THE ROYAL AND ANCIENT CLUB ITSELF HAD ITS ORIGINS THERE IN 1754.

sixty feet long and twenty-five in width and bounded by walls two feet high which the player could employ as he saw fit in his efforts to hit wooden posts placed at each end of the court. John Tunis, one of the most recent writers to enter the fray, sides with the pro-Holland set. According to Tunis, there was no golf in Scotland until shortly after a Scottish vessel, the *Good Hope*, ran aground off the Zuider Zee. A number of the crew, who had been shaken up in the accident, spent the last days of convalescence playing *kolf* and were sufficiently intrigued to take home with them some clubs and balls. The iron egg-shaped ball used on the frozen canals could not be adapted to Scottish links, and a more suitable ball was arrived at by plucking a handful of feathers from the breast of a fowl and encasing them in leather. This is, very probably, a good explanation of the origin of the first feather golf ball, but is the earlier part of the story a bit too convenient? It's hard to know.

One thing is certain, though: the Scots were the first to play a game in which the player used an assortment of clubs to strike a ball into a hole dug in the earth. This is the essence of the game we know as golf. Impartial historians don't go as far as the Scot who laughed off the claims of the Dutch with the crack that *kolf* was no more golf than cricket was poker, but it is generally accepted that golf is the product of Scotland.

By 1457, when we meet the first recorded evidence of golf in Scotland, it is apparent that the game had already attracted a sizable following. In that year the Scottish Parliament decreed that *wapinschawingis be holden by the Lordis and Baronis spirituale and temporale, foure times in the yeir, and that the Fute-ball and Golfe be utterly cryit doune, and nocht usit.* This ban on golf was understandable, for the small highland kingdom had to maintain a stout defense against her enemies, and golf was luring the potential defenders away from their archery practice. Despite this ban and similar and stronger acts by Parliament in 1471 and 1491, the game had such a grip on the Scots that they continued to play it on their seaside linksland. Then, in the sixteenth century, the Church as well as the State began to make it rough for the addicts who played the game on the Sabbath. It was a very fortunate thing for golf and golfers that James VI of Scotland, who later became James I of England, appeared on the scene at that time. James had the golf bug very bad, and shortly after he mounted the throne, he let it be known that he was all for allowing golfers to play on Sundays as long as they had previously attended church. To take care of his own golfing needs, James appointed a Royal Clubmaker and, fifteen years later, to combat the high prices Dutch manufacturers were asking, he set up an official ballmaker and a ceiling of four shillings on balls.

While James I was the most actively sympathetic of the Stuarts, several other members of the house, probably because of their Scottish fiber, had a majestic weakness for the game. Mary Queen of Scots is supposed to have played golf a few days after Darnley's murder to exhibit her indifference to his fate; Charles I was in the middle of a round on the links of Leith when word came to him of the Irish Revolution; in 1681 the Duke of York, who later became James II, partnered himself with John Patersone, a poor shoemaker, in a big money match against two English noblemen at Blackheath, and Patersone won enough that day to build himself a new house. A wonderful family, the Stuarts! They made the game royal as well as ancient.

The focus of Scottish golf was St. Andrews. As early as Queen Elizabeth's day—indeed, as early as the twelfth century, according to some historians—there was a course on the stretch of duneland alongside St. Andrews Bay, although the Royal and Ancient Club was not officially inaugurated until 1754. A century or so later—in 1848 to be exact—the old town was a scene of the controversy that resulted in the first "foreign" expansion of the game. That was the year a few revolutionary sportsmen decided to introduce balls made of the juice of the gutta-percha tree. Allan Robertson, the fine golfer who owned St. Andrews' leading golf shop, declared himself dead set against this new ball. Golf had always been played with a feather ball, he maintained, and, besides, if this gutta-percha ball was adopted, it would ruin the men who owned golf shops. It took a measure of skill to pack and stitch a "feathery" and the ball was worth the half crown for which it sold, but no shopkeeper

could charge that much for a ball he molded from a glob of gum. Robertson personally bought and burned every "guttie" he could lay his hands on, and in his fight he had the cooperation of all the other golf craftsmen except one, Old Tom Morris, his own assistant. Tom was of the opinion that the guttie would give the game a big boost, not only because of the reduction it was bound to bring in the players' expenses but because it could be hit farther than the feathery and golfers would revel in the added distance. There was no patching up the feud that arose between Robertson and Morris; Old Tom went in business for himself and in time became the game's high priest. It wasn't long before the guttie established its marked superiority over the feather ball, and a new age of golf was ushered in. It was the new ball that swept the game triumphantly into England and started the boom that finally swept around the world.

Though St. Andrew's was without question the first golf club organized in the United States that really meant business, golf was played in America before its introduction in Yonkers. It might be well to touch all the bases, however lightly.

Once again the Dutch are on hand to complicate the picture. The first reference to what might have been golf appears in the minutes of the Court of Fort Orange and Beverwyck, a settlement of the New Netherlands that eventually became Albany. This court, in Ordinary Sessions in 1657, reprimanded and fined three Dutchmen who presumed to play *kolven* on ice one Sunday. Two years later the magistrates of Fort Orange and the village of Beverwyck issued a warning to all sportsmen that in the future anyone caught playing *kolven* in the streets would be subject to a fine of twenty-five florins. Both documents were written in Dutch, leaving ample room for argument as to the correct translation of *kolven*. Was it ice hockey or field hockey, was it golf or was it *kolven*? There are no further details to help us.

The next allusion to golf in America turns up in the issue of *Rivington's Royal Gazette* dated April 21, 1779, and this time the game referred to is golf, unmistakably. Rivington, the King's Printer in New York City, was a shopkeeper on the side who stocked sporting goods. On that day he ran

GREAT PLAYERS OF THEIR DAY—INCLUDING PROFESSIONALS ALLAN ROBERTSON, SECOND FROM LEFT, OPPOSITE, AND YOUNG TOM MORRIS, THIRD FROM LEFT—LINE UP FOR A GROUP PORTRAIT IN THE 1840S OR 1850S. THE EARLY PHOTOGRAPH MAY BE THE WORK OF EDINBURGH PHOTOGRAPHERS HILL AND ADAMSON. SHOWN ABOVE IS A MESH-PATTERNED GUTTA-PERCHA BALL AND THE FEATHER BALL, TOP, IT REPLACED.

Hugh Kirkaldy, a St. Andrews professional, contemplates a bunker shot on the Old Course in this 1890s photograph. Broad bunkers, stabilized with steep walls of sod or railway ties, are seen everywhere on the seaside courses that nurtured the game in the 19th century.

an advertisement in his paper to inform the public that he had a supply of the "veritable Caledonian balls." No one knows the response he received, but a few nostalgic Scots may have thought about it, anyway.

Two serious claimants to the honor of being the birthplace of golf in America are Savannah and Charleston. At the close of the eighteenth century a species of the game may or may not have been played in these prospering Southern ports, but in both communities golf clubs definitely existed. From 1788 on, the *Charleston City Gazette* carried the notices of the South Carolina Golf Club—in the main, reminders to the mem-

bers of club anniversaries. Some anniversary meetings were held on Charleston Green, where a putting green may have been maintained, but there is not so much as a word to indicate that golf was played, and none of the implements has been discovered. The purpose of the South Carolina Golf Club would appear to have been purely social, and the same would appear to have been true of the Savannah Golf Club. In addition to the notices of meetings that appeared in the *Georgia Gazette,* through the vigilance of the Johnston family, which has preserved the invitation, we know that in December 1811, "the honor of Miss Eliza Johnston's Company" was requested "to a Ball to be given by the Golf Club of this city." The outbreak of the War of 1812 may have put a damper on social activities, and, in any event, after this date, newspaper references to the Savannah and South Carolina Golf Clubs slowly began to die out.

In 1873 the Royal Montreal Golf Club, the first on this side of the Atlantic, was formed, and at about this time followthroughs began to ripple south of the border. These were the gyrations of Scottish settlers who had brought their baffies and gutties to the new world with them, the way Italians carried their violins and Frenchwomen their needles. In 1883, for example, Colonel J. Hamilton Gillespie, investigating the possibilities of a lumber business in Florida, used to relax after a hard day's work by hitting shots up and down what is now the main street of Sarasota. American boys who had learned the game while studying at English and Scottish universities occasionally carried their clubs back to the States with them, but like Gillespie and other would-be missionaries, none of them was successful in transmitting his enthusiasm for very long. The immune, then as now, ridiculed the idea of "hitting a ball with a stick and chasing after it," and after their supply of balls ran out, the young men's mashies became little more than souvenirs, like that photograph of the Tower of London and the old school blazer.

The Meadow Brook Hunt Club of Long Island had the opportunity of becoming the first American golf club presented to it on a silver platter, and muffed it. In 1887 Horace Hutchinson, the British Amateur Champion, was invited to give the members of Meadow Brook a demonstration of the game. They were bored by his shot-making, and even Hutchinson's great personal charm and eloquence cut no grass. There was for a period a vibrant golf colony at Foxburg, in western Pennsylvania, but it remained for Russell W. Montague, a New Englander, to come closest to setting up a permanent golf club that would have antedated St. Andrew's. Montague owned a summer place in Oakhurst, West Virginia, a few miles from the fashionable spa at White Sulphur Springs. In the summer of 1884, one of Montague's Scottish neighbors had as his guest a young man who had been an ardent golfer in the old country. Montague was not at all indifferent when the suggestion was made that they lay out a course on his property and see what the game had to offer. The group formed the Oakhurst Club and went as far as to hold tournaments on Christmas. Then, after a few seasons, the men lost interest. The course was allowed to grow over and Oakhurst became just another Roanoke colony of golf—like Sarasota and the unknown meadows farther inland where other transplanted Scots had practiced the game but had not continued it. St. Andrew's was different. The club endured.

Within a year after the founding of St. Andrew's, the exclusive colony of Tuxedo Park had built itself a course, and the pros and cons of organizing a club were being discussed at the pleasure patches of the wealthy along the eastern coast. (Across the Alleghenies, entirely isolated from this movement, what may have been the country's first nine-hole course was built about this time in Middlesborough, Kentucky, by English settlers pioneering the iron industry in that region.) The completion of what is generally regarded as the country's first nine-holer at Brenton's Point near Newport in 1890 stemmed from the enthusiasm of Theodore A. Havemeyer, better known to the readers of rotogravure sections as "The Sugar King." Havemeyer had been introduced to the game while wintering at the French resort of Pau, and a violent love affair was underway. From the beginning, Havemeyer was positive golf would be much more than a passing fad. Upon his return to America he talked the game incessantly, built the course at Brenton's Point, fanned the flickers of interest among the members of America's richest summer colony, and became the president of the Newport Golf Club and later of the Newport Country Club, capitalized for $150,000 by Havemeyer, Cornelius Vanderbilt, John Jacob Astor, Oliver Belmont, and other old Newport hands. In time golf almost completely replaced Havemeyer's earlier loves — his horses, his polo, his yachting.

In 1891 the United States for the first time had a golf course that looked like a golf course — Shinnecock Hills. This course was the work of Willie Dunn, a young Scottish professional who doubled as an architect. In 1889 Dunn was designing eighteen holes at Biarritz in France when he was approached by three gentlemen from Long Island, W. K. Vanderbilt, Edward S. Mead, and Duncan Cryder. They had heard a lot about this new game and wanted to see how a real professional played it. Dunn led them to the famous chasm hole, a pitch over a deep ravine to a green about 125 yards away. There he hit several crisp shots, all of them onto the green, some quite close to the hole. It was an impressive demonstration. Vanderbilt immediately remarked that this was, to his way of thinking, the kind of a game that would go in America, and arrangements were made whereby Dunn would come to Southampton and lay out a course for them, once his commitments in France were fulfilled. Dunn finally arrived in America in March 1891, and set to work almost at once transforming four thousand acres along Great Peconic Bay into a twelve-hole golf course. With a crew of 150 Indians from the nearby Shinnecock reservation and a few horse-drawn roadscrapers, Dunn cleared the fairways, removed the blueberry bushes from the rough, utilized the Indian burial mounds as obstacles before the greens or made them into sandtraps, cropped and manicured the sandy turf. By June, in spite of his unskilled help and crude implements, Willie Dunn had finished his job, and

Southampton had a seaside links of which it could be proud.

Vanderbilt was right. The Southampton set was fascinated by the game, and Shinnecock Hills, as the course was called, was given the full Long Island treatment. By September, forty-four men and women had purchased from one to ten shares in the club at $100 a share, and the club was formally incorporated. Stanford White, the renowned architect of the firm of McKim, Mead, and White, was given a free hand in designing a clubhouse. By the time White's clubhouse was opened the following summer, Shinnecock Hills' membership had burgeoned to seventy. The twelve-hole course was unable to accommodate all the players, and a nine-hole course for the women members was undertaken. Scarcely eighteen months after Willie Dunn had first surveyed the treeless stretch by the bay, the inner sanctum of Shinnecock Hills, the prosperity of its project assured, decided to limit membership to persons in the Southampton area whose social status was agreeable. Shinnecock Hills, in addition to being the first golf club on Long Island, the first in America to be incorporated, and the first to have a clubhouse, assured itself one further distinction: it was the first golf club to establish a waiting list. Perhaps, in the long run, Shinnecock lost out by emphasizing the social side of golf-club life, but in the Nineties, it was *the* course. Pilgrims came from far and wide to study the links, to admire the women hacking away with gusto on their own preserve, and to envy the men, restrained and resplendent in their bright red coats with monogrammed brass buttons.

Boston golf had a godmother. Until 1948, she was anonymous, identified only by the limerickish tag of "the young lady from Pau." Now we know that she was an American girl, Florence Boit, who returned to the States after a spell on the continent to spend the summer of 1892 with her aunt and uncle, the Arthur Hunnewells of Wellesley. Florence had picked up the game at Pau and, assuming that there would be several courses around Boston, brought her clubs with her. Her description of the game and front-lawn exhibitions aroused the curiosity of her uncle. Hunnewell's neighbors were his brother-in-law and his nephew, and by pooling their lawns, enough room was found for seven pitch-and-putt holes. Florence added the woman's touch by improvising flowerpots for the cups.

Again it is the same old story: the novices were quickly and entirely won over to the new sport. Laurence Curtis, one of the young men who had been invited to play at the Hunnewells', was so captivated by the game that he wrote a letter to the executive committee of The Country Club, in Brookline, recommending that golf be given a trial. Curtis estimated that a course could be built for no more than fifty dollars, and the executive committee promptly gave

THE EASTERN END OF LONG ISLAND, NEW YORK, SUPPLIED THE SEASIDE TERRAIN FOR ONE OF THE FIRST OUTSTANDING AMERICAN COURSES—SHINNECOCK HILLS, BUILT IN 1891. THE CLUB FEATURED A 12-HOLE COURSE DESIGNED BY SCOTTISH PRO WILLIE DUNN JR., A HANDSOME CLUBHOUSE BUILT BY THE PROMINENT ARCHITECT STANFORD WHITE, AND A SEPARATE 9-HOLE COURSE FOR WOMEN. SHINNECOCK HILLS IS CONSIDERED THE AMERICAN COURSE CLOSEST IN STYLE AND SPIRIT TO THE LINKS OF BRITAIN.

Curtis' suggestion the green light. The following March a six-hole course was constructed and formally opened by an exhibition by Curtis, Hunnewell, and G. E. Cabot. Hunnewell, the first to tee off, amazed himself by stroking his first shot smack into the cup some ninety yards away. The gallery of archery, shooting, and riding enthusiasts were not at all impressed. As they saw it, Mr. Hunnewell had done no more than he had set out to do. As a matter of fact, the archers, riders, and marksmen were rather let down when Hunnewell and the other golfers failed to supply further holes-in-one and went away very skeptical about the future of so imperfect a game.

But golf boomed at The Country Club and at the other early courses— Chevy Chase, Philadelphia, Richmond County, Essex County (Massachusetts), Essex County (New Jersey), Baltusrol, Apawamis, Montclair, Dyker Meadow, Baltimore, and many others. The "firsts" were nicely distributed. The Lake Champlain Hotel built the first hotel course. George Wright of Boston first played the game in a public park, and Van Cortlandt Park in New York was the first authentic public course. The Philadelphia Country Club, with characteristic gentility, was the first to use French-pea cans for holes. Tuxedo was host at the first match between teams representing different clubs, and a side from The Country Club played in the first international team match against Royal Montreal.

As for the first American to gain renown as a phenomenally long hitter, there was no challenging the record drive unleashed one winter's day by "Uncle Samuel" Parrish, the first secretary of Shinnecock Hills. As Parrish tells the story, "We were at the north end of Lake Agawam, Southampton, New York, looking south toward the ocean. There was a strong north wind blowing down the lake at the time, and, as I was able to steady myself on a patch of snow, the drive was a fair success, so that the ball went sailing down the lake until it struck the ice, and then kept on with but little diminution in its velocity. Had the ice and the wind held out, the ball would doubtless still be going, but it finally struck a snow bank on the shore of the lake and stopped. Morton then solemnly paced off the drive and reported its length to have been four hundred eighty-nine and a half yards, being very particular about the extra half yard. He then posted up in the clubhouse a statement to the effect that I, 'under favorable conditions' (no particulars being given) had made a drive of four hundred eighty-nine and a half yards. The result was that for a short time, until the facts became known, I enjoyed a tremendous reputation as a driver, my fame having penetrated to Boston, and I was the recipient of many congratulations."

C. B. Macdonald
Awakens the West

WHILE the oases of wealth in the East were still thinking in terms of six-, nine-, and twelve-hole courses in 1893, Chicago charged straight ahead and built the nation's first eighteen-hole course. The leaders of the new sport in the East were well aware that St. Andrews in Scotland, the game's recognized law-making body, had designated eighteen holes as comprising a round of golf, but certain doubts that the game had come to stay bothered the trustees of these golf clubs and made them wary of rapid expansion. The men in Chicago did not hesitate. Less than twelve months after the game was introduced in that eager metropolis of the Middle West, the members of the Chicago Golf Club, in Belmont, were playing over a full eighteen-hole layout, mighty pleased with themselves, too, at having outdistanced for once their smug cousins along the Atlantic who thought they did everything quicker, better, and on a larger scale than the boys in the backwoods.

Early golf in Chicago is the story of one man, Charles Blair Macdonald, who was recognized by all who knew him, and by Charles Blair Macdonald, as a most remarkable personality. There were only two ways to take Macdonald. Either you liked him intensely or you disliked him intensely. There was no middle ground. Endowed with a massive build and great strength, his natural self-reliance bolstered by a sizable personal fortune, stubborn, loyal, humorless, and intelligent, C. B. Macdonald swung his weight into every controversy American golf experienced until his death in 1928. To his admirers, "Old Charlie" was a genius whose mind never entertained error. In the eyes of his detractors, Macdonald's contributions were far outweighed by his marauding ego.

One reason why Charles Blair Macdonald made staunch enemies was the impression he forced on other men, used to leadership themselves and anxious to have a hand in the growth of golf, that he and he alone had been divinely appointed to supervise the spread of the game in America. They had to admit that the big man with the big mustache played the game very well, probably better than any other amateur in the country, but his attitude toward other people's golf upset them. Why did he insist on being such a stickler for the rules, and why did he hawk his adversaries to detect the slightest infraction of the St. Andrews code? This was America, not Scotland. Golf should be allowed to develop naturally in America, they believed, and if the personality of the game underwent moderate revisions in the new locale, it was a healthy sign. Macdonald's blind allegiance to the way he had been taught the game at St. Andrews was not going to help the sport to find roots in America.

Charlie Macdonald was an extremely articulate man, and through the years his words as well as his acts provided ample data for those who branded him the arch-reactionary. Whenever the growth of the game bred new regulations, Macdonald let it be known that golf had been far better off in the old days when the original thirteen rules and no others governed the play. Subsequent national, sectional, and local rules only made for unnecessary confusion and were superfluous if "the spirit of the game prevailed." He was against all moves for allowing balls to be wiped on muddy greens, against "preferred lies" under any conditions. Touching the ball with the hand was anathema to him. When the campaign to abolish the stymie was the topic of the day, Macdonald declared himself vigorously against a change that would "distinctly lower the morale of the game." He frowned upon four-ball matches as "a degradation" when this form of match threatened to displace the foursome, the type of competition in which partners on two-man teams play alternate shots and drive from alternate tees. "The best people in England and Scotland," he rebuked the upstarts, "adored the foursome." He was saddened when the old red coat, the badge of the golfer, was replaced by the odd-jacket and eventually by the sweater. Toward the end of his life, when golfers carried as many as twenty-five

A DYNAMO OF EGO, ENERGY, AND ENTERPRISE, CHICAGOAN CHARLIE MACDONALD ALMOST SINGLE-HANDEDLY POWERED THE RISE OF AMERICAN GOLF. HE WON THE AMATEUR CHAMPIONSHIP IN 1895, WAS A MEMBER OF THE SPORT'S FIRST GOVERNING BODY, AND, AT SOUTHAMPTON, NEW YORK, DESIGNED THE FIRST EXAMPLE OF GREAT COURSE ARCHITECTURE IN THE UNITED STATES—THE NATIONAL GOLF LINKS.

clubs in their bags, he played with only six, as a protest against the excess.

In locker-room arguments throughout the country over the evils and advantages of Charles Blair Macdonald, there were many golfers who sided with his efforts to keep a noble game noble, and there were some who contended that Macdonald was actually a great liberal. They would remind his critics that the Chicago Golf Club was the first to adopt the out-of-bounds rule, that Macdonald quickly endorsed the new rubber-cored ball, and that the National Golf Links he designed in Southampton revolutionized golf-course architecture in America. Old Charlie had merely stepped out of character on these occasions, his critics would rejoin. In each instance he had a purely selfish motive. The out-of-bounds at Chicago penalized only the hookers, and since Charlie sliced, the new rule simply afforded him a safer means of winning his matches. And his favoring the rubber-cored ball—why, Charlie was beginning to slow up then and needed the extra twenty yards the Haskell ball gave him over the gutta-percha. They could not attack the importance to American golf of the great course at Southampton, but they could insinuate that a reactionary motive had engineered this revolutionary construction. In building the National, Charlie Macdonald was out to show Americans what a first-rate British course looked like.

Macdonald's fans and foes could agree on one thing: the mold of the future

hero, or villain, was determined during his years as an impressionable college student in St. Andrews.

In July 1872, when Charles Macdonald was sixteen years old, his father, a prosperous Chicagoan, arranged for him to be educated at the United Colleges of St. Salvador and St. Leonard's in St. Andrews. The unhurried charm of the old town offered a sharp contrast to the Chicago the young man had left behind, a city still sagging from the Civil War and devastated by the great fire only nine months before his departure. The moment Charles saw St. Andrews he knew he would be happy there. The morning after his arrival, Charles was taken by his grandfather, a resident of the town and a member of the Royal and Ancient Golf Club, to the famous shop run by Old Tom Morris, where the boy was properly outfitted. Charles' grandfather also arranged for him to have a locker in Old Tom's shop, since juniors were not allowed inside the clubhouse of the Royal and Ancient. The first few times he played, Charles was not especially keen about the game, and then, suddenly, it got him. He could not stay off the links. On Sundays, when the course was supposedly closed, Charles and his friends would sneak onto some out-of-the-way hole where they had hidden their putters the evening before, and, safe from observation behind high bushy whins, they would putt back and forth all afternoon.

Charlie Macdonald developed into a fine golfer. He was good enough to play with Young Tom Morris, who had shattered the course record with a 77, and with Davy Strath, who fathered the famous bunker on the eleventh hole that in later years would cause the downfall of hundreds of ambitious invaders. During the long days of June and July, when the light holds until ten thirty or eleven in the evening, Charlie was able to get in several rounds a day and still have the time to practice and to talk golf with Old Tom in the shop. In Charlie's mind nothing in the world could compare to golf on St. Andrews. It wasn't just the links themselves, though they were peerless. It was the whole pervading flavor—the larks floating over the whins, the sailing boats in the Bay that you could see from the High Hole, the old red-brown and gray buildings brooding behind and alongside the eighteenth, the golfers of every class, tailors and authors, grocers and lords, all playing with "the spirit of the game prevailing." Charlie Macdonald could never forget his boyhood in St. Andrews.

Macdonald had planned, to be sure, to continue playing the game he loved when he returned to Chicago. As it turned out, he played only one summer, in 1875, when one of his classmates visited him. They went out to the wide clearing that had been Camp Douglas during the Civil War, and played their approaches to holes they had made from old ration cans that were still lying about. But outside of this one summer, Macdonald was forced to give up play-

ing golf in America. These were the "root, hog, or die" days in Chicago and no one had time for outdoor sports. The gloom of this golfless life, which Macdonald called the Dark Ages, was relieved by his business trips to England. Between 1878 and 1888, Macdonald took at least five trips across and kept his long St. Andrews swing in shape by playing at Coldham Common, Wimbledon, and Royal Liverpool.

Living in Chicago, Macdonald was left out of the first experiments by the Eastern clubs. His chance came in 1892. Sir Henry Wood, England's Commissioner-General to the World's Fair in Chicago, had brought with him a staff of young men who had played golf in their college days and who talked it at all the parties they attended. Macdonald's earlier monologues on the merits of golf had never stirred his friends in Chicago to take any action. The constant golf talk of Sir Henry's young men did. Hobart Chatfield-Taylor decided to lay out a course on the estate of his father-in-law, Senator John B. Farwell, at Lake Forest. He asked his friend Macdonald to act as architect.

The limited plot at Lake Forest afforded Charlie Macdonald little room for self-expression. He had to be content with devising seven midget holes, none of them over 250 yards in length and most of them less than 100 yards. It was a beginning, nev-

MACDONALD'S OBSESSION WITH GOLF IS USUALLY ATTRIBUTED TO HIS EXPERIENCES AS A STUDENT AT THE UNIVERSITY OF ST. ANDREWS. SHOWN OPPOSITE IS A MID-19TH CENTURY VIEW OF THE UNITED COLLEGE OF ST. SALVADOR, ONE OF THE COLLEGES MACDONALD ATTENDED.

ertheless. Macdonald found his friends at the Chicago Club, his downtown hangout, much more willing now to go along with him on a golf venture on a larger scale. Twenty or thirty members of the club agreed to contribute ten dollars to enable him to build a nine-hole course on a stock farm at Belmont, twenty-four miles west of the city. In the spring of 1893, Macdonald added nine more holes to the Belmont course. A year later he was able to sell the members of the Chicago Golf Club an even more ambitious program. For $28,000 — which was money in 1893 — the club purchased the two-hundred-acre Patrick farm in the town of Wheaton, twenty-five miles out of Chicago. Macdonald set out to turn

the lush rolling meadows into eighteen holes that would approach the standard of the finest inland courses of Great Britain. He did a splendid job. The Chicago Golf Club was an outstanding layout, and in the formative days of American golf many important championships were staged on it.

The only members who had reservations about the excellence of the new course in Wheaton were the hookers. Macdonald had laid out the holes clockwise around the perimeter of the property, so the golfer who unleashed a fair-sized hook found himself off the course and playing his recovery from a farmer's cornfield. To appease the hookers, the Chicago Golf Club adopted the out-of-bounds rule. This permitted the golfer who hooked his tee shot, for example, to play "two" off the tee rather than thrash the cornfield until he succeeded in hitting his ball back onto the fairway. Charlie Macdonald, to be sure, was never out-of-bounds. The clockwise layout was made for his slice as perfectly as the short rightfield fence at Yankee Stadium was made for Babe Ruth. When Charlie sliced, the severest penalty he suffered was the rough between holes, and when he was really wild, well, he would be on the adjoining fairway.

After 1895, Chicago went crazy over golf. By the turn of the century twenty-six clubs were operating, among them Hinsdale, Riverside, Onwentsia, Washington Park, Elmhurst, Exmoor, LaGrange, Homewood, Midlothian, Glen View, and Westward Ho. Onwentsia, perhaps, had the most interesting genesis. It was founded by a group of young men, friends of Hobart Chatfield-Taylor, who preferred baseball or tennis to golf. One Sunday Chatfield-Taylor persuaded them to come out to his father-in-law's place in Lake Forest and try the game on the seven holes Macdonald had rigged up on the estate. Four of the holes were under 75 yards in length and only a few were over 200 — "not real golf" at all, as Macdonald commented—but Chatfield-Taylor's friends were sufficiently impressed by the sample to band together and build a nine-holer on the McCormick farm. Five years later, in 1899,

the Onwentsia Club, the beaming possessor of a new eighteen-hole course, was host to the United States Amateur.

Charles Blair Macdonald in later years left Chicago and made New York his headquarters. He did not mellow with age. If anything, his ideas became more fixed, his oaths more explosive, his loyalty to St. Andrews stronger than ever. Whether he was fighting the United States Golf Association or designing his wonderful courses or "replaying" old championship matches on the leather chairs at the Links Club, he remained a law unto himself. Now and then he asked the advice of people he respected, but ninety-nine times out of a hundred, he followed his own judgment. (On the odd occasion he probably listened to Jim Whigham, his son-in-law and an early amateur champion.) The younger men who later came to the leadership in golf found Macdonald a very charming person when he wanted to be. They could also congratulate themselves on a cable they sent him one summer when he went to Britain for a visit: *We hope you are enjoying your holiday. We are.*

Charles Blair Macdonald was not "Mr. American Golf," though this was undoubtedly his life's ambition. He did, however, contribute more to the advancement of golf in America than any other person of his generation.

MACDONALD OFTEN INCORPORATED INTO HIS AMERICAN COURSES DESIGN FEATURES FROM BRITISH COURSES. A WINDMILL SUCH AS THE ONE OPPOSITE FOUND ON THE WIMBLEDON COMMON COURSE NEAR LONDON LOOMS OVER THE 16TH GREEN ON MACDONALD'S GREAT LONG ISLAND COURSE, THE NATIONAL.

The U.S.G.A. and the First Championships

TODAY a golf club would no more think of permitting stone walls to traverse its fairways than Ohio State would lobby to de-emphasize football. In some ways 1894 does not seem so far away, and it is not easy to understand how, pioneer days or no pioneer days, stone walls were esteemed fine golf hazards and a club was considered lucky to have them. When the Newport Golf Club, to keep up with the times, opened a new nine at Rocky Farm, the members appraised the rambling stone walls as one of the chief merits of the new course. Willie Davis from Montreal, whom the club had taken on as pro, further tightened up the layout with a liberal sprinkling of mounds and pot bunkers. These were the accepted "artificial hazards" of the day, easy to build and maintain, hard for a player to avoid. The mixture made for a stiff course rather than a good test of skill, but then few of the golfers in the mid-Nineties appreciated the difference. The Rocky Farm course kindled a new enthusiasm among the members of the Newport club in the summer of 1894, and with one notable result: they voted to invite golfers from all clubs to come to Newport in September and meet in competitions that would decide the champion amateur and professional players in the country.

All the stars accepted. Down from Boston came Herbert Leeds. Laurence Stoddart trained over from St. Andrew's. And out of the West, with a retinue of well-heeled backers, came Charlie Macdonald, supremely confident that he would leave the field of dilettante-sportsmen far behind. Twenty players in all teed off in the tourney, but the toughness of the course and the physical wear and tear of eighteen holes of medal play on two consecutive days killed off all but eight. Macdonald had been established as a heavy favorite from the beginning, and his play on the first day justified that tribute. His 89 gave him a four-stroke lead over his closest competitor, W. G. Lawrence, a member of the Newport club who had put in some time at Pau, in France. On the second day calamity struck the Chicagoan and his supporters. Macdonald blew to 100, and Lawrence's 95 gave him a total of 188, a stroke lower than Macdonald's. A topped shot had cost Charlie the championship. It had rolled into one of the stone walls and died there, and Macdonald had been forced to take a two-stroke penalty.

Charlie Macdonald took the defeat hard. He refused to recognize Lawrence as the champion, claiming that a stone wall was not a legitimate golf hazard and, accordingly, the two-stroke penalty was not a legitimate penalty. He also beefed loud and long that medal play was no proper method of determining an amateur champion. Amateur championships in Great Britain, as any true student of the game could tell you, were invariably match-play tournaments. He suggested that the Newport tournament be ruled "no contest" and that they start all over again, at match play. Macdonald did succeed in stirring up a hot controversy and gained a chance to redeem his reputation when the St. Andrew's club announced that it would be host to a *match-play* tournament in October to settle once and for all who was the American amateur champion. Invitations were sent to twenty clubs, and twenty-seven golfers from eight clubs came to the course at Grey Oaks to stop Macdonald. There was plenty of Eastern money to encourage them.

As at Newport, Charlie Macdonald started out like a house on fire. Fidgeting as always before the ball, champing impatiently while he waited for his opponents to play, he won his first match by the lopsided score of 8 and 6 and his second 4 and 3. The next morning, in the semi-final round, he got sweet revenge by defeating Lawrence, his conqueror at Newport, 2 and 1. Now all Macdonald had to do to prove his point that he was the true master of the amateur field was to win his final match that afternoon from Laurence Stoddart. No one doubted that he would. Stoddart, who had been a member of Hoylake (or Royal Liverpool), gave the long-hitting Chicagoan a good fight. Stoddart refused to crack under pressure, as he was supposed to, and they finished the eighteen holes all square. On the first extra hole Macdonald sliced his tee shot into a ploughed field—this was a counter-clockwise course—and when he took three to get back onto the fairway, he had lost another championship.

Once more Macdonald had an alibi. He had been ill. The night before his semi-final and final matches, he explained, Stanford White had thrown a party for him at the Waldorf. It was five in the morning before Macdonald remembered that he had should doctor himself. White had prescribed a good steak and a bottle of champagne. It was this foolhardy lunch, Macdonald insisted, which had caused his downfall.

Macdonald refused to recognize Stoddart as the national champion. As he saw it, Stoddart had won a tournament, an invitation tournament sponsored by one club. One club could not presume to speak for a

arranged to meet his semi-final opponent, Willie Lawrence, for breakfast at seven o'clock. At White's advice he had taken some strychnine pills after a nap, and thus stimulated was not only able to make his breakfast date but to go out and defeat Lawrence 2 up and 1 to play. At lunch he had confessed to White that he wasn't feeling at all himself and had asked White's opinion as to how he nation. Before a tournament could be designated a national championship, it would have to have the approval of all the clubs in the country, and those clubs would have to be joined in an official organization. He was sorry, but under the circumstances he could not recognize either Stoddart or Lawrence as the national amateur champion.

Macdonald's elaborate post-mortems

BEFORE CHARLIE MACDONALD, RIGHT, ABOVE, WON THE FIRST OFFICIAL U.S. AMATEUR CHAMPIONSHIP IN 1895, HE HAD LOST UNOFFICIAL VERSIONS OF THE EVENT TWICE; FIRST TO W.G. LAWRENCE AT NEWPORT, THEN IN THE MATCH SHOWN HERE TO L.B. STODDART, CENTER, AT ST. ANDREW'S COURSE AT GREY OAKS.

brought about, quite accidentally, the birth of the United States Golf Association. Theodore Havemeyer of Newport, Laurence Curtis of The Country Club, and Henry Tallmadge of St. Andrew's were disturbed by the thought that this war of words between Macdonald's partisans and the gloating East would be only the first of a series of crippling controversies unless some recognized authority was set up to settle points of difference and lay down laws all golfers were bound to follow. Tallmadge wrote to the five clubs the three men had checked as most prominent in their sections of the country—Shinnecock Hills and the Chicago Golf Club as well as Newport, The Country Club, and St. Andrew's— inviting each club to send two delegates to a dinner he was planning in New York for the purpose of establishing a governing body for American golf.

On December 22, 1894, the delegates met at the Calumet Club—John Reid and Tallmadge from St. Andrew's, Theodore Havemeyer and Winthrop Rutherford from Newport, Laurence Curtis and Samuel Sears from The Country Club, Charles Macdonald and Arthur Ryerson from Chicago, and Samuel Parrish from Shinnecock Hills. (General T. H. Barber, the other delegate from Shinnecock, was unable to attend.) Through these representatives, the five clubs agreed to unite and invited other clubs to join them in the Amateur Golf Association of the United States, whose aims would be "to promote the interests of the game of

golf, to promulgate a code of rules for the game, to hold annual meetings at which competitions shall be conducted for the amateur and open championships in the United States." The honor of being the organization's first president narrowed down to two candidates, John Reid and Theodore Havemeyer. Havemeyer won out, largely through the campaigning of Laurence Curtis, who felt that an infant organization could well use the prestige and financial support a man like the Sugar King would provide. Tallmadge was selected secretary; Parrish, treasurer; Curtis, first vice-president; and Macdonald, second vice-president. In this way each of the five original clubs was honored with an office, and the A.G.A.U.S. got off to a harmonious start.

The association was very fortunate in the selection of its key officers, Havemeyer and Tallmadge. Havemeyer was a man of exceptional tact and unusual charm, three hundred and sixty-five days a year. Where other men might have failed, he was able to placate the members of Meadow Brook, Tuxedo, Essex County, and other clubs who had felt slighted by not being invited to attend the original meeting, and to persuade them to join the association. In more material ways, as Curtis had foreseen, Havemeyer was a tremendous help. One of his first acts was to donate a handsome thousand-dollar trophy for the Amateur Championship. Whenever there was a bill that ready funds could not cover, Havemeyer paid it. Tallmadge was a hard-working secretary with the valuable gift of knowing how to handle the rambunctious Macdonald, who from time to time mistook the national organization for the Chicago Golf Club.

The United States Golf Association was the third name the body adopted. The original name, the Amateur Golf Association, was not suitable since the A.G.A.U.S. also dealt with professional golf. The American Golf Association, the second try, was incorrect, too, since the A.G.A. had no jurisdiction over Canadian golf. By any name, the U.S.G.A. through the years has been a competent organization. It has had its moments of weakness—like its ridiculous disbarment of Francis Ouimet from amateur golf, its wavering policy as to whether or not a golf architect was a professional or an amateur golfer, its tardiness in stopping jackrabbit balls from running away with the courses. On the other hand, the U.S.G.A., when still a stripling, stood firm in the face of the R. & A. when that august body barred the Schenectady putter following Travis' incredible exploits in the 1904 British Amateur. It has tried to make rules for American golf that have suited the changing game, agreeing with the R. & A. whenever it was possible but not afraid to break with tradition when it had good reason. The U.S.G.A. has done a very satisfactory job in working with the R. & A. to create a universal set of rules, an excellent job in staging the national tournaments, a superior job in improving turf conditions and aiding the hard-pressed greenkeeper, and a superb job in keeping

golf the one major sport in which an amateur must adhere to the rules of amateur status. Some of the past presidents of the U.S.G.A. would still be voting for Calvin Coolidge or Rutherford B. Hayes if they could, but a far greater number of the organization's officials have not been brass hats and have fought to make the management of the game as democratic as the game itself. The U.S.G.A. looks very good when you compare its record with that of an organization with quite similar functions, the United States Lawn Tennis Association, or, for that matter, with most national bodies governing sports.

The first official United States Amateur Championship, or the first one sponsored by the U.S.G.A., was held at Newport the first three days of October 1895. There was no qualifying round, the players immediately tackling each other in eighteen-hole matches with the final set for thirty-six. Theodore Havemeyer went out of his way to make the U.S.G.A.'s maiden championship an unqualified success. He arranged the parties and personally paid the expenses of the thirty-two entrants. In the main they were gentlemen-golfers (who were more gentleman than golfer), but among the entries there were a few characters, such as the golfing minister, the Reverend William Rainsford, and clubman Richard Peters, who used a billiard cue on the greens, not because he wanted to clown around but because he was convinced he could putt better that way. Society turned out for the tournament, the ladies in their gayest silks and the men in their red jackets. The officials of the U.S.G.A., pleased as schoolboys over their new red-white-and-blue badges, dashed around energetically in circles trying to help out.

Yet, in the minds of the Easterners, a dark cloud hung over the championship—Charlie Macdonald. Macdonald had been playing even better than usual that season, and as the "golfing reporter" of the New York *Herald* stated in between descriptions of what the ladies were wearing, the man from the West was regarded as the "probable champion." None of the Eastern players, as their backers glumly perceived, had scored nearly as low in their practice rounds as Macdonald. Furthermore, Macdonald was avoiding any chance of a repetition of his fiasco at St. Andrew's by going into what for him amounted to training. At no time was he seriously pressed as he marched through

BY 1895, AMERICAN GOLF'S GOVERNING BODY HAD ASSUMED ITS PRESENT NAME: THE UNITED STATES GOLF ASSOCIATION. FIVE OFFICERS, ABOVE, SIGNED THE U.S.G.A.'S CONSTITUTION AND BY-LAWS.

his half of the draw. To make matters worse for the East, Laurence Stoddart, the one man who might have stopped Macdonald—Willie Lawrence was not entered—was eliminated by a much poorer player than himself. Stoddart's conqueror was in turn eliminated in the semi-final round by Macdonald. The other finalist was Charles Sands, a very green golfer from the home club. On the eve of the final between Sands and Macdonald, the East was praying for a miracle, and nothing less than a miracle was needed if the haughty Macdonald was going to be defeated. Young Sands was a fine tennis player, but unfortunately this was a golf championship. He had played his first golf only three months before and had entered the tournament just for the fun of it. No miracle was forthcoming. This time Macdonald would not be denied. Five up at luncheon in the 36-hole final, he won every hole in the afternoon and closed out the match 12 and 11. On his third try Macdonald had made it, and he became the first official Amateur Champion. "I entered this championship in excellent form," he later wrote, "and was well taken care of, stopping with Mr. and Mrs. Henry Clews."

As Macdonald played out the bye holes, rightfully rejoicing in his long-sought triumph, he may have toyed with the thought that winning the Amateur could well become an annual habit for him, one he would not find the least bit objectionable. Macdonald played in the Amateur, without fail, during the ensuing years, and though he was always a dangerous contender until 1900, he never won again. It wasn't that his game deteriorated; if anything, he played a shade better. It was simply that the standard of everybody's golf was improving, and Macdonald was no match for the American college boys and the young men from the British Isles who had come to the States. When the Amateur was held in 1896 at Shinnecock Hills, H. J. Whigham was easily the class of the field. An Oxford man who was doing newspaper work in this country, Jim Whigham wrapped up the qualifying-round honors with an 86 and a great 77, and rolled on until he won his final match 8 and 7. Whigham successfully defended his title at the Chicago Golf Club the next year. His short game was outstanding. He used his wooden putter not only on the greens but also ran up some of his chip-length approaches with this limber-faced club. Whigham married Charlie Macdonald's daughter, so Macdonald at least had the satisfaction of knowing that the championship remained in the family.

In 1898, when the Amateur was played at the Morris County Golf Club, in New Jersey, Whigham failed to qualify. He had recently returned from Cuba, where he had covered the Spanish-American War as a special correspondent, and had not fully recovered from a siege of malaria. (At one time Whigham was rumored captured by the Spanish, and clubmen debated an absorbing question: Should a nation ransom its Amateur Golf Champion?) With Whigham out of the running, the crown went to Findlay Douglas, a twenty-three-year-old Scot who had captained the University of St. Andrews' golf team. Douglas found the 5,960-yard course at Morris County made to order for his aggressive, long-hitting game. More than once he drove into the bunker in front of the green on the 234-yard fourth hole, and since a few of the other contestants also encountered this unusual penalty, it began to look as if the players were getting ahead of the courses. Douglas was favored to repeat in 1899 at Onwentsia. He had little difficulty with any of his opponents until he reached the final, but there he succumbed, quite unexpectedly, to Herbert Harriman by the score of 3 and 2. Harriman was a short, awkward swinger who was never a threat in subsequent championships. However, he was very good on the day it was important for him to play his best game, and his victory at Onwentsia marked the close of American golf's period of infancy: For the first time a foreign-born star had not won the Amateur Championship. For the first time the champ was a "homebred."

Turn of
the Century

GOLF did not graduate into a truly popular sport in America until the Open Championship of 1913, when Francis Ouimet, an unknown ex-caddie, stunned the nation into acceptance by defeating the celebrated British professionals, Harry Vardon and Ted Ray. However, as early as 1900, the year that Vardon made his first American tour, the game had established itself as more than the coddled crush of the gilded set—something more than hard rackets or court tennis, to use a modern analogy. Only twelve years after its introduction in Yonkers, golf had come to be regarded by Americans of that day more or less as skiing was by mid-century Americans: an outdoor recreation, open to both sexes and a wide range of ages,

whose environment was as attractive, if not more attractive, than the exercise itself; a sport whose first professionals came from overseas and whose leading missionaries were the college crowd, and which offered its followers an occasion for dashing outfits, endowed them with the bright aura of being fashionable, and demanded from them a good slice of their incomes.

Findlay Douglas may have been a trifle exuberant in estimating that by the turn of the century 250,000 Americans had seen the light and were spending over $20,000,000 annually on golf, but there was no denying that the game was growing and growing fast. The length and breadth of the United States were dotted with golf courses, over a thousand of them. There was at least one course in every state. The Atlantic seaboard states New York and Massachusetts led with 165 and 157 respectively, but there were 57 courses in Illinois, 43 in California, 17 in Florida, and already 5 in Texas. Cincinnati, Philadelphia, Boston, and Providence were some of the cities that supported courses that were open to the public. Chicago had created its municipal course by filling in Jackson Park with the bricks, concrete pillars, and other debris from the World's Fair buildings. Van Cortlandt Park in New York, the original public course, sported a 700-yard finishing hole, and after hitting his four or five brassies on that hole, a player was finished.

In the other direction, men who could afford it—like Theodore Havemeyer, John Jacob Astor, and A. G. Spalding—built private courses on their estates. In the beginning, Spalding and the other manufacturers of sporting goods had been afraid to touch the game, but now they were setting up plants especially tooled for turning out gutta-perchas as well as the baffy spoons, cleeks, iron and wooden niblicks, mashies, and the other weapons demanded by the increasing number of players.

America looked more and more like the promised land to Scottish professionals, and the Mackies and the Nicholls and the Rosses and the Smiths headed West *en famille* to make their fortunes. Alex started the wholesale migration of the Smiths from Carnoustie in 1898. His brother Willie followed him a year later. George came over and then Jimmy. Shortly afterwards, Mr. and Mrs. John Smith, the boys' parents, joined them in the greener pastures, bringing with them the baby of the family, Macdonald, who developed into the greatest golfer who never won a major championship.

The Scottish professionals—and the other British and Irish emigrant professionals— found themselves playing and teaching on layouts remarkably different from the true links back home—that belt of sandy soil deposited by the receding ocean along the coast of the British Isles. Lacking this linksland, with its natural bunkers and dunes, Americans had used their native genius, often excessively, in providing themselves with comparable hazards for their inland courses. Stone quarries, pigeon traps, ploughed fields, railroad tracks, and wooden pavilions were accepted

A POPULAR ILLUSTRATOR OF THE DAY, EDWARD PENFIELD USED GOLF AS HIS SUBJECT IN A CALENDAR FOR THE YEAR 1899, ABOVE. OPPOSITE, SCOTTISH GOLF PRO ALEX SMITH, SHOWN STANDING, IN SHIRTSLEEVES, WITH HIS BROTHERS, WAS THE FIRST OF THE CARNOUSTIE CLAN TO TEACH AND PLAY IN THE STATES.

as obstacles that added interest to the game, and self-appointed architects remedied Nature's absent-mindedness by digging cross-bunkers the width of their fairways and scooping circular pits—pot bunkers— around their greens. To many Americans, these devices were not a substitution for the natural hazards of a seaside links; they were an improvement on them.

The men who banded together to finance golf courses in their communities discovered it was an expensive proposition. By the time a syndicate had purchased its two hundred acres, built its course, and added an adequate club-house, the costs had already soared to $200,000—a figure to be respected in 1900. The syndicates were always faced with the possibility that the game might not catch on in their particular community, and to protect their investment they usually purchased wooded land. Then, if the venture collapsed, the land could be cut up and sold to prospective builders, who were always partial to leafy lots. Apart from the considerable initial outlay, it took money to operate a golf club; the artificial hazards, greens, and watering systems had to be maintained, and there was always the clubhouse to think about.

After Stanford White had showed the way at Shinnecock Hills, every self-respecting club had to have a clubhouse. The social advantages of a good clubhouse were inextricably bound up with definite economic factors. Wealthy men would join a golf club that possessed a well-appointed clubhouse, even if they were not attracted to the game itself. Many of these men would, sooner or later, be converted to golf and grow to love their eighteen holes as much as their drinks and their dinner; yet, however they reacted to life in the rough, wealthy members were essential if a club was to remain solvent. And unless it could point to a handsome clubhouse, no golf club could hope to attract the women of the community, without whose presence the project would not click socially. For these reasons, golf clubs were forced, or thought they were forced, to charge high initiation fees and healthy annual dues, and golf grew up in America as a rich man's game, viewed with a certain antagonism by the average working-man, who distrusted any diversion pursued almost exclusively by the wealthy. The man who didn't play golf glibly shrugged it off as an effeminate sport for old fogies with one foot in the grave.

The adoption of golf by the college boys helped to spotlight the sport as one that could be enjoyed by vigorous young men. Outside of the contestants, few Americans cared who won the Intercollegiate title, but many Americans, consciously or unconsciously, had to revise their opinions of the game when the Amateur Championship of 1904 was won by a strapping, clean-cut young man named Chandler Egan who was still an undergraduate at Harvard. On the other hand, the endorsement by the college crowd did not make the game any more democratic, immediately. Harvard, Yale, and Princeton men took turns in winning the Intercollegiate Championship, and the golf teams at these universities were the especial preserves of the very social set.

Egan the collegian thrilled the galleries with his recoveries from the rough, a type of shot he had mastered through practice, since, like most young golfers, he was extremely long and extremely erratic off the tees. At Chicago, where he successfully defended his title in 1905, there were three

Chandler Egan, above, attained momentary fame by winning the Amateur Championship in 1904 and 1905 as a Harvard undergraduate. Turn-of-the-century women players are, clockwise from upper left, opposite, two U.S. Women's Amateur Champions — Peggy Curtis and Genevieve Hecker — and an unidentified player.

degrees of rough: a width of five yards cut fairly close; then a really formidable growth; and finally a hayfield that looked much tougher than it actually was. Egan fortunately was wild enough to reach the hayfield quite consistently.

The early golfers liked to find pretty women lounging on the verandas of their clubhouses, but they were not in favor of women playing the game. To keep them off the course, the men invoked stringent club rules, argued the fantasy that golf developed unbecoming muscles, and talked loud and laboriously about the dangers lurking on the wild frontier bordering the holes farthest away from the clubhouse. A favorite story at every course was the close call George had the other day when that wild bull in the adjoining pasture caught sight of his red coat and charged through the fence and would have gored poor George if he hadn't had the quick wits to dive into the water hazard. The hardier girls refused to be intimidated by these frock-and-bull stories and investigated life on the frontier for themselves. Others played golf for the very sufficient reason that they wanted to. In 1893 an enterprising group of New Jersey ladies got back at the men by organizing a course "for women only" in Morris County. Two years later they held their first national championship at Meadow Brook, Long Island, with Mrs. C. S.

Brown carrying the day with a sporty 132. By the turn of the century the women had won their fight. In Beatrix Hoyt they had a champion who could play in the eighties, on a calm day, and Peggy Curtis could bang a brassie farther than most strong men.

To accomplish these wonders the women had shortened their skirts—they now reached to the *top* of the ankle—and defrilled their blouses. "For once," said H.L. Fitzpatrick, writing in *Outing*, "comfort and fashion united in the attire of the sex." Down through the years as the demands of sports, more than any other single factor, encouraged abbreviation in feminine styles and brought the age of the sweater and sensible skirt a little nearer, man was always on hand with an appreciative word.

Golf's popularity among the "best people," of both sexes, was not overlooked by the established summer resorts nor by the men transforming the South into a winter playground. By 1900, Poland Spring, Saratoga, Manchester in Vermont, Shennecossett near New London, and the Lake Placid Club had added golf courses to attract the couples who wanted to play the game during their vacations. Henry M. Flagler, who opened up the east coast of Florida, and Henry B. Plant, who concentrated on the west coast, talked up the game as a year-round sport: there was no need any longer for golfers to stow away their clubs during

In 1900, 29-year-old Donald Ross, top, arrived at a fledgling resort in North Carolina and set to work, using man- and horse-power, to create his first masterpiece—the Number Two course at Pinehurst.

the winter months, now that Palm Beach and Ormond Beach and Tampa and Belleair were waiting for them. The Belleview Biltmore at Belleair assured them of grass greens, built from topsoil imported by the carload from Indiana. Pinehurst, the colony founded by James W. Tufts in the sandhills of North Carolina, had a good eighteen-hole course, and Donald Ross, just over from Scotland, was starting work on the famous Pinehurst #2. There were courses at Aiken, South Carolina, Jekyll's Island in Georgia, Hot Springs, Virginia, Del Monte in California, and the resorts without a few holes were writing interesting letters to the best Scottish pros.

Realizing that golf had come to stay, newspaper editors allotted increased space to accounts of the tournaments, and golf reporters learned the names of a few of the sticks. W. G. Van Tassel Sutphen wrote *The Golficide* and other tales, and led the way in publishing periodicals in which an addict could read about the game in those rare moments he wasn't talking about it. Golf acquired a literature, or at least many books on golf were published. Charles Stedman Hanks, who gloried in the pseudonym of "Niblic," was one of the first to write an "instruction book." In *Hints to Golfers*, Niblic advised "keeping the eye on the ball and not on the ground behind it" and generally explained his credo that "no other game requires such a variety of physical and mental adjustments." William Garrott Brown, who had written biographies of Andrew

Jackson and Stephen Arnold Douglas, was one of the "minds" who tried to get down in black and white the overpowering fascination the game had for him. Was it the delicate adjustments and self-control the game demanded of its players? Brown wasn't sure. But he knew that the red-coated hordes issuing from the city each weekend to play golf were in for a *moral* outing. H. W. Boynton's tribute, *The Golfer's Rubaiyat*, contained such hedonistic sentiments as—

A Bag of Clubs, a Silvertown or two,
A flask of Scotch, a Pipe of Shag—and Thou
Beside me, caddying in the Wilderness—
Ah, Wilderness were paradise enow.

The humor of golf and golfers began to get around, and insinuated itself into the he-she jokes magazines used as fillers.

There was the joke about the specialized language golfers used—

Sphinx-like Magistrate: "What are these prisoners charged with?"
Policeman: "I arrested them for fighting, your honor. They are a couple of golf players, and—"
Magistrate: "Send for the court interpreter."

And the one about the suitor—

"Hasn't Willoughby Perkins proposed yet?"
"No, Mamma. His approach is all right, but then he gets nervous and foozles."

And a switch called "Cruel Treatment"—

"I proposed to her in a smooth, well-modulated tone."

THE CAROLINA HOTEL, SHOWN ABOVE IN 1900, WAS THE CENTERPIECE OF THE PINEHURST RESORT.

"Well?"

"She rejected me in her golf voice."

The year 1900 brought into the focus of American golfers three men whose talents were to prove invaluable in promoting the growth of golf in this country: Walter J. Travis, Harry Vardon, and Coburn Haskell.

Walter J. Travis was Australian-born, but learned his golf in the States, and was regarded as an American golfer. Travis had taken the game up in his middle-thirties, at an age when few men are able to master a sport they have never played before because their muscles are "set" and their reflexes slowed. Travis, a man with a mind of his own, entered the United States Amateur less than two years after he had started the game, and made his way into the semi-final round before being ousted by Findlay Douglas. That was in 1898, and the next year the "Old Man" was back for more. Again he reached the semi-finals and again it was Douglas who put him out, but the score was closer this time and Travis was encouraged. He met Douglas for the third time in the final of the Amateur at Garden City, Long Island, in 1900, and this time Travis turned the tables on the long-hitting Scot, defeating him 2 up.

After the tournament, newspaper men approached the new champion and asked him how he had managed to add 25

yards to his drives, to hit them 200 yards now where he had averaged 175 yards in previous years. Guarding his elation over his victory, Travis remarked indirectly, "I am only just learning this game."

"Do you think you will work your game up to a greater degree of proficiency?"

"I should say so," Travis answered. "Why, I am now just scratching on the outside, and if I don't improve my game by at least another three strokes by another year, I shall be very much surprised."

Walter Travis went on to win the Amateur twice more and to do things in the British Amateur of 1904 that left Americans gasping, particularly those Americans who wanted to believe that golf could begin at forty and could see from Travis' example that it could.

Harry Vardon, who is regarded as one of the four greatest golfers of all time—a distinction he shares with Bobby Jones, Ben Hogan, and Jack Nicklaus—made his first trip to America in 1900. The impeccable swinger from the Isle of Jersey had already won three of the six British Open titles he would amass. He had grooved his rather upright swing so perfectly that his opponents declared that when he played his second nine on a nine-hole course, his drives ended up in the divot marks he had cut from the fairways his first time round. Americans had heard about his deeds, and had a chance to see the peerless one himself when the Spalding company arranged for him to tour the country to promote their new guttie, the Vardon Flyer. The tour came on the eve of the emergence of the new rubber-cored ball, and from this point of view it was not successful. But the tour sold golf.

In a long series of exhibitions, Vardon played against our best homebreds and the outstanding Anglo-American pros, and dropped only one match. He took time off to compete in the U.S. Open and finished nine strokes ahead of the field. Most important, he showed Americans, much more convincingly than the transplanted pros who had won the earlier championships, how the game could be played. With his brassie he could pick the ball cleanly from any lie and propel it high and floating to the green, where it sat down abruptly. With his irons he merely brushed across the turf with the clubhead instead of taking a large divot, and faded his shots into the pin from left to right. He hit the ball with an utter absence of visible effort, and yet his timing was so fine that he sent his shots yards farther down the fairways than his straining opponents. After they had seen Harry, American golfers knew that the game, in the hands of a master, could be an art.

Coburn Haskell was a fair golfer who lived in Cleveland. Not unlike many other golfers of his day, Haskell was not at all satisfied with the performance of the gutta-percha ball and had frequently thought about substances from which a superior ball could be developed. One day in 1898 he called in at the Goodrich Rubber Company to pick up a friend, an official of that company. Haskell's friend found himself unable to get away immediately and suggested that Haskell take a turn around the plant and look things over. On his walk Haskell's attention was caught by a pile of thin rubber stripping, and he was struck by the idea that an improved ball might be built by wrapping these strippings tightly around a rubber core and covering them with a sheath of gutta-percha. With the assistance of his friend at the Goodrich Company, Haskell worked out the new rubber-cored ball, which revolutionized the game as thoroughly at the turn of the century as the guttie had done fifty years earlier. The tendency of the first rubber-cored balls to "duck" in flight was corrected by impressing a bramble marking on their smooth covers. Later the gutta-percha for the covers was replaced by balata.

The "Bounding Billies," as the new balls were called, were harder to control around the green than the old gutties, but a golfer did not have to strike them perfectly to get a reasonably straight shot, and, far more important, the average golfer found his drive a full twenty yards farther down the fairway. Now the game was really enjoyable for the weekend player. Now it took only one long whistling drive with the rubber-cored ball to convert an infidel.

*GOLF'S **FIRST MODERN** SWING BELONGED TO THE PEERLESS BRITISH CHAMPION HARRY VARDON. VARDON'S STYLE, AS SHOWN IN THIS SEQUENCE OF EARLY 20TH CENTURY PHOTOGRAPHS, FEATURED AN OVERLAPPING GRIP AND AN OPEN STANCE.*

*VARDON'S **DOWNSWING** AND FOLLOW-THROUGH BROUGHT HANDS, FEET, AND BODY GRACEFULLY THROUGH THE BALL. "TO ACCURACY," WROTE BRITISH GOLF WRITER BERNARD DARWIN, "HE ADDED SOMETHING MORE OF POWER WHICH PUT HIM FOR A WHILE IN ONE CLASS WITH ALL OTHER GOLFERS IN ANOTHER."*

Walter J. Travis—The Great Old Man

GOLF fans in Great Britain have a far clearer idea of who Walter J. Travis was than most Americans do. Should a Briton's picture of Travis begin to blur, a torrid round by some American in a British championship is all that is necessary to evoke golf writers' references to 1904 and that unforgettable first invader, Travis. In America today, however, the name of Travis rings few bells, and those who claim to remember him well too often have his doings confused with those of his homonymous contemporary, Jerome Travers. And Walter J. Travis is worth the knowing.

The thing about Travis that first startled the golfers of his day was the thoroughgoing way he blasted the current idea that a man had to play golf from the cradle on if he nurtured any ambitions to score in the seventies, let alone become a champion. Born in the state of Victoria in Australia, Travis had come to America when still a small boy. He was athletically inclined, but golf seemed a waste of time to him, and he spent the leisure hours of his young manhood playing tennis or cycling. On a visit to England he took a house in Streatham, close by the course at Tooting

BADMINTON.

Bec, and on his daily strolls stopped to watch the players. This closer inspection only confirmed his previous opinion: golf wasn't a game for him. While in England, however, he did purchase a set of sticks but only because his friends at the Niantic Club in Flushing, Long Island, had written him that they were thinking of starting a golf course, and Travis thought he should support such a venture. He started to play the game with these friends at the Oakland course on Long Island when he got back in the fall of 1896. Travis was then thirty-five.

Walter Travis was one of those men who saw no sense in doing a thing at all unless he did it well. Since circumstances had led him to take up golf, he made up his mind to become something more than a dub. During the winter he gathered around him the best books on the game he could

acquire. He realized that learning from books could be dangerous unless the reader had great powers of concentration and an extraordinary diligence in investigation, but he knew that he had those abilities and kept on reading, setting aside Horace Hutchinson's theories in the Badminton Library series as worthy of more detailed study, marking Willie Park, Jr.'s, manual as material that should be helpful, tossing aside the books by other authorities who advocated methods he felt were not in harmony with his slight physique and limited brawn. Travis recognized the fact that a good golfer plays half of his shots on the putting green, and slowly, scientifically, arrived at what he approved of as a sound putting method for himself. This was to use a short-shafted putter and grip it well down the shaft, the palms working in direct

THE BADMINTON LIBRARY OF SPORTS AND PASTIMES, WHICH COMPRISED 23 VOLUMES INCLUDING ONE ON GOLF, WAS EDITED BY HIS GRACE THE 8TH DUKE OF BEAUFORT, WHOSE RESIDENCE APPEARS ABOVE.

opposition to each other to produce a pendulum stroke, the body held absolutely motionless. The next spring he played three or four rounds but chose to spend the bulk of his time practicing his self-taught swing. A few months more and he terminated this trial-and-error period, satisfied with the product of his disciplined search. It wasn't the prettiest swing in the world and it may have had a homemade quality, but it was Travis' and he knew and controlled every inch of it. He did not hit the ball far but he hit it straight, and from the beginning he was far too good for the other players at Oakland. In his second year he was ready to test his skill against the country's best in the United States Amateur, and got to the semi-finals. Two years after that, less than four years after he had started golf, Travis led the fast field in the Metropolitan Championship and topped off his season (as noted previously) by winning the Amateur, no less.

When he won his first national championship, Travis wore a heavy dark beard that, along with the Rough Rider type of hat he then favored, gave him the aspect of a junior-sized Stonewall Jackson. His opponents found him a tough customer. He was always perfectly polite, but he had little to say and preferred the company of his long black cigar. Even when he shaved off his beard, his opponents could not read his emotions. They knew only that the Old Man was out to win and did not want to risk disturbing his concentration by any social bantering. His accuracy nullified the greater length of his rivals, and on the greens he putted them to death, dropping the 20-footers as smoothly and as confidently as the 7-footers. Then, with just the slightest flicker of pleasure in his menacing dark eyes, he was off to the next tee, taking a careful practice swing, stroking his drive down the middle and walking slowly after the ball, his neck stuck out like a turtle's, the smoke of his cigar curling over the rim of his rolled-up twill hat.

During the winter of 1901, Travis' health was poor and he went to Scotland for a rest. By summertime he was back on the fairways stalking his foes not one whit more leniently and proving beyond a doubt that he was no flash in the pan. He finished third in the United States Open. Playing the rubber-cored ball for the first time, he won the qualifying medal in the national Amateur at Atlantic City by three strokes. In the semi-finals of that tournament, though putting less devastatingly than usual because of the more resilient ball, he eliminated his most dangerous challenger, Findlay Douglas. In the final he won as he pleased from Walter Egan.

Travis' hopes of making it three in a row the following year were smashed when

When Walter Travis won the 1904 British Amateur crown, he did it over the Royal St. George's Golf Club at Sandwich, England, where golfers are tested by acres of sandhills, like the "Sahara," opposite, which once dominated the course's par-3 third hole.

he came up against young Eben Byers in the third round at Glen View. Travis shot a fair enough 78 but Byers came up with a 77 and won 1 up. In 1903, Byers and Travis again met in the Amateur, this time in the final round. Playing almost errorless golf, Travis went around the Nassau Country Club course in 73 on his morning round and coasted to a convincing 5 and 4 victory. The Old Man was not to be trifled with.

During his holiday in Britain in 1901, Travis had played several matches against the ranking Scottish and English players. He had lost most of these matches, and his experience had pointed out to him the deficiencies in his game. By 1904, when he had won three of the last four United States Amateur crowns and had clearly established himself as the nation's leading amateur golfer, he was filled with the desire to return to Britain and prove to himself that he was now just as good if not better than the men who had licked him three years

before. He decided to enter the British Amateur Championship in 1904, to be held at Royal St. George's in Sandwich, Kent. Deep down in his heart, the Old Man believed his game was good enough to win despite his shortness off the tees and the length of the links at Sandwich—6,135 yards of harsh duneland whipped by the winds off the North Sea. With the same detached calculation that had marked his efforts to learn the game without a teacher, this man who loved a fight mapped his conquest of the British Amateur: He would arrive in London three weeks before the start of the tourney; he would tune up for a week and a half at St. Andrews and North Berwick; then he would go down to Sandwich and spend the last ten or twelve days before the tournament getting to know the championship course and practicing his shots in the wind and rain.

When he found himself playing very badly at St. Andrews, Travis had to scrap this plan. He stayed on in Scotland, trying to discover why he wasn't hitting the ball. He played worse and worse. He bought himself some new clubs, hoping these would give him a psychological lift, and found they were no help at all. He was still in this slump, the worst of his career, when he arrived at Sandwich seven days before the start of the tournament. He wanted to get in as many practice rounds as possible, and at the same time he was loath to make his first round at Sandwich a bad one and become antagonistic toward the course. He debated the dilemma a full morning and decided to go out with only one club, the new putting cleek he had bought at North Berwick, and simply beat the ball for a few holes. With the first shot he hit, he felt his old timing returning. The next day he went out with his full set, and gradually his game came back during his practice rounds and his frame of mind began to improve. Only one thing about his golf was bothering him now. He couldn't hole a putt. He tried putting off his left foot, off his right foot. He opened his stance, closed it, opened it again. He shortened and then lengthened his stroke, tried new grips, varied the arc of the club, and still could not sink a putt of over three feet. In desperation he borrowed a friend's Schenectady putter the day before the tournament began. This was a putter with the shaft inserted in the *center* of a mallet-shaped head. It was called the Schenectady, since it was a resident of that city, Mr. A. W. Knight, who had introduced this unconventional model. Finding he could putt a little better with the Schenectady, Travis decided to sink or swim with it during the tournament.

In addition to his purely golf worries, the Old Man's spirits were weighed down by several extracurricular irritations during that week preceding the start of the tournament. He and the Englishmen in charge of the Royal St. George's Golf Club did not hit it off, at all. The English thought him cold and impolite, and he felt the same way about them. There are, of course, two sides to the story. From the viewpoint of the Englishmen running Sandwich, Travis had responded uncivilly to their attempts at friendliness. When they had asked him to join them for a dinner party or an after-dinner drink, Travis had firmly rejected their invitations. This went against all their ideas of the guest's role in the English code of hospitality; in the eyes of his hosts, it was about the same as if Travis had entered a house without wiping off his muddy shoes. They concluded that he wanted to be left alone, and in the future they left him alone.

Travis, for his part, believed he had suffered a series of consciously wrought insults. He was not able to obtain quarters in the buildings usually reserved for guests of the Royal St. George's, and he and his

To become the first American citizen to win the British Amateur, Walter Travis, opposite, accomplished the following: he defeated two British champions, Hilton and Hutchinson; overcame an inept caddie; neutralized a hostile gallery; and putted like a god.

American friends were obliged to take rooms at the Bell Hotel. He had asked to play his practice rounds with some of the star British golfers, but this was not arranged. He was assigned a cross-eyed caddie whom he believed to be a congenital idiot, and was not able to get him replaced. He and his American friends, he claimed, were cut dead by the same Oxford and Cambridge golfers whom they had entertained royally when the combined team had visited the States the year before. Travis felt like a pariah. As he saw it, he had done nothing wrong but his hosts had gone out of their way to frustrate his every simple request and render him ill at ease. Under the smart of these real and/or imagined discourtesies, Travis pressed

his thin lips even tighter and made up his mind to get even the only way he could: he would carry that precious championship home with him. He talked himself into the state of mind where he asserted he was damn glad the English had treated him so poorly. Now he would never relax for a moment in his efforts to win. "A reasonable number of fleas is good for a dog," he told his American friends gathered sympathetically around him at the Bell. "It keeps the dog from forgetting that he is a dog."

Travis' opponent in the first round—all the matches in the British Amateur except the final were eighteen holes—was a Mr. Holden of the Royal Liverpool Golf Club. Travis started out well by rolling in a couple of good-sized putts with the Schenectady, and went on to win 4 and 3. On the seventh hole Travis "called" Holden for soling his club in a bunker, and the remainder of the match was played in a very disagreeable atmosphere.

It had rained and rained hard that morning, and when Travis came off the course at ten minutes before two, he was soaked from head to foot. He asked the officials to allow him time to change into dry clothes, but he was informed that he was due on the first tee for his second-round match at twenty-eight minutes past two, unless he wished to default. Travis toweled himself in the hallway—he had not been given a locker—and went out in the same wet clothes to play his second-round opponent, James Robb. Robb was as fresh as a daisy. His morning-round opponent had defaulted, so he had avoided the downpour. On the out-nine, Travis hung on, and then, encouraged by a few long putts that found the cup, worked himself up to a two-hole lead with three to play. Robb halved the sixteenth and won the seventeenth, but the Old Man lasted out a half on the eighteenth for a tight 1-up victory.

Again the match had been marred by an unpleasant incident. On the eleventh hole Travis' idiot caddie, who had been making his usual quota of mistakes, had flagged the hole improperly for Robb. Robb was momentarily upset, but he was a sportsman and made no protest. When the match was over, Travis asked Robb if he could have his caddie, now that Robb had no further need for his services. Robb was perfectly willing, but the caddie-master, while not definitely turning down Travis' request for a change in caddies, managed to find some reason for inaction. Travis was stuck with the cross-eyed idiot for at least another day, if he remained in the tournament that long.

In the third round Travis defeated A. M. Murray 3 and 1. In the fourth round he came up against H. E. Reade, a golfer with a good all-round game. When Reade reached the fifteenth tee 2 up with only four holes to play, it looked as if the foreign invasion had been quelled. Travis chewed hard on his cigar and gave no outward sign of his distress. On the long fifteenth, he knocked in a fine 4. That made him one down with three to play. He followed with a birdie 2 on the 180-yard sixteenth, dropping his putt after sticking his tee shot twelve feet from the

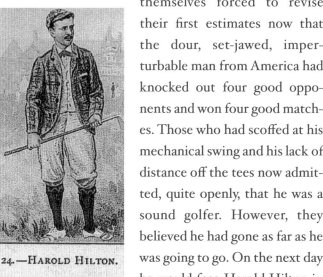

24.—HAROLD HILTON.

pin. Now Travis had drawn even with Reade. On the seventeenth, a 350-yard par 4, Reade just missed his putt for a 4 and Travis holed his. One up now with one to play, Travis held on with a halving 4 on the eighteenth, and that was the match—1 up.

Many Britishers who had not conceded Travis a chance of winning even one match against first-class golfers found themselves forced to revise their first estimates now that the dour, set-jawed, imperturbable man from America had knocked out four good opponents and won four good matches. Those who had scoffed at his mechanical swing and his lack of distance off the tees now admitted, quite openly, that he was a sound golfer. However, they believed he had gone as far as he was going to go. On the next day he would face Harold Hilton in the fifth round. Hilton had won two British Opens as well as two British Amateurs and stood forth as the greatest amateur in the world. He had trounced Travis when they had played in 1901. Against a master of Hilton's class, Travis was bound to fold. Sooner or later his drives would catch the high dunes down the fairways that they had been clearing by a scant matter of feet. Sooner or later those 40-footers and 20-footers he had been sinking with that center-shafted putter would begin to slide off.

In the enemy camp—and that term is

not too strong, for Travis had urged his pugnacity upon his seconds—the Old Man's friends did everything in their power to steady and stimulate their hero. To take his mind off the championship, they played cribbage with him and fed him large portions of stout. To keep him on his toes, they extolled the abilities of Hilton and his other possible opponents. The British Amateur was now more than a golf tournament in their minds; it was an international feud.

On the next morning Walter Travis went out and defeated Hilton in their "return match." Travis won the first three holes and protected that lead by going out in 34. Hilton cut the margin to two by winning the eleventh, but the Old Man snapped back hard, won the next three holes in a row and the match 5 and 4. Hilton had not played up to form, and Travis had not cracked.

For the first time now, the men who had been waiting for the invader to be ousted were confronted by the black thought that he could win, could very definitely win. In the sixth round—the semi-final—he would face Horace Hutchinson, and that was not too good. Hutchinson was now an old man, well past his peak. It would have been better if Hutchinson had lost to Robert Maxwell, as he had been expected to. By defeating Maxwell, Hutchinson had eliminated a man who could have probably stopped the

21.—H. G. HUTCHINSON.
Literary Golf Champion.

foreign threat more robustly than himself. These forebodings proved correct. Against Hutchinson, Travis went out in 34 to go 3 up, but coming in he played his worst nine holes of the tournament. He took two 6s. Maxwell might have seized this opening and marched to victory. Hutchinson didn't. Where Travis faltered, he faltered. Instead of picking up holes, Hutchinson actually lost one. Travis closed out the match on the sixteenth green, 4 and 2. He had reached the final.

The one man who now stood between Travis and victory, or between Great Britain and calamity, was Edward "Ted" Blackwell. A tall, strong man, with heavy eyebrows, Blackwell could drive a golf ball farther than any man, pro or amateur, on the island. Once he had banged a guttie 358 yards on the straightaway, and another time he had driven the eighteenth green at St. Andrews, an even more colossal wallop. On the eve of the final Travis was nervous but confident. He had overcome his complex about his caddie. Now he regarded his chronic irritant as a being designed by Fortune to remind him at every glance of the full importance of his conquest.

Both Travis and Blackwell started out shakily. Neither had a 4 on the 366-yard first hole, but Travis' 5 was better than Blackwell's 6. Both men were on the second green in two, and then Travis, to the great consternation of the gallery, sent his 36-foot putt into the bottom of the cup for a winning 3. Neither of the players had spoken a word to each other on the first two holes. On the third tee, Travis ventured to break the ice with a complimentary remark on Blackwell's driving. Possibly because he was 2 down at the time and in no mood for conversation, Blackwell's answer was a sort of monosyllabic grunt and nothing more. Travis never again addressed Blackwell during their match nor did Blackwell at any time say so much as a word to Travis.

The men halved the third in 5s, and then Travis played an excellent 4 and a perfect 3 to win both the fourth and fifth and increase his lead to four holes. He lost the sixth, the treacherous Maiden, when he missed his first putt of the round. The gallery was so on edge that they applauded the miss. At the turn Blackwell was still 3 down. He won the tenth to cut his deficit to two holes, halved the eleventh, and the twelfth, and looked to be in position to pare away another hole on the thirteenth. Two good woods into the teeth of the wind left Blackwell with an easy pitch, while Travis, 100 yards farther back, had a long, difficult iron to play. Travis hit a low, boring shot well onto the green, and when Blackwell hooked his pitch badly, he lost the hole and went 3 down where he had stood the chance of being only 1 down. The next hole, the 505-yard Suez Canal, was a repetition of the thirteenth. Both hit good drives, with Blackwell some 35 yards in front. Travis played his brassie second about 25 yards short of the Suez Canal, the deep ditch running the width of the fairway. Blackwell also elected to play safe. He took out his cleek, and hitting the shot too cleanly, sent it into the ditch. Travis pitched on . . . and down went another long putt. The way he did it was what hurt. After he stroked a putt, he would stand absolutely still and eye the ball like Svengali as it dipped off the rolls and found its way into the cup. He acted as if there were no other possible outcome for the stroke.

Travis made no mistakes on the last four holes, and went to lunch with a comfortable 4-up lead.

When Travis started the afternoon round with a 7, the English gallery, which had been looking for any sign that the Old Man was cracking, thought that this moment had at last arrived. Travis killed off this hope by winning the second. He lost the third, and then roared back to take the next three holes with a 4 and two 3s and go 6 up with twelve holes to play. Blackwell managed to shave this down to 4 up at the turn, but coming in he was unable to do any better than halve five consecutive holes and carry the match to the fifteenth. When he failed to beat Travis' 5 on the long fifteenth, Blackwell had lost the match, 4 and 3, and Walter J. Travis had become the first "foreigner" ever to win the British Amateur Championship.

AFTER TRAVIS USED A SCHENECTADY PUTTER, OPPOSITE, TO WIN THE BRITISH AMATEUR, BRITAIN BANNED THE CLUB FOR 41 YEARS.

Travis' winning putt was greeted by a loud silence. Though the inevitability of his victory had been impressing itself upon the spectators hole by hole, the end of the match had left them stunned and still unbelieving. Then gradually, as the shock began to wear off, the gallery for the first time began to see Travis as he really was: a great golfer with a great heart. One man, who had been rooting against Travis all the way, turned to his fellows in the gallery and shouted, "Well, I'm damned glad. I'm damned glad." Another galleryite shook his head in admiration and soliloquized, "Travis could *write* with his putter if you put a nib on it." Some of the spectators still argued that Travis' win, much as they respected the man,

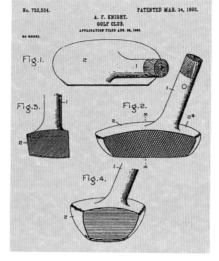

was a fluke. He had putted his way to victory, won the championship solely because of the wizardry of his weird Schenectady. The men who really appreciated the game knew better. Inspired as Travis' putting had been at Sandwich, he had played excellent golf the entire week. In the rough cross-winds on his final rounds, when the least flaw in shot-making was exaggerated into a punishing error, he had stroked the ball cleanly down the fairways with his compact, controlled swing.

Exultant as he was over his victory, Travis was hurt by some of the remarks made by Lord Northbourne during the cup presentation. Northbourne's family had lived for centuries in the old castle on the hill close by the course. From time to time Northbourne came down from the hill to lend a hand in the ceremonies at Sandwich, regarding this as a genial display of interest in the affairs of his tenantry. His speeches were invariably long and maladroit. On this occasion Lord Northbourne spoke for almost an hour—dwelling at length on the early history of the county of Kent under the Romans, rehearsing the glories of British golf and British golfers, and then, very briefly, congratulating Mr. Travis on his triumph and piously hoping that such a disaster would never again befall British sport. Travis hid his annoyance and made a short, graceful acceptance speech. The conquest was over.

Several years later, under a ruling by the R. & A., the Schenectady putter—and its cousins—was barred from British tournaments.

The Old Man grew older, but he got a few more licks in before he closed his tournament career. In the United States Amateur of 1904, it took three 2s by George Ormiston to knock him out. Ormiston played an orthodox 2 on the tenth, holed a full mashie for a 2 on the twelfth, and clinched the match by rolling in an approach shot from 125 yards out for a 2 on the seventeenth. (One of Travis' sympathizers sought to console him with the obvious remark that Ormiston had been extremely lucky. "You seem to forget," Travis answered him calmly, "that luck is a part of the game, and a good golfer must be good at all parts of the game.") Three times after this the Old Man won the medal in the Amateur, and in 1909 he led all the other amateur entries in the national Open. He never won the Amateur again, though. He could play superb golf for two or three rounds—rather similarly to the way Bill Tilden, after he reached fifty, could still hold his own with any tennis player for one set. But the Old Man's stamina was failing, and toward the end of the tournament week the youngsters could take him. He devoted more and more time to his other golf interests: the Old Guards clique at Palm Beach; the *American Golfer*, which he inaugurated and edited with a clear, bold hand; the designing and remodeling of golf courses. As a golf architect he was not noted for his inventiveness. Rather, he was a tightener-up of courses, a follower of the penal rather than the strategic school of design.

One day when he was remodeling some holes at the Essex County course in Massachusetts, Travis inadvertently disclosed the secret of his success as a golfer and, particularly, as a putter. He and the consulting parties were discussing the probabilities of turning a stretch of land into a new short hole. Asked how far he thought it was to a certain tree, Travis estimated the distance to be between 155 and 157 yards. "Why not say between a hundred and fifty-five and a hundred sixty yards, Walter?" one of the group asked. "It isn't," Travis answered. "It's between one fifty-five and one fifty-seven." He hadn't meant to be dogmatic, but he had seemed so sure of his estimate that the group decided to measure the distance and see how close the Old Man actually was. He was a little off. The tree was 157 1/2 yards away. This incident impressed upon those to whom it was related a fact about Travis that they had always sensed but had never quite known: he was an infallible judge of distance, probably the greatest in this respect of all American golfers.

The Old Man finally gave up tournament golf in 1915 when he was well into his fifties. He finished like a true champion. He won the Metropolitan Amateur. On his route to victory he defeated five capable young men, including Jerry Travers. In his final match against John G. Anderson he sealed his victory on the home green with a gesture so completely fitting that it has the ring of high fiction: He lined up a 30-foot putt, and with the palms of his hands in direct opposition to each other to produce a pendulum stroke, tapped the ball and watched it meander off the roll and make its way confidently into the center of the cup.

Jerome D. Travers— The Great Young Man

F R O M Jerry Travers down through Bill Campbell, a very high percentage of the ranking American amateur golfers have been the sons of well-to-do families, who were able to start the game young, develop under the guidance of the best teachers, play and practice whenever they chose. These factors, and particularly the last, afforded young men like Bob Gardner, Max Marston, Bobby Jones, Jess Sweetser, George Dunlap, Charlie Yates, Dick Chapman, and Frank Stranahan—to name a few of the many blessed with the advantages of life—a much easier avenue to championship golf than amateurs who had to work five days a week for a living, or, more precisely, to work when they would have liked to have been out on the course perfecting the intimate timing required of the topflight golfer. The amateur without a provided income could solve his problem of work versus golf by combining the warring elements and becoming a professional golfer—as did George Von Elm, Lawson Little, and, more recently, Cary Middlecoff, Gene Littler, Ken Venturi, and Johnny Miller, to name some of those who come first to mind. Failing this, he could ride on the prestige of a

series of good showings into a job where a sympathetic boss, almost a sponsor, allowed him to take off for the fairways and get in the practice he needed in the weeks preceding an important tourney—as Chick Evans did, for instance, or Johnny Goodman or Harvie Ward. The amateur confined to weekend golf by the necessity of earning a living cannot hope to stand up to the rigors of championship play, no matter how talented he may be.

The story of Jerome D. Travers is more than the story of a rich man's son who made good in golf. It is the story of a pertinacious student and a gifted match-player. But it is still the story of a young man who had every assistance in his quest for championship honors, and as such it is nicely typical of the pattern that through the years has produced some of our finest shot-makers.

Jerome Dunstan Travers' adventures in golf began on the lawns of his father's estate at Oyster Bay on Long Island. When he was nine years old, Jerry tried out the game by hitting midiron shots from the windmill on the back lawn toward the house, 100 yards away. The next year, home from school, he teed a ball at the windmill and drove it through a window in the house. At his father's suggestion, Jerry then shifted the area of his industry to the larger front lawn. Here he improvised three shatter-proof holes. The first ran from the flagpole to an old oak 150 yards away; the second, from the oak to a narrow tree in the right-hand corner of the lawn 180 yards off; and the third stretched from the small tree back to the flagpole. Jerry set to work mastering his triangle. The first time he hit the tree on the first hole in one shot, he became highly excited and went to pieces; it took him seven blows to hit the narrow second "hole."

When he was thirteen Jerry began to play regularly at the Oyster Bay course. Matches with the three Mahon boys—two of them were caddies and one gave lessons—brought the youngster's game along in the right channels. Two years later Jerry's father joined the Nassau Country Club at Glen Cove and Jerry became a junior member. One day after he had lost a match to a boy his own age, Jerry was approached by Alex Smith, the pro at Nassau.

"Do you want to become a real golfer, kid," Alex asked, "or are you just going to dub around at the game?"

The fifteen-year-older said he wanted to become a real golfer.

"All right," said Alex. "Now that we understand each other, let's see what you can do."

Smith watched the youngster hit out a batch of balls and gave him his first lesson. He pointed out three distinct faults. The youngster was overswinging. He held his arms too stiff. His right hand was too much on top of the shaft.

Two years later, after constant practice and regular lessons with Smith, Jerry Travers won the Interscholastic Championship. That same summer—1904—he attracted national attention by defeating Walter Travis in the final of the Nassau Invitation tournament. Two holes down with five to

play, Travers squared the match by the eighteenth and won it with a birdie on the 21st. His father was so jubilant over his boy's triumph that when Jerry asked him for two dollars to pay his caddie, he handled him a twenty-dollar bill by mistake.

This was the first of a long series of duels between Travers and Travis. It was a serious rivalry. The young man and the Old Man were of the same basic temperament: they always went out to win, not just to play well. It was also a friendly rivalry. After his defeat in the Nassau tournament, for example, Travis had remarked, "There is no aftermath of bitterness in such a defeat. It is a match I shall always recall with pleasure." For his part, Jerry Travers never forgot that the Old Man was a remarkable golfer and a fine sportsman. At the time Jerry may have regarded their rivalry as one hard match after another from which he derived intense pain or pleasure, depending on the outcome. In retrospect, however, his duels with Travis formed the crucible in which a talented young golfer was made into the greatest match player of his decade.

In 1905 Jerry, who was then all of eighteen, defeated Travis 7 and 6 in the Metropolitan Amateur Championship. At Westbrook, Travis retaliated measure for measure. He overwhelmed Jerry 8 and 7 and thought that after that thrashing the boy would never be able to beat him again. He looked to be right when they met next

JERRY TRAVERS, OPPOSITE, WAS A STYLISH PLAYER FROM LONG ISLAND WHO, BETWEEN 1907 AND 1915, WON FIVE NATIONAL TITLES AND THEN RETIRED FROM CHAMPIONSHIP PLAY.

at Shinnecock, for he pulled out the match on the 21st green when it was Jerry who had the openings in the extra holes. But at Nassau, Jerry came back to win 4 and 2. For ten more years after this, the two bulldogs went after each other, and sometimes the young bulldog beat the old bulldog and sometimes he didnt. It was a rivalry from which both, really, emerged victorious.

The following year Jerry Travers captured his first big championship, the Metropolitan. The "Kid Champion" caught the fancy of the Eastern golf fans, and one New York reporter pulled out all the stops. "The feature of the winner's game," he wrote, "was the length of his full shots and their perfect direction. W. J. Travis in his palmiest days was never truer on line. Then again the youngster had a versatility in playing various iron and approach shots which few veterans could surpass, and what slight weakness there might have been in his game was an occasional lack of strength in his approach putts."

Travers was knocked out of the United States Amateur that year by Travis, with an assist going to the young man's loss of temper after a camera clicked as he was about to hit a shot. The next season, 1907, a more mature Travers climaxed his steady improvement by winning the Amateur at the Euclid Golf Club in Cleveland. Travers was then just twenty-one, a medium-sized young man of wiry build and the deceptive strength that usually accompanies it. Alex Smith had not been able to shorten his swing appreciably. The new champion's backswing was overly fast as well, but his

hands were good and he brought the club-head beautifully into the ball. He had corrected his tendency to lapse on the putting green. In the final of the Amateur against Archie Graham, he putted like a Travis, and came to the thirteenth green in the afternoon needing only to hole a simple 4-footer to close out the match. Then, under the unnerving realization that he would win if he sank the putt, Travers froze. He found he had no feel of his hands or the putter. Walking away from the ball, he explained to Graham that he just couldnt begin to go through the motions of the shot. "Oh, drop it anyway and end the agony," Graham told him shortly. "You couldn't miss it with your eyes shut." He dropped it.

Travers successfully defended his title in 1908 when the Amateur was played at the Garden City Golf Club. Stern-faced and uncommunicative, the twenty-two-year-old veteran of twelve golfing seasons marched relentlessly through one match after another and defeated Max Behr 8 and 7 in the final. His only moment of danger came in his semi-final match with Travis. All even coming to the seventeenth in an eighteen-hole match, the young man fired a magnificent second, a 240-yard brassie that hooked into the opening to the green and left him with a short putt for his birdie. To keep the match alive, Travis now had to win the eighteenth. The eighteenth at Garden City, Travis' home course, is a devilish short

hole over water to a green surrounded flamboyantly by bunkers that Travis himself had designed and had refused to eradicate or make shallower in the spite of the vigorous objections of the members. One bunker in particular struck the members as unfair— a pit six feet deep with perpendicular walls, to the left of the green. It was this bunker that Travis found with his tee shot. Travers put his tee shot on the green and stood by his ball as the Old Man lowered himself into the pit and passed out of sight. From the pit came the sound of a heavy thump, and then a spray of sand flew up, but no ball came into sight. Then another thump, another spray, but still no ball. The Old Man then pulled himself out of the bunker, walked over and congratulated Travers. One member of the gallery could not resist commenting in a stentorian stage whisper, "I guess the Old Man dug his own grave that time." Travis accepted the humor, nodded and smiled.

Travis was extremely pleased with the triumphs of Jerry Travers. He devoted the key pages in the first issues of the *American Golfer* to a pictorial analysis of the champion's game. Travis' editorial comments left no doubt that he believed that any young man learning the game would do well to adopt the basic features of Travers' style, if not his slightly open stance, very full pivot, and effortful followthrough. For this series of photographs the champion wore his

TRAVERS' SWING WAS PRAISED BY WALTER TRAVIS BUT HIS DRIVES WERE SO ERRATIC THAT HE OFTEN USED HIS CLEEK, A LONG IRON, OFF THE TEE; OPPOSITE, HE USES IT TO PLAY A PITCH-AND-RUN SHOT.

favorite golf attire: a small cap, a regular white shirt buttoned at the neck but without a tie, cardigan sweater, white duck trousers, and white low-cut sneakers. He also wore his favorite expression: a bland poker face.

Jerry Travers made a disappointing showing in 1909 when he attempted to repeat the triumph of Walter Travis in the British Amateur. He was knocked out in the first round. He did not choose to defend his American Amateur crown that year—Bob Gardner, the Yale pole vaulter, won it—nor did he enter the event in 1910, when it went to Bill Fownes of Oakmont. The following spring

Jerry returned to tournament play in earnest, having learned during his two lean years that a young man cannot be both a professional playboy and an amateur golf champion. He won the Metropolitan and the New Jersey Amateurs—he was now playing out of the Upper Montclair Country Club—but Harold Hilton beat him in the third round of the national Amateur. Travers put up a stout fight against Hilton after a poor morning round, but looked up on a 2-foot putt when he had the Englishman worried.

The Amateur of 1912 was called "the Blazing Championship." Only a few days before the tournament, the clubhouse of the Chicago Golf Club burned down; the weather was torrid; and in the final Jerry Travers cut loose with some of the hottest stretches of golf ever played in the championship. His opponent in the final was Chick Evans, a young Chicagoan who looked as awkward as a farm boy until he took his stance before a golf ball and released the prettiest one-piece swing on the continent. Three times before, he had reached the semi-final round of the Amateur. Now that Evans had chased his semi-final jinx and, moreover, was playing on home ground, his supporters could not see how the local star could be beaten. Travers had been playing much less convincing golf than Evans, but the Easterners who had come out to watch the championship were confident that their man would rise to the occasion and produce his best golf when he had to. On the eve of the final, sectional feeling ran high and the wagering was heavy.

Travers was lucky to finish the morning round only 1 down. Where Evans was stroking the ball from tee to green with his lyrical accuracy, Travers was all over the course. Jerry could not correct the hook he was getting with his woods off the tee, and was forced to drive with an iron most of the time. He hung on by some courageous scrambling, playing deft pitch-and-run shots on the sun-baked course and canning three putts of over twenty feet. The last of these was a 35-footer on the eighteenth green that cut Evans margin to 1 up and, simultaneously, pared away some of Chicks confidence. Chick had been "inside" of Tra-

vers and had visions of going to lunch 3 up, and certainly not lower than 2.

The fourth hole of the afternoon round decided the match. Evans had now lost his lead, and the partisan gallery was beginning to feel uneasy as they saw his usually smiling face grow long and fretful. Maybe Chick could pull himself together if Travers would do something wrong. On the fourth tee Travers made a mistake, a bad one. His drive was a wide, sweeping hook that flew over the edge of the fairway and headed for the high, tough rough that would cost him one or possibly two recovery strokes. The ball, however, slapped into a mound and rebounded back onto the fairway. This break shattered whatever fight was left in Evans. Travers won the hole and saw to it that his opponent had no further openings. He raced to the turn in 34 strokes to win six of the nine holes and go 5 up. He won the tenth as Chick plodded down the fairway in a daze. Two holes later he ended the slaughter, 7 and 6. On the walk-in Jerry allowed himself to relax for the first time. During the match he had spoken to only one person, Freddy Herreshoff, a golf crony of many years standing who caddied for him in the final.

In 1913 the national Amateur was played once again over the tight, multi-trapped course of the Garden City Golf Club. Never noted for his medal scores, Travers this time barely qualified. On the

CHICK EVANS, OPPOSITE, AN EX-CADDIE FROM CHICAGO WHO FACED PLAYBOY-GOLFER JERRY TRAVERS IN THE FINALS OF THE 1912 U.S. AMATEUR, AND LOST, LATER BECAME THE FINEST PLAYER OF HIS DAY.

famous last hole, the short one over the pond, Jerry took a 7. One more shot and he would have been out. As it was, he gained the chance to defend his title by winning a place in the most amazing playoff of all times. Twelve players fighting for eleven places teed up on the first hole to determine which one of them would not qualify. This distinction fell to Heinie Schmidt, the man who had the best drive of the lot. Instead of making sure that he hit his second shot well over the bunker protecting the green, Heinie elected to go for the pin with a niblick, caught the far edge of the bunker, and that was that. There was a further note of irony in Schmidt's elimination. Had he used his head and played in the clothes the steaming weather demanded, Heinie would have been among the lowest scorers. Instead, Heinie wore the heavy tweed golf suit he had just purchased in England—cap, jacket, and knickers in a large hound's-tooth check. Any sensible man would have discarded this English-winter outfit, but Heinie—he had added red socks and a matching bow tie—was going to show the boys how the well-accoutered Britisher dressed, and he balked at peeling off his new suit even when the men in shirtsleeves were feeling the heat.

Once assured of a place in the match-play rounds, Jerry Travers got down to business. Bellwood, the pro at Garden City, showed him what he was doing wrong: his left wrist was breaking in toward his body as he started the club down. After this correc-tion, Jerry was able to squeak by in his early matches although he was far from his top form. He shanked his irons periodically, and was getting that perniciously sharp hook with his driver. He practiced between rounds, and when his woods still gave him trouble, decided to use his black driving-iron off the tee in his semi-final match should his opponent, an unheralded youngster from Boston named Francis Ouimet, put up a bat-tle. Ouimet put up such a battle that Travers used his driver only twice during, the morn-ing round—he hit one fair and one very poor shot with it—and on the second eighteen Travers did not use his driver at all.

Against Ouimet, Travers went to lunch with a 1-up margin produced by a 20-foot putt on the home green. In the afternoon Jerry won the first hole, but then the cool young man from Boston came fighting back to take the second and the third and square the match. Ouimet went 1 up when he took the seventh, and appeared to be on his way to add to his lead on the eighth when he planted his second shot, a 180-yard iron to an uphill green, eight feet from the cup. Travers took a little more time than usual before hitting his second. It would be a cru-cial stroke and he wanted to think it out fully. A mild practice swing and finally he was ready to play. He came through with a shot that covered the flag all the way, sat down smartly on the green, and ended up ten inches from the hole. Ouimet missed his try for a birdie, and knew then that he was licked.

In the final Jerry had a comparatively easy time with John G. Anderson, 5 and 4. At the ripe old age of twenty-six the erstwhile Kid Champion had won his fourth, and what proved to be his last, Amateur Championship. No player before had won the crown four times, and the best golf heads, with reason, could not see any later golfer equaling this record. With the exception of Jones, no one ever has.

Off the course Jerry Travers was an amiable person, but during a match he was as cold as a halibut, and as expressionless. He was aware that his manner distracted many of his opponents, but this was secondary and somewhat accidental. What was important was that alone with his game, keen but not tense, Jerry could play winning golf. Along with Hagen, although Hagen's temperament was quite different, he stands out as a golfer who could somehow win matches when he was far off his game. He had the ability to hit an iron ten inches from the cup, like that crusher against Ouimet, at the critical moment. He developed into a remarkable putter, one to be ranked in the same category with Travis, and in this department again his forte was the unexpected ones—which means the putts his opponent did not expect him to drop and which broke hearts and hopes when they did. Like most rich men's sons who have played a sport well, Travers could afford to play the game as if his next meal depended on winning.

In the semi-finals of the 1913 National Amateur, an unknown player named Francis Ouimet, above, gave eventual winner Jerry Travers a run for his money.

Childe Harold's Pilgrimage

IN the interim between Jerry Travers' two-year reigns in 1907-8 and 1912-13, the United States Amateur Championship acquired an international flavor when Harold Horsfall Hilton crossed the Atlantic to play in the event in 1911. Hilton held a position among British amateurs akin to Harry Vardon's unquestioned supremacy among the pros. In 1900, 1901, and 1911, Hilton had triumphed in the British Amateur, and before that, in 1892 and 1897, he had done the unthinkable for an amateur and won the British Open. In the spring of 1911, just when it looked as if he would carry off his third Open title, he had stumbled.

On the short sixteenth at Sandwich, the 70th hole of the grind, Hilton had caught a trap with his iron off the tee. A 3 on that short hole would have won for him; his 5 left him one stroke behind Vardon and Arnaud Massy, who tied for first. Had Hilton won, the thought of coming to America might never have entered his mind. He lost, and set out to drown his sorrows in the wine of victory, in our Amateur.

As Harold Hilton sailed for America, the press came up with a bright tag for his purposeful visit—"Childe Harold's Pilgrimage." It was a good phrase and deserved to stick, although, as the literal-minded pointed out, Hilton was a middle-aged man and not a child and rather devoid of the other qualities that made a Byronic hero. He was medium-sized, suave, contained, and worldly—the kind of chap you would expect to take plenty of time choosing the colors in his hose and who would have H. H. H. neatly engraved on his cigarette case. He smoked fifty cigarettes on the days he played golf—another record that Jones beat—and in the evenings exhibited a continuous concern for the King's health and the health of the American president. He appreciated the nuances of the English language and expressed himself with practiced delicacy. He was sensible about his golf. He knew precisely how well he could play, and experience had taught him that few amateurs could keep up with him, so he played his own game and let nature take its course.

WILLS'S CIGARETTES.

ARNAUD MASSY.

Hilton's challenge in 1911 altered the attitudes of the Americans assembled at the Apawamis Club in Rye, New York. For the first time since Harriman's victory in 1899, the dominance of the native-born players was endangered. The customary rivalry between the Eastern stars and the Western stars was momentarily shelved, and the homebreds united their energies to throttle the foreign threat. (In many ways Hilton's invasion was Travis in reverse.) Chicagoans would have preferred one of their own boys—say, Chick Evans or Albert Seckel or Paul Hunter—to gain the glory of stopping Hilton, but if Jerry Travers or Oswald Kirkby or some other Easterner could turn the trick, well, the honor of America came ahead of that of Chicago. Every loyal American prayed for a week of sunshine to sere the turf and harden the ground. On a wet, slow course, they confided to one another, Hilton would be a much tougher man to beat.

It rained. As everyone feared, Hilton found the soggy turf to his liking. But even on the dryer days, he played crisp, steady golf. There was nothing poetic about his swing. Before playing each shot, he planted his feet with deliberation, waggled his club for a moment, and then, with a little jump forward onto his toes, took the club back quickly and brought it down into the ball with a rapid hitting action. It was a deceptive style, for beneath this fast smash of a swing the studied art of controlling the ball lay concealed. Hilton thought out each shot well in advance. Whenever the wind or the topography advised it, he played intentional slices or hooks—or perhaps it is more accurate to say that he played the shot for drift or draw. This is an easier thing to do with

irons than with woods, but in his wood play Hilton had a phenomenal skill at bending the shot to order. Unlike Joe Kirkwood, the trick-shot artist of later days, Hilton could also hit the ball straight when he wanted to. Sometimes he played his approaches in the pitch-and-run style and at other times he lofted the ball to the green with a dancing backspin. When he appeared at Apawamis, Hilton was a shot or two past his peak but he showed the record galleries some subtleties of the game the native sons had not yet mastered.

Hilton started off by taking the qualifying medal with 76-74—150, two strokes better than Bob Gardner and Albert Seckel. In the first round, playing well within himself, he disposed of Samuel Graham of Greenwich 3 and 2. Next he took care of Robert C. Watson, the secretary of the U.S.G.A., by the score of 11 and 10, carding a nice 73 on the first eighteen. Moving into the third round, he met Jerry Travers. On the first eighteen Hilton did not play his best game, but Travers was very erratic and stood 4 down to the Englishman at lunch. Travers shook some great golf shots out of his bag in the afternoon, and by the 27th had reduced the Englishman's margin to one hole. Calm and assured, Hilton stalled him off with four halves in a row, won the 32nd and 33rd, and shut the door on Jerry, 3 and 2, with a half on the 34th. C. W. Inslee of Wykagyl fell an easy victim to Hilton's steadiness in the semifinal round; Hilton led by one hole at the ninth and slowly drew away to be 4 up at the eighteenth, 6 up at the 27th, and 8 up with six holes to play. In making his way to the final, Hilton had had to exert himself only during his match with Travers.

Hilton's opponent in the final was Fred Herreshoff. Herreshoff had been there before—in 1904, when he was a boy of seventeen and not good enough to stay with Chandler Egan. This nephew of Nat Herreshoff, the famous boat designer, had grown up into a broad, easygoing giant who could paste his tee shots ten or fifteen yards beyond the best efforts of men who prided themselves on their long-hitting. Herreshoff took an understandable delight in his slugging prowess, and perhaps the other departments of his game suffered from lack of attention. In any event, his irons were inconsistent and his putting was weak. When his driving was on, it took inspired golf to beat Herreshoff. When it was off, he was just another golfer. Freddy drank a good deal, but he apparently played as well after a big night as he did after an evening by the fireside. At Apawamis he fell into a hot putting streak that helped him through a much harder bracket than Hilton faced. In the semi-finals he had been expected to lose to Chick Evans but had stormed back after being 3 down at the halfway mark and put Chick out on the 34th green.

Hilton started off to make short work of Herreshoff. Actually, he did nothing exceptional himself but kept his shots online and let Herreshoff hand him three holes on the first nine through spotty driving and multiple putting. On the in-nine Hilton ran into errors himself and made no further headway until the eighteenth green, where he got down a 12-footer to give himself a comfortable four-hole lead to work on. When the match was resumed in the afternoon, Herreshoff presented Hilton with another hole when he pulled his drive on the first. Freddy topped his drive on the second but a fine chip enabled him to halve in 4s. Still 5 down. On the 310-yard third, Freddy tried to win the hole with his tee shot, lost his timing by pressing, and hooked his drive into an almost unplayable lie. It took him three strokes to reach the green and, of course, this cost him the hole. He was now 6 down. It looked like a rout. Freddy managed to halve the fourth, and the fifth as well when Hilton, with a chance to become 7 up, three-putted. Encouraged by this reprieve, on the 330-yard sixth he played three fine shots, the last a sizable putt for a winning three. This was Herreshoff's first birdie of the day, and it gave him a terrific mental lift. He went on to halve the seventh and win both the short eighth and the 612-yard

Urbane British amateur Harold Hilton, opposite, had won numerous titles in the U.K., including 3 Amateur titles and 2 Opens, before he entered and won the 1911 U.S. Amateur.

ninth. He reached the turn only 3 down.

Herreshoff had played himself back into the match. On the fourth (or 22nd) tee, all that the three thousand spectators had hoped for was some sort of a comeback by the American that would prolong the match a respectful number of holes and prevent Hiltons winning by too humiliating a margin. Now that Herreshoff had taken three of the last four holes, the spectators discovered that they would be satisfied with nothing less than an American victory. They realized that it would take very hot golf for a man to pick up three holes down the stretch from a campaigner of Hilton's caliber, but then, Herreshoff was now playing very hot golf. He was beginning to hit the ball fairly straight as well as for distance off the tees, and he had regained his putting touch.

Herreshoff did not let up, now that he had Hilton on the run. He pulled his drive on the tenth, but a chip shot stone-dead to the pin enabled him to halve in par 4s. He won the eleventh, to become only 2 down, when Hilton sent his tee shot out-of-bounds. Now, Herreshoff and his excited gallery knew that the Englishman, for all his studied composure, was feeling the pressure. On the twelfth, a 241-yard par 3, Freddy boomed his drive onto the green, won

the hole, and was now only 1 down. He was moving but the holes were running out and one error might ruin the stirring rally that had won for him five out of the last seven holes. On the thirteenth Herreshoff left himself a hard 15-foot putt for a half in 4 — and made it, when he knew he had to. He played the long fourteenth in a poor 6, but Hilton also messed up his fairway shots and could do no better than a 6 himself. With four holes to go, the Englishman still retained his narrow one-hole lead and was playing wisely if not too well. He appeared almost as debonair as when he had stood 6 up, and he hit his shots with the same cool urbanity, and yet it was obvious that he was not striking the ball at all well for him and was trying to avoid errors rather than gambling on bold winning shots. He was going to force Herreshoff to do the gambling.

On the fifteenth, the 33rd hole of the match, Herreshoff smashed out a long drive, and a lofted approach left him a birdie putt of some fifteen feet. He pushed the putt off-line. Still 1 down. On the 217-yard sixteenth (or 34th) he socked his tee shot hole-high but was off in the rough. Then he played a beautiful recovery to within four feet of the cup. Again he had the putt for the hole, and this time he made it. The match was now all square. Herreshoff's courageous comeback had won six holes for him, and he had not lost a hole since the 21st. Freddy was now in the driver's seat. When a player rallies down the stretch and catches his opponent, in golf, like in all sports, nine times out of ten his momentum, and his opponent's loss of confidence, will carry him on to victory.

Freddy had a chance to win the 35th but he rimmed the cup from five feet in his try for a birdie. He had a 7-footer for the hole and the match on the 36th, and again he failed to get it down. The gallery groaned, and then was off for the first hole, where Hilton and Herreshoff would begin their sudden-death struggle now that they had finished all even after thirty-six holes of grueling attack and counter-attack.

The first hole at Apawamis is a testing par 4, slightly uphill after the drive. In 1911 it measured 377 yards and called for two good shots. There was trouble on the right—rough, rocks, and woods. To the right of the green the ground sloped up moderately, and players might have used it as a bank for their approaches had the incline not been studded with rocks. There was less trouble on the left, and practically none whatsoever as Herreshoff and Hilton mounted the tee, for a wall of spectators lined that edge of the fairway all the way from tee to green.

It was Herreshoff's honor. He hit a good one, long and down the middle. Hilton faded his tee shot a bit but the ball sat down before it reached the rough. As usual, he was shorter off the tee than Herreshoff and prepared to play the odd. He looked the shot over, and asked for a spoon. He set his feet heavily in place, made that little spring onto his toes, and brought the club down fast. If Hilton had been playing for drift, he had overdone it. The ball streaked off to the right, heading straight for the rocky slope—and trouble. It was a poorly hit shot and deserved whatever harsh ricochet befell it; it would probably end up deep in the woods. The ball struck the incline hard—and dribbled easily down the slope and onto the green, well onto the green. For Hilton it was the luckiest of breaks. For Herreshoff it was the kiss of death. He half topped his approach short of the green. He was still twenty feet short of the pin with his chip. Hilton would almost surely get down in two for a 4, and to keep the match alive, Herreshoff had to sink his 20-footer. It was never in. Hilton, 1 up, thirty-seven holes.

Hilton's spoon to the 37th green became the most-discussed single shot ever played in an American tournament. Eyewitnesses could not agree as to what actually had happened when Hilton's ball struck the incline. Some men who were in a perfect position to see the shot were positive that the ball had evaded the rocks and taken a normal carom off the turf. Others who were in an equally good position were equally certain that the ball had struck a rock—and

HAROLD HILTON, RIGHT, OPPOSITE, AND FRED HERRESHOFF WERE SO EVENLY MATCHED IN THE 1911 U.S. AMATEUR FINAL THAT IT TOOK A LUCKY BOUNCE ON THE 37TH HOLE TO GIVE HILTON THE TITLE.

they could point out the exact culprit. In time, golf fans throughout the country, undoubtedly because the rock story made Hilton's victory seem less deserved, adopted this explanation. Golfers who visited Apawamis for the first time were let down when they found out that they had heard wrong and that there was no Hilton Rock nearby the first green duly inscribed with the grim facts of the extra hole.

Hilton had no comment to make on the winning break or on his campaign in general. However, his traveling companion, a Mr. Philip Samson, got some things off his chest when the London reporters interviewed him. Samson explained that he had never seen a gallery as unruly as the three thousand who had dogged the players at Apawamis. They didnt know the first thing about golf or golf deportment. Whenever Herreshoff won a hole they hollered and shook rattles. The officials, Samson opined, were just as bad. They were continually yelling at the crowd through megaphones, often when the players were hitting. Now the reporters could understand why Hilton had not been his usual impregnable self during the latter stages of the match.

Hilton's victory proved to be a blessing in disguise for American golfers. In the cool of reflection, the ranking amateurs came to understand how faulty they had been in presuming that they had already caught up with the best standards of play in Britain. Bizarre ending or no bizarre ending, the middle-aged Britisher had played better golf during the week at Apawamis than any of the homegrown hopefuls. Now they knew that they would have to work harder if they wanted to be the best golfers this side of the Nizhni Novgorod Country Club.

The effect of Hilton's victory on Americans who did not play golf was even more significant. Travis' overseas heroics in 1904 had never been circulated beyond the clubhouses, but the Hilton–Herreshoff match, because of its native setting, became a topic of the day for thousands of Americans. They were not at all pleased that a foreigner had carried one of our championship cups out of the country, and men who had never cared a straw about golf before now wanted to know the real inside story. The press was a good touchstone. A New York newspaper that had referred to the Englishman as "Horace H. Hilton" on his arrival got the name right when he left.

If it was solace American golf fans were seeking, they could find it in the fact that in the same year Hilton carried off the U.S. Amateur trophy, a homebred for the first time won the U.S. Open. Not that Johnny

JOHNNIE McDERMOTT MADE GOLF HEADLINES WHEN HE BECAME THE FIRST AMERICAN-BORN PLAYER TO WIN THE U.S. OPEN. A STEREO VIEW, OPPOSITE, OFTEN DEPICTED A HERO OR MONUMENT.

McDermott's victory could balance Hilton's. In the first place, McDermott had not beaten any "real foreigners," just the Scottish-and English-born professionals who had become as permanent a part of the American scene as Swedish masseurs and Chinese laundrymen. And, in the second place, in 1911 the Open was not as important a championship as the Amateur, for the very ample reason that no native son had ever

which one of the old familiar faces was playing the best golf that week. The winner received $300 and became even more godlike in the eyes of his pupils.

The two outstanding champions in the early days of the Open were Willie Anderson and Alex Smith. Anderson picked up his first title in 1901 when he defeated Alex in the playoff at Myopia, north of Boston, after they had tied at 331. Before he

953. J. J. McDERMOTT.—Grip. Mashie.

won it. From its unofficial inception in 1894—when Willie Dunn beat Willie Davis and Willie Campbell, and many Americans had deduced that every golf pro had to be named Willie—the Open had been a gathering of the clans. The Smiths and the Nichollses and the Rosses and the McLeods exchanged news from home, chatted about the courses they were designing and the wealthy duffers they were stuck with, and topped off their annual convention with seventy-two holes of medal play to see

succumbed to a lingering illness, Anderson won the Open three more times, in '03, '04, and '05. Along with Jones and Hogan, the dour, flat-swinging Scot stands as the only four-time winner of the event. Alex Smith won it twice. (His brother Willie had crashed through before him in 1899.) After many seasons as a top contender, Alex finally made the grade in 1906. In winning, he totaled 295 for his four rounds, the first time anyone had broken 300 in the championship. (At the time, this performance was viewed as nothing short of miraculous, and experts doubted if Smiths record would ever be broken. Only three years later, George Sargent returned a total of 290 in winning the Open over the moderately easy Englewood Golf Club, in New Jersey. Then the experts were just as positive that no one would ever again come close to Sargent's mark.) Alex Smith was a hearty man with a grand sense of humor and a temperament that is often the crucial difference between a splendid player and a champion. He never took his golf too seriously, never dawdled before a shot. His motto for putting was "Miss'em quick." Alex won his second championship in 1910 when a person of less equable temperament might have groaned himself groggy. On the 72nd green he missed a simple 3-foot putt that would have given him the championship outright then and there. He grinned it off—and meant it—and the next day went out and won the playoff hands down from his kid brother Macdonald and Johnny McDermott.

The victory by a homebred, when it finally came in 1911, was a surprise and a shock, and yet it should not have been. The American pros had been gradually closing the gap between themselves and the foreign-born professionals. In the 1909 Open, Tommy McNamara of Boston had scored a remarkable 69—to become the first man to break 70 in major competition in America—and had gone down the homestretch neck and neck with the winner, Sargent. The next year, McDermott, the chesty little pro from Atlantic City, had reached the playoff only to lose to Alex Smith. Sooner or later a homebred was bound to snap the monopoly of the transplanted, and McDermott did it in 1911 at the Chicago Golf Club, when he again tied for first and this time won the play-off. The following year McDermott demonstrated that he was a worthy champion by successfully defending his title at the Country Club of Buffalo before a happy gallery that included a young assistant pro from Rochester, Walter Hagen.

McDermott had expected to win at Chicago and Buffalo. He expected to win every tournament he entered. As shy as Mark Spitz and as reserved as Howard Cosell, McDermott feared no man. He was willing to wager on his ability to outplay any golfer in the world—Vardon not excepted—any time, any place, and for any amount of money. For two or three seasons, while his nerve held high, the 130-pound bantam-cock was almost as good as he thought he was. In the Shawnee Open of 1913 he did defeat Vardon. And then, almost as quickly as he had appeared, McDermott vanished. The nerves on which he had relied so heavily to carry him to the top suddenly snapped. By 1915 he was forced to retire from active tournament competition. Four scant years after Johnny McDermott had won at Chicago, golfers had to pause a moment and ponder before they could remember the name of the little firecracker who was the first American to win the United States Open.

The Shots Heard Round the World

WHENEVER the peerless Harry Vardon came to America, something of great consequence invariably happened. Vardon made his second tour of this country in 1913, with the backing of Lord Northcliffe, the owner of the *Times* of London. For his series of exhibition matches, Vardon had in Edward "Ted" Ray the ideal partner, a perfect Pythias for their four-ball matches and a dramatically long hitter born to attract galleries. Whereas Vardon's swing was a flawless fusion of grace and power, Ray was all power. A bulky, slope-shouldered man standing an inch over six feet and weighing about two hundred pounds, Ted Ray threw all of his weight and strength into his strokes. He broke the rules of correct body movement right and left. He swayed on his backswing and came into the ball with a lurch, but he could get away with it because of the fundamental rhythm of his swing and the grooved arc of his clubhead. He could be wild, all right, but he had won the British Open at Muirfield in 1912 and had done this by clearly outplaying Vardon, James Braid, J. H. Taylor, Sandy Herd, and the other formidable British professionals. A large laissez-faire mustache gave Ray's otherwise mild face a rather fearsome aspect. He played in a long, loose tweed jacket and a crushed felt hat, and was never seen on or off a golf course minus a pipe, usually a big Sherlock Holmes model.

The Vardon–Ray tour of 1913 was an unprecedented success. Wherever they played, record or near-record crowds turned out to learn from watching Vardon how easy the game became in the hands of the master and to gasp at Ray's Brobdingnagian tee shots and his surprisingly delicate touch on the greens. Bobby Jones, a boy of eleven, saw the Englishmen when they played an exhibition in Atlanta after the national Open, and he always remembered one recovery played by Ray as the greatest golf shot he ever saw. After a long but wild drive, Ray found his line to the green directly stymied by a spreading tree more than forty feet high. Since his ball lay about thirty feet from the base of the tree, lofting over it was out of the question, and the spectators speculated as to whether he would try to slice or hook it around the obstacle. Ray took a look at the green 170 yards away and pulled out his mashie-niblick. Then, as Jones tells it, "he hit the ball harder, I believe, than I have ever seen a ball hit since, knocking it down as if he would drive it through to China. Up flew a divot the size of Ted's ample foot. Up also came the ball, buzzing like a partridge from the prodigious spin imparted by that tremendous wallop—almost straight up it got, cleared the tree by several yards, and sailed on at the height of an office building, to drop on the green not far from the hole."

Another stop on the Vardon–Ray tour was Chicago, where one of their opponents was a left-hander. He played way over his head during the match and, bent on doing a little fishing afterwards, approached Vardon and asked him whom he considered to be the best left-handed golfer he had ever seen during his lifetime on the links. "Never saw one who was worth a damn," grunted Vardon.

Ray and Vardon interrupted their tour in mid-September to play in the national Open, held at The Country Club in Brookline, outside Boston. Two other European professionals were in the field assembling there—Wilfred Reid from Banstead Downs, in England, and the diminutive French star Louis Tellier. Johnny McDermott was primed to defend his title, and Mike Brady, Tommy McNamara, and Jerry Travers, among the homebreds, and Macdonald Smith and Jim Barnes, among the transplanted Britons, were on hand for what loomed as the most turbulent tournament ever staged in this country.

The 1913 Open was the big leagues, the big test for American golf—no question about it. The United States had demonstrated that it could hold its own in international sports competition by defeating teams representing Great Britain in tennis, yachting, and polo, but was it still too early to hope for a declaration of independence on the golf course? It could be done, of course. McDermott had confessed to his countrymen that he was just as good as Vardon, and Brady and McNamara knew The Country Club course by heart. Yet when Americans weighed the mild talents of the native-born players against the furious talent of Ray and the genius of Vardon, they reluctantly concluded that it might probably take another few years.

Because of the large number of entries, the qualifying round of thirty-six holes was divided into three sections, with some of the players assigned to the first day of play and the rest finishing up on the second. Vardon led the first-day qualifiers with a total of 151, a stroke ahead of twenty-year-old Francis Ouimet, a local boy who held the Massachusetts State Amateur title and had given Jerry Travers quite a tussle in the semi-finals of the national Amateur. Mac Smith had played two steady 77s and would bear watching. On the second day, Ted Ray paced the qualifiers with 148, three strokes better than his countryman Reid. McDermott and Brady played poorly, though they managed to qualify. A kid named Hagen playing his first national tournament hit the ball impressively in posting a total of 157.

With the formality of the qualifying round out of the way, and no casualties among the favorites, the players started the championship test—seventy-two holes of medal play (thirty-six on both days) over a hard par-71 layout. At the halfway mark Reid and Vardon were tied for the lead with 147, two strokes ahead of Ray and three ahead of Mac Smith and Barnes. The youngsters, Ouimet and Hagen, were still in the running with 151, as was Tellier with 152, but McDermott and Brady were still having trouble. Travers was too far behind at 156, and McNamara had blasted his chances by adding a wretched 86 to his opening 73.

At the end of 54 holes, Vardon, Ray, and Ouimet were tied for the lead at 225. Ouimet had caught the two favorites with a round of 74, but no man in his right mind could expect the inexperienced amateur to stand up to the enormous pressure of the last round of a major tournament. Reid had blown sky-high. Tellier had not made up enough ground. Hagen, Smith, Barnes, and McDermott would have to play sub-par golf to catch the leaders, and the sodden condition of the course definitely argued against the realization of any such hopes.

Ray was the first one of the leaders to finish his fourth round. He had taken a 79 on the rain-soaked course and would have to stand by at 304 and see how his rivals fared. One by one they faded. Vardon straggled home with a 79, which was only good enough for a tie with Ray. Harry's putting, his old Achilles' heel, had let him down. Back to the clubhouse over the grapevine came the news that Barnes' rally had petered out. Hagen and Smith were done too. Tellier had a fighting chance until he reached the twelfth, and then he had cracked wide open. Simultaneously the report came in that Ouimet, the one man left who could catch Vardon and Ray, had gone to the turn in 43 and had killed off what slim chance remained for him by taking a 5 on the short tenth. To get his 304 now, Francis would have to play the last eight holes in one stroke under even 4s, and under the circumstances that was asking for the impossible. The young man deserved enormous credit for sticking with the Englishmen as long as he had.

WILL'S CIGARETTES.

EDWARD RAY.

Ouimet did not think he was finished. Even when he had taken a 5 on the par-4 twelfth after getting his par on the eleventh, he did not give up the fight. On the thirteenth tee he figured out that he would now have to play the last six holes in twenty-two strokes, 2 under par, to gain a tie. He went over the six holes in his mind and selected the thirteenth and the sixteenth as the ones on which he had the best chance to pick up the two birdies he needed. He had been putting for 3s regularly on the thirteenth, a short par 4; the sixteenth was a relatively easy par 3, but Francis had not gotten a deuce there all week and had a hunch that this could be the time.

Francis got his birdie on the thirteenth, but had to hole a chip from the edge of the green to do it. On the fourteenth, he got his par 5 comfortably enough. He hit a nice drive on the fifteenth, a testing par 4, and then completely mishit his approach. To stay in the hunt, Francis had to get down in 2 from a snug lie in the rough, and did this by playing a superb chip shot less than a yard from the pin. He came to the short sixteenth, the hole he had a hunch he might birdie. His hunch was wrong. Francis had to sink a 9-foot putt to get his par.

To tie now, Ouimet was faced with bagging that all-important birdie on either the seventeenth, a dogleg to the left, or on the eighteenth, a somewhat lengthier par 4. The gallery appreciated as clearly as the boy himself the full size of that task. There was an almost tangible tension in the air as Francis followed his drive down the seventeenth with a jigger shot some twenty feet from the pin. On the green the young man did not fidget or pose. He looked over the sliding downhill, sidehill putt, and concentrating so intensely that he did not hear the blare of automobile horns that unnerved the gallery, stroked the ball boldly for the cup. The ball took the roll nicely, slipped rapidly down the slope, struck the back of the cup hard, and stayed in. The keyed-up spectators crammed around the seventeenth green could not contain themselves. They yelled, pummeled each other joyously, swatted their friends with umbrellas, and shouted delirious phrases they had not thought of since boyhood. Jerry Travers, the icicle himself, jumped three feet in the air. The stirring battle of the hometown David against the two Goliaths had cut deeper into their emotions than the gallery had been aware.

Francis Ouimet was the calmest man on the course as he walked to the eighteenth tee. He needed a par 4 now to tie Ray and Vardon. He forgot about everything else but getting that 4. His drive was satisfactory, straight and long enough. He hit his second shot accurately and saw it kick up the mud at the top of the soft bank in front of the green. His chip shot left him five feet short of the cup. Then, with a complete disregard for the feelings of the spectators, he stepped up to his putt as if he had not the vaguest idea that history was riding on that shot. He placed his putter in front of the ball once, took a

look at the hole, and hit the ball firmly into the back of the cup.

The moment the ball entered the hole, the rarefied air of The Country Club was filled with a mass cheer and individual outbursts the like of which for pure spontaneity and heartfelt joy may have never been equaled on any golf course. The impossible and the historic had happened, and the spectators felt it in the pits of their stomachs. In what was a positive ecstasy, they mobbed their hero and hoisted him on their shoulders and might have done him physical damage with their demonstrations of affection and congratulation had some cool head not reminded them that Francis Ouimet had to play off the next morning with Harry Vardon and Ted Ray.

Americans turned to their newspapers the following morning and read about the incredible accomplishment of Francis Ouimet. Outside of Massachusetts, no one had ever heard of him. Who was this Ouimet? What had he done before? How was that name pronounced—*Oymet* or *Umet* or *Weemay* or what?

The name was pronounced *Weemet.* In time the country received the answers to the other questions and learned that its hero was ten-tenths a hero, compounded from the very best parts of Charles Dickens and Booth Tarkington with a touch of Horatio Alger.

When Francis Ouimet was starting grade school, his father moved the family from a thinly populated section of Brookline to a modest house he had bought across the street from The Country Club. Mr. Ouimet was a workingman with no interest in golf, and had it not been for the proximity of the course his sons might have emptied their childhood enthusiasm in other channels. Francis first walked the fairways as a trespasser, on his way to and from the Putterham School. On these walks he found a few gutta-perchas now and then—Silvertowns, Ocobos, Vardon flyers, Henleys, and the other popular brands of 1900. No one ever seemed to lose a club on the course, though, so Francis' golf for several years consisted of hoarding his collection of balls. One afternoon in 1902, while kicking his way home through the rough, he uncovered his first rubber-cored ball. He recognized that it was different from his other balls, but had no idea why it was different. It was a beat-up arc, so Francis painted the ball and put it in the oven to dry, beside the bread his mother was baking. Shortly afterwards a terrific stench came from the oven. The heat had melted away the gutta-percha cover and left a smoking glob of elastic bands. Mrs. Ouimet had to throw out the batch of bread, which was the least of her worries since she had first thought that the

house was on fire. This incident may have been at the bottom of her distrust of golf. Mrs. Ouimet was sure the game would be the ruination of her boy.

Shortly after Francis' older brother Wilfred had become a caddie at The Country Club, a member had given him one of his old sticks. While Wilfred was off caddying, Francis practiced swinging with the club. He watched the tournaments across the street, and whenever he saw someone play an exceptionally good shot, he photographed the golfers form in his mind's eye and then rushed home to try out the swing himself. Wilfred was as crazy about the game as Francis. It was his idea that they convert the land behind their house into three golf holes—slightly more primitive than Jerry Travers triangle, since they took in a gravel pit, a swamp, a brook, and patches of long rough grass. The first hole was 150 yards long, with a brook crossing the "fairway" about 100 yards from the tee. The second was a 50-yard pitch, and the third was a combination of the first and second played backwards. The boys built themselves some greens and sank tomato cans for their cups.

On one of his trips into downtown Boston, Wilfred learned that the Wright and Ditson Company would trade a good golf club for three dozen balls. The boys exchanged thirty-six balls from their collec-

BRITISH PRO TED RAY WAS KNOWN FOR HIS LENGTH OFF THE TEE, TOP RIGHT, OPPOSITE, BUT THE POWERFUL MAN ALSO HAD A SUPERB PUTTING TOUCH, TOP LEFT, OPPOSITE, AND DISPLAYED PRODIGIES OF STRENGTH AND SKILL WHEN ESCAPING HAZARDS, STEREO VIEWS, OPPOSITE. DURING THE FATEFUL FINAL OF THE 1913 U.S. OPEN, RAY WAS THE LEADER IN THE CLUBHOUSE WITH A 304.

tion for a mashie and, via a similar transaction, later added a brassie. Francis was still too young to caddy, so he spent all of his time practicing in the backyard. It paid dividends, as practice always does. One Saturday morning he drove across the brook on the fly with the brassie. He had never been able to do this before, and he couldnt wait until he could unveil the new Francis Ouimet, the long-hitting Ouimet, before his brother. His first exhibition was a failure, but the next morning after the boys had returned from Sunday school, Francis drove over the brook on two of his three attempts. After that he was never worried about that tee shot.

When Francis was eleven, he followed Wilfred to The Country Club as a caddie. During the big tournaments he saw his heroes at close range — Chandler Egan, Jerry Travers, Fred Herreshoff, Walter J. Travis, Alex Smith, Willie Anderson. He loved the atmosphere of the golf course, and the members were fond of the bright, clean-cut boy. One day after Francis had caddied for Samuel Carr, Mr. Carr gave him four old clubs from his locker—a driver with a leather face, a lofter, a midiron, and a putter. Nothing could stop him now. He got up at four thirty or five in the morning and practiced on the big course until the greenkeeper shooed him off. These early-

morning sessions didn't satisfy the boy's hunger for golf, and occasionally on Saturdays Francis and a school friend would spend the whole day on the nine-hole public course at Franklin Park. One Saturday the boys played fifty-four holes and would have gone on indefinitely had the light permitted.

The first red-letter day in Francis Ouimet's life was the afternoon he first played the eighteen holes at The Country Club. Francis was assigned to caddy for Theodore Hastings, who usually played by himself. Before they set out, Hastings asked Francis if he played golf. Francis said he did. He asked him where he lived. Francis told him across the street. Hastings then told him to run home and get his clubs and they would play a round together.

It was against the rules for caddies to play at the club, but Francis was so excited that the rules completely slipped his mind. He tore home and got his bag and joined Hastings at the first tee. He played the first nine in thirty-nine strokes. He was doing nicely coming in until he came to the fifteenth hole, which passed by the caddie-shed. As Francis came over the hill to play his second, he saw the caddie-master taking it all in. Francis became so nervous that he topped his second, missed his third, put his fourth in a bunker, and ended up with a 10. Even with this figure, he finished the round

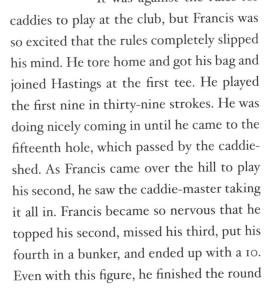

in eighty-four shots. Hastings straightened things out with the caddie-master.

In the summer of 1908, when Francis was fourteen and about to enter Brookline High, he turned up for the Greater Boston Interscholastic Championship. The officials told him he was not eligible to play since he was not attending high school, but the boy argued that he didn't see why he couldn't represent the school he was going to enter in the fall, and won his point. He qualified with an 85, but was eliminated in the first round by J. H. Sullivan. He later married Sullivan's sister.

While a freshman, Francis was the driving force in organizing a golf team at Brookline High. The team, with Francis in the number-one position, played twice a week against Fessenden, Worcester Classical, Newton High, Roxbury Latin, and other schools where a handful of boys played golf and had formed a team. Francis and his teammates brought their clubs to school on the days matches were scheduled and came in for a lot of good-natured kidding—such as the notices chalked on the blackboard to the effect that the marbles or tiddlywinks team would meet at Woodland at 1:00 p.m. The golfers at Brookline High put their riders in their place by winning the high school team championship held at Commonwealth. Francis, who was only fifteen, won the Greater Boston Interscholastic Championship, overwhelming his final-round opponent 10 and 9.

In 1910 the United States Amateur was

scheduled to be played at The Country Club and Francis decided to enter. To be eligible for the Amateur, a golfer had to be a member of a recognized golf club. Francis applied for a junior membership at the Woodland Golf Club. He prevailed on his mother to advance him the twenty-five dollars it cost to join, and paid her back with the money he earned while working that summer for four dollars a week in a Boston drygoods store. Francis failed to qualify by one stroke in the Amateur that year, and was dogged by that same one-stroke margin when he tried the Amateur again in 1911 and 1912. Around Boston, though, he soon established himself as one of the up-and-coming young golfers. In 1912 he reached the final of the Massachusetts State Amateur, where Heinie Schmidt, the well-dressed man, defeated him. In 1913, when the State Amateur was played at Wollaston, Francis won it. In his semi-final match against John G. Anderson, he went completely berserk on the last six holes, playing them 2-3-3-3-3-3, 6 under par. In addition to his astonishing natural ability, Francis had a quality even rarer among young athletes: he used his head. He learned something from every match he lost, and from some matches he won. He did not copy the mannerisms of other players and allowed his admirable competitive temperament to develop unforced. He knew himself.

In 1913, in his fourth try, he succeeded in qualifying for the Amateur and gave Jerry Travers a good match in the semis before

HARRY VARDON WAS, THROUGHOUT A TWENTY-YEAR CAREER THAT SAW HIM WIN 6 BRITISH OPEN TITLES, A BEAUTIFUL SWINGER. HE ADOPTED THE OVERLAPPING GRIP, ABOVE — THE SO-CALLED VARDON GRIP THAT HE POPULARIZED BUT DID NOT INVENT — BECAUSE IT KEPT THE RIGHT HAND FROM DOMINATING THE SWING.

bowing on the 34th green. The Open was scheduled for The Country Club, but Francis did not plan to play. He had to be talked into entering by Robert Watson, the president of the U.S.G.A. Once entered, the boy achieved the impossible, tied the untieables, Vardon and Ray.

The circumstances of the playoff and its outcome made it the most momentous round in the history of golf. Embellishment would only obscure the drama. The full impact of the historic match comes through if the story is told simply, stroke, by stroke, hole by hole—the way it happened.

After tying with Harry Vardon and Ted Ray, Francis Ouimet went home and took a bath. He went to bed at nine thirty and slept until eight. He ate a light breakfast, and then walked to The Country Club and hit some practice shots out to his ten-year-old caddie, Eddie Lowery. The shots felt fine. Johnny McDermott, who had watched Francis practice, took him by the arm and said, "You are hitting the ball well. Now go out and pay no attention whatsoever to Vardon and Ray. Play your own game." Francis promised Johnny he would do his best. A few minutes before ten he joined the Englishmen on the first tee for eighteen holes of medal play.

In the tent beside the first tee, the three contestants drew straws to determine who would have the honor of hitting first. Francis drew the longest straw, and teed up. He was nervous but got off well. Vardon and Ray also hit good drives. As the players walked down the first fairway, they were followed by a gallery that swelled to 3,500 as the match progressed. Thirty hours of continuous rain had turned the low stretches of the course into a quagmire, and a drizzle was still coming down, but this was a match that even the old and the gouty had to see for themselves.

The first hole at The Country Club was a lengthy 430-yard par 4, and under the sopping conditions only Ray had a chance of reaching in two. Ray, however, pushed his second into the mounds off to the right of the green, and had to be satisfied with a 5 when the wet grass held up his chip. Vardon took a 5, and Francis got his when he holed a 3-footer. That putt was very important. The instant it dropped, Francis lost all sense of "awe and excitement."

Ouimet was down the middle with his tee shot on the second. So was Vardon. Ray's timing was still off, and he again pushed his drive, into the rough just off the fairway. All three played orthodox pitches to the green, and all got their par 4s.

On the third, a testing two-shotter measuring 435 yards, Ouimet and Vardon were again nicely down the fairway, Francis ten yards in front. Ray once more was off to the right. Vardon was on with his second. Francis followed him on with a well-played midiron. Ray's line to the pin was blocked by a big oak tree, and he elected to play an intentional fade into the green. The shot did not quite come off as Ted had planned it, but it kicked off the slope on the left and onto the corner of the green about forty feet above the cup. Ray was left with a difficult downhill putt, which he stroked five feet short of the hole. He missed that putt and went one stroke down to Ouimet and Vardon, who made their 4s.

To make certain he got his ball up quickly enough to clear the abrupt rise in front of the fourth tee, Ouimet used a wooden cleek with a small head and narrow face. He got the results he wanted. Vardon, as usual, was down the fairway. Ray pulled his drive off to the left, overcorrecting his errors off the first three tees. None of the players was attracted to the cross-bunker cutting across the fairway thirty yards short of the long, low green. All three played tidy pitches to the green and got down in two putts for their 4s.

The fifth proved to be a very interesting hole. On this long par 4, a player drove from an elevated tee and tried to keep well away from the woods hugging the right-hand side of the fairway. On his second shot, which on wet turf was a brassie or spoon for even the good golfer, he avoided the pot bunker to the right of the green, if he could.

WILLS'S CIGARETTES.

HARRY VARDON.

He worried about the green slanting from right to left, when he got there. All in all, a very tough par 4—420 yards long. Ouimet, still up, continued his steady driving. Vardon was a little behind the amateur but down the middle too. Ray was off to the left again in the high grass. His second was short of the green. Vardon cut his brassie a shade too much and was off to the right. Ouimet also elected to play a brassie. The ball streaked crazily off to the right and crashed into the overhanging branches of the trees—out-of-bounds. It was the first error the young amateur had made. Had the shot been just a little awry, Francis might have started to worry about what he had done wrong. Fortunately, it was such a totally bad shot that Francis was able to dismiss it immediately. He didnt alibi to himself that his hands had slipped on the wet shaft, nor did he change his club. While the gallery was speculating on the effect his loose shot would have on Ouimet, he dropped another ball quickly over his shoulder and played his third without the briefest hesitation. It was a ringing brassie that ended up on the edge of the green. Ouimet got down in 2 from there, and came out of the hole with a 5. When Vardon and Ray both needed a chip and two putts, Ouimet had gained a half and a valuable psychological boost. His opponents had failed to capitalize on the opening, and this reinforced Ouimet's confidence in his ability to keep pace with them. Vardon and Ray were not infallible. Then, too, he felt that he had been lucky when that second shot had ended up out-of-bounds, for if he had been forced to play it out of the brush, he might have dropped several strokes to par instead of just the one.

The sixth was a shortish 4 uphill, the sort of hole on which a player might well pick up a birdie. All three were down the middle, with Ray, straight for the first time, the longest. Vardon played first and sent an elegant little pitch close to the cup. Ouimet and Ray could not match it. They two-putted for their 4s, and when Vardon sank his putt for a birdie 3, he went into the lead, one stroke in front of Ouimet, two in front of Ray.

It was Ray's turn at the seventh. None of the three was on the green on this stern one-shotter. Ray and Ouimet were both short—Francis had played his midiron—and Vardon, though nearer the pin, was in the high grass fringing the left side of the green. Francis went twelve feet by with his chip and Vardon was even stronger. They missed their putts for 3s and lost a stroke to Ray, who had played a brilliant run-up. Ray had now drawn back on even terms with the American and was only one stroke behind Vardon.

There was not much to choose among the drives on the eighth. The players were left with approaches of about 160 yards from the valley at the foot of the incline on which the large green was perched. Ouimet played a mashie, and the wild shout of the spectators gathered around the green told him that the shot was near the cup. Absolutely stone-dead, Eddie Lowery, his caddie, thought. Francis wanted to think so too, but as they walked up the hill, he guarded against disappointment by reminding himself that approaches that looked stony from a distance often turned out to be ten or fifteen feet away. But it was dead, eighteen inches from the hole. Francis got his birdie, but Ray matched him by rolling in a curving 35-footer. Vardon got his 4. Now, after eight holes of play, Vardon, Ray, and Ouimet were tied at 33 strokes apiece.

Ray was feeling better now. He had picked up two strokes on Vardon and one on Ouimet on the last two holes, and his length gave him the best chance of snagging a birdie on the ninth, a 520-yard par 5, which dropped from an elevated tee into a flatland crossed by a brook 350 yards out and then broke sharply up to a well-trapped green. Ray played his tee shot down the right-hand side of the fairway, which gave him the shortest line to the green if he was going to try to get home in two. Francis declined to press and was comfortably down the middle. After Vardon had hit, Ray commented, "Nice shot, Harry," the only words that passed between the Englishmen during the round, as Ouimet remembered it. Actually, Vardon's drive was not a nice shot. It was off-line, remarkably off-line for Vardon, and his lie in the rough made it necessary for him to play his second safe, short of the brook. Ray had to forgo any ideas he might have had about putting everything into his second in an attempt to reach the green when he found that his drive had ended up in a close lie on sloping ground. He played a regulation 5, on in three and down in two, as did Ouimet. Vardon had to work harder for his 5, but he got it by hitting his midiron third close to the green and chipping up for one putt.

Everything had happened and yet on the scorecard nothing had happened. All three were out in 38.

They started in. Ray, Ouimet, and Vardon, in that order, put their iron shots onto the Redan-type green of the 140-yard tenth. Ouimet was nearest the pin. The Englishmen were about thirty-five feet away, with Vardon's line to the cup stymied by the hole his ball had dug when it landed on the soft green. Harry three-putted. Ray also three-putted. Francis got his 3 and for the first time in the match he was out in front.

Vardon and Ray both had chances to get that stroke back on the eleventh, a 390-yarder, but they missed holeable putts for their 3s and halved with Ouimet in 4.

Ouimet had been outdriving Vardon regularly, and on the twelfth he outdrove Ray as well. The approach to the twelfth green was not blind, but the green lay at the bottom of a contoured slope, and this made for a certain difficulty in judging the distance to the pin. Ouimet was the only one to get home in two; he hit a superb mashie ten feet from the cup. Vardon was short, halfway down the slope, and Ray was down the embankment to the left. The Englishmen could do no better than 5s. Ouimet was timid on his try for his birdie, but his comfortable par increased his lead to two strokes.

On the thirteenth, the short par 4 on which Ouimet had picked up a birdie the day before, all three were on in two—Ray on the edge, Vardon about nine feet away, and Ouimet just inside Vardon. Ray made a fine bid for a 3 with his long putt. Vardon holed his 9-footer. Ouimet missed his. Vardon was now only one stroke behind Ouimet, the perfect position for the experienced campaigner with five hard holes left. On the long fourteenth, however, Vardon played poorly although he got his par 5. He hooked his drive into the rough, and after an adequate recovery, hooked his mashie third. This was not like Harry. If he didn't hit his irons perfectly straight, he faded them. Linde Fowler, the pioneer golf reporter, had not been looking for indications that Vardon was feeling the pressure, but Harry had hit that hooked approach so

IN 1913, FRANCIS OUIMET DID MORE THAN WREST THE U.S. OPEN TITLE
FROM TWO FORMIDABLE BRITISH OPPONENTS, HE MANAGED IN A SINGLE
WEEKEND TO ATTRACT TO THE SPORT THE NATIONAL ATTENTION AND
AFFECTION IT HAD LACKED UNTIL THEN. FOR THIS VICTORY PHOTO-
GRAPH, FRANCIS, TOP, WORE HIS JACKET AND BROAD SMILE WHILE
EDDIE LOWERY, HIS 10-YEAR-OLD CADDIE, CENTER, BOTTOM ROW, USED
A TOWEL TO PROTECT THE WINNER'S CLUBS FROM THE RAIN.

uncharacteristically that Linde could only deduce that Vardon was becoming worried. Ouimet apparently was not. He topped his brassie second on the fourteenth—his first poor shot since the fifth—but he put his third confidently onto the green as if he had already forgotten his second. The young man's poise was amazing. On one hole, when a member of the gallery had stupidly buttonholed him between shots and asked for some advice on his own golf troubles, Ouimet had patiently answered the intruder's questions. Ray seemed to be getting restless about his inability to do the things he wanted to do. He also played the fourteenth badly, pushing his second far to the right, but he took advantage of a lucky opening to the green and also got his 5. Three pars on the scorecard.

Ray finally went on the fifteenth, the par 4 over the hill and across the driveway. Ted's tee shot was headed for the rough on the right when it hit a spectator's derby and rebounded onto the fairway. (The spectator was incensed and left the playoff then and there.) Ray, however, did not take advantage of this break. He underclubbed himself on his second, and his soaring mashie thudded into a trap. He took two to get out, and only a good putt prevented him from taking a 7. But Ray's 6 put him four strokes behind Ouimet and three behind Vardon—who had taken 4s—and with only three holes remaining, Ted was out of it. On this hole Vardon, who never smoked on a golf course, lit a cigarette.

On the short sixteenth, Vardon and Ouimet got their 3s. Ray three-putted carelessly for a 4. He had given up the fight.

They came to the seventeenth, the 360-yard dogleg to the left, with Ouimet still protecting his one-stroke lead over Vardon. It was still Vardon's honor. Harry elected to play his drive close to if not over the corner—a risky shot, but he had decided that the time had come to gamble and he wanted to be in a position after his drive to stick his approach very close to the pin. That drive proved to be Vardon's undoing. His right hand got into the shot too much, and he hooked it into the bunker in the angle of the dogleg. From his lie in the bunker, Vardon could not go for the green and was forced to play out to the fairway. He put his third on, but not stone-dead. He had to take a 5. Francis had driven straight down the fairway to about the same spot from which he had played his jigger approach the day before. This time he selected his mashie—and hit a lovely shot eighteen feet from the hole. His long-shafted, narrow-blade putter had not let him down all morning, and now he called on it to get him down safely in two putts for the 4 that would give him that valuable insurance stroke over Vardon. He tapped the ball over the slippery grade . . . and holed it.

Francis now held a three-stroke lead on Vardon as they came to the home hole. He did not let up. His drive was down the middle, his second on. His approach putt, however, left him with a good 4-footer for his 4. As Francis lined up his putt, he realized for the first time that he was going to win, and with that awareness the astounding calmness that had sheathed him from the first hole on instantly disappeared. The boy felt himself shivering all over. He steadied himself as best he could, and made the putt. It was quite irrelevant that Vardon had taken a 6 and Ray a birdie 3.

The crowd who had slogged around the course in the drizzle, worn out from playing every shot with Ouimet, still staggered by the boy's nerveless poise and his brilliant golf, reeled around the eighteenth green and the clubhouse in the gayest stupor many of them ever experienced in their lives. They recalled the great shots the new champion had played—that brassie to the fifth green after he had knocked his first out-of-bounds, that mashie to the eighth and that equally fine mashie to the twelfth, that conclusive putt on the skiddy seventeenth, which perhaps more than any other single shot was the one heard round the world. In the visitors' party there was no rancor. Bernard Darwin, the Englishman who became the greatest of all golf writers, had been scoring for Ouimet during the playoff. Naturally, Darwin had been hoping that one of his countrymen would win, if he played the better game. By the seventeenth hole, when it looked as if Ouimet would do it, Darwin had stopped hoping for a comeback by Vardon. The slim, mild-faced youngster had played the better game, and Darwin rooted Ouimet home with his

whole heart. Vardon and Ray, though disappointed, could have nothing but praise for the boy who had not only beaten them but had nearly beaten their best-ball.

THE CARDS OF THE MATCH:

	OUT	IN
PAR	444 444 345—36	344 454 344—35—71
OUIMET	544 454 435—38	344 454 334—34—72
VARDON	544 453 445—38	445 354 356—39—77
RAY	545 454 335—38	445 456 453—40—78

And what about the new champion? After the battle he was the same exceptional young man—exhilarated but modest, still unbelieving and still unbelievable. "I am as much surprised and as pleased as anyone here," he said in accepting the trophy from the U.S.G.A. secretary, John Reid, Jr. "Naturally it always was my hope to win out. I simply tried my best to keep this cup from going to our friends across the water. I am very glad to have been the agency for keeping the cup in America."

The next day, when The Country Club was the scene of an all-out celebration, Francis Ouimet walked over from his house across the street and joined in the merriment by tossing down, one after another, a drink called a Horses' Neck, a compound of lemon juice and ginger ale.

PART TWO
THE DILIGENT DECADE

AFTER OUIMET

CHICK EVANS—TO HIM WHO WAITS

THE WAR YEARS

SAM'S BOYS AND JOHN'S BOYS

SIR WALTER

JONES BREAKS THROUGH

The
Diligent
Decade

1913—1923

After Ouimet

ENJOYING ONE OF SEATTLE'S GOLF COURSES, OLYMPIC MOUNTAINS IN BACKGROUND

AMERICAN golf has always been fortunate in the men who have been its champions. Macdonald, Travis, and Travers were sharp personalities. Jones, Hagen, and Sarazen were mature and four-square men with the power to communicate with their idolators. Though less articulate individually, Hogan, Nelson, and Snead produced excitement through the clean, metallic perfection of their golf. Palmer, Nicklaus, and Trevino, each in his own way, have exerted a tremendous influence on galleries here and abroad. The luckiest thing, however, that happened to American golf was that its first great hero was a person like Francis Ouimet.

Had a pleasant young man from a good Fifth Avenue family or some stiff and staid professional defeated Vardon and Ray, it is really very doubtful if his victory would have been the wholesale therapeutic for American golf that was Ouimet's. Here was a person all of America, not just golfing America, could understand—the boy from "the wrong side" of the street, the ex-caddie, the kid who worked during his summer vacations from high school—America's idea of the American hero. Overnight the non-wealthy American lost his antagonism toward golf. He had been wrong, he felt, in tagging it a society sport. After all, the Open Champion was a fine, clean-cut American boy from the same walk of life as himself.

The hundreds of thousands of Americans who had been inspired by Francis

Ouimet's victory to take up golf found that their hero was an even greater person than most heroes: he was a fine man. He never allowed his successes to swell his head. He remained free from affectation. He was an instinctive gentleman. He was the great boy who became a great man. If the hero-worshipping American boy accidentally learned of some of the "real details" about his heroes in baseball and football, his ideals were frequently shattered. The more Americans learned about Francis Ouimet, the more they admired him. American golf was lucky, very, very lucky, that it was Francis who won at Brookline.

Under the impetus of Ouimet's victory, within a decade golf became an all-Americans' game. Less than 350,000 played golf in 1913. Ten years later there were 2,000,000 golfers in the country. The man who took the trolley to his club, wearing his knickers and carrying his sticks, still attracted comment, but fewer and fewer people snickered out loud and referred to him as Reginald or Little Lord Fauntleroy in tones he was supposed to overhear. During this decade, and largely because of the game's increasingly democratic base, the quality of American players improved. Slowly but surely they caught up with the best British amateurs and professionals—and then passed them. By 1923 golf was a game Americans played better than any other people in the world.

Following Ouimet's epic victory in the Open, the members of the Woodland Golf Club tendered their favorite son a whopping banquet at which high-flying poems were recited and his deeds commemorated in song—such as this one, in which the words were sung to the tune of "Marching Through Georgia":

Hurrah! Hurrah! There's Ouimet on the tee!
Hurrah! Hurrah! The smallest of the three.
The boy who trimmed the British when
    they came across the sea.
When he goes playing to victory.

The members of the Woodland Club also presented Ouimet with a trip to England so that the boy could play in the British Amateur of 1914. Francis met with no more success than the other Americans, the Old Man excepted, who had tried to beard the lion in his own den. Francis was ousted in the second round by a golfer of little reputation. In that same championship, Jerry Travers was whipped by an elderly gentleman suffering from lumbago who barely broke 90. Chick Evans, in his second try overseas, played well but had the misfortune to run into a man named MacFarlane, who went completely mad and played the first nine at Sandwich in thirty-one strokes. That was the way it went with American professionals, too, when they tried for honors on foreign soil. For some reason or other, four out of every five rounds American pros played overseas were three or four strokes higher than the scores they made on American courses of almost comparable difficulty. On the rare occasions when they played well, some Britisher always played better. The best showing an American pro had ever made in Great Britain was Johnny McDermott's tie for fifth in the 1913 Open. Even in France, where the going should have been easier, our pros could not win. An American team composed of McDermott, Brady, Alex Smith, and McNamara lost all four matches in a team competition in 1913 with the best French professionals.

In Ouimet, America was backing a thoroughbred. After his wobbly performances in Great Britain, Francis showed the European skeptics the golf he was capable of when he won the French Amateur Championship. He had profited from his experiences in England, too, which was more than his less conscientious compatriots could claim: he had changed his style of iron-play to the punch method advocated by Hilton, and so bolstered what had been the weakest department of his game. In the U.S. Open played at Midlothian, near Chicago, that summer, he fired a first round of 69 and finished in a tie for fourth place, a more than creditable performance. (That young pro from Rochester, Walter Hagen, won the Open, defeating Chick Evans by a stroke.) When the amateurs gathered at Ekwanok, in Manchester, Vermont, for their tournament, young Ouimet proved that he was just as good at match play as he was at medal by winning that champi-

onship. On his way to the final he defeated two former champions, Bob Gardner and Bill Fownes, and in the final against Jerry Travers, *the* match player, Francis took seven straight holes and beat him soundly, 6 up with five to play. Against Travers, Francis was off-line only once in thirty-one holes; on his morning round he hit his approach a few yards to the right of the fifteenth green. Curiously enough, winning the Amateur thrilled Ouimet more than his victory in the Open. He had never given much thought to the Open, but as a boy he had dreamed of winning the Amateur—and now he had.

The next season, 1915, Francis was eliminated in the second round when he attempted to defend his Amateur crown at Detroit. The winner, and a most deserving one, was Bob Gardner. When he had taken the Amateur for the first time in 1909, Gardner was an undergraduate at Yale who could play all the golf he wanted. When he repeated six years later, he was an executive in a coal company in Chicago who took time off from business only for the major tournaments. Bob always played well, once he had the chance to warm up. Pole-vaulting (over thirteen feet) had developed his arms and shoulders, and he was long off the tees. He coupled this with a great flair for competition. For example, in an early-round match in the Amateur against Tom Sherman, he watched Sherman put his tee shot twelve inches from the hole . . . and then holed his. He was 2 down with five to go against Max Marston in the semi-finals, won back those two holes with 15-foot putts, and beat Max on the 37th green. In the final he defeated John G. Anderson 5 and 4.

In 1914, one year after his triumph at the U.S. Open, Francis Ouimet, above, completed his sweep of national titles by winning the U.S. Amateur at the Ekwanok course in Manchester, Vermont.

Considering the little competitive golf he played, Gardner compiled a truly remarkable record in the major tournaments. In 1916, despite an infected finger, this handsome collar-ad man stopped the challenge of the youthful phenomenon from Atlanta, Bobby Jones, and went all the way to the final before surrendering his title. Though he never won another national championship, Gardner went to the final of the British Amateur in 1920, the best showing an American had made in sixteen years, and in 1921 he was a finalist against Jesse Guilford in our Amateur. Bob Gardner never beat himself. It took fine golf to beat him.

Jerry Travers' loss of his Amateur crown in 1914 and his failure to recapture it in 1915 did not get him down, for in 1915 he became the second amateur to win the United States Open. No one could argue Jerry's ability in match play. As a medal player, however, he was looked on as just one of the boys, and his victory in the 72-hole test at Baltusrol came as a decided surprise.

Jerry's first two rounds left him in fourth place. A 73 on his third round gave him a one-stroke lead on the field. He was one of the last starters on the nerve-racking last round, and knew all the way the exact number of strokes he could take and still come in a winner. Knowing what they have to do is, for most golfers, an invitation to crack. They fight against cracking, they overfight, they outthink themselves, they play too safely, they worry, they weave, and they lose. The easy way to win a medal tournament is to come in early and coolly smoke your panatela as the reports filter in that, one after another, your rivals have blown up trying too hard to catch you. When Jerry came to the tenth tee on his final round to play the 64th hole of the Open, he learned that he would have to play the last nine holes in one stroke under par in order to beat Tom McNamara's total of 298. To make certain he hit his tee shot down the middle on the tenth, a drive-and-pitch par 4, Jerry used his driving-iron. He sliced the ball far out-of-bounds. Then he wrapped himself around his second tee shot and hooked it into the wheat drifts. For all intents and purposes, Travers had cooked his goose through these two loose shots. The green on the tenth was completely encircled by a water hazard, and Jerry would be lucky to get out of the hole with anything less than a 6, and could take even more if he went for the green. Jerry hunched over his ball, and rapped a magnificent biting iron over the water and onto the green two feet from the pin. He holed for his 4.

He got his par on the eleventh when a player of less courage would have again thrown in the sponge. He took a chance on his always-treacherous wooden driver and topped his tee shot barely forty yards down the rough. Two mashies got him to the green, and there he dropped a 35-footer for his par 4. He played his pars on the next three holes without having to call upon himself for further true-tempered evidence of his resourcefulness. On the fifteenth he nailed the birdie he was looking for, in typical Travers fashion. On this par 5, he gambled on carrying a deep cross-bunker with an iron on his second shot, and won this gamble by four yards. Then he got down in 2 from off the green. Pars on the last three holes would do it now, and concentrating with frigid fervor, this spiritual ancestor of Ben Hogan reeled off his par on the 70th, his par on the 71st, his par on the 72nd. Perhaps he had won because he had known what he had to do, just as in match play.

This was Jerry Travers' last championship victory and he made it a good one. Soon afterwards he retired from competitive golf save for some Red Cross exhibition matches during World War I. When he tried to come back after the war, this great putter could no longer putt. In other ways, too, he was not the same Jerry Travers who had won four Amateur titles and the 1915 Open.

Now that Ouimet had once and for all taken the curse off golf as a diversion for the rich and the elderly, each warm summer weekend saw the ranks of the converts swelled by the thousands—men who had "made their pile" and had the time for relaxation; men who were making their piles and saw the advantages of good contacts afforded by the friendliness of the locker room; college and high school athletes no longer in shape for body-contact sports but keen for some competitive outlet; women who had been sold on the game by the prowess of their new champion, Dorothy Campbell Hurd. At the strongholds of society in the East and at many strata-conscious golf clubs throughout the country, the cost of joining and playing remained prohibitively high, but, as the game spread, an ever-increasing number of clubs—golf clubs as distinct from country clubs—supplied the demand for golf at popular prices. That helped. Jerry

Travers, in the cool of retirement, estimated that it now cost the average golfer less than $200 a year to play the game. Travers broke it down this way:

INITIATION FEE	$50.00	
ANNUAL DUES	50.00	
BALLS	20.00	
(1 ball to every 36 holes)		
CLUBS	17.50	($2.50 apiece for 7)
CARFARE	20.00	
CADDIES' FEES	25.00	(40 cents a round)
	$182.50	

If, as Travers suggests, a golfer could average two full rounds with one ball, the caddies in those days must have been a distinctly different breed from the present-day crop—what remains of it. In some ways they were. For many ambitious boys in junior high and high school, the golf course was the land of opportunity—the place where they could earn more money than by mowing lawns, learn to play a game they could carry with them through life, and meet men who often became their valuable friends off the course. Many clubs, following the example set by Alexander H. Revell of the Chicago Country Club, fixed up "caddie shacks" for the boys, with lockers for their clothes and lunches, and cleared adjacent fields for baseball diamonds and putting greens. The atmosphere of the golf course was a salutary change from tenement life, as were the "caddie camps" organized at summer resorts where underprivileged kids from the city

"paid" for two months of sunlight and air by toting the bags of the vacationers. For quite a number of youngsters about to be swallowed up by the necessity of going to work to support their parents, the summer at Bretton Woods or Poland Spring was the bright spot in their childhood, and sometimes in their lives.

Throughout the country the expansion of the game produced many local heroes, golfers who never cut much of a swath in national tourneys but who were practically invincible in their own sections. Sam Reynolds won the Nebraska Amateur seven times, and Larry Bromfield hung up a similar record in Colorado. Harry Legg in Minnesota and E. J. Barker in Montana won their state Amateurs nine times. George V. Rotan took the Texas title five times and shared the rule in that realm with that strange and wonderful character, Commodore Bryan Heard of the Houston Country Club. The Commodore stumbled into golf at the age of forty-five only because he was unable to get up a poker game one afternoon. His golf grew better as he grew older, and at sixty-five he was "shooting his age." At seventy-five, he played a 74. It looked as if he would keep going forever, when an automobile accident and cataracts in both eyes finally forced the doughty Commodore to give up competitive golf. Bobby Jones was only one of the infant prodigies the Commodore helped up the ladder by giving him a sound trimming.

Happily, as the game began to make

considerable headway in the various sections of the United States, the aberrations of the first golf architects were corrected and Americans began to play on bona-fide golf courses. Gone were the days of the "Sunday architects," the snowy-haired Scots who six days a week "proed" at their respective clubs and on the seventh hustled around the countryside "designing" at least one and sometimes as many as three courses for communities newly golf-conscious. These oldtimers forgot about Prestwick and Leven, for speed was of the essence and so were the desires of their clients. Few of the Sunday architects went so far as to suggest a sporty little railroad track before the green—though some American golfers still regarded tracks as a legitimate and enviable hazard, better even than a quarry or a stone wall—but their layouts had been littered, prodigally and unimaginatively, with chocolate-drop mounds and pot bunkers and tantalizing combinations of these fashionable, now-obsolescent hazards. One obvious deficiency of this all-I-need-is-an-afternoon school of designers was their necessary addiction to formula. For some, a good course and a billygoat course were synonymous—the more blind shots, the better; for others, no hole except a dogleg was a worthwhile challenge, regardless of the natural contours of the terrain.

More than any one other architect, it was Charles Blair Macdonald who opened the eyes of American golfers to the shortcomings of the pioneer trends in this coun-

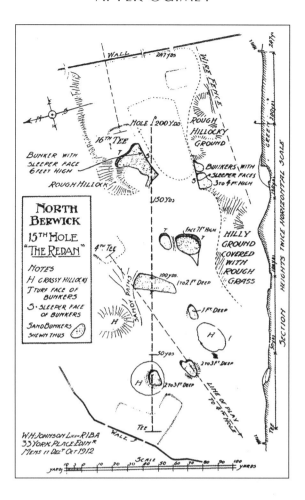

try. Near Southampton on Long Island, old Charlie built the National Golf Links, America's first heroic course. The character and beauty of the National became the subject of prose poems by the leading British and domestic authorities. A walk around the course, and syndicates preparing to build in New Mexico, Tennessee, and Idaho tore up their first blueprints and adopted the National as their criterion. It influenced the members of the Olympia Fields club drawing up plans for four courses (on 627 acres twenty-seven miles south of Chicago's Loop) and, to a lesser extent, the budget-bound designers of the nation's public courses. The National Golf Links dramatized for Americans what a real golf course looked like.

The inspiration for the National had come to Macdonald as early as 1901, when he read an opinion poll conducted by the English periodical *Golf Illustrated*. Called "The Best Hole Discussion," this consensus disclosed that the best one-shot holes on the island, in the minds of the British golfers, were the Eden (the eleventh) at St.

CHARLIE MACDONALD MODELED THE 4TH HOLE AT THE NATIONAL ON THE MUCH-ADMIRED 15TH HOLE, THE REDAN, AT NORTH BERWICK, SCOTLAND, ABOVE. EACH IS A LONG PAR 3 WITH A DEEP BUNKER ALONGSIDE A GREEN THAT IS PLACED AT AN ANGLE TO THE LINE OF FLIGHT.

Andrews and the Redan (the fifteenth) at North Berwick; similarly, the most-favored two-shotter was the Alps (the seventeenth) at Prestwick, with the fourteenth (the Long) and seventeenth (the Road) at St. Andrews awarded the distinction among the long holes. It was Macdonald's idea to build in America a seaside links in which the holes would be duplicates of the most famous British holes. Charlie made several trips to Britain to research his project, and came home loaded with sketches and surveyors' maps of the holes he had in mind. Always a shrewd salesman and organizer, he persuaded seventy men to put up $1,000 apiece to back his venture, and found the natural links he wanted in an undulating, untouched stretch of duneland along Sebonac Bay, three miles from Shinnecock. The development of the land was begun in the spring of 1907, and four years later the course—ultimately 6,650 yards of great golf—was opened.

The National had many features altogether new to American layouts. It was a lengthy course, several hundred yards longer than many that had been adjudged to be of championship caliber. This added length was important, because golf balls were becoming more and more lively as manufacturers vied for the patronage of the golfers who wanted more distance, which meant all golfers. The course was also a blessed departure from the penal type of architecture that had become epidemic from coast to coast. Macdonald did not traffic with the artificial. Cross-bunkers and pot bunkers and symmetrical mounds had no place at the National. His hazards conformed to the contours of the ground. His bunkers were the sides of slopes that cried out to be made into bunkers. Starting from the land and not from a blueprint, Macdonald "found" one natural hole after another, his Redan and his Alps, his Road and his Eden. He was wise enough to let his copies modify their originals as the topography suggested. He implanted the strategic spirit of these fine Scottish holes in the original holes he designed, or, more in the spirit of his approach, which he "discovered" as he walked his acres tirelessly looking for golf holes.

Whereas a *penal* hole is designed to punish the player who strays from the straight and narrow, a *strategic* hole places the emphasis on initiative. The player is given a choice of several routes to the green. On a one-shotter like the Redan, for example, he can generally get a 4 by steering away from the one serious hazard, a large, harsh bunker cut into the bank just below the front edge of a raised green built on a traverse. The player who goes for the small unbunkered opening to the corner of the green can get his 3, but he leaves himself a long putt and just about forfeits his chance for a possible 2. The player who goes for the pin and gambles on carrying the bunker,

A typical Macdonald-designed hole is the fifth at Bermuda's Mid-Ocean Club, opposite. It offers a choice of routes, with the most dangerous being the most rewarding if negotiated successfully.

suffering the consequences if he plays his stroke inadequately, is rewarded for hitting the required shot with an easy 3 and a good chance for his 2. In other words, on a strategic course boldness is repaid. The man who carries a fairway trap with his tee shot has a shorter and easier route to the green on his second than the man who has elected to play short of the trap or to one side or the other of it. The man who goes for the pin on his approach is the man who has the chance to get down in 1 on the contoured green. While making low scoring harder for the good players with its banked plateau greens slanted behind hungry hazards, Macdon-

ald's National was not unfair to the average golfer. In truth, his off-line shots were dealt with more leniently than on penal courses. By using his head and taking the discreet routes, the golfer who could play a 95 at Thorny Lea could play a 95 at the National. If he tried to play the pros' game, then the average golfer invited disaster. Macdonald's hazards carried out his dictum that "the object of a bunker or trap is not only to punish a physical mistake, to punish lack of control, but also to punish pride and egotism."

Charlie Macdonald's revolutionary achievement at Southampton led to many offers from wealthy Eastern groups to construct comparable courses for them. Macdonald was happy to oblige. Working with his engineer, Seth Raynor, he built such Churrigueresque courses as Lido, Mid-Ocean (in Bermuda), Piping Rock, and Yale, spending hundreds of thousands of dollars in his pursuit of perfection. They were all interesting layouts, and yet they lacked something the National had: the true breath of the game. On the dunes off Sebonac Bay, old Charlie had built himself a majestic monument.

Teddy Roosevelt, as was to be expected, found golf too mild a sport for his tastes, but, with each passing month, the leading men in the country were becoming increasingly golf-conscious and rabid to spread the gospel. Ex-President Taft, his ardor intact although his figure in profile now resembled Fujiyama standing on end, proclaimed that "golf is in the interest of good health and good manners. It promotes self-restraint and, as one of its devotees has well said, affords the chance to play the man and act the gentleman." Where else could you find a game that made you a better man for having a good time? A prominent churchman gave golfers his blessing: "They walk with saints and poets whose souls have been lifted by contact with the lowly violet and the snow-crowned mountain peak."

And yet, in candor, there was something to be said against the game. Good men, who could take liquor or leave it alone, who smiled at pretty women but kept on walking, who remembered their wife's birthday and their children's names, went to the dogs once they became golfers. Under the spell of the game, they lived on the golf course, trying to break a hundred or ninety, pitifully oblivious that back home in those little white cottages or hulking Gothic showplaces sat the "golf widows" of America. Many reformers spoke of the inroads that golf, with all its insinuating sinuosity, had made on American family life, but it remained for Russell W. Hobson to immortalize in verse the new menace to our mores.

"Who's the stranger, Mother Dear?
Look! He knows us! Ain't he queer?"

"Hush, My Own! Don't talk so wild;
That's your father, dearest child."

"That's my father? No such thing!
Father died, you know, last spring."

"Father didn't die, you dub!
Father joined a golfing club.

"But they closed the club, so he
Had no place to go, you see—

"No place left for him to roam
That's why now he's coming home . . .

"Kiss him, he won't bite you, Child!
All those golfing guys look wild."

Chick Evans–To Him Who Waits

THE
AMATEUR CHAMPIONSHIP CUP,
(GOLF).

T H E January 1912 issue of the *American Golfer* carried a rather provocative verse. Charles (Chick) Evans, Jr., the author, had entitled it "A Chronic Semi-Finalist":

> I've a semi-final hoodoo, I'm afraid.
> I can never do as you do, Jimmy Braid.
> I've a genius not to do it,
> I excel at almost to it,
> But I never can go through it,
> I'm afraid.

Chick Evans was not one to keep his joys and his sorrows to himself. He had to get them out of his system verbally or in writing, and this verse was only one of his many attempts to shoo his hoodoo by look-

ing it squarely in the eye. Everyone who had watched Evans in action recognized that he owned a champion's game. No amateur could match him as an iron-player. As a matter of fact, from tee to green he was the superior of the best American professionals. He could be a shaky putter in crises, it is true, but it wasn't his putting alone that kept him a bridesmaid whenever he entered the national Amateur. It was something deeper, and deepening—a complex that gained a tighter grip on him the harder he tried to free himself.

By the winter of 1912, when he tried to exorcise his complex with poetry, Chick had played in three Amateurs and been ousted in the semi-finals each time by opponents whom he had definitely out-played. In 1909 he had lost 1 down to Chandler Egan. (He balmed the wound by winning the playoff for the medal from the new champion, Bob Gardner.) In 1910 he allowed Bill Fownes to beat him when he had stood 2 up with only three holes to play. (He rationalized that it was his putting that had licked him.) In 1911 he had again reached the semis and had again wilted like a morning glory, losing to Fred Herreshoff after he had built up a commanding lead over the first eighteen. By this time Chick was no longer amused by his inability to win the Amateur. Blaming his putting, blaspheming his opponents' luck, and other such intellectualizations now failed to assuage the sting of losing. He would have been hurt had his friends not consoled him with the bromide that he was the uncrowned champion, and he was hurt when they did. What good did it do to be the best amateur golfer in America when some other guy always won the title?

It looked as if Chick, perhaps with the help of his poem, had finally chased his jinx in 1912. For the first time he got safely through the semi-final round of the Amateur. In the final, surrounded by his host of fanatic Chicago admirers who had come out to watch him finally win the big one, he had played himself into a three-hole lead over Jerry Travers on the morning round. Then, with the crown he dreamed about at his fingertips. Chick had petered out like an exhausted skyrocket. Travers captured one hole after another in the afternoon, and Chick had not been able to fight back. The score was 7 and 6, and Chick was inconsolable. Depressed and bewildered, he dodged the parties at the clubhouse and wandered aimlessly down a country road, trying to forget what had happened. He walked for several hours and was well into the country when he heard the sound of music and merriment coming from a barn across a field. At the door of the barn he stood watching the squaredancers for a heavy moment, and then joined in. By morning he had danced himself healthy.

Chick's tribulations (and the dramatized versions concocted by emotion) were far from over. In 1913 at Garden City his semi-final hoodoo caught up with him again. None of his previous disappointments had been so hard to bear. All year long he had played irresistible golf. On a spring tour through the Northwest he had broken course record after course record, and the fans in Tacoma, Portland, Salt Lake City, Kansas City, and Omaha had reiterated the superlatives of his earlier worshippers. He had won the qualifying medal in the Amateur for the third time, and had

CHICK EVANS DRIVES FROM THE TEE OF THE PAR-4 SECOND HOLE AT ROYAL ST. GEORGE'S AT SANDWICH DURING THE 1914 BRITISH AMATEUR CHAMPIONSHIP, OPPOSITE. THE DRIVE MUST CARRY A LARGE FAIRWAY BUNKER, WHICH IS JUST VISIBLE AT THE RIGHT OF THE PHOTOGRAPH.

won it sensationally by playing the in-nine on his second round in 32 strokes. He had continued to hit the ball beautifully as the tournament moved into match play, and then, once again, his putting touch had evaporated, just as it always seemed to do under the pressure of championship match play. Against Eben Byers, Chick had put on an exhibition on the greens that was both tragic and comic. On hole after hole, bee-line approaches had left him with "gimme" putts for wins, and on hole after hole, switching desperately from one to another of his four putters, he foozled these short putts. He teetered through to the semis, where John G. Anderson put him out of his misery.

Well, maybe 1914 would be the year. Chick went over for another shot at the British Amateur. In 1911, in his first try, he had been ousted in an extra-hole match by a left-handed Tasmanian. This time an outgoing nine of 31 by a man named Macfarlane was too much even for the good golf Chick was playing. Back home, he took the Western for the third time—those sectional tournaments, match play or medal, never bothered him. His putting appeared steadier than it had been for years. In the Open at Midlothian, near Chicago, he amazed even his most adoring supporters by flashing two out-of-this-world finishing rounds that brought him to the last hole needing an eagle 2 to tie with Hagen. And Chick had

almost done it—his chip had ended up nine inches from the cup. But in the Amateur at Ekwanok that year, for the first time he was eliminated before he had reached the semi-finals. He lost to Eben Byers, who had taken ten putts on the first nine holes while Chick was helping himself to twenty.

1915 made it worse. With the exception of Jerry Travers, the winner, Chick did better than any other amateur in the Open. In the weeks before the convocation for the Amateur, he was unbeatable around Chica-go, and then he was whipped and whipped badly in the first round of the big event by Ned Sawyer, a fellow-Chicagoan whom Evans had trampled on all summer.

Nothing insucceeds like insuccess. By 1916 one searing disappointment after another had made Chick Evans a far more complicated person than he was intended to be. He had been born, the son of a librar-ian, in 1890 in Indianapolis, in a brown shingled house four minutes away from President Benjamin Harrison's home.

Nineteen sixteen was the year Chick Evans, shown above with a center-shafted putter, broke through: he won both the U.S. Open and the U.S. Amateur championships.

When Chick was three, the Evanses had moved to Chicago. At eight, he had started to caddy at the old Edgewater Golf Club, earning his ten cents for nine holes, his fifteen cents on the weekends. A friendly, freckled boy, Chick became the most popular caddie at Edgewater because of his sunny disposition and his record for rescuing lost balls. When a ball was buried in high grass and no amount of poking could uncover it, Chick would stretch out full length in the rough and keep rolling until his body struck something round and hard. He quit the caddie ranks the day before he reached his sixteenth birthday so as not to jeopardize his amateur standing. By that time he had developed the smooth, flowing, thrillingly simple swing that had made him a champion among boys and would, Chicagoans were positive, earn him many national titles. At the age of sixteen he qualified for the Western Amateur and started on the golf career that brought him both glory and grief.

Golf galleries liked Chick Evans. He talked to everyone, he remembered faces and names, he laughed and he joked, and he could really hit the ball. Chick Evans liked golf galleries. Something of an extrovert—in the East they called him a "Western" type—he opened himself to their affection and plaudits with a readiness the super-concentrators like Travers could not understand. Some contemporaries of Chick's always maintained that he loved to play in front of crowds so much that he purposely lost holes when he was ahead in some matches in order to prolong his sessions before the galleries.

Whenever he was playing well and a gallery was whooping it up at his heels, Chick was a happy young man—a slim, sandy-haired kid with something attractively rural about him even after he had joined a brokerage firm. On the other hand, during or just after the heat of defeat, he was prey to a streak of bitterness. Without being fully aware of it, he resented Francis Ouimet. It wasn't so much Ouimet the person as Ouimet the young man who had done what Chick had wanted to do—captured the Open and the Amateur and gained center stage as America's darling. Chick felt that he was a better golfer than Ouimet and did not hesitate to discuss in public their comparative records in national events, especially in the qualifying rounds of the Amateur and other medal affairs in which he knew his record was incomparable. He prided himself on the judgment expressed by Harry Vardon, who everyone knew had lost to Ouimet, that Chick Evans was the best amateur he had played with in America. And, quite understandably, he loved to hear statements that supported his frustrated ego, like the one by Jerry Travers that "if Evans could putt like Walter J. Travis, it would be foolish to stage an Amateur tourney in this country." He didn't know whether to be insulted or pleased when the gag went around Chicago that, in his search for a remedy for his woes on the green, Chick had raced toward a store with the window inscription "New Way of Putting," only to discover that the words "On Soles" followed below in smaller type.

And then, in 1916, it came. Just like that.

A siege of illness had forced Chick to forgo the junket to Del Monte for the Western, but he was back in shape by the time the national Open was scheduled to get underway at Minikahda, outside Minneapolis. He brought to Minikahda his own caddie from Chicago, a good-luck Billiken a friend had purchased in Hawaii, and, for the *n*th time, a new method of putting. The night before the Open began, the parched course came to life under a heavy downpour. The turf was fine and gripping, and Chick raced to the turn in 32 before he knew what had happened. He got a little frightened of his score coming in, but a 38 gave him a 70. He went out in good spirits in the afternoon, and repeating the word *Relax* to himself before each shot, added a 36-33—69 for a total of 139 and a three-stroke lead over the nearest man, Wilfred Reid. The next day was a blazer. Reid crumpled under the heat, and Evans, playing streaky golf, was lucky to go no higher than 74 in the morning round. He missed his shots at the right time. He still retained a three-stroke lead over the man in second place, lanky Jim Barnes, the Cornish-born professional who had dug in with a 71. Now if he could only hang on.

On the fourth hole of his tense last round, Evans buried himself in a bunker, three-putted for a 7. For once Chick did not

interpret the 7 as a sign from the gods that he was not supposed to win. He accepted the 7 and kept on going. Information reached him at the turn that Barnes, playing three holes behind, had caught him. He kept on swinging. As he prepared to play the 540-yard twelfth hole, he was told that Barnes had hooked his drive badly on the ninth. That would give him a one-stroke lead, Evans reflected on the tee, but he would lose that advantage unless he went for his birdie 4 on the twelfth, as Barnes was sure to do. Chick split the fairway with his drive, and after checking his lie, made up his mind to go for the pin on his second rather than play short of the creek that crossed the fairway twenty yards before the green. He came through with one of the finest fairway woods he ever hit, an arrow-straight whizzer that cleared the creek and pulled up on the green. The birdie was easy. Chick stayed in there, dropping those troublesome 3- and 4-foot putts, and it mattered little that he three-putted the home green for a 73. His total of 286—an average of 71 1/2 per round and a new record for the Open—gave Evans a margin of four strokes over Barnes and two over Jock Hutchison, who had come flying home in 68. Chick Evans, the chronic disappointment, had not come close this time. He had *won* a major championship.

The Amateur in 1916 was held at the Merion Cricket Club, outside Philadelphia. Chick was the man to beat, and no one could beat him. He played his way to the

Two competitors for best American amateur of the period between 1910 and 1920 were Chick Evans, left, above, and Francis Ouimet, photographed at the 1920 U.S. Amateur. When the two met in the finals of the event, Evans used brilliant iron play to defeat Ouimet 7 and 6.

final through Nelson Whitney, the New Orleans crack (3 and 1), John G. Anderson (9 and 8), Clarke Corkran (3 and 2), and in the final against Bob Gardner defeated the defending champion with an exhibition of the new staying power he had acquired by winning the Open. Between seven and eight thousand spectators parked over two thousand cars and followed the two Chicagoans over the sunbaked course. They witnessed a vibrant battle. Evans started with a birdie 3 and fought off Gardner's challenges to lead by three holes at the halfway mark. Curiously enough, Evans had gained his advantage by outplaying Gardner, the great clutch putter, on Merion's difficult greens. In the afternoon Gardner rallied to be only 1 down at the turn and seemed to be on his way to squaring the match on the tenth, but Evans staved him off by sinking a sweeping 40-footer. That putt was the Gettysburg of the match. Chick had halved a hole he should have lost, using the same weapon so many others had used against him. He won three of the next five holes, playing with confidence and forcing Gardner into errors. On the 33rd green the match was over— Chick, 4 and 3. Chick Evans had become the first American to win the Amateur and the Open in the same year.

Chick's erratic public relations added a needless wrangling footnote to his great double victory. Instead of ignoring the taunts of die-hard Easterners that the absence of Ouimet and Travers had made his triumph at Merion much easier than it

might have been, Chick popped off. Francis and Jerry, he declared, would not have won had they entered. "There is a certain provincialism about the East," Chick continued, "a sort of ostrichlike spirit that believes that when its own eyes are hidden no other eyes can see. . . . In the West it is generally understood that when a leading player fails to enter an event, he knows he has little chance to win it." Once again he recalled Vardon's opinion that Chick Evans was the best amateur in the country. The Eastern critics, rushing to the defense of Ouimet, asked Chick if he remembered his tussle with Francis in the East–West matches just before the 1915 Amateur in which Francis, 3 down with three to play, won out on the first extra hole.

Quite a batch of bitterness was brewed and it did neither of the disputing parties any good, especially Chick. He should have been satisfied that at the end of his rainbow he had found two pots of gold. It had been a long and arduous journey, but Chick had stuck with it, and no golfer in the country, whether he was irritated by the vagaries of Chick's personality or hailed them as further halos, could debate the record: From 1909 on Chick Evans had been one of the country's best golfers; in 1916 he had proved himself the best.

The War Years

IN April 1917 the United States entered World War I. Under the first sobering realization of how serious life could be, the nation abandoned all that was trivial. Then, just as during World War II, Americans tempered their attitudes to the task of winning a long struggle and gradually came to endorse a duration species of sports as a necessary balance for the increasing strain thrown on the home front. A man worked better if he could get out and exercise now and then, and cast off that heavy-hearted mood.

Americans filed back to their golf courses, occasionally to contracted courses in which three or four or nine holes had been given over to growing food. Some golfers ridiculed these miniature grain gardens as a bogus ascetic gesture—rather like wearing a hairshirt with matching plus-fours. A person either played golf or he didn't, and there was no sense kidding ourselves about the tremendous good sacrificing the ninth and tenth holes was going to do for our boys Over There. The bulk of American golfers knew that fact supported the cynics, but it made them feel less guilty about indulging their pleasures when they saw the wheat tossing on the old tenth. Some clubs spared their holes and satisfied their consciences by turning other tracts they owned into farms.

As 1917 wore on, the issue of "to golf or not to golf" gave way to measures for manipulating the Saturday and special tournaments so that they were in some way integrated with the war effort. On Independence Day, Liberty Tournaments, held concurrently at 485 golf clubs in forty-four states, grossed a total of $72,000 in war bond subscriptions; the members of the Allegheny Country Club showed the way by subscribing over $4,000 worth. Many clubs voted to divert 50 percent of their tournament fees into a fund for buying an ambulance. Nearly all clubs substituted War Savings Stamps and Liberty Bonds for the traditional tournament prizes. In a favorite type of war tourney, each entrant bought a bond, ranging from $50 to $5,000, before teeing off; the prizes for the winners were checks for one-tenth of the purchase price of their bonds.

Shortly after the nation's declaration of war, the U.S.G.A. canceled the national championships. No official Open or Amateur was held during the war, but the U.S.G.A. answered the public demand for a meeting of the "name golfers" by staging a tournament called the Patriotic Open and

A 1917 RED CROSS MATCH IN CHICAGO—WITH PROCEEDS GOING TO BENEFIT THE WAR EFFORT— ATTRACTED, AMONG OTHERS, U.S. OPEN AND U.S. AMATEUR CHAMPION CHICK EVANS, SECOND FROM LEFT, AND A TEENAGER, FAR RIGHT, NAMED BOBBY JONES.

distributing the receipts among war-service organizations. The Professional Golfers Association, which had been formed in 1916, took the cue and encouraged its stars to offer their services gratis for all exhibitions in which the proceeds went to war charities. However, it was the Western Golf Association that, more clearly than any other golf organization, perceived the role exhibition golf could play in raising funds and carried out the most ambitious wartime program.

The scope and progressiveness of the W.G.A.'s activities made the U.S.G.A. look moribund in comparison, and this was all right with the large majority of American golfers. In the winter of 1916 the U.S.G.A. had made itself highly unpopular by barring Francis Ouimet from amateur golf. Technically, the association had a good case. At that time the U.S.G.A. definition of a professional was, in a nutshell, a person engaged in any business connected with the game of golf. Ouimet had been warned that he would forfeit his amateur standing if he went through with his announced intention to open a sporting goods store with his friend Jack Sullivan. Francis had persisted in his plan, and the U.S.G.A. had no other alternative than to consider him a professional—at least in the opinion of President Frank L. Woodward. Over the agonizing months in which Ouimet's status hung fire, his conduct, as always, was above reproach. He thought the action grossly unfair, but kept his thoughts discreetly to himself. He

obeyed the U.S.G.A.'s order to refrain from amateur competitions until the summer of 1917, when his patience was exhausted and he entered (and won) the Western Amateur. If ever a golfer possessed the true spirit of the amateur, it was Ouimet. Close upon his epochal victory in 1913, he had been besieged with many attractive offers, including contracts for vaudeville and movie appearances that would have netted him $15,000. He had turned them all down flatly. He had worked in sporting goods stores before deciding to go into partnership with Sullivan. If the new ruling of the U.S.G.A. made him a professional—okay, it made him a professional. He had given Sullivan his word and intended to keep it. As Ouimet's friends pointed out, had Francis wanted to be cute, he could have accepted any number of jobs offered him by wealthy admirers that would have assured him a handsome income and would not have endangered his amateur status, technically. Obviously what was wrong was the definition of what constituted a professional, but this was lost on President Woodward, who went gunning for his man, won his legal case, saved face, and lost the day.

No one attacked Woodward and the U.S.G.A. with more vituperation than Walter J. Travis. The Old Man had a personal grievance to settle: under the new definition, Travis, like all architects, was judged a professional. In his column in the *American Golfer* Travis lambasted the U.S.G.A. for its failure to be a body truly representative of the country's golfers, for the "intense conservatism" of its self-perpetuating clique, its archaic constitution, and, to be sure, its highhandedness in L'Affaire Ouimet. The most penetrating remarks on the controversy were made by W. O. McGeehan. "Some of the men who compose the U.S.G.A.," commented that outstanding sports writer, "seemed to believe that there was some intensified stigma attached to the word *professional.* Personally I prefer the professional writers from the late Mr. Shakespeare down to George Ade to talented amateur authors. I would rather hear Caruso sing one aria than I would a gifted amateur tenor sing a dozen—much rather....And I would rather see Nazimova on the stage than the most talented amateur actress-lady in all the Middle West."

For its jampacked schedule of exhibition matches, the Western Golf Association had a willing workhorse in Chick Evans. While he was sweating out acceptance into the Aviation Service, the double champion gave up every weekend during the golfing seasons to play exhibitions for the Red Cross and other charities. In 1918 he traveled twenty-six thousand miles in the course of performing in forty-one different cities, and assisted in raising $300,000. Some Sundays he teamed up with his amateur colleague, Warren Wood, and fought it out in four-ball matches with the ranking professionals, Walter Hagen, the Western Open Champion, Jim Barnes, the P.G.A. Champion, and Jock Hutchison, who had bounded to fame by winning the Patriotic Open by seven strokes. At other times Evans filled out a foursome in which the other players were pros, and, as often as not, was low man for the round. When Warren Wood fell ill, Bobby Jones stepped into his shoes, and Jones and Evans made a very successful swing through the East.

Previous to teaming up with Evans, fifteen-year-old Bobby Jones had played the full exhibition circuit with three other youngsters—Perry Adair, Alexa Stirling, and Elaine Rosenthal. Elaine was the best woman golfer in the Middle West, and Alexa, when she was only nineteen, had carried off the United States Women's Championship in 1916. Perry was the Atlanta neighbor and boyhood rival of Bobby Jones and a youthful prodigy in his own right. The troupe usually played mixed four-ball matches. One day Bobby would team up with Elaine, the next with Alexa. Now and then the girls would sit out a date and watch the Dixie Kids, Jones and Adair, fire away against players twice their age. No one who saw the kids ever forgot Alexa and Elaine

In 1916, Bobby Jones, opposite, appeared in his first national competition. It was the U.S. Amateur at the Merion Cricket Club in Ardmore, PA; the 14-year old made it to the quarter-finals.

clouting their mashies as naturally as most girls took to dancing, or Bobby and Perry wearing their red Swiss Guard berets and having the time of their lives making the hard game of golf look as easy as hopscotch.

While he was awaiting induction into the army, Francis Ouimet participated in many Red Cross exhibitions in New England. Francis' regular partner was Jesse Guilford, a big bruising fellow from New Hampshire who had earned the sobriquet of "The Siege Gun" when he appeared at Ekwanok in the 1914 Amateur and had walloped tee shots that had to be seen to be believed. Jesse's drive on the first hole, for instance, had *carried* a bunker 280 yards from the tee. Francis and Jesse made a formidable combination, and their matches against Mike Brady and Louis Tellier were packed with good and exciting golf. (Brady, incidentally, had tied a record on Labor Day 1917 by scoring holes-in-one on the sixth and thirteenth holes during the course of a round at Siasconset on Nantucket.) In the winter of 1918 when Ouimet was inducted at Camp Devens, he was reinstated as an amateur by the U.S.G.A. There was no strict legal logic behind the reinstatement. The *good* reason given by Howard W. Perrin, the new U.S.G.A. president, was that things were different now that Francis had severed his connections with his sporting goods firm upon entering the service. The *real* reason was that the Perrin administration was anxious to right the wrongs that had brought down upon the head of the U.S.G.A. such

deserved unpopularity. An opportunity to make amends to Ouimet had presented itself when he was inducted, and Perrin's alacrity in seizing it met with the approval of every golfer in the country.

Because of its record in raising millions of dollars during World War I, golf achieved a new dignity in the eyes of Americans. They came to know the star players as respectable citizens, and to re-evaluate the professionals in particular. The non-golfers were startled and agape at the generosity of the fairway fraternity—men who shelled out hundreds of dollars for the privilege of acting as caddie or fore-caddie for Evans and Barnes, who paid thousands of dollars for the balls used by Jones and Hagen or for the favorite clubs of Travers and Hutchison. The two hundred members of the Lake Shore Country Club in Chicago set the record high when they contributed $35,000 to the Red Cross the day Evans played their course and Julius Rosenwald came out from Washington to act as auctioneer.

The afternoon before the Armistice, Findlay Douglas and Walter Travis, those two arch-rivals of turn-of-the-century golf, pulled themselves together and played a bang-up exhibition match. Travis was the winner, 1 up. In the auction following the match, the Schenectady putter the Old Man had used in winning the British Amateur went for $1,700. At that price, it was a steal.

Sam's Boys and John's Boys

1925 GREATEST YEAR IN HISTORY OF SPORT

Kings and Queens in Sporting Realm

ORLD War I ended in the autumn of 1918. Compared with the suffering of nations nearer to the battlefields, the United States had got off lightly, but there had been strain and sorrow and sacrifice, and the Armistice found Americans in a furious hurry to enjoy themselves. The post-war neurosis led to many excesses, and perhaps the national mania for sports that erupted was excessive too, but it seemed so healthy and innocent, so prophylactic, almost, in contrast with some of our other enthusiasms that it struck most Americans as the perfect fusion of the good old days and the brave new world. The nation played sports and watched sports with a wild-eyed seriousness it has never abandoned and modified only slightly in times of depression and war. The nation asked for champions, and got them aplenty in the "Golden Age of Sport" that followed—Jack Dempsey, Babe Ruth, Bobby Jones, Charlie Paddock, Bill Tilden, Red Grange, Helen Wills, Johnny Weismuller, the Four Horsemen, Glenna Collett, Gene Tunney, Aileen Riggin, and hordes of satel-

lites who, in less abundant heavens, would have been stars of the first magnitude.

Golf rode forward on the crest of the wave. Golf courses cut their grainfields and resurrected the plans for enlargement that the war years had postponed. The men newly rich from the war became the most ardent of the ardent recruits, the country-clubbers made architecture a paying profession, the golf ball manufacturers started their search once again for balls that would go ten yards farther and possibly develop an allergy to sand traps and rough. This fever

for doing things bigger and better communicated itself to our leading players, amateur and professional. The war had, of course, prevented our amateurs from taking a crack at the British Amateur, and now they were burning to make up for lost time and show the world that they had outgrown their ineptitude at playing good golf in Britain. The American pros, spurred on by the unexpected esteem they had earned during the war, set their sights on the British Open. Winning this championship would be the quick way to rid themselves of the inferiori-

In June 1920, British professionals Abe Mitchell, far left, above, and Jim Duncan, far right, met American players Jim Barnes, second from right, and Walter Hagen, the reigning U.S. Open champion, in a $1,000 match in Croydon, England. The Americans won.

ty complex acquired through their previous humiliations on foreign courses. A period of high-pitched international rivalry was in the making, for on the other side of the Atlantic the British had returned to their links after five years of war with a similar eagerness for the game and great expectations for their new stars and renascent champions.

The year 1919 was one of preparation for both sides. Though no national championships were conducted in Britain, the British golfing fans studied the form and the competitive spirit of their golfers, and marked down the men on whom they could rely to uphold the nation's supremacy. Among the pros, George Duncan and Abe Mitchell looked to be the logical successors to the now superannuated Great Triumvirate of Harry Vardon, James Braid, and J. H. Taylor. Duncan was playing perceptibly better than before the war, and if he would only stop his interminable theorizing, there was no knowing what heights George could reach with his sound, stylish swing and those not infrequent "mad rounds" in which he could do no wrong. Mitchell wasn't in a class with Duncan for style—his followthrough was the shortest ever sported by a first-rate golfer—but he could score and he could do wonderful things in match play. Behind these two

standouts in the professional ranks came golfers like Charles and Ernest Whitcombe and young Arthur Havers, who apparently had the stuff from which champions are made. Ted Ray was now in his forties, and while Britishers recognized that their stars had a miraculous longevity that enabled them to continue in competition at an age when their American contemporaries were content to give lessons—well, anything that Ted won would be so much velvet. And that went double, naturally, for Sandy Herd, the colorful Scot who had made nineteen holes-in-one during his long career on the links and now, approaching his fifties, was beginning to show signs of slowing down.

And how about the British amateurs? Two of the best bets were those youngsters up at Oxford, Tolley and Wethered. Cyril Tolley was a rugged fellow with a leonine head who had spent thirteen months in a German prison camp. Roger Wethered was a big chap, too, rangier in build than Tolley, long off the tees though inclined to be wild, and with an understanding of shot values as instinctive as his sister Joyce's. Willie Hunter, the son of the professional at Deal, Tommy Armour from the Braid Hills of Edinburgh, Robert Harris, Sir Ernest Holderness—they were all good and getting better, though it was a pity Holderness spent so much valuable time working at the Home Office. All in all, both the amateur and professional contingents were strong, and Britons were not worried about the assaults being mapped in America.

After the wartime hiatus, the United States Open and Amateur were restored in 1919. No Britishers had come over to play in them, and Americans were able to scan the new and old faces of our native golfers with the impersonal objectivity of a football coach watching his squad work out on the Wednesday before the big Saturday game. Davy Herron, who won the Amateur at Oakmont, was a competent golfer—anyone who won the Amateur had to be—but it was questionable if Davy had a game that, day in and day out, was in a class with those of the other rising amateur stars, such as Jesse Guilford, Max Marston, Fred Wright, and especially the youthful veteran whom Herron had whipped in the final of the Amateur, Bobby Jones. From all sections of the country reports were coming in on the

dazzling scoring feats of kids barely out of high school. Let them get a little more experience under their belts and they would be playing low-seventy rounds in big-league competition as well as on their home courses. And to steady these youngsters, we had Francis and Chick and Bob Gardner, who seemed old only because they had come upon the scene at such tender ages. They were still young men and topnotch golfers.

American golf fans also liked the looks of our pros. At the head of the heap there was Walter Hagen—he took the Open again in 1919—and close behind "The Haig" were Jock Hutchison and Jim Barnes. Both Barnes and Hutchison had been born overseas, Jim in Cornwall and Jock in St. Andrews, but they had developed their games in the States and were looked upon as American golfers. Barnes was six foot three, as lean as Chile, with a thatch of undisci-

Two top American professionals in the early 1920s were diminutive Jock Hutchison, opposite, and lanky Jim Barnes, above. Notice the gaze and garb of Hutchison's young gallery: evidently golfers had become objects worthy of admiration and imitation.

plined light-brown hair swirling above his studious face. There was a bit of a loop at the top of Barnes' crouching swing but even the loop was grooved and Jim had very few off-days, as his sweep in 1919 of the North and South, the Western, the Shawnee, the Southern, and the P.G.A. Championships well corroborated. On and off the course, he was serious-minded but relaxed, and Americans came to associate him with the cloverleaf he liked to chew in the corner of his mouth. Hutchison's temperament was the antithesis of Barnes'. In a friendly round or off the links, Jock was talkative, high-spirited, and a contagious chuckler. In competition, he was dourness itself and as nervous as a mosqui-to. He walked around restlessly between shots. He sweated lav-ishly and took to waving his arms in the air to dry them. He literal-ly twiddled his thumbs. Jock, who had the map of Scotland written all over his face, was in some ways our George Duncan.

ABE MITCHELL

He had a theory for everything. He had his moods. When he shifted into a brilliant streak, Jock could play one plus-perfect hole after another, each shot, like mountain views in Switzerland, seemingly more breathtaking than the one that went before. Along with the swaggering Hagen, "Hutch" and "Long Jim" comprised our Triumvirate. Their supporting cast consisted of seasoned players like Mike Brady and young pros like

Leo Diegel working their way to the top step by step—caddie, caddie-master, assistant pro, pro at a small club, pro at a large club, with the last jump more often than not depending on their degree of suc-cess in sectional and national tournaments.

In 1920 the Americans were ready for light attacks on the British citadels, the Open and the Amateur.

The assault force on the British Amateur at Muirfield, east of Edinburgh, consisted of gentleman golfers like Nelson Whitney and Bob Gardner (who was in Britain as the representa-tive of the U.S.G.A. to discuss rules and regulations with the Royal and Ancient). Gardner started slowly. M. M. Burrell of Troon carried him to the eigh-teenth green, and Ted Blackwell, the man Travis had defeated away back in the final in 1904, held on until the sixteenth. As had often happened in the past, Gardner's stamina made him an increasingly dangerous opponent as the tournament progressed and players less bountifully endowed physically began to fold under the strain of playing two match-es a day. Bob moved safely through the fourth round (where Whitney was ousted), and his 36 on the out-nine sewed up his fifth-round match. In the sixth, he shook off the challenge of Gordon Lockhart by birdieing the eighteenth for a 2-up victory, and he won his semi-final match with Michael Scott by once again playing the home hole superbly. In the other half of the draw, Cyril Tolley, the burly Oxfordian, had played his way into the final. On his march Tolley had never given his opponents a look-in, and Britishers, now that Gardner had worked his way into a position where he could repeat Travis' triumph, were prepared to cheer Tolley on to still greater heights in the final.

The Tolley–Gardner match was a hectic battle between two stalwart athletes. It was a hard match to lose and a great match to win. With thirty-two holes behind him and only four to play, Tolley stood 3 up. Gardner cut it to 2 up by winning the 33rd when Tolley over-pitched the green. He cut it to 1 when he took the 34th. Both players holed missable putts to halve the 35th, and this brought Tolley to the home hole dormie 1. Gardner followed his drive on the 36th by fading a cleek beautifully into the pin, won the hole, and sent the match into sudden death.

The first hole at Muirfield in those days was a one-shotter. Gardner, up first, found the green with his iron. Tolley hit an even better shot, about fourteen feet from the pin. Gardner put his putt up close and

WILLS'S CIGARETTES.

GEORGE DUNCAN.

stood by helplessly as Tolley rolled his bid for a deuce straight into the back of the cup and was immediately engulfed by his ecstatic countrymen. It had been touch-and-go but Britain had held.

Gardner's performance at Muirfield had given British golfers the jitters. The mediocre play of Barnes and Hagen's ignominious debut in the British Open restored their aplomb. Hagen had come to Deal, on the coast of Kent, ballyhooed as the greatest golfer ever produced in America, a dashing competitor who time after time cut loose with a finishing kick as irresistible as Snapper Garrison's. At Deal, Hagen failed to break 80 on any of his four rounds. His finishing kick was a hot 84, and he ended up in 55th place, twenty-six strokes behind the winner, George Duncan. Duncan had made up a deficit of thirteen strokes on Mitchell on the third round, a comeback and a crash that were debated in the pubs for many weeks afterwards but scarcely interested Americans. Barnes had finished sixth at Deal, but that was cold comfort.

To make matters worse, Ted Ray topped off a British counter-offensive by taking *our* Open in 1920. Ray and Vardon, grayer now and shaggier at the mustache, had come over that summer for a second tour, another financial and artistic success.

But when it came to the Open, much as Americans respected the evergreen prowess of the two Jerseymen, we were less awed by their reputations than we had been in 1913, when we had practically conceded them the title. In 1920 we looked to Hagen and Barnes to make up for their fiasco in the British Open, and Hutchison, Evans, and Jones could be counted on as a second tide.

All the Opens from 1909 on had been rich in excitement, but the 1920 championship at Inverness, in Toledo, topped every one except the classic Open of 1913 in the tumultuous, nerve-tingling drama that unfolded on the afternoon of the final round. Old Harry Vardon, the master himself, led the field at the three-quarter mark. Vardon's 218 gave him a one-stroke lead over Hutchison and inexperienced Leo Diegel, two over Ray. (Hagen and Barnes were not far back but they never looked like winning.) Harry was playing the same immaculate golf he had exhibited a quarter of a century earlier in winning his first British Open, and all transatlantic rivalry was momentarily forgotten as the gallery spilled over the course to pay homage to Vardon and watch the great man win what would probably be his last championship. At the 64th tee it looked as if Harry would do it. He had gone out in 36 with no trouble. He could take as many as forty-one strokes coming in and still top the best total so far posted, a 296 by Jack Burke, a young homebred who had turned in a last-round 72. Harry began the long voyage home with a par on the tenth and a birdie on the

eleventh. As he stood on the twelfth tee preparing to play that 522-yard hole, the sky suddenly grew indigo and a vicious gale blew off Lake Erie and ripped across the fairways. Playing into the teeth of the gale, Vardon needed four shots to get home on the twelfth, and took a 6. He stood firm against the smashing wind on the thirteenth until he set himself to sink a 2-footer for his par, and jabbed it wide. The fifty-year-older was utterly weary now. He three-putted the fourteenth, and try as he did to summon one last measure of skill, he three-putted the fifteenth and the sixteenth. On the seventeenth, he failed to carry the brook before the green with his second shot and limped home, spent and forlorn. Vardon had gone 7 over par on the last seven holes, and his 78 was good enough only for a tie with Burke. The storm had been too much for his years.

The crowd raced back from the clubhouse to find Ray, Diegel, and Hutchison.

Ray had swept out in 35. His putter had compensated for his early lapses. On the first four holes he had gotten down putts of thirty, twenty-five, forty, and fifteen feet. He really couldn t kick when he missed comparatively short ones on the eighth and ninth. Like Vardon he wobbled badly coming home, but his 40 gave him a 75 and a total of 295, a stroke better than Vardon's and Burke's.

Deigel, from Lake Shore, had gone out in 37. The young man was becoming more and more nervous as he moved into the in-nine, yet he was still hitting the ball handsomely. He had putts for birdies from four feet and seven feet on the tenth and twelfth, and although he had missed them both, pars would see him through. Chick Evans had taken over Diegel's bag from his caddie in an effort to lend the youngster the benefit of his years of tournament experi-ence, and by the thirteenth hole an ever-swelling gallery had clustered around the neo-phyte to pray him home. The fourteenth finished Diegel. He half-topped his drive when a spectator coughed. His tenseness mounted. As he was lining up his brassie, about to play his second, a homebred pro, trying to be helpful, broke through the front line of the gallery to report a high score by Ray. Understandably upset by this interruption, Diegel threw his brassie to the ground. "I don't care what Ray took," he said in disgust. "I'm playing my own game." When he finally hit that brassie, Leo hooked it into trouble and could do no better than a 6, two over par. He came to the seventeenth faced with birdieing either that hole or the eighteenth to tie with Ray, but missed a 10-footer and a 25-footer and had blown the first of his many chances to win the Open.

Like Diegel, Jock Hutchison needed a birdie and a par on the last two holes to tie

WILLS'S CIGARETTES.

WALTER J. HAGEN.

WILLS'S CIGARETTES.

ABE MITCHELL.

Ray, and couldn't get the birdie. On the 69th green, Jock had commented after choking on a 3-foot putt, "That shot cost me the championship." It had at least cost him a crack at a playoff.

Ray won the championship on the dogleg seventh. On each of his four rounds, he had thrown all of the power in his rough, sloping shoulders into his tee shot and carried the trees in the V of the dogleg 275 yards out. Twice he had driven the green, and on all four rounds he had snared his birdie 3. Ray was forty-three years old at Inverness, the oldest golfer ever to win our Open.

A fragment of our national honor was salvaged in the Amateur of 1920, played at the Engineers' Country Club on Long Island. Tolley, Tommy Armour, Lord Charles Hope, and Roger Wethered had come over for the event, but Armour was the only one to get by the qualifying round and he went out early in the match play. Chick Evans, who won the tourney, almost came a cropper in the second round when he had to sink a wicked 14-foot sidehiller on the last hole to tie Reggie Lewis and then had to last out five extra holes before the ordeal was over. In the final Evans faced Ouimet, who

had eliminated Jones. This was only the second time Evans and Ouimet had met in a national championship. The year before Francis had taken Chick 1 up. This time it was Chick s turn. In winning 7 and 6, Chick covered a stretch of nineteen holes in 71 strokes, was trapped only twice all day, and didn't miss a putt he should have holed. Chick was rightfully pleased with all this.

American golfers did better in 1921. In the two of the four major championships played in the United States, the British entries were held in check. Neither Duncan nor Mitchell, who came over for the Open at the Columbia Country Club, in Chevy Chase, Maryland, could keep up with the torrid pace set by Long Jim Barnes—and for that matter, none of the homebreds could. Jim finished with a margin of nine strokes over Hagen and Freddy McLeod, who tied for second. In the Amateur at the St. Louis Country Club, Willie Hunter, the British postal clerk who had won the British Amateur earlier in the year, looked dangerous when he upset Bobby Jones in the third round, but Bob Gardner stopped Willie in the semis. In the final, played over a waterlogged course, Jesse Guilford put on an astounding exhibition of slugging and golfing—in one spurt he tied four birds together—and gave Gardner a bad beating.

(Jesse was as shy as they came and, for laconic honesty, his acceptance speech has yet to be equaled: "If I am expected to give a speech," Jesse drawled, "I am sorry I won the title.")

In the spring of 1921, well before these domestic championships had taken place, a half dozen or so American pros and a larger group of amateurs had sailed to England on their first full-scale invasion. Because of their disappointing records in both the Opens of 1920, we were not overly sanguine about the chances of our pros. Gardner's success, on the other hand, had hoisted our hopes that the British Amateur crown might be carried off by one of the young men in the party Bill Fownes' was taking across. It turned out just the other way.

In what was more or less a warmup for the British Amateur, Fownes' boys met a team of British amateurs at Hoylake in an informal match that set the pattern for the Walker Cup competition officially inaugurated the next season. At Hoylake the American team—Francis, Chick, Fownes, Jones, Guilford, Paul Hunter, Woody Platt, and Fred Wright—won all four of the foursomes and five of the eight singles matches. This convincing 9–3 victory, coming on the eve of the Amateur, reinforced our faith in the chances of the American players and spread a corresponding gloom through Britain. The fans in Scotland and England steeled themselves to accept an American

Scotsman Tommy Armour learned the game at the Braid Hills public courses in Edinburgh. The photograph opposite was taken during his first visit to the States in 1920.

champion. Sooner or later a foreigner was bound to break through again, they rationalized, and if this was destined to be the year, there was nothing to do except to get it over with.

In the Amateur our players failed to hold the form they had displayed in the team match. One by one they fell by the wayside, and often at the hands of "unknowns" who had entered the tournament principally because it gave them a more intimate view of the proceedings. Jones' showing was typical. In the second round against a nobody by the name of Hamlet, who clocked an 87, Bobby had all he could do to win 1 up. He was more like himself in winning his third match, but in the next round Allan Graham, an old gentleman with a brass putter, went out after Jones from the first tee and nailed his man 6 and 5. By the fifth round, Paul Hunter and Freddy Wright were the only two Americans still surviving. In that round Hunter was defeated by Bernard Darwin, and it was Darwin who also accounted for Wright in the sixth. The evening after he had ousted Wright, the last American threat, Darwin, the famed golf correspondent of the *Times*

of London, walked into a marvelous incident. He was shuffling in a happy mood down a village street when he found himself the object of an inquisitive stare from a man advancing up the sidewalk from the opposite direction. Darwin didn't place the face, and, concluding that the stare was just an idiosyncrasy of the stranger's, made up his mind to keep on walking. As Darwin was about to pass him, the stranger suddenly shifted over, intentionally it seemed, and blocked Bernard's path. "Sir," said the stranger solemnly as he looked Bernard in the eye, "I would like to thank you for the way in which you have saved your country."

The British Open in '21 was scheduled for St. Andrews, Jock Hutchison's hometown, and the local boy who had made good in America decided to combine a long-delayed visit with a try for the title. He arrived in St. Andrews in the winter, long before the other contenders. In the months before the Open, Hutchison gave his admiring townsmen something to look at—the most consistent low scoring on the Old Course since the days of Young Tom Morris. If he continued to play golf of that caliber, Jock would be a hard man to beat, but his supporters were afraid that he might go stale before the championship got underway. Jock had done that before. At Brae Burn in 1919 and Inverness in 1920, he had spent his brilliance during the qualifying

rounds and was relatively played out when the championship proper began.

In the qualifying round for the Open, Jock was up to his old habits. Two effortless rounds gave him a total of 146, and if he could stay in that groove, he would take some beating. Jock's first round in the championship was a 1-under-par 72 in which the popular native son just missed scoring holes-in-one on two consecutive holes. He got an ace on the 135-yard eighth, and on the ninth, then 278 yards long, Hutchison smacked a drive that ran onto the green and, trickling up to the hole as softly as if it had been putted, caught a corner of the cup, twisted out, and just stayed out. Jock's second round, a 75, kept him up with the leaders but at the same time worried his backers. He did look over-golfed. Then in the crucial third round—all rounds of an Open are crucial but the third is often the real killer—Hutchison fell apart. A 79 gave him 226 at the three-quarter mark and left him four strokes behind Barnes, who had played three 74s, and Sandy Herd, the 1902 Open Champion, who refused to act his age. Jock was also a stroke behind Roger Wethered, whose 225 included an unlucky penalty stroke; Roger had accidentally kicked his ball on the third round as he backed up to play an approach after sighting the terrain ahead. Hutch was one of the last to go out on the final round, teeing off

BERNARD DARWIN, THE GREATEST OF ALL GOLF WRITERS, WAS AN EXPERT PLAYER WHO IS SHOWN, OPPOSITE, DURING THE 1921 BRITISH AMATEUR AT THE ROYAL LIVERPOOL CLUB AT HOYLAKE. TWICE DARWIN REACHED THE SEMI-FINALS OF THE EVENT: IN 1909 AND, AGAIN, IN 1921.

at about the same time that his father, caddying for another entry, came down the
eighteenth. Hutch's work was cut out for
him. Herd and Barnes had soared to 80s but
Wethered had added a final 71, and to tie,
Jock had to play a 70, 3 under par. His 36 out
looked to be a little too much, but Jock sent
his home-town gallery into raptures by
turning on his maddest golf just when he
had to and played the difficult last nine in
34. He came within a hair of holing his putt
on the home green for an outright win. In
the 36-hole playoff against Wethered, Jock
caught the amateur on one of his more
erratic days, and playing a
heady 74 and 76, won the title
with nine strokes to spare.

C. A. WHITCOMBE.

That was something,
Hutchison's victory in the
Open. For the first time
since Arnaud Massy of
France had won at Hoylake
in 1907, the cup had gone to a
foreigner, and this time to a
foreigner from a distant
country. Some Britishers per-
sisted in viewing Hutchison as one of their
own, but Jock was an American citizen
when he won, and indeed an American
golfer, and back in the States his spectacular triumph was acclaimed the first twist in
the lion's tail by "one of our boys." Subsidiary praise was in order for Barnes,

Hagen, and Tom Kerrigan of Siwanoy. Kerrigan finished with a pair of 72s to come
within two strokes of the winning total.
Though he had played indifferently for
him, Hagen had tied for sixth, and this was
at least an improvement over his performance the year before at Deal.

The climactic victory came in 1922. Hagen
won at Royal St. George's, in Sandwich. This
time there was no escape from the facts for
the British, as there had been the year before
in Hutchison's dual nationali-
ty. Hagen was a homebred,
as American as apple pie—or
perhaps a mint julep would be
a more appropriate symbol.
Walter's break-through at
Sandwich, in the minds of
both the American and
British publics, signalized suc-
cess-at-last for the American
invasions of the island where
golf was born.

Hagen was himself at Sandwich. He
led off with a mediocre 76, but a 73 in the
wind put him in the lead by one stroke at
the halfway mark. His bad round, a 78, could
have been much higher had he not come
through with sensational recoveries several
times when it looked as if he had again

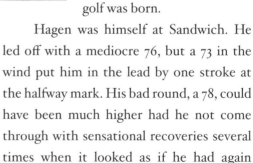

*AMERICAN PRO JOCK HUTCHISON, RIGHT, OPPOSITE, AND BRITISH AMATEUR ROGER WETHERED
DUELED FOR THE 1921 BRITISH OPEN ON THE OLD COURSE AT ST. ANDREWS. THE TWO WERE TIED AFTER
72 HOLES; HUTCHISON WON THE 36-HOLE PLAYOFF BY NINE STROKES.*

played himself out of the championship. At the end of fifty-four holes, even with the 78, he was bracketed with Jim Barnes and Charles Whitcombe just one stroke off of the pace set by Jock Hutchison. On the last round, all of the leaders stood up fairly well. Barnes played a 73, Whitcombe a 75, Hutchison a 76. Hagen won because, for the first time in Britain, he uncorked his tremendous finishing kick, what we in American termed a "Hagen finish." His 72

put him one stroke ahead of Barnes, and all he had to do now was sweat out George Duncan. George, well behind the leaders all the way, was off on one of his dream rounds, putting for birdies from twelve feet or less on every other hole as he snubbed the elements and the gathering darkness. Duncan came to the 72nd needing a par 4 to tie Hagen. All his valor went for nought when he tightened up on his chip and had to take a 5. Hagen was in.

The British Open was the only one of the four major championships in 1922 with a robust international flavor. In winning our Open at Skokie, Gene Sarazen, a new name, had surprised a field that included only two British entrants—Duncan and Mitchell. None of our ranking amateurs went over to try for the British Amateur (which Ernest Holderness won), for they were too busy preparing for the first official Walker Cup Match, to be played at Macdonald's National. While the British title still eluded them, U.S. amateurs demonstrated that on American soil, at any rate, they were now more skillful than the men from the British Isles. The American team took the Walker Cup competition 8 points to 4, and in the national Amateur, which followed shortly afterwards at The Country Club, in Brookline, our golfers quickly converted the foreign threats into innocent spectators. As it turned out, Jess Sweetser, the strong boy from Siwanoy who won our Amateur that year, became some four years

NINETEEN TWENTY-TWO BROUGHT TO CENTER STAGE TWO IMMORTALS: GENE SARAZEN, OPPOSITE, WHO CARRIED OFF THE U.S. OPEN TITLE AND IS HIMSELF ELEVATED BY FANS, AND BRITISH OPEN WINNER WALTER HAGEN, ABOVE, IN A POLO COAT, WHO CUT A FIGURE ELEGANT ENOUGH TO ECLIPSE EVEN THE PRINCE OF WALES WHO STANDS TO HAGEN'S RIGHT ON THE WINNER'S PLATFORM.

later the first American-born golfer to win the British Amateur.

In the four years that had elapsed since the end of the war, American players had completely altered the complexion of international golf. Our amateurs had won one unofficial and one official team match against their British rivals, and while they had been repulsed in their efforts to take the British Amateur, it was clear that it would be only a matter of time before that enemy citadel would fall. Our pros, led by a homebred and a naturalized American, had captured the British Open two years in a row and were on their way to creating what

would be, for over a decade, virtually an American championship. There would be times when British golfers, pro and amateur, would rise and demonstrate with authority that America did not have a monopoly on the first-class shot-makers, but these British triumphs were few and far between, sporadic protests rather than the clarions of a national resurgence.

By 1923, the leadership in golf had passed from Great Britain to the United States. Here at home our first successes ignited the ambitions of a younger generation to become the builders of a golfing empire of more grandiose proportions. In

Great Britain, the golf fans began their long wait for an emancipator, yet there was no mourning. Harold Hilton, the old victor at Apawamis, voiced the feelings of the nation when he said in his most delicate phraseology: "There can be no doubt that the American player of the game has somewhat rudely annexed that presumptive hereditary right of ours. Recent events have proved beyond dispute that the standard of the game as played in the United States is at least of a more consistent and accurate description than that which we are in the habit of witnessing on courses in the British Isles. To put the matter in the very plainest of language, American players of the present day are better golfers than their British cousins."

Jess Sweetser was a fine player whose career somewhat paralleled that of Bobby Jones. Here, he smiles after defeating Jones on his way to winning the 1922 U.S. Amateur.

Sir Walter

UNLIKE many of the golfers who went before and after him, the long career of Walter Hagen does not present one great year, one great tournament, or even one great round towering high and as incontrovertible as an Everest over the ridges of his other accomplishments. If charted on a graph, Hagen's two decades and more as a top tournament golfer would show a series of peaks, many of similar altitude, with the tallest peaks invariably following a sizable depression. The reader of the graph, as a result, is able to make out a fairly good case for whatever peak in the zagging line strikes him as the man's finest hour—winning the U.S. Open in 1914, the U.S. Open in 1919, the British Open in 1922,

the British Open again in 1924, 1928, and 1929, or taking the P.G.A. title four years in a row, overwhelming Jones in their one "private" match, leading our Ryder Cuppers, or urging his ancient bones in a last brave challenge in the Open at Oakmont in 1935. They were all great moments, and it can be argued that the sum of the man's deeds is more readily appreciated because of the absence of any one overriding climax.

Hagen's essentially dramatic personality made him acutely conscious that there was something unfinished, something incomplete, about his career. In one tight spot after another, he had demonstrated to his own satisfaction and to the delighted astonishment of the public that he, like no

other golfer, could call upon himself for the one shot he needed and come up with it. In the latter stages of his career, believing that in his bag one last parade of winning shots lay unplayed, he continued to appear in tournaments hoping that under the stress of competition he would be able to summon these shots and win that crowning championship. Hagen never quite got them out, and so he never went into an abrupt retirement, but continued to make one farewell appearance after another, very much in the tradition of Sarah Bernhardt.

Somehow it is difficult to picture Hagen having a childhood or a period in which he put his game together by stern, unglamorous practice. He etched his personality so deeply on the minds of sports followers that the mere mention of his name still evokes the full image of the man—hair brilliantined, face tanned and smiling with an almost Oriental inscrutability, clothes that would have looked showy on anyone else, the haughty stride back onto the fairway after punching a recovery shot through the brambles and onto the car-

WHEN WALTER HAGEN WASN'T WINNING TOURNAMENTS HE WAS ELEVATING THE STATUS OF THE GOLF PROFESSIONAL TO NEAR-MOVIE-STAR LEVEL. IN THE PHOTOGRAPH ABOVE, HAGEN BOARDS A 1933 CADILLAC PARKED OUTSIDE THE WILSHIRE COUNTRY CLUB IN LOS ANGELES.

pet. This man, you felt, had always been that way. Like Athena, he had undoubtedly emerged full-blown from the forehead of some twentieth-century Zeus.

Walter Hagen, who was of Dutch extraction, was quite a boy. Like the other kids in his neighborhood in Rochester, Walter was crazy about golf and baseball. He had far more talent for both games than any of the fellows he grew up with. In baseball he pitched, naturally. He had no brothers so he taught his sister how to catch in order that he would have someone to hold his stuff in the backyard. He threw with either hand. In time Walter became the best pitcher in the district, and for many years could not make up his mind as to which sport he would make his profession, golf or baseball. A few weeks before he won his first national Open, he finally decided on golf. He had just been offered a contract by the Philadelphia club of the National League, but the way he looked at it, in baseball there were eight other men who could lose a game for you. In golf, there was only yourself. Even so, baseball never lost its fascination for Walter. As late as 1934, when he resembled a third-base coach in portliness, he climbed into the flannels and spikes and worked out with the Detroit Tigers in spring training. There is no knowing how far Walter would have gone in organized baseball or how it would have shaped his personality, but there are many folks who believe he would have attained the same eminence he did in golf. They believe that

Walter Hagen was one of those rare ones who would have been an unqualified success in whatever profession or business he chose as his lifework.

Walter caddied at the Country Club of Rochester. Noticing how adept the boy was at fielding any sort of a ball, Andy Christie, the pro, picked out Walter to shag balls for him whenever he gave lessons. Walter graduated to the pro shop and helped with the caddies. On the slow mornings he played nine holes with Christie, and worked in the shop until six. He practiced then until it was dark, took a dip in the creek, and walked home to eat the supper that his folks had left in the oven.

When the Open was played at Buffalo in 1912, Hagen asked Christie for a week's leave of absence from his duties as assistant pro to play in the tournament. Christie couldn't see it. The kid was only twenty years old, too inexperienced for that sort of competition. If Walter wanted to take a couple of days off to watch the tournament, all right, but there was no sense letting the kid make a fool of himself trying to keep up with the gang who played in the Open. Walter went to Buffalo and watched Johnny McDermott win the championship. He picked up a few pointers from studying the stars, but by and large he was not impressed by what he saw. The big boys weren't as good as he thought they would be.

The next season, 1913, Hagen tested his belief that he could stick with the best professionals by playing in the Shawnee

Open and the national Open. He didn't set any worlds on fire at Shawnee, but he didn't disgrace himself, and in the Open he finished in a tie for fourth. That was the year Vardon and Ray were expected to take the title out of the country. None of the leading pros gathered at The Country Club knew the black-haired assistant from Rochester and they got quite a boot when the kid introduced himself to Johnny McDermott in the locker room and explained that he'd "come down to help you fellows stop Vardon and Ray." Ouimet did the stopping, but Walter outscored every American pro except McDermott and brought in the same total as the ex-champion. He was in the running until the last nine, when the pressure told on him. He took a 7 on the fourteenth and sprayed his way home.

Having decided not to be a ballplayer, the kid was on the firing line for the Open in 1914. He turned up at Midlothian wearing what he thought was the last word in rakish straw hats. He liked clothes and had a horror of looking like a hick. When he had made his Open debut at Brookline, he had worn a checked Scottish cap, a fancy bandanna, a striped silk shirt, gray flannels, and shoes with the tongue stylishly doubled back over the instep. He'd show them that he knew how to dress! At Midlothian, a long course for those days, measuring 6,355 yards, Walter jumped into the lead by shooting a 68, a new competitive record for the course.

A 74 and a 75 kept him up front, four strokes ahead of Chick Evans as the field entered the last round. All Chicago, it seemed, was following Evans. Playing about three holes ahead of Chick, with no gallery to speak of, Hagen heard one mighty roar after another come from Evans' mob. That could only mean that Chick was hot. He was. He took 35 for the out-nine and had shaved Hagen's lead to one stroke. All the way in, Hagen heard the bursts of applause from Evans' gallery telling him that Chick was still coming. To make it the more menacing, these shattering salvos often split the air just when Walter was engaged in digging himself out of trouble. Walter tried to erase Evans from his mind and to concentrate on his own score. He made up for a hooked mid-iron on the thirteenth by sinking a 12-footer for his par. One the sixteenth he pulled his brassie and stubbed his chip, but coolly got down a long putt for his birdie. He missed from seven feet on the seventeenth, but on the last green he sank an 8-footer. This last putt constituted Walter's margin of victory.

Hagen had won the Open the right way; he had got out in front and stayed there. He had displayed unusual control of his nerves and seemed to have the physical equipment necessary for a topflight golfer—good hands, good wrists, good forearms. His swing, though, had too much body in it, a good deal of sway. The kid didn't swing really. He brought the club into position and then *hit* the ball. Walter was a cocky, unapologetic young man, but at the same time he was neither boastful nor disrespectful, and when the older pros commented that the new champion might be only a flash in the pan, their judgements were based on no personal antipathy (apart from a natural touch of jealousy) but on a distrust of Hagen's somewhat unorthodox style.

The new champion was not champion long. He made a poor showing defending his title at Baltusrol, and in 1916 he was not a contender. The experts who had criticized his form could point to these and other disappointing performances as bearing out their prediction that Hagen was not a fundamentally sound golfer...and yet some weeks they weren't quite as sure as they would have liked to have been. Walter never went very long without winning some kind of tournament. In 1915 he had to be content with the Massachusetts Open, but in 1916 he took the Metropolitan Open, a big championship in those days, the Shawnee, and the prestigious Western; in winning the Western he had played five holes in thirteen strokes, two 2s and three 3s, terrific golf whether you swayed or you pivoted. Walter always made it a practice never to be without a title during his long career. He preferred it to be a United States or British Open, but during the years he missed out on the big ones, he always had the P.G.A. or the Western or the Metropolitan or the North and South to put under his name. Even when he was supposed to be slipping—and Hagen was supposed to be slipping from 1914 on—he would shift into high long enough to garner a Canadian or some other tournament of distinction, which was a lot more than most of his detractors could say for themselves.

Whether you liked his style or not, by 1917 Walter Hagen had left all the other native-born professionals far behind and was the unanimous choice to captain the team of Homebred Pros when they faced the English Pros, Scottish Pros, and Amateurs in a four-cornered exhibition for war charities. By the close of the war he had joined Jim Barnes and Jock Hutchison as the triumvirate dominating the money-golfers and had earned a reputation as the most colorful shot-maker in the country. He was an amazing finisher. In an exhibition four-ball match in Rochester, for instance, with his side 3 down with five to play, Walter pulled out the match by playing the last five holes in birdies. He could take a course apart in medal play with the best of them, but there was something about match play, the chances it offered for dealing with one crisis after another, that seemed to bring out the sharpest shots in his repertoire. Above all, Hagen was interesting to watch. The other star golfers made the game look easy: all you had to do was knock the ball down the fairway, pitch it on the green, and

get down in two putts. Hagen made the game look hard. Once or twice a round he hooked or sliced a drive as savagely as a 90s-golfer, leaving himself a shot that looked absolutely unplayable until he executed a fantastic recovery. These violent errors by a champion had the same effect on the spectators as if they had watched a supposedly flawless tight-rope walker suddenly lose his balance and go hurtling through space into the net below. Then when the performer went back to his perch and this time successfully waltzed on the wire, the spectators realized how hard it really was to walk a tightrope, or play par golf.

A born showman, Hagen could feel the grip he gained on galleries. He discovered that they liked him best when he gave full rein to his developing personality—his unruffled poise in the face of disaster, an unmalicious condescension toward his opponents and toward the galleries themselves, a touch of bravura at those very moments when he could have been forgiven for quailing. But he built his performance on good golf. He was the best putter of his day. His mashie-niblick and spade-mashie play, from 70 to 165 yards, was without peer. This made him especially destructive on a short course. His fairway woods were either very good or very bad, and in important tournaments he preferred to play a long iron to the green if the shot resolved itself into a choice between an iron and a wood. The drive, which for most professional golfers is the easiest shot in the game, always gave

Hagen difficulty. He would hit seven or eight straight and long, and on the next tee, with no advance intimation, he would lose the rhythm of his sway the faintest fraction and whack the shot on a vicious curve to either the left or the right—he was impartial. He threw his right side into a drive with such force that on his followthrough his right shoulder was the part of his body nearest the green.

Until the twilight of his career, when whisky fingers destroyed his putting touch and nullified his tardy straightness from tee to green, Hagen was seldom able to play eighteen holes without hitting at least one or two weirdly loose shots. Nine hundred and ninety-nine golfers out of a thousand would have been ruined by this affliction, would have worn themselves out worrying about when that wild shot was coming and fretted themselves helpless when it eventually raised its ugly arc. Hagen didn't let these errors upset him. He was a philosopher, an honest one. He accepted the fact that three times or so a round he would hit a very poor shot—and what was so calamitous about that? No golfer could expect to hit every shot perfectly. As a result, Walter was able to forget about a bad shot almost instantly. Other golfers, knowing that the index of the ideal golfing temperament is the ability to ignore a costly error and keep hitting the ball, asserted that they, too, never let a mistake eat into their confidence, but most of the time they were simply saying words. Hagen was genuinely able to forget his laps-

es. Equally unique and invaluable was his penchant for remaining relaxed at all times. He regarded this gift as the key to whatever success he enjoyed, and it is significant that he devoted the first chapter of an instruction book he never finished to the importance of relaxation.

In the Open at Brae Burn in 1919, worldly at twenty-seven, as fearless on the golf course as Cobb was on the diamond, Walter won the crown from Mike Brady. It was a triumph of temperament. Walter came to the last nine holes knowing that he had to match par to equal Brady's total. On the 65th hole, he hooked out-of-bounds and lost what could have been a critical stroke. "I'll get a birdie and make up for that little error," Hagen told his fretful friend Harry Martin. He got that bird on the 67th. He stayed with par from then on and arrived at the 72nd tee needing a par 4 on that demanding hole to tie with Brady. Hagen's drive left him with a long iron to the green, a two-level dipper with the pin positioned on the upper deck. Most golfers would have played for a safe 4, aimed for the middle of the green and allowed themselves two putts to get down for a tie. Hagen wasn't built that way. A stone wall fringed the back of the green, ready to punish the bold golfer who overshot the upper level, but Hagen eschewed all cautious tactics and hit a screaming midiron straight for the pin. The ball faded slightly, landed on the dangerous top terrace, and spun itself out eight feet to the right of the hole—a really wonderful

shot. Before attempting the putt that could give him an outright win over Brady, Hagen brashly had Mike summoned from the club-house so that he would be on hand to watch his own funeral. Mike obliged and shivered in his spikes as Walter tapped his sidehiller into the corner of the cup, only to have it twist out again and linger on the lip.

In the playoff the following day, Hagen defeated Brady by a single stroke. A golfer of less spontaneous shrewdness than Hagen might have lost. On the seventeenth hole of a nip-and-tuck battle, Hagen hit one of his typical loose drives, slicing the ball into the spongy rough. After a lengthy search, the ball was found deeply imbedded in the earth. It looked to Hagen as if some specta-tor might have inadvertently stepped on his ball, and he requested a free lift. The officials ruled against this: they were not sure the ball had been stepped on. Hagen then asked the officials for permission to identify the ball as his own, a request they were bound to grant. Before the identification was completed, the ball was loosened and some of the mud uncaked. Hagen was able then to play one of his most awesome recoveries.

Such tactics as these time and time again upset the concentration of his adver-saries and, just as often, made them so

HAGEN PLAYS TO A LARGE GALLERY ON THE 72ND HOLE OF THE 1919 U.S. OPEN AT THE BRAE BURN CLUB NEAR BOSTON. NEEDING A BIRDIE TO WIN, HAGEN JUST MISSES THE PUTT SEEN HERE BUT WON THE TITLE THE NEXT DAY IN A PLAYOFF WITH MIKE BRADY.

grimly determined to outthink the resourceful Haig that they ended up out-thinking themselves. It was this psychological aptitude of Walter's, supplementing his versatile shot-making, which made Americans confident that if any American could bag the British Open Championship, it would be Hagen. There was, as always, a clique of old-school golfers who did not share the general optimism concerning Hagen's chances of beating the British. By 1920 they were willing to admit that on American courses under American conditions Walter was our best tournament scorer but they didn't think he had the shots for the winds that would be swirling over the seaside links at Deal, where the 1920 British Open would be played. Walter, they advanced, hit his shots too high. They would get caught in the wind and blown all over the course. Walter replied to his belittlers that "there are no bunkers in the air." He intended to hit the ball at Deal the way he always did, and he expected to win.

At Deal there were no bunkers in the air but there were plenty on the ground, and Hagen visited a good many of them. The critics of his game had been absolutely right. While shots of low trajectory could bore into the wind and hold their line, Hagen's arching woods and irons were scattered as ruthlessly as the Spanish Armada. He was far behind the leaders after his first round, and with each ensuing round he fell farther and farther back, finishing a dismal 55th. On his four rounds he had averaged over 82

strokes—undoubtedly the most painful comeuppance a national champion ever received. Hagen did not alibi. He never alibied. "I tried too hard, just like any duffer might play," he said, and added with as much audacity as he could collect, "Guess I figured these boys were tougher than they were."

Walter managed to win the French Open at La Boulie on that trip across, and back home he licked Jim Barnes in the playoff for the Metropolitan, but in the U.S. Open, in which he had a chance to redeem himself by stopping Vardon and Ray, he finished with two disappointing 77s. 1921 was a duplication of 1920. He won his first P.G.A. crown and gobbled up his share of minor affairs, but in the pay-off tournaments Walter didn't have it. In the British Open at St. Andrews, though he finished a respectable sixth, he played unimpressively. In the U.S. Open at the Columbia Country Club, he was nine strokes behind the winner, Jim Barnes. These failures in major events reduced the public's faith in Hagen. In 1919 they had sincerely believed that no one could stop him. Now, ever since that awful beating at Deal, American golf fans no longer felt that Hagen would come tearing down the stretch in one of his famous finishes and drive all other scores off the board. Perhaps they had oversold themselves on him back in 1919. Or maybe he was simply past his peak. Whatever the reason for Hagen's decline, they had been wrong in considering him in a class by himself. Obviously, he was just another good pro.

Hagen changed all this by winning the British Open of 1922, at Sandwich. One stroke behind the leader as he set off on his last round, Walter came through with a 72 that gave him a total one stroke below Barnes'. He sat placidly on a mound by the first tee smoking a big cigar as he waited for the last man to come in. The last man was George Duncan, and Hagen went over and watched Duncan blow himself to a bogey 5 on the final hole when he needed a 4 to tie. From fifty-fifth to sixth to first! That was more like it. Hagen went home with the title and made a fortune.

When he defended his title at Troon the next year, Walter failed to catch the winner, Arthur Havers, but was glorious in defeat. When Havers added a 76 to his three 73s, Hagen was left with a 74 to tie. (A 74 may seem like tall shooting today, accustomed as we are to fancy figures in the sixties in *tour tournaments;* a review of the scoring in the major championships will readjust a too glib condescension toward the scores of the Twenties.) After a tough battle in a wild wind, Hagen reached the home hole confronted with the necessity of playing a birdie 3 for that 74. A good drive left him an iron of some 160 yards to the green. He hit a firm spade-mashie but it faded off as it came up to the pin and overran the green into a bunker.

WALTER HAGEN

Unperturbed, Hagen marched into the bunker and lined up his shot as carefully as if it were a putt and not an explosion shot he had to hole. He studied the texture of the sand, the distance between the bunker and the pin, the rolls of the green...and then he played an absolutely beautiful stroke that almost did find the hole. He nonchalantly rolled in the putt that didn't count.

Walter Hagen had a sterling contempt for second place. He believed that the public only remembered the winner, that a man might as well be tenth as second when the shooting was over. At Troon as at Brae Burn before and in many crises still to be faced, Walter went all-out for victory, disdaining a sure second place and several times finishing farther back than second when a one-in-a-million shot for first failed to come off. When the Open was held at the Worcester Country Club in 1925, Walter was informed on the 72nd tee that a par 4 would gain him a tie with the lowest man in. Hagen decided to gamble on a 3, although this meant shaving an approach inches over a brutal bunker backing right up to the pin on the extreme front edge of the terraced green. Walter cut that shot a shade too fine, caught the bunker, and ultimately finished in a tie for third. In the 1926 British Open at Lytham and St. Annes, Walter had a probable second place all wrapped up, but that wasn't good enough. If he could somehow get an eagle 2 on the 72nd hole, he could tie with Bobby Jones for first, and then he would have a chance to win the title in the playoff. Hagen put everything he had into his drive on this last hole, and then all he had to do was to sink a full iron approach. Before playing that shot, Walter strolled down the fairway to the green, the better to study the terrain. He then ordered his caddie to stand close by the hole so that he could remove the flagstick if his approach, after landing on the front of the green, was headed for it. He then walked back to his ball and played an heroic shot which came extremely close to entering the cup on the fly...and Walter was not the least bit regretful when he holed out in 6 after playing back from the hazard into which the approach had rolled.

Hagen's order to his caddie to, in effect, flag the hole on the home green in the Open would have been absurd had any other golfer ordered it. Coming from Hagen, it was wonderfully in character. On and off a golf course, the ex-caddie and sandlot hurler comported himself in a manner as imperial as a king or a Hollywood star. He loved the high life. He drank what would have been for other people excessive quantities of liquor. While it was not exactly habitual, it was not uncommon for him to drive directly from an all-night party to the first tee of the tournament in which he was involved. Some of the other pros who

tried to live like Hagen were back mowing greens in Keokuk in a very short time; Walter broke eleven of the Ten Commandments and kept on going. He knew how to take care of himself. He had the right words and the right tie for every occasion. Loving clothes as he did, whenever he had the time he changed into a new outfit between his morning and afternoon rounds. His favorite diversions during the off-season were fishing, shooting, and big-game hunting, and he indulged these tastes with the same lack of restraint that made him so attractive a playmate for those who could afford to play. He liked the big gesture— ordering the pin to be tended or keeping the Prince of Wales waiting or giving his prize money for winning the British Open to his caddie. He refused to enter British clubhouses by the back door, the traditional entrance for professionals; if he was good enough to enter at all, he would use the front door with the other gentlemen, and there was nothing contradictory about being a professional golfer and a gentleman. Sir Walter, as he came to be called, was proud of his profession. More than any other golfer, he brought it a new stature. However, for all his sophistication and velour, Hagen never lost his love of battle or that brash badinage he cultivated on the way up. Sir Walter was only half kidding when he quipped as he teed up on the first hole, "Well, who's going to be second?"

Hagen's never-say-die spirit made him a terror in medal competition. The low man could never relax until Hagen was in, regardless of how poorly Walter seemed to be playing, for it was common knowledge that though Walter hit more rank bad shots in a single round than most pros hit during an entire tournament, somehow he could always score. In match play, when he confronted his opponents in person, not indirectly over the grapevine but solid and satanic in the flesh, Hagen was even more to be feared. His personality was completely dominating. If you tried to kid along with him between shots you could never get down to business when the strokes had to be played, but Walter could. If you tried to shut him out of your mind, the harder you fought to ignore him the more strongly his presence enveloped you. You were attacked by the uneasy feeling that he knew everything you were going to do well in advance, and though you laughed when people attributed sinister powers to him, there were times when you privately agreed with this explanation. There you were, beating your brains out and playing far from your best golf when you wanted more than ever to play your best. And there he was, so damned casual, polite as hell, but with that indelible smirk of superiority playing over those bland features. You could understand from your own experience how a seasoned big-timer like Leo Diegel could lose to Hagen even when he stood 5 up with six holes to play.

Hagen won the P.G.A. Championship, a match-play tourney, five times in all and four years in a row. He had won twenty-two consecutive matches when Diegel finally stopped him in 1928. Only Gene Sarazen, who was as intrinsically cocky as Hagen and could fight fire with fire, was able to stand up against him in man-to-man combat. In 1926, when Bobby Jones was playing some of his finest golf, he and Hagen hooked up in a 72-hole match in Florida, and Walter crushed Bobby 12 and 11.

There are many tricks to match-play psychology and none escaped Hagen's attention. Against pertinacious foes, Hagen occasionally resorted to playing his approaches purposely short of the green to lure his opponent into unconsciously letting up on his shot. Hagen knew he could get down in a chip and a putt, and that the percentage would be working against his opponent. In one P.G.A. tourney he picked up a hole he had to win by an involved yet rather simple piece of chicanery. He and his opponent were about even after their drives, with Hagen a little in front. Hagen drew a long iron from his bag, as if he meant to use that club on his second shot. Observing Hagen's selection, his opponent asked his caddie for a similar iron. His shot ended up yards short of the green. Hagen then replaced his iron, took out the wood he intended to play all along, banged it home, and won the hole. Against players who were weakest on the greens, Hagen was generous in conceding putts in the early stages of a match; then, more likely than not, his opponents would miss the 2-footers that Hagen did not concede at crucial junctures. In later years, when his rivals were on the alert for his wiles, Hagen always gave a truthful answer to the questions they asked. This policy paid off for Hagen as richly as it had for Bismarck in diplomacy; the other fellow persisted in thinking he was being misled. Hagen's reputation as a match player reached such proportions that each error he made was interpreted as a deliberate move to set up some stratagem. In one P.G.A. final, for example, he sliced his drive into a cluster of trees. He frowned as he studied the possible avenues of exit, and shaking his head as if he would be forced to play a sacrifice shot, glumly surveyed the lateral line to the fairway. He returned to his ball and lo! why, he could play it to the green through that small aperture he hadn't seen before. Hagen got the ball on, nicely. His opponent, who thought he

had the hole in his pocket, received such a jolt that he mishit his approach and handed Hagen the hole and the match. The gallery was convinced that Walter had sliced into the rough on purpose.

In the Twenties, Hagen established a record in the P.G.A. Championship no one has ever approached. Season after season his average per round for the winter tournaments in the South surpassed the averages of 90 percent of the campaigners. From 1920 through 1930, with the exception of Jones, he had the best record in the Open. That was the title he wanted to win the most, just one more time, yet try as he would, Walter was never quite able to do it. His very best golf seemed to come out in England and Scotland.

Hagen won his second British Open in 1924 at Hoylake with one of his most arresting last-ditch spurts. As they set out on the final round, Hagen and Ernest Whitcombe were locked at 224 in what was virtually a two-man duel. Whitcombe started out ninety minutes before Hagen. Ernest dropped four strokes to par on the first five holes and didn't really get hold of himself until he had reached the turn in 43. However, he fought his way home in 35 strokes over one of the toughest finishing stretches in golf, and his 78 began to look like more than a courageous effort when Hagen, in an erratic mood, ran into three 6s and used up 41 strokes going out. Hagen had been built up by the press as a man who reveled in a chase, and no doubt he did like to set out behind his man and chew up the distance between them, but to beat Whitcombe Hagen had to play home in 36 strokes, and on Hoylake that is a very tall order indeed.

He seemed licked at the par-4 tenth when he lay twenty feet from the pin after playing his third. He took what was, even for Hagen, an exceedingly long time before he was satisfied with his line on the putt. Then he rapped it in. On the eleventh, Walter was on the ropes again when he steered an iron into a bunker, but a fine out and a fine putt saved him. On the twelfth he was in another trap, and again pinched the ball perfectly with his niblick. He lined up his 11-footer for his par off his left toe and stroked it into the middle of the hole. How long could he keep this up, this desperate scrambling? He missed his iron on the short thirteenth, and yet once again he managed to get down in 2 from a trap when he followed a delicate cut shot with another nerveless putt. Then he settled down, and where he had been holding on by sheer strength of will, now he began to hit his shots right on the nose, and his pars came easily. At the seventeenth he rifled a 2-iron through the narrow opening to the green and eight feet from the cup, but he failed to drop the birdie putt that would have put him one stroke under even 4s coming in and given him some leeway for error on the last hole, a short par 4. He still needed that par for victory. There was nothing wrong with his drive, but his second shot was too strong and his chip back left him a 9-footer for that 4. The man who could sink the crucial ones sank this putt, and did it so coolly that many spectators wondered if he

had realized its importance. "Sure, I knew I had to make it to win," Hagen explained with characteristic bravado, "but no man ever beat *me* in a playoff."

One week before the British Open in 1928, Walter walked into the most humiliating defeat of his long career. Just off the boat after a session before the cameras in Hollywood, badly out of practice, Walter met Archie Compston in a special 72-hole match at Moor Park when that rawboned giant was playing nothing but sub-par figures. Compston clipped off a 67, 66, and a 70, and the fourth round had hardly begun when the match was over — Compston 18 and 17, the most ignominious drubbing ever inflicted in a match between ranking professionals. While the London press was joyfully building up Compston as the native son who would restore British prestige in the Open, Hagen took himself down to the seaside and went into intensive practice. His lacing at Moor Park had fired his old will to win, and he meant to show the world that at thirty-seven, with fifteen years of competition behind him, he was far from finished.

Walter later admitted that he never started a tournament feeling shakier than when he teed up at Sandwich in 1928. He got himself a fair enough 75 to start with, and his confidence returned as he hit the ball more convincingly on each succeeding round. A 73, a 72, and another staunch 72 gave him an aggregate of 292, two strokes lower than Sarazen's and three lower than Compston's. Hagen's margin over Sarazen actually depended on a great recovery he played on his final round. Hagen, out first, was moving along in good style until he slapped his second on the fifteenth into a bunker just before the green with a full Chevalier lip. An explosion shot was not an easy stroke, but under the circumstances it was the safest shot to play, certainly less risky than attempting to pick the ball clean off the sand and hazarding quick and absolute ruin if the blade caught the ball a fraction of an inch too high or contacted a grain too much of sand. So Hagen cut the ball out as cleanly as if it had been the top of the dandelion, got down in one putt; he was safely past his crisis.

The British never learned to leave Hagen alone. Having won the Open three times, Walter had no ardent designs on the 1929 championship. However, in the Ryder Cup matches played at Moortown previous to the Open, George Duncan made the mistake of mauling Hagen 10 and 8, a defeat as personal and as humiliating as the one at the hands of Compston, since Duncan had rubbed it in over the 36-hole route. There was no other course open to Walter but to take the Open at Muirfield and restore his prestige.

This was a championship that showed Hagen at his best. His opening salute was a 75 that might have been an 82 in the hands of a less dauntless golfer. Hagen went four strokes over par on the first four holes. He had to play through a punishing rainstorm the early starters escaped. Again he showed his unapproached courage for staying with a bad round, fighting it out by will power alone until he had made it, from the standpoint of figures, a fairly decent round. He went out the next day and broke the British Open mark for a single round with a 67, and Muirfield is a course that resists a 70. He topped off this sacrilegious performance when his mashie second to the eighteenth, overhit, caught the flapping flag of the flagstick and ended up in the middle of the green. This 67 brought Walter from a tie for eighteenth to second place. On the last day, when the third and fourth rounds were played, a furious storm blew over Muirfield. It sent Diegel and Sarazen reeling into the 80s, and none of the top five finishers broke 75. Walter collected two 75s for 292. No Britisher was under 300. To keep his shots low in the storm, Hagen had switched to a deep-faced driver and, according to Henry Longhurst, hit no drive more than twenty feet off the ground. This was the fellow who nine years before had been blown to fifty-fifth at Deal.

Hagen completes his record-breaking round of 67 on the 18th green at windy Muirfield during the second round of the 1929 British Open. Hagen won the title by six strokes.

As a young man, a highly realistic young man, Walter Hagen had eyed the world and concluded that the golfer who didn't win was forgotten overnight. Hagen's triumph at Muirfield proved to be his last victory in a major championship, but Walter was never forgotten. Great as he was as a golfer, he was even greater as a personality—an artist with a sense of timing so infallible that he could make tying his shoelaces seem more dramatic than the other guy's hole-in-one. Whenever he entered a tournament, buoyant crowds ran out to find him, passing up the pacemakers so that they could watch Sir Walter. On his tours back and forth across the country, Hagen would step, shining and uncon-cerned, from the limousine his chauffeur had moored near the first tee, always a lit-tle late for his matches, since he had no idea of time and had once kept the Prince of Wales waiting; he would have disap-pointed the crowds if he had arrived on time. With hardly so much as a practice swing, the ex-caddie from Rochester, the closest thing to a "noble" many Americans had ever seen, would take a disdainful look at the first hole and rock himself into his drive. He would stride erect down the fair-way, his black hair gleaming above his weather-beaten face, and not until he had holed out on the last green did he relin-quish, even for a moment, the attention of every person in the gallery.

Jones Breaks Through

THE last hole at Inwood, on the southern shore of Long Island, is a terror.
Four hundred and twenty-five yards long,
its narrow fairway fringed with clumpy
rough and shut in by trees along the length
of the drive, it would be a stern enough par
4 without the additional menace of a water
hazard. But just before the green a deceptively mild lagoon stands guard, and this
makes the eighteenth at Inwood, along
with the eighteenth at Pebble Beach and
Carnoustie, one of the most frightening
finishing holes in golf.

One golfer who apparently knew how
to play the eighteenth at Inwood was Bobby
Jones. On his first three rounds in the

national Open in 1923, Bobby had picked up
two birdies and a kick-in par on this hole by
the simple expedient of hitting two brilliant
shots on each round. From the day he first
strode onto the championship stage back in
1916 as the fourteen-year-old wonder from
Dixie, no one argued Bobby Jones' genius
for hitting golf shots. There was no room
for argument. The chubby youngster had
everything—a graceful full swing, perfect
hand action, a nice feel in his fingers, and a
pretty fair competitive temperament for a
child prodigy. The puzzling thing was that
Jones, head and shoulders above the other
amateurs and as good as the best professionals, had won none of the ten national

championships in which he had appeared.

Walter Hagen had predicted that Jones would win the Open before he won the Amateur, and Walter looked to be right when the young man from Atlanta placed his ball on a high peg on the eighteenth tee at Inwood for the fourth time during the championship and set himself to play the 72nd hole. Rounds of 71, 73, and 76 had given Bobby a three-stroke lead on the field when he began his final spin around the difficult Long Island layout. He had gone out in 39, better golf than it appears to be at first glance, since the par on that nine was 37.

Starting with the tenth, his putting and his niblick recoveries had made up for his minor lapses, and his start back of 3-4-3-4-4-3 had given him just the cushion he wanted for the bogey 5s he ran into on the 70th and 71st holes. Bobby had probably made all the 3s he was going to get on that last hole, but a 4 would give him a 74 and 294 for his four rounds. That total would be too good for the one man who still stood a chance of catching Jones, wee Bobby Cruickshank.

Jones cracked another fine drive up the eighteenth. The wind was blowing slightly against him, so he took a spoon for

A GLIMPSE OF PERFECTION IS SEEN IN THE PHOTOGRAPH ABOVE OF BOBBY JONES ON HIS WAY TO WINNING THE 1923 U.S. OPEN—HIS FIRST NATIONAL TITLE—AT THE INWOOD COUNTRY CLUB ON LONG ISLAND.

his second rather than press a long iron over the lagoon. The ball came off the clubhead fast, heading for the front left-hand corner of the green, and then it began to hook and it kept on hooking until it finally came down in the rough near the twelfth tee. Not a shot to be proud of but nothing to worry about. Bobby had a simple little pitch left over a pot bunker, so he could still get his 4, and, anyway, his 5, and that would probably be good enough. The officials removed the chain around the twelfth tee. Bobby took a comfortable stance and pitched the ball smack into the pot bunker. When it took him three to get down from the bunker, Bobby had taken an inglorious 6, and his 294 had become 296.

Playing well behind Jones, Bobby Cruickshank, one of the strongest hearts the game has ever known, was meanwhile banging away at the three-stroke lead Jones had held going into the last round. When he was all over the course on the first five holes, it looked as if Cruickshank could never do it. When he followed his 2 on the sixth with a 3 and a 3 and a 4 and then another 3 and a 4 and still another 3—an incredible burst of one over 3s for seven tough holes—Cruickshank had forged ahead of Jones' figures. He could do it now, very definitely. Cruickshank slipped to 5-5-4, three strokes over par, from the thirteenth through the fifteenth, but he could still win now that Jones had stumbled so pathetically with two 5s and that miserable 6 on the last three holes. Three pars, three 4s, would give Cruickshank a winning total of 295.

And then the picture suddenly changed once more. Cruickshank pushed his approach to the sixteenth into the rough. He played a weak recovery, and going too hard for one putt, took three—6 costly strokes. Winning was out of the question now. To draw even with Jones, Cruickshank would have to shoot a par and a birdie. He hooked his drive on the seventeenth but fought back and got his par. Now he needed a birdie 3 to tie.

Cruickshank bisected the fairway with his drive on the eighteenth. With everything depending on his second shot, the courageous little Scot rose to the occasion and played one of the finest clutch shots of all time, a slashing midiron that cleared the lagoon, braked itself on the green, and ended up six feet from the hole. Cruickshank looked his putt over carefully, and holed it. He had caught Jones.

That evening Bobby Jones was way down in the dumps. It wasn't Cruickshank's valiant finish that hurt. If there was a silver lining in Bobby's clouds, it was the opportunity he would have the next day to go out in the playoff, now that Cruickshank had tied him, and prove that he could win a championship, not back into one. He couldn't get over the way he had butchered the last hole. When his great friend and biographer, O. B. Keeler, had met him as he dragged himself in disgust off the eighteenth green, Jones had refused to be cheered up. "Well, I didn't finish like a champion," Bobby had said, shaking his head. "I finished like a yellow dog." He brooded over his collapse all through dinner at the Engineers' Club and was still thinking about it when he turned in for a night's rest back at Inwood in the room he shared with Francis Ouimet.

The 6 on the final hole of the 1923 Open epitomized for Bobby his failures to produce at the critical junctures the golf he knew he had in his system. There was always something wrong. At one time it had been inexperience. He had outgrown it. Later it had been a wicked temper. He had con-

BETWEEN BOBBY JONES AND THE 1923 U.S. OPEN CHAMPIONSHIP HE COVETED STOOD BOBBY CRUICKSHANK, A BRITISH PROFESSIONAL WHO HAD CLOSED WITH A FLOURISH TO TIE JONES AFTER 72 HOLES. THE PLAYOFF AT INWOOD WENT TO THE FINAL HOLE BEFORE JONES WON IT.

quered it. Sometimes it had been just plain bad luck. It seemed that all a golfer needed to play the hottest golf of his life was to find himself matched with Bobby. Frequently it was Jones' own lack of intelligence. It took Bobby many seasons and many heartaches before he learned to stop worrying about what the other fellow was doing and to pit his skill against the proper opponent, Old Man Par. When he finally learned this lesson, there was no one who could stay any place close to Bobby Jones.

In a country so over-flowing with infant prodigies that the child who couldn't break off a curve sharper than Christy Mathewson's, dash off a song hit, or exhibit some other startling precocity appeared to be an out-and-out case of arrested development, Bobby Jones was the infant prodigy. He had taken up golf at five. His mother and his father, a well-to-do Atlanta lawyer, had joined the Atlanta Athletic Club's East Lake golf course that summer, and while they were learning their fundamentals from Jimmy Maiden, the new pro, Bobby knocked a ball up and down a road bordering the course. A digestive ailment had prevented him from eating any substantial food until he was five, and Bobby was a frail, thin little fellow. The next summer the Joneses took a cottage on the East Lake property near the old thirteenth green. Bobby used to follow his parents around the course, batting the ball with a cut-down cleek, worried more about keeping up with the grownups' pace than hitting the ball correctly. He liked to follow Stewart Maiden, who had succeeded his brother as the pro at East Lake, but Stewart paid no attention to the little fellow with the oversized head, and after being ignored for five or six holes, Bobby would wander home. He didn't dislike golf, but then, he liked all sports. He inherited his father's passion for baseball; Jones, Sr., had been such an outstanding ballplayer at the University of Georgia that the Brooklyn club had tried to sign him. At one period in his childhood Bobby had the tennis bug, at another the fishing bug. An old dodge of his was to tread in all the puddles he could find on his way to school so that he would be sent home; then he would pick up his rod and go fishing.

When he was nine, Bobby won the junior golf championship of the Atlanta Athletic Club, trouncing a boy seven years older than himself in the final. Young Bobby had a talent for imitation. One of the standard entertainments the Joneses provided for their guests was to call on Bobby to give his impressions of the odd addresses and the patented followthroughs of the East Lake characters. Bobby could also imitate the flat Carnoustie swing of Stewart Maiden's, which was a very good thing. A few years later when he had grown to Stewart's height and had added some poundage, he was often mistaken for Stewart by golfers who had watched him swing from a distance. Bobby's attitude toward golf, however, was always a little patronizing until he read about the 1913 Open and later saw Vardon and Ray play when they visited Atlanta. The exciting aspects of Ouimet's triumph and the first-hand thrills he felt when Ray uncorked one of his leviathan shots and Vardon nursed the ball so neatly persuaded Bobby for the first time that golf was a game that deserved a young man's full attention and respect. Later that same autumn—Bob was eleven then—he shot his first 80. Two years later he carried off the club championships at East Lake and Druid Hills, scoring a 73 in the final of the latter tournament. Bob never took formal lessons from Stewart Maiden but would search him out whenever he felt he was doing something wrong or had struck a sour streak. Stewart could straighten him out in three minutes.

Bobby's father was rightfully proud of the progress his son was making. In 1916, when Bobby was fourteen, Robert Tyre Jones, Sr., sent him around to the various tourneys sponsored by the principal Southern clubs. George Adair, an old friend of the Joneses and a leading figure in Southern golf, looked after the youngster and reported enthusiastically on his improvement, and sometimes this must not have been the pleasantest thing in the world for Mr. Adair, since young Jones was eclipsing the brilliance of his own boy, Perry, a lad a little older than Bobby who had the infant phenomenon field to himself before Bobby came along. That summer Bobby won the invitation tournaments at the Cherokee Club in Knoxville and the Birmingham Country Club (with a 69), defeated Perry Adair to win the East Lake tournament, and defeated Perry again in the final of the Georgia State Amateur Championship. Bobby's father rewarded him by sending him to Philadelphia with the Adairs for the United States Amateur.

When Bobby appeared at the Merion Cricket Club, in Ardmore, about ten miles from downtown Philadelphia, he was fourteen and a half, a chunky boy five-feet-four and weighing 165 pounds. Cocky as they came, too, not the least bit impressed by any of the names assembled for the meeting, and rather

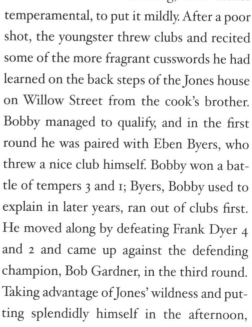

temperamental, to put it mildly. After a poor shot, the youngster threw clubs and recited some of the more fragrant cusswords he had learned on the back steps of the Jones house on Willow Street from the cook's brother. Bobby managed to qualify, and in the first round he was paired with Eben Byers, who threw a nice club himself. Bobby won a battle of tempers 3 and 1; Byers, Bobby used to explain in later years, ran out of clubs first. He moved along by defeating Frank Dyer 4 and 2 and came up against the defending champion, Bob Gardner, in the third round. Taking advantage of Jones' wildness and putting splendidly himself in the afternoon,

Gardner stopped the kid on the 31st green, but not before he had been called on to play every bit of golf he knew. Jones was the sensation of the tournament. Everyone went home raving about the boy from Atlanta who hit the ball so naturally and hit it so perfectly in the bargain that, even at fourteen, he was one of the longest drivers in the field. Old Walter Travis, a tough man to please, was bowled over by the shots he had seen the youngster play. "Improvement?" snorted the Old Man when someone asked him about Jones' potential. "He can never improve his shots, if that's what you mean. But he will learn a good deal more about playing them."

Bobby did learn more about putting his shots together as he toured the country playing Red Cross exhibitions during the war, but it took him a good while longer to learn how to control his temper. Young Jones knew he was a crackerjack golfer, but Bobby was not a prima donna in the sense that he demanded special attention and kid-glove handling. On the contrary, he was an exemplary sportsman in all his dealings *with other people*, so much so, as he grew older, that more than one of his rivals remarked that a chief reason why Bobby had never won a championship was that he went out of his way too much to comfort and cheer his opponents when they hit a bad streak. But *with himself* Bobby was rough. The target of Jones' tantrums was always Bobby Jones, the dope who was continually making some inexcusable error, missing some silly shot through carelessness and lack of con-

centration. Bobby would storm around getting more and more worked up with himself, playing with decreasing effectiveness, of course, in his petulance. On one round, according to Glenna Collett, Bobby blew up so fast when an errant shot of his ended up in an old shoe that he could not see the humor in the situation and grimly gave the shoe a terrific belt.

Though he had stopped throwing clubs at helpless elms by 1919, rub-of-the-green incidents continued to upset Bobby more than a tournament golfer could afford. In the final of the 1919 Amateur against Herron, Bobby was 3 down with seven holes to play yet still very much in the fight as he prepared to hit his wood second on the long twelfth at Oakmont. Jones was already into his swing when some megaphone-happy official started to shriek directions to the gallery. Jones not only mis-hit his shot but allowed himself to become so irritated by the official's stupidity that he never got back in the match. Francis Ouimet was playing grand golf the day he opposed Bobby in the semis of the 1920 Amateur and would have undoubtedly defeated the young star anyway, but Jones made it easier for him by chasing a pesky bee that had alighted on his ball clear off the 25th green, and eventually three-putting. Fortunately for Bobby, in the 1921 British Open he was guilty of an impetuous gesture of which he was so ashamed after he cooled down that, once and for all, he graduated from adolescence. On his third round in that tournament, it had taken him 46 strokes to reach the turn. He was burning up. On the tenth, Bobby ran into a double-bogey 6, and when he had played five strokes on the short eleventh and was still not in the cup, he picked his ball up—the equivalent in golf of throwing in the towel. Bobby Jones had quit in competition. This, as he saw it, was an unforgivable breach of the sportsman's code, and the ever-rankling memory of what he had done on the eleventh at St. Andrews, as much as any single factor, was responsible for the magnificent standard of deportment Bobby Jones created in later years.

In 1922, after he had failed to overhaul Gene Sarazen in the Open at Skokie, the maturing Jones eliminated another bad habit. He had steadily improved his position in the Open, moving from eighth in 1920 to fifth to second. Second was not bad, but it was still a long ways from first, and as Bobby and his friend O. B. Keeler reviewed the week and analyzed the various elements that might have contributed to Bobby's chronic inability to get really hot in a big championship, they came to the matter of Bobby's diet. O. B. had often mentioned to his young friend that stuffing himself at luncheon between rounds wasn't likely to be conducive to playing sharp golf in the afternoon, but Bobby had continued to go in for heavy luncheons topped off with apple pie à la mode or, when there was no ice cream, with something on the order of loganberry sherbet. O. B. was able to convince Jones that these gustatory adventures

could quite possibly have accounted for the stroke difference between tying Sarazen and being second. From that time on, the reforming Jones was a tea-and-toast man between rounds.

All that Bobby needed to win a championship, now that he was emerging from the cocoon of adolescence, was a little more patience and a little more luck. Someday the law of averages would come out of hiding and Jones' opponents would not take a quick look at Bobby and then shoot one of the dizziest rounds of their lives. Jones' experience at the hands of Jess Sweetser in the 1922 Amateur was typical of this curious bad fortune that dogged him. Jess played crushing golf at Brookline before and after beating Bobby, but against Jones, the favorite, he put on his most devastating exhibition. Over the first nine holes Jess piled up a six-hole lead. Bobby hadn't played his best golf, but he had hit a number of fine shots—at precisely the wrong times. On the second hole, for example, he had stuck his second, a full mashie-niblick, six inches from the pin, and yet this birdie merely boiled down to a brave but futile try for a half since Jess had already put his spade-mashie approach right into the cup for an eagle 2. From the tenth through the eighteenth, Bobby used only 34 strokes, and for all his pyrotechnics won back only one hole from Jess. In the afternoon Jess kept pumping his irons next to the pins, and Bobby, not playing badly at all, could make no headway whatsoever against the Yale undergraduate and went down 8 and 7, the most humbling defeat he had ever encountered in tournament competition.

While Bobby had never won a major title, the consistent excellence of his golf stamped him as the nation's leading amateur. The press and the public agreed that he was fulfilling the promise of his earlier youth and was bound to break through to a glorious triumph sooner or later. Bobby could not share these sanguine feelings. His game had never really caught fire during a championship, yet year in and year out he had played good enough golf to win and hadn't. He resigned himself to the probability that something would always pop up to prevent him from winning—that is, if he continued to play in tournaments. On more than one occasion Bobby was on the verge of retiring from competitive golf, a game so grueling for him that he lost as many as eighteen pounds during a championship with no victory to compensate for the punishment. He had entered the Open at Inwood in an I'll-give-it-one-more-try frame of mind. He had hoped he would win, and yet by this time he had reached the point where he genuinely believed that winning and losing were out of his hands. Where competitive golf was concerned, Bobby had become a fatalist. He would go out on the course and play his heart out, but his efforts didn't really matter unless some larger destiny had marked him down as

the man who would win. All golf tournaments, Jones was firmly convinced, had been settled before the players stepped on the course, and the shots that they made and the scores they turned in had been ordained by Fate well in advance.

If Fate was looking for a deserving fellow to tap for the 1923 Open, Bobby Cruickshank's credentials were in order. Long before he had come to the 72nd hole at Inwood, Bobby had shown the stuff he was made of in some of the most severe tests of life. As a foot-soldier in the British army in World War I, Cruickshank had been in the thick of the fighting. He had seen his brother blown to bits two yards from him. He had been captured and assigned to the same prison camp as Sandy Armour, Tommy's brother. Sandy was weak with dysentery and Cruickshank had deprived himself of most of his scanty rations so that Sandy might have them. Then Bobby had escaped and rejoined his outfit. This tiny thoroughbred had gone back to golf when the shooting was over, turned professional in 1921, and come to the States to make his living. Bobby Cruickshank was a very good man.

Because of the psychological advantage he would draw from his marvelous finish, Cruickshank went to the first tee in

THROUGHOUT HIS COMPETITIVE CAREER, BOBBY JONES USED CLUBS WITH HICKORY SHAFTS THAT COULD TWIST OR BEND, MAKING THEM DIFFICULT TO CONTROL. IN THIS 1923 PHOTOGRAPH OF JONES' FOLLOW-THROUGH, HIS DRIVER SHAFT LOOKS SLIGHTLY BENT; IT PROBABLY WAS.

the eighteen-hole medal playoff a 10 to 7 favorite over Jones, the chap who had taken a 6 on the last hole. Both men went out to win on their own shots, not on the other fellow's errors. Only three of the eighteen holes were tied. By the fifth, Cruickshank had snared three birdies and Jones had got one. Jones rode back into the fight, rubbed out his deficit, and built up a two-stroke lead by the thirteenth. Then back came Cruick-

shank to pick up one of these strokes on the fourteenth and the other on the fifteenth. Jones attacked again and went out ahead by a shot on the sixteenth, but the determined Scot dug himself out of the trap by the seventeenth green and went down in one putt to retrieve that stroke and square the playoff.

And so the two battlers, Bobby Jones and Bobby Cruickshank, came to the eighteenth at Inwood all even. Cruickshank,

Should he play safe from his extremely poor lie and gamble on wearing down his pertinacious adversary in extra holes? Or should he go for it? If he decided to try for the green and found the lagoon, he would be playing 4 where Cruickshank was playing 3 and . . . Jones eyed his ball in the loose dirt and glanced at the flag rippling on the green over the lagoon 190 yards away. Without hesitation, he took his midiron, one of the most difficult clubs to play even from the most perfect of lies. Back came the club and down it went, and *swick!* the ball came up like a rifle shot and, white against the gathering storm clouds, drilled itself directly for the flag. Over the lagoon it went and onto the green and up, up, up to within six feet of the cup.

That was the match. And the championship. And if anyone had ever won it like a true champion, it was Bobby Jones. With that gallant shot, the young veteran had finally broken through. An era had ended and the Age of Bobby Jones had begun.

with the honor, tried to keep his ball low in the face of the stiff breeze and hit a half-topped drive that hooked into the rough. Jones laced a long tee shot down the right side of the fairway; at the last moment, the ball bobbled into the loose dirt at the edge of the rough. Jones stood by his ball and watched Cruickshank play the only shot he could from the rough—a safety short of the lagoon. It was now squarely up to Jones.

JONES'S MIDIRON APPROACH SHOT TO THE FINAL GREEN AT INWOOD IS PROBABLY THE SHOT THAT LAUNCHED THE JONES LEGEND. IT CLEARED THE LAGOON, SEEN ON THE LEFT SIDE OF THE PHOTOGRAPH ABOVE, AND ALLOWED JONES TO PUTT OUT FOR THE 1923 U.S. OPEN TITLE.

PART THREE
THE AGE OF BOBBY JONES

THE ONE AND ONLY

THE MASTER BUILDERS

THE WOMEN

THEY ALSO PLAYED—SUPERBLY

THE GRAND SLAM

The Age of
Bobby Jones

1923—1930

The One and Only

Bobby Jones

THERE are three types of golf—golf, tournament golf, and major championship golf. The difference between the three is one-tenth physiological and nine-tenths psychological. It is hard enough for a man to play a good round of *golf*, the informal game most of us play with a putt conceded here or there and double-or-nothing on the eighteenth. It is three or four strokes harder to play a round of *tournament golf*, although the rules are just the same and a player merely has to hole those insignificant putts he was conceded only because he was a cinch to make them.

These are the very putts he misses when he plays in competition; along with this, he half-hits those explosion shots he plays so confidently on his friendly rounds, is short on his approaches although he keeps reminding himself to be up, slices on the dogleg to the left that he always plays with a slight intentional hook—and all for no apparent reason. There is a reason, of course, and it is readily apparent. The knowledge that he is playing for keeps and for glory makes the tournament golfer a worrying golfer, forces him to be ever-mindful that a 2-foot putt may be the barrier between him and victory, drives him to adopt half-unwittingly a negative attitude whereby he concentrates on avoiding error, playing safe, taking the conservative route. When victory is beyond his reach, only then does the average tournament golfer throw caution to the winds and release the shots that have been stifling inside him.

It takes time and experience and some intelligence for the talented professional or amateur to digest the rigors of tournament play so that he can feel almost normal as he goes about the business of winning the Greensboro Open or the Colonial or the Crosby. After a while the professional professional or the professional amateur becomes adapted to his environment. If he can shoot a 68 in a practice round, you can count on him to approximate that figure during the tournament, and often to improve it. The men who are used to playing under fire have long ago learned how to harness their nervousness. They seldom lose because of a jumpy feeling in their stomach, and contradictory as it seems at first, they worry about not being worried, about becoming phlegmatic

and missing that little tingle that keeps a player sharp and dangerous. But put the seasoned campaigner of *tournament golf* into a *major championship*—say the United States or British Opens—and he begins to sweat like a novice, that welcome little tingle becomes a nauseating thump, and the golfer finds himself playing his shots by some cloudy memory of his formula and praying that his trained reflexes will see him through. There are some exceptions, but for most big-time golfers the jump between *tournament golf* and *major championship golf* is as wearing and as real as the jump between *golf* and *tournament golf* is for the less cultivated players. The results are about the same—three or four strokes more. The reasons are about the same—the greater glory and material rewards for winning, the consequent greater strain. Occasionally a golfer can hold himself together long enough to carry off one major championship, and he merits enduring respect regardless of how fluky his victory seemed or the quick oblivion his subsequent flops cast over him. But the men who have won more than one major

BY THE MID-1920S, BOBBY JONES SO DOMINATED THE FIELD THAT HE WAS FAVORED TO WIN ANY EVENT HE ENTERED. HE IS SHOWN ABOVE AT MERION FOR THE 1924 U.S. AMATEUR, WHICH HE WON.

championship—they are the true champions. They are a select body. Since 1919, among American amateurs, only Jones, Lawson Little, Johnny Goodman, Bud Ward, Willie Turnesa, Frank Stranahan, Harvie Ward, Dick Chapman, Jack Nicklaus, Deane Beman, Bob Dickson, and Steve Melnyk have won two national titles. (Across the water, Joe Carr has won three British Amateurs and the amazing Michael Bonallack five.) The only repeaters among the pros in the two big Open Championships have been Hagen, Sarazen, Barnes, Armour, Ralph Guldahl, Henry Cotton (of England), Bobby Locke (of South Africa),

Ben Hogan, Peter Thomson (of Australia), Cary Middlecoff, Arnold Palmer, Jack Nicklaus, Gary Player (of South Africa), Julius Boros, Billy Casper, Tony Jacklin (of England), and Lee Trevino.

Only Harry Vardon, Ben Hogan, and Jack Nicklaus merit comparison with Jones as *major championship golfers*. Over a period of eight years, Bobby won the U.S. Amateur five times, the U.S. Open four times, the British Open three times, and the British Amateur once. Approach this record from any angle, and its mold looms more and more heroic. In eight cracks at the U.S. Amateur between 1923 and 1930, Jones was defeated once in the first round, once in the second, and once in the final; he was victorious the five other times. In the U.S. Open over the eight years between his first victory in 1923 and his last in 1930, Jones once finished in a tie for eleventh but on no other occasion was he worse than second; he won twice without a playoff, won twice after a playoff, lost twice after a playoff, and the other time was an untied second. In other words, in six years out of the eight, Bobby either won the Open outright or finished in a tie for first, necessitating a playoff. He won the British Open in three of his four attempts—he picked up at St. Andrews on his maiden effort and then was successful in his last three starts. The most difficult championship for Bobby, and perhaps the most difficult championship for anyone to win, was the British Amateur, with its seven rounds of 18-hole matches before the 36-hole final. It took Bobby three cracks before the finally won it. No one except Jones, of course, has ever won the two big national Amateurs and Opens in one golfing season. And while history has demonstrated how foolhardy it is to predict that certain sports records will never be equaled or broken, it does seem reasonably safe to predict that men will be pole-vaulting twenty-two feet and women will be running the four-minute mile before another golfer comes along to match Jones' Grand Slam of 1930.

There are some elderly fans who contend that Harry Vardon, peerless in his own age, was the equal of Jones. Those who would rank Vardon with Jones have a fairly good case, since he was as outstanding in his age as Jones was in his. In Vardon's period there was really only one major championship, the British Open, and he won it six times—in 1896, 1898, 1899, 1903, 1911, and 1914. (The other two members of the illustrious Triumvirate, J. H. Taylor and James Braid, each won the British Open five times.) In addition, Vardon won the U.S. Open in 1900, lost it in the historic playoff with Ouimet and Ray in 1913, and again lost it by a whisker in 1920 at Inverness when he was unlucky enough to catch the full force of the gale off the lake as he was coming down the last nine holding the lead. To maintain one's form for a quarter of a century—from 1896 through 1920—was something in those days, particularly when your golf possessed Vardon's picture-book quality. Old Harry's left arm may have been bent as he took the club back, and he may have taken it back in a very upright arc in the eyes of his contemporaries, but that was, in a way, the plane of the future, just as his overlapping grip was the grip of the future and his elegant left-to-right fade was, possibly, the flight of the future. Old Harry was something, but was he really as good as Jones? In the long run, that is a matter of opinion, as is, for instance,

BOBBY JONES, LEFT, OPPOSITE, AND HARRY VARDON POSED FOR A PHOTOGAPH EARLY IN THE TWENTIES DURING THE TWILIGHT OF VARDON'S CAREER AND THE DAWN OF JONES'. FROM 1896 TO 1930 THESE TWO MEN SUCCESSIVELY REIGNED AS THE TWO GREATEST CHAMPIONSHIP GOLFERS IN THE WORLD.

one's reaction to the inescapable argument waged during World War II as to whether Byron Nelson's achievements matched, if not exceeded, Jones'.

The indecent precision with which Nelson clicked off one tournament after another in 1944 and 1945 gave his supporters sturdy grounds indeed for pressing their argument: What other golfer had ever finished in the money in over a hundred consecutive tournaments, won eleven consecutive P.G.A.-endorsed tournaments, or averaged 69.67 for 85 rounds as Lord Byron did in 1944, or his even more stunning 68.33 for 120 rounds in 1945? It was this last feat, in particular, which convinced Nelson's supporters of his superiority over Jones, for, as they shrewdly noted, the old Emperor had never approached a sub-70 average. All very well and good, all very wonderful, rebutted defenders of Jones' pre-eminence, but . . . Nelson had rung up his records in relatively minor tournaments held on courses far easier to score on than the arduous championship layouts, and he had worked his wonders against a field depleted by the exigencies of war.

Back and forth it went, and the controversy soon bristled with rhetoric about Nelson's failure to win more than one national Open, what Jones would have done if he had gone in for the minor tourneys, how Nelson would have swept every major championship in sight had the war not canceled these meetings, why Nelson had played such high scores in all but one Open, what Jones might have done in the line of scoring if the hypoed balls, the foolproof blasters, the steel shafts and other refinements of the Forties had been available to the stars of the Twenties. The controversy was filled with speculative *ifs* that couldn't be settled in combat, to be sure, and so it ran its course, a forum between two generations.

Quite similarly, especially after Ben Hogan's banner year in 1953, when he swept the Masters, the U.S. Open, and the British, many admirers of the fabulous Texan asserted that he had demonstrated a skill not only equal to Jones's but of an even higher order. The Hoganites pointed to Ben's superior scoring. Marvelous, but under vastly different conditions, replied the partisans of Jones, who felt that this argument suffered from a lack of objectivity. Moreover, continued the Jonesmen, all that talk about Bobby's compiling his record against a weaker group of adversaries than Hogan faced was way off the mark; his contemporaries, in fact, may have been finer players than the modern gypsy band who were so accustomed to driver-wedge-putter courses that they were all at sea when they came to a championship course that made them play the full bag. Not at all, answered the Hogan-

THE JONES SWING FEATURED A NARROW STANCE, A FULL TURN, AND FORCEFUL ROTATION OF THE TORSO DURING DOWNSWING AND AT IMPACT, THIRD ROW. HE CONTROLLED HIS SWING WITH HIS LEFT SIDE, AND KEPT HIS LEFT ARM EXTENDED UNTIL ALMOST THE END OF HIS FOLLOW-THROUGH.

ites, who felt that this argument suffered from a lack of objectivity. And so it went. No one, of course, will ever know for certain how the Hogan of 1953 and the Jones of 1930 would have come out had they met in a prolonged series of tournaments. And, actually, the comparison is unfair to both, since neither could have accomplished more than he did. They belong in a class by themselves along with Vardon and the phenomenal Jack Nicklaus, whom many today rate the best golfer of all time. In some ways, each was incomparable. Bobby Jones certainly was.

From 1924 until Jones' retirement, major championship golf is the chronicle of Jones versus the field. The amateurs were a so-so lot, but the professional troupe was filled with colorful and capable golfers—Walter Hagen, Gene Sarazen, the brilliant but unfortunate Leo Diegel, the equally brilliant and more unfortunate Macdonald Smith, Tommy Armour of the whistling irons, Johnny Farrell the immaculate, Joe Turnesa, Bobby Cruickshank, Wild Bill Mehlhorn, the young Harry Cooper, Denny Shute, the young Horton Smith, Craig Wood, George Duncan, Abe Mitchell, Archie Compston, and the usual collection of in-and-out tournament golfers like the Espinosas, Abe and Al, Willie Klein, and Wiffy Cox. Any one of these men could get red-hot, yet 50 percent of the time Jones defeated them *en masse*. Perhaps the full dev-

astation of the Georgian's march through golf can be best appreciated if one reviews his annual campaigns during the seven great years that followed his seven lean years. Such a retabulation, year by year, tournament by tournament, runs the risk of sameness, but, then, there was a sameness to golf in the Twenties: Jones nearly always won.

After his victory at Inwood in 1923, Bobby was an odd-on favorite to win the Amateur when the "gentlemen" gathered at Flossmoor, near Chicago. Max Marston eliminated him in the second round. From the seventeenth hole in the morning through the seventeenth in the afternoon, Max was 5 under par, and this was too good for Bobby. This early-round defeat at Flossmoor had beneficial repercussions. As he was going through his usual post-tournament analysis, Bobby decided that the time had come to examine the causes for his continual unsuccessful play in match competition. He concluded that he was chucking strokes away by playing his opponent when he should have been battling Old Man Par, as he did on his better medal rounds. This was not a victory-proof formula, Bobby realized. If his opponent made more headway against par than Bobby, as Marston had, then his opponent would win, and this would be perfectly agreeable with Bobby. What he did want to eradicate was his tendency to toss away matches in which he had not been outplayed. After Flossmoor, Bobby adhered to a policy of dueling exclusively with par, and from that time on he was defeated only three times in championship match play, on each occasion by a foe who had given Old Man Par a thorough going-over.

The 1924 Amateur was all Jones. The steep margins by which he routed his adversaries—6 and 5 (W. J. Thompson), 3 and 2 (Clarke Corkran, the medalist), 6 and 4 (Rudy Knepper), 11 and 10 (Francis Ouimet), 9 and 8 (George Von Elm)—testified to the effectiveness of his new philosophy of match play. For the sixty-one holes on his afternoon rounds at Merion, Bobby's card added up to one stroke under par: forty pars, ten holes in a stroke above par, and eleven birdies, and this over a layout heavily scarred with hazards. Early in the tournament week, the rains had made the fairways heavy with moisture, and in a rather interesting move, Jones allowed his clubs to grow rusty rather than have the faces regularly buffed after a round; he deduced that on the soaked turf the ball was likely to skid off polished faces and could be gripped more effectively by the rougher blade; in any event, Bobby got remarkably good results. Everything went well. Never an exceptional putter before, Bobby was so consistently expert on the big greens at Merion that Jerry Travers, who knew a good putter when he saw one, exclaimed that he had never observed a better stroke than Jones' during the championship. Hard work and intelligent experimentation lay behind this reformation. In the winter Walter Travis

had looked over Jones' putting style and had recommended that the young man strive to have his wrists work more in opposition to each other. He also suggested that Jones concentrate on taking the club back with the left hand, and pounded home in his emphatic fashion the other theories that had served him so well during his long career. Jones also changed his putting grip, overlapping the index finger of the *left* hand—the reverse overlapping grip. As a final alteration, to check the nervousness that sporadically visited him on the greens, he adopted a breath-control tempo that was slow and easy—what Bobby called "tranquillized breathing." His new dietary discipline justified itself. In addition to watching his noonday snack, Bobby ate sensible breakfasts of a sliced orange, cornflakes, and coffee. In the evenings he let himself go and stowed away whatever he wanted, yet his over-all menu was one that would have received the approval of Bunny Austin, the fragile English Davis Cupper of later years and one of the most accomplished dieticians sport has ever known. All in all, the week at Merion was a joy. All of Bobby's investments paid dividends, and one accurate shot after another poured from his clubheads.

This triumph in the Amateur followed a respectable if not wholly satisfying showing in the 1924 Open—not wholly satisfying because Jones did not win, respectable since he finished second to Cyril Walker, although he skied to a last round of 78 in one of those gales off the Great Lakes. (Any time you want to amaze your friends with your powers of prophecy, one of the surest bets, it would seem, would be to predict a gale on the last day of the Open.) By losing, Bobby inadvertently wrote a happy ending to a short-short story. A month before the Open, Cyril Walker, the little 118-pound pro at Englewood, confided to his wife Elizabeth that he was absolutely certain he was going to win the Open that year. Walker had never been close in his previous shots at the title. Furthermore, he had not fully recovered from the ravages of insomnia, which had made his slight frame a bundle of nerves. Cyril seemed so sincere about his chances that Elizabeth, or "Tet" as he called her, told him that by all means he should go to Oakland Hills if he felt that way. Tet went along too, for moral support and protection against Cyril's staying up all night with the boys. Walker began with a pair of 74s that put him up with the leaders for once, since the high winds militated against any fancy scoring. On the last day, when the winds really roamed the course, Walker, another one of that army of good golfers trained on the links at Hoylake, found that his seaside education served him in good stead. The gale that blew over fellows almost twice his size did not bother Cyril. He kept his shots low, and his last two rounds, a 74 and a 75, gave him the only sub-300 total among the eighty-five players. Walker never again came close. His victory was labeled a freak. But as

Tet never let him forget, he had played like a champion in winning, and no one could ever take away from him that wonderful week at Oakland Hills.

Jones formed the habit of carrying off either the Amateur or the Open each year. In 1925 it was not the Open, although Bobby played himself from thirty-sixth to tenth to fourth and into a tie for first with Willie Macfarlane. The double playoff between Jones and Macfarlane was a fitting climax to a tournament that will hold its own with any when it comes to thrilling finishes. *Eight* men came down the stretch at the Worcester Country Club, each of them with the championship in his grasp if he could fashion a 70. All eight were golfers accustomed to playing 70s—Hagen, Diegel, Farrell, Jones, Ouimet, Macfarlane, Sarazen, and old Mike Brady. That afternoon none of these stars could get his hands on the figure he wanted. As the afternoon wore on and one by one they came to the 72nd hole, seven of them, all but Brady, were still in the hunt. Diegel was the first to try the 335-yard eighteenth, a drive and a pitch—but a wickedly touchy pitch—to a sloping, raised green surrounded by a bodyguard of deep bunkers. Leo proceeded to break his heart with an awful 8. Next came Johnny Farrell, and he nailed his 4. This gave Johnny an aggregate of 292 and the lead at

WILLIE MACFARLANE, OPPOSITE, AN EXPERIENCED CLUB PRO, TIED JONES WITH A CAREFUL PAR ON THE 72ND HOLE OF THE 1925 U. S. OPEN AND CAPTURED THE TITLE BY A STROKE AFTER TWO 18-HOLE PLAYOFFS.

this point. Francis Ouimet, looking for all the world like a Chinese mandarin in his straw tropical helmet, calmly played himself into a tie with Farrell when he got his 4. Sarazen needed a birdie 3 for his 292. He had to be satisfied with a 4. A 4 would have given Hagen his 292, but Walter had his eye on 291 and, passing up a certain par, went all out for his birdie by trying to drop his approach inches behind the front bunker so that he would be close to the pin on the very front edge of the green. This time The Haig just couldn't pull it off. He caught the back wall of the bunker, and got a 5 for his daring. Then Jones came along needing a 4 for 291, which would make Farrell and Ouimet also-rans. Bobby made no mistakes: on in 2, down in 2. One man, Willie Macfarlane, could catch Jones by getting his 4 on the eighteenth, and Willie did it by getting down in 2 after he had placed his approach on the high back slope of the green.

The calm, observant manner in which he made sure of his two putts on the 72nd was a succinct sample of the intelligence that had steered Willie Macfarlane through many rough passages from the first hole on. On the last green Willie paid close attention as his partner, Francis Gallett, with practically the same ticklish 40-footer as Willie, sent his approach putt slowly down the dip and saw it keep on sliding until it was well past the cup. Willie would have played his putt just that way, had he not been able to profit from Gallett's example, but now he hardly stroked his downhiller, barely nudged it on its way and let it crawl down the slope and peter out a foot from the cup. Willie still had a golf shot left, for in marking his ball before Gallett putted again, he noticed that his ball had ended up in a pitch-mark left by some player's approach. Willie thought it wisest not to use a putter from that indentation, for the ball might hop off-line as it came out. He took his midiron and hit it into the cup.

Without his glasses, tall, gaunt, aquiline Willie Macfarlane looked like a country schoolmaster, and when he wore his rimless glasses, he looked like a professor of poetry at Princeton. Willie had no love for tournament golf, preferring to play the game for the fun of it. But when he did enter the New York area tourneys at the coaxing of his pupils at Tuckahoe, he always gave a fine account of himself and occasionally went off on mad streaks that brought to mind the purple patches of Old Jock Hutchison. Willie didn't mind if it got around that he could play in the 90s left-handed and in the 80s with one hand, but this was the extent of his vanity. He had entered the Open because it was one of the few tournaments he liked to play. He had no dreams of winning it. When the opportunity for winning did present itself, however, Willie made the most of it.

The playoff at Worcester was as exciting as the championship proper. Macfarlane appeared to be on his way to victory over the regulation eighteen-hole route. As the players came to the fourteenth green, Willie had a stroke lead and was in a position to pick up another stroke, or maybe two. After his second shot, Willie's ball lay eight feet from the cup, and Bobby was playing his third out of the rough fifty or sixty feet away. Bobby struck his chip smack into the cup. Willie missed his 8-footer and had lost his lead instead of going two or three strokes up. But Macfarlane was a placid operator and kept right on stroking the ball. He quickly took the play away from Bobby and made the young man can a 5-foot side-hiller on the eighteenth green to come out of the morning round all-square and force the match into a second eighteen holes. In the afternoon Jones slowly drew away from the Scot. At the halfway mark, when Bobby had built up a four-stroke advantage, the gallery concluded that it was all over except the handshake, since no one could ever hope to make up four strokes against Jones in nine holes. Willie picked up five. The break came on the long fifteenth, where Jones, forgetting his friend Old Man Par, attempted to shut off Willie's rally by pressing his second shot to the green and setting

himself up for a birdie. Instead, he wound up with a 6. Willie went evenly on his way. His 33 home included two 2s. Scores: Macfarlane 75-72, Jones 75-73.

The 1925 Amateur, on the other hand, was one of the dullest tournaments in the history of that championship. Some parties had objected to the old tournament form as taking too long, so something new was tried in 1925 at Oakmont, north of Pittsburgh: only sixteen players would qualify for the match play, and the matches would all be over the 36-hole distance. On paper, the innovation did not look too bad. If a good percentage of the leading amateurs succeeded in qualifying, there would be no scary 18-hole matches in which they could get knocked out before they were warm by some reputationless upstart playing way over his head; ultimately, the two best golfers in the field would meet in the final. Well, it didn't pan out that way. Jess Sweetser, Jesse Guilford, George Von Elm, and Jones were the only name players to sneak under the qualifying wire, and Guilford and Sweetser were eliminated in their second-round matches. Perhaps if the new system had been tried out on some course other than Oakmont, it would have stood up better. On that penal institution, with its abundant hazards, one or two bad shots could always ruin an otherwise adequate round, and the Fowneses never seemed to think that Oakmont was sufficiently maddening. When word was received that Oakmont had been awarded the championship, they had toughened the course up once again. Several new traps were added, which was like carrying coals to Newcastle. Nine heaping railway carloads of sand from the Allegheny River were spilled into one excavation on the eighth that was though to be the largest trap in the world.

The unyielding sterness of the new-and-improved Oakmont not only kept many of the best amateurs out but conspired against the chances of those who were in for giving Jones any competition. In winning his matches by scores of 11 and 10, 6 and 5, 7 and 6, and 8 and 7, Bobby finished 32 up on his opponents and had an even easier time of it than at Merion, where he had been 36 up over his span of five matches. The championship would have been little more than a string of sad statistics had Watts Gunn not introduced a chunk of human interest. Watts was Bobby's protégé, a small but well-knit twenty-year-older who had attracted Jones' attention by shooting a 69 at East Lake and a 67 at Druid Hills. Jones had persuaded Watts' parents that some seasoning in the Amateur would do the boy a world of good. At Oakmont, Watts vindicated Jones' faith in him by qualifying in fifth spot, and got hotter and hotter. He slaughtered his first opponent 12 and 10, winning *fifteen holes in a row* after he had stood 3 down at the eleventh. He went out in the wind and the rain against Sweetser and shot himself a 71, which on Oakmont is the equivalent of a 65 on the average non-championship course. Watts accounted for

Jess, 11 and 10. He cooled down a little in his semi-final match with young Dick Jones but took it 5 and 3 to enter the final with R. T. Jones Jr., his friend and idol.

For a while in the final Watts Gunn acted as if he had forgotten that Jones used to give him three or four strokes during their informal matches in Atlanta and all week long at Oakmont had watched over him like a father. Watts went out in 35, and it was all Jones could do to keep up with that terrific pace. Watts took the tenth, and Jones had to fight and fight hard to save the eleventh and the twelfth. Then the senior Atlantan called on his great reserves. On the last six holes of the morning round and the first two in the afternoon, Jones had a relatively short putt for his birdie on each green, helped himself to five 3s, and won seven of these eight holes to go 6 up. This majestic burst of power settled the contest. On the 29th green Watts broke out into a big smile and walked across the green to congratulate the winner.

The year 1926 turned out to be Bobby's biggest to date, but it began quite inauspiciously. Tuning up in Florida in the winter, Bobby was scoring as well as usual and hitting the ball crisply when he and Walter Hagen were matched in a 72-hole exhibition between "the amateur and professional champions," the first thirty-six to be played over the Whitfield Estates Country Club at

Sarasota, where Jones had been stopping, and the second thirty-six at Hagen's course in Pasadena, Florida. Walter put it all over Bobby. The final score was 12 and 11 as Walter moved out in front early and continued to add to his lead by his own ingenuity on some holes and Jones' errors on others. One of Hagen's more productive rounds prompted the crack that Walter had gone around in 69 strokes and Bobby in 69 cigarettes.

As this was the year that Walker Cup matches were set for St. Andrews, Jones had to do something about the weaknesses in his game that the overwhelming defeat by Hagen had uncovered, and he had to do it fast. Bob had first realized at Skokie in '22 that his iron play was liable to periodic depressions, and against The Haig his irons had been more off-color than the rest of his game. He put himself in the hands of Tommy Armour and Jimmy Donaldson, Tommy's assistant at Sarasota, and they quickly diagnosed the illness. Bobby had been playing his irons with too much right hand in the shot. Jimmy, in particular, worked with Jones on left-hand control, bringing the club down and through the ball with the left hand in charge and the right hand simply supplying momentum. Bobby began banging his irons on line again.

The British Amateur that year preceded the Walker Cup congregation, and with the other members of the American squad,

Bobby Jones went up to Muirfield to see what he could do about winning for America the old mug that had never left the island since Travis' day. Bobby moved along, taking good care of himself in the treacherous 18-hole matches that constituted the British Amateur all the way to the final, where thirty-six holes were decreed. On the morning of his fifth-round match with Andrew Jamieson, a steady golfer from Scotland's West Coast, Bobby woke up with a stiff neck. As the day grew warmer, the knots loosened up—Bobby's stiff neck was not an alibi; it was a stiff neck—and Jones shot about the same brand of golf he had been playing in his previous victories, only this time Jamieson played even better. Over fifteen holes the young Scot, a very tidy pitch-and-run artist, posted thirteen pars and two birdies and was never behind and never flustered. So Jones went out, 4 and 3, and Jess Sweetser of the Walker Cup team went on to win the final from the chap who had taken care of Jamieson in the semis.

In the 1926 Walker Cup Match Bobby won his singles from Tolley 12 and 11 (a score that must have brought back memories of Florida) and teamed with Watts Gunn to defeat Tolley and Jamieson in the foursomes in which partners play alternate strokes and drive from alternate tees. He had his passage back to the States, and the U.S. Open, booked on the *Aquitania*, but at the last

IN THE 1926 WALKER CUP COMPETITION BETWEEN TOP BRITISH AND AMERICAN AMATEURS, THE AMERICAN TEAM, OPPOSITE, WHICH INCLUDED BOBBY JONES, CENTER, SEATED, AND FRANCIS OUIMET, FAR RIGHT, SEATED, DEFEATED GREAT BRITAIN 6 TO 5 AT THE OLD COURSE, ST. ANDREWS.

moment Jones canceled his passage and stayed on for the British Open. His decision was compounded from the still-rankling memory of quitting in the Open at St. Andrews in 1921 and from the desire to show the British golfing public that he could "sometimes play good stuff." Jones had never quite got going in Britain. His subsequent performance in the Open was all that he wanted it to be.

In the qualifying round of thirty-six holes in which Bobby was one of the entries assigned to the Sunningdale course, the Georgian smashed all records for that test with a 66 and a 68 for 134. The 68 was all right. The 66, in the opinion of the British critics, was definitely the finest round of golf ever played in their country. It deserves

close inspection. First of all, Sunningdale is a testing course. While no figures from the back tees are available, it must have stretched to somewhere in the neighborhood of 6,500 yards. Whatever its exact measurement, it was long enough to compel Jones, who was a fairly long hitter, to play all but three approaches over his thirty-six holes with a 4-iron or more; twice he hit his second shot with a mashie (a 5-iron) and once he was able to get home with a mashie-niblick (a 7-iron). A 66 over such a layout is great going, no matter how you get it, but it was the way in which Bobby manufactured his 66 that set it apart from middle-and-low-60 scores of earlier and later years. On every hole except the short thirteenth, Jones was *on the green* with the shot that should have been on—that is, on every par 3 (except one) he was on in one, on every par 4 he was on in two, and on the four par 5s, where on-in-three would have been regulation, he was also on in two. His one slip from perfection on the thirteenth, a 175-yarder, was a 4-iron he pushed into a bunker off the edge of the green. By chipping six feet from the cup and holing his putt, Bobby kept his card free from bogeys. Here is his card for that round.

	OUT	IN
PAR	554 344 434—36	544 353 444—36—72
JONES	444 334 434—33	434 343 444—33—66

Had "Calamity Jane," Bobby's putter, been functioning that round, Jones' 66 would have been at least several strokes lower. Bobby missed several banal 5-footers, and a 25-footer on the fifth was the only putt of any length that went down for him. On seventeen of the eighteen holes he was putting for birdies, or, more accurately, for eagles on four and birdies on thirteen. He used 33 shots going out and 33 back; he hit 33 putts and 33 tee-to-green shots. There was not a 5 or a 2 on the card, just 3s and 4s.

Bobby was not able to carry this streak with him when the qualifiers assembled at the Royal Lytham and St. Annes course for the tournament that marked the lowest ebb in Britain's golfing fortunes. At no point in the tournament was a Briton in the picture, and seven of the first nine finishers were Americans. Bill Mehlhorn, the venerable Freddy McLeod, and George

Von Elm were contenders until the last nine holes, and Walter Hagen refused to be counted out until he had missed holing his approach to the 72nd green, yet the 1926 Open, in effect, narrowed down to a fight between Jones and Al Watrous, the young professional from Grand Rapids who had gone over with the Ryder Cup team. Jones, with two 72s, held a two-stroke lead on Watrous when they were paired to play the last thirty-six holes together. Watrous put together a grand third round, 33 out and 36 back for a 69 that took him from two strokes behind Bobby to two in front. Bobby was lucky not to have yielded more ground, for he was scrambling all morning long. During the noon intermission, Bobby and Al went back to the room Jones and Keeler shared in the Majestic Hotel to grab some rest. Bobby stretched out on his bed and Al on Keeler's. They removed their shoes and gabbed away until the tea, toast, and cold ham that O. B. had ordered were sent up. Keyed up as he was, Al managed to get down a slice of the ham. Then it was time to return to work, and the two friendly rivals put their shoes back on and tried to shake off their nervous tiredness.

Bobby hit his shots with more authority in the afternoon, but, as often happens, when the zip returned to his tee shots and his irons, his putting began to slip. On three greens on the first ten holes Bobby required three putts, and yet he chopped a stroke off Watrous' two-stroke lead. Realizing only too vividly how much a victory in the Open would mean to his career, the husky blond pro was beginning to tighten up. He made one last offensive thrust by tying together three neat shots and a nice putt for a 4 on the thirteenth (or 67th) to go two ahead on Jones again, but he three-putted away one of these strokes on the next hole and the other on the fifteenth. All even now. Watrous looked rickety in halving the sixteenth, but it was Jones who broke on the seventeenth tee, hooking his drive into the stretch of loose sand at the angle where the fairway breaks to the left on that 411-yard dogleg. Watrous hit an easy, safe, straight tee shot and played his approach onto the front edge of the green. Considering that it could have been partially buried in the sand, Jones' ball was lying well. Jones could still keep up with Watrous if he played a strong, perfect shot off the sand, although, on second thought, by picking the ball up cleanly and hitting it hard enough to carry the 175 yards over the dunes to the green, the only way the shot could be played, there was bound to be a lot of run on the ball and it would probably bounce on over the hard green into trouble—a minor type of trouble, to be sure, but sticky enough in a situation like this when anything higher than a 4 would lose the championship. He would have to play it blind, too, but . . . there was no other shot to play. He selected his mashie-iron—sort of a strong 4-iron—and the old frown of concentration came over his face. Then, into that deceptively lazy pivot, and into the ball. He got the ball, all

of the ball, on the face of the club, and it came whistling out in an arching arc and sailed over the duney rough toward the green. The shot was high enough so that the wind held it up a helpful fraction, and when it came down on the green it had far less legs on it than Jones had anticipated. It curled up inside of Watrous' ball. Once again, Watrous took three putts after misreading the speed of the green. Jones got down in two for his par. He was in front again. Watrous dropped another stroke on the last hole but that was inconsequential.

Jones' winning total at Lytham was 291—72, 72, 73, 74—a more than creditable job despite the fact that only on the final eighteen had he hit the ball with approximately the same precision he had at Sunningdale, and then he had messed up his tee-to-green play by taking thirty-nine putts.

Bobby sailed for home, the British Open Champion, fairly well pleased with himself and unable to find anything much wrong with the world. His family and closest friends met him at Quarantine, and with Jimmy Walker as chaperone, Bobby rode in triumph down the canyons of New York to City Hall, and the band played "Valencia."

Two weeks later Bobby was back at work. Stale as he was after two full months of tournament golf, he announced his presence at the Open at Scioto, in Columbus, Ohio, by firing an opening 70, two strokes under par. He was a machine, an errorless machine, the reporters exclaimed, so Bobby went out and shot himself a very wild and very human 79. His 7 on the last hole was superhuman. Fighting to rescue a 76 with a birdie 4, Bobby pressed his drive into the rough on the right, slashed the ball twenty yards down the rough foolishly trying to get home with his 2-iron, hooked the ball clear across the fairway without changing clubs, fell short of the green with his pitch, rolled a chip five feet from the cup, and missed the putt. On that round, however, Jones did one of those little things that endeared him to the public and which explained, in part, the adulation that was showered on him wherever he went. On the tenth hole he had incurred a penalty stroke when his drive ended up against a stone wall that was ruled part of a water hazard. He had rallied after this bad break and was rolling to a probable 74 when he reached the fifteenth green. He placed his putter in front of the ball, as he always did to square the blade, but in doing this he cut off the breeze that had been holding the ball on the grade, and the ball moved a scant, unnoticeable fraction of an inch. Jones promptly called a penalty stroke on himself.

A third round of 71 put Jones back in the running, three strokes behind the pacemaker, Joe Turnesa, a very pretty swinger and the most accomplished member of that family of fine golfers growing up in Westchester. Joe was a good front-runner, and with only eighteen holes to go, he would take some catching.

Turnesa started out two pairs ahead of Jones and, playing steadily, increased his lead to four shots when Jones, for the fourth time in four rounds, failed to par the short ninth. Turnesa got his 4 on the tenth . . . and his 4 on the eleventh as well, Jones gathered from the applause that came from the eleventh green as he walked down the tenth. Jones matched those pars, and came to the twelfth with his first big chance to whittle away some of Turnesa's lead. Joe had taken a 6 on that 545-yard par 5 when his brassie second had lacked the distance to carry a bulge of the rough he tried to bite off. Joe hadn't wilted, not by any means. Maybe he was wrong to have gambled when he was ahead, but the alternative to gambling was playing conservatively, and Joe was wise enough to know that aggressive golf is usually winning golf. Jones slammed a long drive into the wind on the twelfth and followed it with a low, long brassie that rolled to the apron of the green. A chip and an 8-footer, and he had his birdie. Now with six holes to go, Jones was only two strokes down.

Turnesa meanwhile had played the 445-yard thirteenth. He drove nicely into the cross-wind, keeping his ball on the fairway. He played his spoon second for the right-hand corner of the green, trusting that the strong wind, blowing from right to left, would coddle it into the pin. It didn't take. The ball bounded into a green-high trap, and Joe took a 5. Jones' second on this hole finished up in a shallow trap at the left of the green. Using his bean, Bobby elected to roll the ball out, brushed it up and over the flattish face of the trap to within four feet of the cup. He sank the putt, and now he was within one stroke of Turnesa. A hole-and-a-half ahead, Turnesa knew exactly how he stood.

No blood on the fourteenth. Or the fifteenth. But Jones caught his man on the sixteenth, where Turnesa had missed a 9-footer for his 4 after a delicate downhill chip. Jones was on with his second and down in 2, for his seventh 4 in a row. And then Jones went out in front with a 3 on the seventeenth. Here Turnesa had made his only real mistake; he had been short with his iron, and his chip had not been close enough. But Turnesa had showed his mettle by playing a birdie 4 on the 480-yard eighteenth, making up for a pushed second by pitching out of the rough eight feet from the pin and holing his putt. To win, Jones would have to duplicate that birdie.

Jones hit a beauty off the tee, almost 300 yards down the fairway. (Under tension Bobby made it a practice to lengthen his backswing a notch to counteract the tendency of the under-pressure golfer to hurry his timing.) There was no mistake about Bobby's iron either. It came up to the green as big as a grapefruit, on the pin all the way, and finished about sixteen feet past. Bobby stuck his first putt up close and tapped in the winning shot.

In the privacy of his hotel room, the strain finally got to Bobby. He sat down and cried—he was that exhausted from the demands that the week of high pressure and the final chase had made on his nervous system. The spectators at Scioto would never have guessed that the man who had played sub-par golf down the stretch with such consummate grace was, inside, as keyed up as a playwright on opening night. Jones was high-strung by nature and during some tournaments became so nervous that he couldn't get his fingers to unknot his tie. But before a shot, he somehow drew himself together, and the average spectator received the impression that Bobby was all placidity. Jones was one of those great athletes who could never exterminate his basic nervousness but who controlled it and made it work for him and extracted from it an extra-something his more phlegmatic rivals were denied. But controlling one's nerves taxed an athlete severely, and sometimes he ended up, when the battle was over, crying in a hotel room in Columbus.

After Scioto, the Amateur Championship should have been a breeze for Bobby. He made his way to the final, where he met George Von Elm, the slick, blond challenger from California. In two prior bouts with Bobby, George had been made to look like just another amateur, and he wasn't just another amateur. Along with Jones, Von Elm was the only non-professional whom Hagen and Company had to watch out for, a player with all the shots. At Baltusrol, George came onto his game gradually, and in the final was under par for the thirty-five holes he needed to defeat Jones. With Von Elm's victory, for the first time a national championship trophy was taken west of the Rockies.

Bobby's 1927 campaign got off to a slow start when he finished eleventh in the Open at Oakmont, lengthened to 6, 915 yards and so extravagantly trapped by the Fowneses that you couldn't see the greens for the bunkers. Jones may have treated his preparation for this tournament a trifle too cavalierly, may have been guilty of regarding his competition too lightly because of the success he had been enjoying against the pros in "their tournament." After the amateur had again led the field at Scioto the year before, Hagen, the natural leader of the pros, had told off his colleagues in no uncertain terms. They were losing face by letting Jones romp home in front so regularly, he lectured them. Once he (Hagen) had played himself out of the running, the other pros seemed to lose their fight. It was about time they stood their ground. It may have been Hagen's appeal to their sense of pride—it certainly wasn't his last two rounds at Oakmont—that spurred the pros on to leaving Jones far in in their wake for once. Or it may simply have been Jones' mediocre play. He turned the 3-pars into *faux pas*. Not once did he hit the short sixth, and when he took a 6 on the short thirteenth on his third round, he was done for. Bobby's aggregate of 309, and a tie for eleventh, contained no round under 76.

Jones' loose golf at Oakmont deeply disconcerted his best friend, O. B. Keeler, and his severest critic, Bobby Jones. In the two championships that remained on his itinerary for 1927, Jones drove himself relentlessly in his determination to make up

for Oakmont. He was rewarded with one of the finest scoring sprees of his career. In the British Open and the United States Amateur, Jones played 224 holes, the equivalent of more than twelve rounds, in seventeen strokes under par, and, in the process, carried off both championships.

In successfully defending his British Open title, Bobby fulfilled one of his strongest desires: "to win a championship at St. Andrews." Along with most foreigners, Bobby's first estimate of the hallowed Old Course was that it was grossly overrated. Walker Cup warfare revised his opinion, and by 1927 he had learned to love St. Andrews like a native and to play it like one. Bobby began his defense with a 68, which equaled the competitive record for St. Andrews, and turned the tournament into a one-man show by adding a 72, a 73, and a 72 for 285, six strokes ahead of the second man and a new record for the championship. After holing his putt on the 72nd green, Jones received a terrific ovation from the Scottish spectators, the most astute golf galleries in the world, since golf to them is an extension of their lives as natural and as implicit as jazz is for Americans. They cared little that Bobby had taken St. Andrews apart on a week in which the Old Course wasn't really itself, the fairways baked hard by the sun and with hardly so much as a breeze stirring the whins. They were delighted that Bobby was the one who had done it, for in the judgment of the Scots he was the perfect player. In their minds they had conjured up the faultless golfer, in about the same way a man has his ideal woman, and when Jones came along they knew right off the reel that here was their dream-golfer. With a modicum of oral interchange, the Scottish galleries and their idol shared the bliss of complete communion. On the course the Scots knew instinctively when to let him alone, but once the tournament was over, they mobbed him and hoisted him high on their shoulders and carried him tenderly but triumphantly to the R. & A. clubhouse. Jones made a charming speech of acceptance when the cup was presented and then insured an everlasting place for himself in the hearts of the nation by signifying that he wished the trophy to be left in the keeping of the R. & A. If the Scots recognized their perfect golfer when they saw him, Jones was no less adept in sensing that they were his most intelligently enthusiastic admirers.

Splendid playing conditions also collaborated in the dazzling rounds Bobby turned in en route to his third victory in the U.S. Amateur Championship. After studying the weather conditions that prevailed during the fifteen previous summers and discovering that the third week in August invariably offered the coolest weather, the committee at Minneapolis' Minikahda Club, which had been awarded the tournament, settled on the week of August 22nd. Sure enough, the weather was delightful all week, almost sweater weather. Minikahda's famed "Sea Serpent" sprinkler took care of the patches that had been burned brown by the summer sun.

After qualifying easily, Jones got a bad round out of his system, a 78 that was no more than sufficient for an eighteenth-green victory over Maurice McCarthy, Jr. He was even par in taking Gene Homans, and then he really turned it on. In his morning rounds against Harrison "Jimmy" Johnston, Ouimet, and Evans, he shot a 68, a 69, and a 67, and coasted in to lopsided victories — 10 and 9, 11 and 10, 8 and 7. Chick Evans, returning to the scene of his first national triumph eleven years earlier, was playing his irons with a much shorter backswing but getting the same beautiful results. He went all the way to the final, and, against Bobby, Chick gave a demonstration of mashie-play that might have got him home against any other amateur but Jones.

There weren't as many tournaments in the Twenties as there are today, when the various circuits are in action almost the year round except for a short layoff between Thanksgiving and New Year's. Nevertheless, the big guns had a fairly full calendar to shoot at — the California and Florida tournaments in the winter, the mid-continent affairs in the summer. Jones, however, rarely entered the lists. While his legal work did demand an increasingly large slice of his time, he could have probably sneaked off from the office had he not been convinced that there was such a thing as too much tournament golf. Some observers felt that Bobby might have

been able to sharpen his game even finer if he played in more tournaments, but he remained steadfast in his view that continual competition would take too much out of him and leave him dried up and dull-edged when the major events came along. In 1928 he passed up defending his British Open Championship and confined himself to the two big domestic affairs.

Olympia Fields, that colossal installation below Chicago called a country club, was host to the Open. A glance at Jones' four rounds—73, 71, 73, 77—would forward the inference that Bobby, who tied for first, had tossed it away on the last eighteen. There was a bit more to it than that. During the championship proper and the first half of the playoff with Johnny Farrell, he was decidedly off his game. His driving, ordinarily one of his strongest points, was erratic, and Jones was perpetually struggling for his pars. By the fourth round he was so tired that the pupils in his eyes were drawn to pinpoints, and he felt more like flipping a coin with Farrell than going out the next morning to settle the tie via a 36-hole playoff. Farrell won. He threw a 70 at Jones over the first eighteen and held on bravely in the afternoon when Bobby, for the first time in the week at Olympia Fields, started to hit the ball and forced the slim Irishman to finish in birdies to win by one stroke.

The pros had managed to stop Jones two years in a row but among the amateurs he was still the boss. The field through which he made his way at Brae Burn, west of Boston, was rather strong one, too. In addition to the players of the Ouimet–Evans generation and George Von Elm, it included new stars like Don Moe from Oregon, George Voigt (who had taken the Long Island Open from the pros), Phillips Finlay, Ducky Yates, and other young men with ambitions of their own. The British Walker Cup team was also entered, and Phil Perkins, the number-one man, was itching for a chance to square accounts with Jones for that 13 and 12 shellacking he had received in the Cup Match. At Brae Burn, Bobby had his customary close calls in his eighteen-hole matches, but once he was safely into the double-eighteens, he was as good as home. John Beck of Britain was a beaten man on the 23rd green; Phil Finlay was able to carry Bobby only one hole farther; and in the final Phil Perkins, who had earned his chance for another shot at Bobby, was stampeded almost as badly. Up to 1924, Jones' opponents in the Amateur had, more often than not, played over their heads. Now, with rare exceptions, they played "under their heads," if there is such a phrase, and, in any event, never seemed to be able to do themselves justice when they

PRECEDING PAGES: MOMENTS AFTER SINKING THE FINAL, WINNING PUTT AT THE 1927 BRITISH OPEN, JONES IS CARRIED OFF THE GREEN BY THE ST. ANDREWS' CROWD. NOWHERE WAS JONES' COMBINATION OF MODESTY AND SUPERIOR PERFORMANCE MORE APPRECIATED THAN IN SCOTLAND. OPPOSITE, JONES PLAYS FROM THE SAND AT PEBBLE BEACH DURING THE 1929 U.S. AMATEUR.

faced the great Atlantan. Perkins, for example, had used only 52 strokes over the fourteen holes of his afternoon round against Voigt. Against Jones, over the same distance, Perkins needed 66 on the morning round, and went down 10 and 9.

Had all matches been over the 36-hole route, the mature Bobby Jones might never have known what it was to *watch* a United States Amateur. However, in the very first round of the 1929 Amateur at Pebble Beach—the first national championship, incidentally, to be staged west of Minneapolis—Jones came up against a dogged youngster from Omaha named Johnny Goodman who jumped off to a lead over the first nine, hung on grimly as Jones came back, staved off Jones' last assault with a magnificent spoon shot to the green on the dangerous seventeenth, and succeeded in halving the eighteenth and winning the match 1 up. For years Jones had been frightened of being eliminated in the early 18-hole matches, and now that it had happened, he felt relieved, though at the same time it took him a while to get used to the idea of being a spectator in what had become his personal championship. He was himself an interesting tournament in which the oldtimers more than held their own against the youngsters. The average age of the semi-finalists—Jimmy Johnston, Doc Willing, Francis Ouimet, and Chandler Egan—was thirty-nine. Johnston from Min-

nesota and Willing from Oregon won through to the final where the thirty-four-year-old Johnston, the baby of the quartet, outsteadied the steady dentist.

The Amateur, as usual, had been held later in the year than the Open, and Jones' upset at the hands of the unknown Goodman was all the more shocking since Bobby had again captured the Open. For the fourth time he finished in a tie for first, this time with Al Espinosa. On the thirteenth tee of the last round, no one would have given an enchilada for the chances of the slow-moving Spaniard from Monterey, California. Starting out before Jones, Espinosa had to make up four strokes on the Georgian but fell further off the pace with a 38 on the first nine. After taking an 8 on the 66th, Espinosa, believing that he had kicked away his opportunity neatly and completely, played out the rest of the holes simply as a matter of routine. With no pressure to distract him, he covered the last six in 22 strokes and was startled to discover that, for all his blunders, he had the best four-round total among the early finishers. Jones meanwhile was marching along with par until he was trapped on his approach to the eighth green. He exploded clean across the green into another trap, then exploded out of that trap across the green and back

into the first trap. He ended up with a 7 and was understandably trap-shy after this experience. Over the rest of the route, Bobby managed to stay out of the traps that guard the typically Tillinghast narrow-opening greens at Winged Foot, though this protective type of golf was not getting him any birdies. However, with four holes to go, he had pars in for a 75, a three-stroke lead over Espinosa's comparative figures. Then, on the 69th, a not particularly rough par 4, the Georgian completely lost his concentration. He punched his third shot much too forcefully into the wind, and the ball bounded well over the green. He chose to loft it back, over a little knoll, and

flubbed his pitch smack into the knoll. The galleries that had come out to watch the flawless Jones play a 69 as he had on the first round watched an embarrassed man take his second three-over-par 7 of the day. They saw him throw away what looked like a sure birdie by three-putting the 70th from twenty feet. They shuddered for him when he left himself a touchy 12-footer on the 72nd to tie with Espinosa.

If Bobby Jones had failed to sink that putt on the 72nd green at Winged Foot, he would have blown a three-stroke lead on the last four holes, and there is no knowing how such a collapse might have affected a golfer as hypercritical of himself as Jones. There are many who think that the career of Bobby Jones would have tapered off then and there, that there certainly would have been no Grand Slam had he missed that curving 12-footer. He sank it, of course, borrowing perfectly off the slope and sending one of his "dying ball" putts into the exact center of the cup. Bobby Jones had won a reprieve. He went out the next day and shot two great playoff rounds of 72 and 69 and overwhelmed Espinosa by twenty-three strokes. Bobby Jones remained the champion of champions.

In chart form Bobby's major tournament record from 1923 through 1929 would look like this:

	BRITISH AMATEUR	BRITISH OPEN	U.S. AMATEUR	U.S. OPEN
1923			eliminated 5th round	1 (playoff)
1924			1	2
1925			1	2 (playoff)
1926	eliminated 5th round	1	2	1
1927		1	1	tied for 11th
1928			1	2 (playoff)
1929			eliminated 1st round	1 (playoff)

NO STROKE WAS MORE IMPORTANT TO JONES' GRAND SLAM ASSAULT IN 1930 THAN THE ONE HE FACED IN 1929, OPPOSITE, TO SALVAGE THE U.S. OPEN AT WINGED FOOT. JONES HAD LOST A SIX STROKE LEAD; HAD THE SIDE-HILL 12-FOOTER NOT DROPPED THE DEFEAT MIGHT HAVE SHATTERED HIS CONFIDENCE.

Emperor Jones' appearance in a national tourney was the signal for five to eight thousand golfing fanatics to inundate the course and form a tense, idolatrous, noisy, frenetic, marshal-mangling gallery. Each person in the thousands wanted to touch his hero. Fans who couldn't get to the tournaments and who followed Jones' triumph by newspaper or radio felt an almost equal closeness to their hero. During the week of a national championship, the residents of every golfing community in the United States acted as if it were Atlanta. Bobby's victories were their victories, and his defeats were their defeats.

For a man who exerted so compelling a magnetism over American sports fans, Jones was an exceptionally restrained performer. He did not dramatize himself like Tilden or Hagen. He made no appeal to primitive human emotions, like Dempsey. He was no happy extrovert like Ruth. Jones' stupendous popularity—unprecedented in what had been a minor sport until he emerged—rested partially on a skill so apparent that it needed no showboating, and partially on the type of man he was.

There was a clear, cold aesthetic thrill in watching Jones hit a golf ball. The other leading players had excellent form that a duffer could appreciate, and they got results that spoke for themselves. Compared to Jones, though, they didn't look so finished. You noticed a little bumpiness in their backswing, a vague departure from the blueprint at impact, the expenditure of brute force in the followthrough. You looked at Jones and you saw the copybook form that you and two million other American golfers were striving for. You saw a one-piece swing in which the man had somehow incorporated every "must" your pro had enumerated—the left arm straight but not rigid on the backswing; the weight shifted from left to right going back and then gradually returned to the left side again as the club started down and the hands moved into position to unleash their power; the hit through the ball; the finish with the weight entirely transferred to the left side and the hands high—the million other integrated contributions of the chin, the hips, the balls of the feet, the knees, the grip, the left shoulder, the right ankle, the wrists, the eyes. If you could buckle down and remember to do all those things, then you, too, would play like Jones. No, you couldn't at that. You would always lack that something which lifted Jones above mechanical perfection. It was hard to put your finger on it. It had to do with a certain *je ne sais quoi* quality that made Bobby's swing so rhythmically singular, made it appear so effortless though you knew it was built on effort. Bernard Darwin came as close as anyone to tagging the genius of Jones when he said, without any gingerbread, that there was a strain of poetry in Bobby.

Dissected position by position, Jones' swing was, of course, not markedly different from those employed by the other stars. He did stand with his feet closer together than most of the other champions in order to facilitate the freest, fullest body turn the game has ever known. The shifting of weight is a very unglamorous facet of correct form to the average golfer. He would much rather hear that the key to playing par golf is the sturdy left elbow at contact or the machinations of the big toes. But Jones intimated that if there was any one most-important "secret to his success," it was that mundane, colorless chore, the free body turn, on which the correct execution of his shots depended.

A picture-postcard golfer like Jones had few idiosyncrasies. He teed the ball on his drive opposite his left arch, a bit farther forward than most players, since he preferred to hit his wood shots at the beginning of the upswing. He teed the ball high since he inclined toward woods with deep faces about four degrees straighter than the average clubs. He was of the opinion that his pitches from 60 to 125 yards were the weakest department of his game, but none of his rivals noticed this foible. If he had a weakness, it was his periodic unsureness at fading an approach. The shots he thought he hit best were the 3- and 4-irons.

Around the golf course, Jones, who could have gotten away with vanities and eccentricities, behaved as if he were just another golfer. A few soured also-rans griped that Bobby was always given the preferred starting times at the big tournaments. This was true, but it was the doing of the U.S.G.A. officials, who naturally were aware that Jones was an unrivaled drawing card. Jones' galleries were a trying lot, but no matter how deeply or how often he was disconcerted by individual gestures of love and devotion tendered at the wrong times, he never addressed a rebuking word to the offenders. His rivals were confounded by his regard for their feelings. The first word that came to Tommy Armour's mind in describing Jones was *considerate*.

Jones had rather simple tastes. There were stretches when he liked to be alone, such as tournament weeks. His evening ritual at these times consisted of two drinks (the first swallowed as he luxuriated in a hot tub), a relaxing dinner with Keeler and one or two other close friends, some conversation or a few chapters in a book like Papini's *Life of Christ* before retiring. But there was nothing prissy about Bobby—or Bob, as he preferred to be called. He loved the atmosphere of the locker room. He enjoyed a good story and told a good story. He used a man's language in expressing his emotions and had a nice gift for inventing phrases to describe his golf. (A hard, dangerous shot, for example, was one which demanded "sheer delicatessen.") Bobby was an intelligent person—he had studied at Harvard for two years, after getting his B.S. degree in mechanical engineering at Georgia Tech, and he later prepared for his legal career at Emory Law School. He was a man of many interests, to say the least. He was a good husband, a good father, and a good son. He and his father, "The Colonel," got a real kick

out of each other. Paul Gallico, one sports-writer who never called a spade a sable instrument for delving, wrapped up Robert Tyre Jones, Jr., as well as anyone when he said of him: "I have found only one [sports figure] who could stand up in every way as a gentleman as well as a celebrity, a fine, decent human being as well as a newsprint personage, and one who never once since I have known him has let me down in my estimate of him."

The American sports public didn't know the intimate personal habits of Jones, but what they saw of him was an accurate index of the man. They liked the way he acted in competition. They liked the way he looked—clean-cut, boyish and grown-up at the same time. A decade or so before they had flocked to Ouimet because he was a young American they understood and admired, and it may not be at all excessive to say that they worshipped Jones, and formed an enduring enthusiasm for the game he played, because, of all the heroes in the Golden Age of Sport, he stood forth as the model American athlete.

JONES' POPULARITY HELPED TO TRANSFORM GOLF INTO A MAJOR SPECTATOR SPORT. WHEREVER HE PLAYED, LARGE GALLERIES FOLLOWED, AS ABOVE AT THE ENGINEERS' CLUB ON LONG ISLAND.

The Master Builders

ON the fairway Americans tried to keep up with Jones, and off the fairway they were busy keeping up with the Joneses. The Joneses were going in for golf in a great big way, more avidly, even, than they pursued the latest bridge systems, the inside story on murder trials, the new subterranean address the indispensable Tony had moved to, Clara Bow's formula, and a college education for their fair-haired progeny. The Joneses liked golf and would have stuck with the game once they took it up for the right good reason that it fascinated them. But there we other reasons for playing golf, more right and better. The fact that

the Joneses were able to spend so much time at the course marked them as a family that was doing all right financially. Then, too, if they "made" an *exclusive country club*, a snazzier bazaar than the Smiths belonged to, they need not bow their heads to anyone socially. Membership in an exclusive country club—on rare occasions the three words were not yoked together—was the salient badge of distinction in the Twenties. Mrs. Jones was happy about it, for her kiddies' sake, she said. Mr. Jones was more honest. He got as much business done in the locker room and on the course as he did at the office. It was the environment that he favored as well for those hours when his second business, that wonderful invention called the stock market, made money for him even as he carded his 46 on the back nine with his new MacGregor Chieftains.

As the country club came of age in America, the Joneses and Americans of greater and less equilibrium puffed the ranks of the nation's golfers. Now there were over two million of them. Each year they spent $10,000,000 for caddies, bought about 24,000,000 balls and about $20,000,000 worth of implements, and contributed toward the $120,000,000 that went into new mowers, seeds, watering systems, and other equipment requested by the green committees. Some of them furnished their golf bag with all the items Hagen carried in the British Open: in addition to clubs and balls, they were fortified with an umbrella, ball-cleaner and brushes, thermometer, clock, a case for tees, wind gauge, rule book, a second pair of shoes, an extra sweater, and a caddie whistle. Also a second pair of argyles, one of the 6,876,192 pairs of golf hose Americans purchased in a single year. There was hardly enough room to carry around that Pivot-Sleeve jacket—the one Ph. Weinberg and

Sons had shown for years in the *American Golfer*—but jackets were going out anyway. The old golfers had been blinded by tradition when they had persevered with the jacket; obviously, the smart thing to wear with knickers and cap was matching sweater and socks, like that sharp checkered combination George Von Elm had on at the Amateur.

Room had to be found for the new thousands who wanted to play golf, and from seacoast to seacoast kidney-shaped traps were scooped out and oaks were felled and split for tee benches as the country went back-to-the-soil. By the middle Twenties, the 300,000 Oregonians living in Portland had twenty courses to choose from. Seattle had only seventeen, but they were all within thirty minutes drive of the totem pole in the center of town. Miami and Miami Beach were building new courses at the rate of over one a year. The size of the community, though, was of small importance. The folks in York, Nebraska, had twice attempted to finance a golf course and twice the project had died on them, but they wanted a golf course and on the third try they made it. Enough $100 bonds were sold in three drives to purchase forty-three acres of blue grass and clover turf cut by a snaky

Properly outfitted in up-to-date golfing attire—a jacket with knitted waistband and cuffs, knickerbockers, and patterned hose—a 1920s golfer, above, prepares for a round. At the time, a sand wedge cost $12, a bag $30, and the Pasadena Municipal course, opposite, $52,000.

little brook, and to add a modern frame club-house for $15,000. George Ade, the humorist and a golf pioneer, had his own course in Hazelden, Indiana, with a rustic clubhouse fashioned from three hundred burr oaks. Almost a hundred towns in Kansas had their golf courses. Cloudcroft in New Mexico built one nine thousand feet above sea level. By the late Twenties there were more greens in the United States than savings banks and libraries.

The clubs with a problem were the pioneer layouts near the larger cities. At the turn of the century the land purchased by the syndicates had been truly rural, fifteen or twenty minutes from the heart of the city. Now, as the cities spread out, many of these old clubs found themselves hemmed in by houses, stores, and factories, their land no longer ample enough to take care of the holes they wished to build or remodel to keep up with

the livelier golf ball, their locations uncongenial to the commodious clubhouse their members were discussing. Most of the time these clubs solved their problem by buying new land farther out in the country and selling their old plot to the city. Municipal golf courses were a paying investment. Norfolk, Virginia, for illustration, constructed nine holes at the cost of $1,500. The green fee for a day's play was only fifteen cents, but six months after the course had been opened, it had paid for itself and returned the city a clear $2,000 profit. Norfolk then decided to extend the course to eighteen holes, and soon after this, started work on the first of three public courses on a 575-acre farm owned by the city. San Antonio could boast of the $45,000 clubhouse, modeled after a farmhouse of the Marie Antoinette period, which it had ordained for the Brackenridge Park municipal course over which the Texas Open was played. Port Townsend, Washington (population 3,300), had a private club but the town officials at length gave in to the demands of that golf-happy community for a public course, and never regretted it. Everyone wanted to be a golfer, and if the man in the low-income bracket was stymied in joining an exclusive country club, thanks to the public course he could still play the same game that hypnotized his boss and after a good round he could experience that "g-r-r-rand and gl-l-l-lorious feeling" Clare Briggs had delineated in his matchless cartoons. Over five hundred non-private courses mushroomed across the country, some just unkempt acres with flags on the flattest spots, others too short for a long-hitter and overcrowded on weekends, but a fair percentage of them excellent tests of golf.

Looking for *lebensraum*, the wealthy clubs pushed deeper into the sticks. The little towns of America, Ade commented dryly, had succeeded in foisting Prohibition on the large cities but now they were being shackled with golf in retaliation. No land within thirty-five miles of a large city was safe, and if it had a winding stream and a

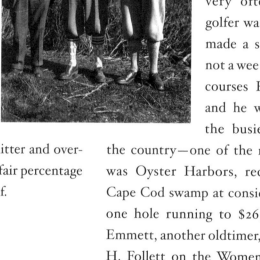

hill suitable for a spreading clubhouse, it was as good as under construction. The golf architects went to the country and went to town. A. W. Tillinghast built his imaginative and pleasant-to-play courses in all parts of the country. Donald Ross had gotten away from his penchant for placing his greens on the crowns of graded hills and for sticking his traps so close to the greens that very often the average golfer was better off if he made a sizable error and not a wee one. Of the later courses Ross designed— and he was undoubtedly the busiest architect in the country—one of the most interesting was Oyster Harbors, reclaimed from a Cape Cod swamp at considerable expense, one hole running to $26,000. Devereux Emmett, another oldtimer, worked with W. H. Follett on the Women's National, the fine course in Glen Head, Long Island, financed by and operated for women exclusively. Marion Hollins, the former women's champion who had spearheaded the promotion of the Women's National, called on Dr. Alister Mackenzie when she fell in love with California, and Mackenzie did two first-class jobs for Miss Hollins—Pasatiem-

THREE CALIFORNIA GOLF ARCHITECTS PROMINENT IN THE 1920S ARE, RIGHT TO LEFT, ABOVE, ALISTER MACKENZIE, FAMOUS FOR CYPRESS POINT, OPPOSITE; GEORGE C. THOMAS, JR.; AND BILLY BELL, WHO BUILT THE PASADENA MUNICIPAL COURSE SHOWN ON THE PRECEDING PAGE.

po at Santa Cruz and Cypress Point on the Monterey Peninsula. In the astonishing range of its beauty, Cypress Point stands almost alone among golf courses—green forests edging down to the blinding whiteness of the sand dunes, cypresses fringing the craggy headlands that drop with an awful suddenness into the blue Pacific. Mackenzie wisely winked at the principles of golf architecture when the rugged terrain suggested untraditional measures, such as two par 3s in a row. The fifteenth is a pitch over an inlet that is Stevenson's pirate cove come to life. The sixteenth is a carry (which must be all of 210 yards) across a deep elbow of the Pacific to a green that is a miniature Heligoland. Mackenzie and Robert Trent Jones, the young man who with Stanley Thompson did the thrilling

courses at Banff and Jasper Park, were not showboat architects—indeed, quite the reverse of it. They share the credit for bringing back into American golf-course architecture the natural dune bunker and for replacing the multitude of penal headaches with a few strategically positioned hazards that punished a poor shot in direct proportion to its inaccuracy. They were also the first to realize the role that sharply contoured greens with several pin positions could play in making courses stiffer for par golfers while rendering them no more difficult for the average player.

One of the great courses of the world, Pine Valley, was the work of a non-professional architect, George Crump. One day when Crump was out hunting in the harsh stretches of sand and pine in western New

Jersey, the idea came to him that this was the perfect land for building a golf course that would be fundamentally fair and yet be a course that would stand up to the wizards who were making scores in the 60s seem as prosaic as brushing your teeth. A few years later, Crump, a successful Philadelphia hotel man, turned all of his exceptional energy into making his dream come true. He engaged H. S. Colt, the highly respected English architect, to help him with the plans for his undertaking, and moved into a bungalow he built on the property. For eight years he lived practically the life of a hermit, hunting in the odd moments he wasn't occupied with turning his primeval domain into the most carefully planned golf course in the history of the game. George Crump died before he had completed his project, but he had finished fourteen of the holes, and his estate and a generous friend from Morristown furnished the necessary funds for carrying out Crump's plans for the last four holes. (These holes were executed by Hugh Wilson, another remarkable amateur architect from Philadelphia and the creator of Merion.) Pine Valley emerged the course George Crump had visualized—just about the toughest layout in the world, "an examination in golf," as Bernard Darwin phrased it. In 1922 George V. Rotan succeeded in getting around in 70, and down through the years, in the face of innumerable assaults by the best golfers, that 70 remained the lowest score made in competition at Pine Valley until 1939, when Ed Dudley played an astonishing 68.

The courses designed in the comparative country were handsome and ingenious, and yet at many of the country clubs the course was somewhat in the same position as the juggler who made the mistake of hiring a female assistant of such incandescent beauty that no one had the vaguest idea if he were twirling Indian pins or dishes. The clubhouse, of course, was the assistant that became the star of the show. Starting as Stanford White's modest lounge and locker room at Shinnecock Hills, the clubhouse had now become the center of the social life of America's middle-middle, upper-middle, and upper classes. At the clubhouse you lived with the people you wanted to associate with, played your bridge, drank your gin rickey, ate your guinea hen, danced your foxtrot, traded your tips on stocks, and gave your daughter away in marriage. Home was where you brought your dirty laundry—although the country club, in time, came to offer laundry service, valet service, a complete barber shop, a masseur, a dancing instructor. . . . Just name what you wanted and your country club had it. It was like some magnificent luxury liner that someone had forgotten to launch.

Bigger and better installations went up all over the country. The members of the Birmingham Country Club in Alabama spent over $300,000 on their new place in Shades Valley but they believed it gave them the most spacious clubhouse in the South. $250,000 was about par for a new clubhouse, and then there were the fixings—tennis courts, bridle paths, dancing pavilion, swimming pool, perhaps a polo field, and yes, a golf course or two. In Chicago, a thousand Shriners, building the Medinah Country Club at a cost of $1,500,000, planned to have the whole works, plus toboggan slides and ski runs. The Los Angeles Country Club had one of the largest memberships—three thousand. The Glen Oaks Country Club, occupying the former mansion of William K. Vanderbilt, had one of the nicest nooks, a sunken Italian garden. The richest was the Detroit Golf Club, founded in 1906 and still sticking with its original course, since its 212 acres now formed the heart of the city's residential district; the land was now valued at $100,000 an acre, and a Class A membership (entitling the holder to stock and voting power) went for $7,500. The most snobbish was Chevy Chase, outside of Washington, which barred local businessmen on the grounds that they were "persons engaged in trade."

Olympia Fields was the daddy of them all. Conceived in 1914, this gargantuan retreat in the woods below Chicago was at

GEORGE CRUMP, OPPOSITE, WAS A PHILADELPHIA SPORTSMAN WHO DREAMED OF BUILDING HIS OWN COURSE. COMPLETED IN 1921, CRUMP'S PINE VALLEY IS STILL CONSIDERED ONE OF THE WORLD'S BEST.

length completed in 1925. "The world's largest private golf club" was the first to offer its members seventy-two holes of golf. (Over two thousand caddies were enrolled.) The clubhouse was a liberal translation of English Tudor with a dining room seating eight hundred, a cafe seating six hundred, only one outdoor dancing pavilion but five hundred feet of veranda. The club operated its own ice-making plant and its own hospital. One hundred families owned cottages in the dells of the club's 692 acres. Through some oversight Olympia Fields never made provision for its own college and a major league baseball team, but it was possible to live out your life there if your wants were not exotic.

More and more celebrities played golf—Charlie Chaplin, Pola Negri, Uncle Joe Cannon, Harold Lloyd, Vilma Banky, President Harding, Douglas Fairbanks, to name just a few of the stars of stage, screen, and government. Magazines and newspaper editors never tired of photos showing Babe Ruth twisted like a corkscrew after smashing a drive, or Aileen Riggin, the reigning pin-up girl, bestowing her come-hither on a mashie, or cartoonist Rube Goldberg inventing some zany stroke at the Artists and Writers annual tournament. Earl Sande, the hero of the race tracks, became a convert. So did Ty Cobb, except during the baseball season. Frank Craven

was impatient for the Broadway run of *The First Year to* end, for he had been neglecting his game. Rex Beach, a fairly good player, made a hole-in-one and won a free case of Canada Dry, among other things. John D. Rockefeller's spontaneous statements to the effect that golf was the best insurance of longevity sold more people on the tycoon's humanity than the artful campaigns of his publicity man, Ivy Lee.

The American Golfer, now a glossy job thick with advertising, tastefully edited by Grantland Rice and Innis Brown, conducted a "contest" in which various celebrities were asked to respond humorously to the question: What do you find the hardest shot in golf? Many of the boys came through nicely:

GROUCHO MARX: I find the hardest shot in golf is a hole-in-one.

RING LARDNER: I am undecided as to which of these two is the hardest shot in golf for me—any unconceded putt or the explosion shot off the first tee. Both have caused me more strokes than I care to write about.

W. C. FIELDS: I am stumped when it comes to saying which is the hardest shot in golf for me, but I know the easiest one—the first shot at the Nineteenth Hole.

Golf humor was no longer "society stuff." The office boy knew the game:

BUSINESS MAN TO OFFICE BOY:

IN THE PHOTOGRAPH OPPOSITE, HOLLYWOOD STAR DOUGLAS FAIRBANKS, LEFT, SHARES TABLE, NOTEBOOK, AND A SCHWEPPES WITH GOLF COURSE ARCHITECT, ALISTER MACKENZIE. FAIRBANKS WAS ONE OF MANY CELEBRITIES TO TAKE UP THE GAME IN THE 1920S.

When people want to see me, do you know what to tell them?

OFFICE BOY: Sure. I've worked for business men before. When you're playing 9 holes, you're out-to-lunch—18 holes is in conference—27 holes, sick—and 36 holes is out-of-town.

As always, some of the best humor was unintentional. When Los Angeles was host to the P.G.A. Championship, the movie luminaries decided to give the tournament that extra Hollywood touch; before each twosome went out, a Hollywood star introduced the players to the gallery. Fay Wray,

whose job it was to introduce Hagen and his partner, was doing fine in her breathless way until she referred to Walter as "the Opium Champion of Great Britain."

To play good golf was a gilt-edged social and commercial asset, so Americans beat a path to the door of the local pro, the doctor who could trim three strokes off anyone's game, maybe more if the instruction could be hammered home over a long series of lessons. In the Twenties the career of the average golf pro was no longer a precarious one, and the boys who had made a name for themselves in tournament golf had drawing rooms on the gravy train. The Open title was now worth about $25,000 to the winning pro, and after his victories in the Open and the P.G.A. in 1922, Gene Sarazen parlayed them into many more thousands by an astute understanding of the public's appetite. In addition to playing the numerous exhibition and special matches that every champion comes into, young Sarazen cashed in on his big year by opening a golf correspondence school in New York, signing with the Wilson Company to promote and design clubs, endorsing his favorite golf ball (and the cartridge the Open Champion liked to lock in his barrel when he went trap-shooting), making movie shorts, putting out an instruction book, and accepting the highest salary ever offered a professional to go with Briarcliff Lodge, Chauncey Depew Steele's combination country club and resort in Westchester.

As the money became easier, some of the top golfers chose to spend the winter as resident pros at select spas in Florida rather than follow the tournament caravan winding from California across the Southern states and up to the Carolinas with halts for $1,500 and $2,000 tournaments. To lure the likes of Sarazen and Hagen to their tournaments, the sponsors had to increase the prize money. The $6,000 San Antonio Open, once the richest pot on the winter march, began to look rather emaciated as the Los Angeles Open upped its prize money to $10,000, Miami countered with $15,000, and Agua Caliente placed the maraschino on the sundae with a $25,000 affair. (It was rather characteristic of Sarazen to come onto his game just in time to carry off the first-place check in the first Agua Caliente Open.) One reason why Bobby Jones faced so little competition in the amateur field was that nearly every young golfer of promise without a private income no longer hesitated to turn professional. Hagen had led the way in wiping out the old social stigma of being a professional, for one thing, and a tidy living awaited the young man who could shoot his way to a place among the nation's top twenty. Whole families of golfers became pros, the two outstanding examples being the Turnesas and the Espinosas. Six of the Turnesa boys were pros—in order of seniority, Phil, Frank, Joe, Mike, Doug, and Jim. Abe and Al were the only two Espinosas who earned national reputations, but Romie, Henry, Raymond, and *Annette* all made golf their career.

By 1929, the Joneses of America were playing golf on over 4,500 courses and were members of clubs whose collective real estate was

WARM-WEATHER GOLF BECKONED TO SNOWBOUND GOLFERS IN ADVERTISEMENTS LIKE THE ONE OPPOSITE FROM THE NOVEMBER 1929 ISSUE OF THE AMERICAN GOLFER. DEL MONTE, ON CALIFORNIA'S MONTEREY PENINSULA, OFFERED FOUR GOLF COURSES, INCLUDING THE FAMOUS PEBBLE BEACH COURSE.

valued at over a billion and a half dollars. The Joneses who lived in some small towns, in the Middle West in particular, belonged to clubs that remained free from arbitrary social distinctions, such as the one in Sheffield, Illinois, where the holes had been laid out by John Stapleton, the chauffeur for the town's leading banker and his boss' equal in the shower room and the sand trap. But by and large the class-conscious country club was the thing, and the Joneses were seldom resentful, and then only if they were left out, as the spirit of the country club cut deeper and deeper into the mores of the country, obliterating, for everyone except Rodgers and Hammerstein, some of the healthier attitudes of non-metropolitan America. The Joneses liked to hear that private companies, like the Cudahy branch in Kansas City, had opened golf courses for their employees. This was Progress, and, besides, the Joneses were all set to spend the summer occupying

This Winter . . . Revel in Springtime at Del Monte

One of the World's Most Beautiful Playgrounds

The Bel-Air Country Club course was built in 1927 by George C. Thomas, Jr. (assisted by Jack Neville and Billy Bell) on canyon-land between Los Angeles and the Pacific shore. A suspension bridge connected the course to the Mission style clubhouse, above.

two of the four hundred rooms at the Westchester-Biltmore's hideaway in Rye. They saluted golf as the great common denominator when the final match of the Cleveland District Amateur Championship brought together Ellsworth Augustus, the section of a very affluent family, and Eli Ross, his gardener—and didn't think the perfect story had been sabotaged when Augustus trounced his gardener 10 and 8.

The Joneses read everything that was written about the game they doted on. They got a big bang out of the cranky scorn of a Mr. Quale, the Federal Director of Prohibition Enforcement in Minnesota, who declared that golf "encourages idleness, shiftlessness, and neglect of business as well as family responsibilities; that it deprives many wives of their husbands, and children of their fathers, and that it tempts hundreds of young men into extravagance that sometimes leads to crime." They knew why they played golf: it was a good game, a damn good game that took you outdoors—a damn fashionable game, too, and you didn't have to be a three-letter athlete to play it. Nevertheless, they ate up any and all dissertations by the posse of scholars who were hunting basic sociological explanations for the craze. The Joneses were delighted when Charles Merz in "The Great American Bandwagon" released his theory that golf had created a new frontier for the bored, frontierless modern world, that plus-fours were a substitute for leather chaps, and loud argyles were "the

war paint of a nation." In their rude fortresses the Joneses and other frontiersmen ordered soda water at a dollar a bottle and talked about the lighter arts. Broadway was readying a show with a golf background, *Follow Through*. Indefatigable William Haines had included golf among the many sports he played so well on the screen. In *Spring Fever* he had won the girl by holing a full brassie shot on the last hole, just when things looked blackest. (When it was remade into a talkie with Robert Montgomery and called *Love in the Rough*, Montgomery's heroics were sublimated to making an impossible recovery shot and negotiating a stymie.) The Joneses planned their trips abroad to include golf in romantic locales and made gay references to Cheops' Pyramid as the oldest tee in the world. They attended indoor golf schools, if they stayed north for the winter, and turned up at the National Golf Show to study the exhibits on country club layout, caddie welfare, clubhouse structure, green committee work, etc. The country club had come to stay, and rain or shine the Joneses could always be found at Bubbling Bay. At seven-thirty sharp, Mrs. Jones was at her regular table in the café—not the dining room or the informal grill, but the café—reading a few of the two million words sent out over the wires to describe the Open at Olympia Fields. Mr. Jones was detained a moment. He was down at the putting green watching his star salesman practice missing the short ones.

The Women

MISS GLENNA COLLETT

THE best woman golfer in America in the Twenties was a graceful, strong, and appealing girl from Rhode Island with the euphonious name of Glenna Collett. In christening Glenna "the female Bobby Jones," the apostles of apposition were paying the logical tribute to Glenna's comparable dominance over the field of women golfers. Yet, if you pushed the analogy further, it stood up surprisingly well. Glenna was like Bobby in many ways. She came from the same stratum of society, took advantage of her assets with the same sensible determination to succeed, and reached her goal after the same painful but invaluable passage through the shoals of despondency. As a champion, like Jones she was more than the best in her business. She exuded quality. Young men wrote poems about her infinite charms as she stood silhouetted against the horizon at Pebble Beach; older men claimed that she was the exact type William Dean Howells had in mind when he had stated that the crowning product of America was the American girl; and women had a good word for Glenna.

Like Bobby, Glenna liked all sports. Blessed with a fluid coordination that set her apart from the other girls in her neighborhood in Providence, she was an accomplished swimmer and diver at nine. At ten, she drove her first auto. Mrs. Collett, with a mother's natural concern for her daughter's tomboy predilections, tried to steer her into tennis when Glenna began to blossom as a star on her brother Ned's baseball team. Glenna did develop a promising tennis game to please her mother but continued to play on Ned's club. The girl could throw a ball farther than most of the boys. One afternoon in 1917, when Glenna was fourteen, her father took her along when he went to the Metacomet Golf Club for a round with his cronies. This was Glenna's first meeting with golf. She watched the men for a few holes, and then asked if she could hit one. Not knowing how ornery a game she was trifling with, Glenna banged a beauty straight down the fairway. The men smiled uncomfortably at each other and asked her to play along. Her score was nothing to post in the ladies' locker room, but Glenna came off the course both excited and sobered by the strange feeling that she was meant to be a golfer. Mr. Collett, a famous bowler and a former national cycling champion, went out of his way to see that Glenna had every assistance possible in improving her game, and there were times when he might have overdriven the girl in his desire to have another champion in the family. Mrs. Collett was relieved. She didn't care

if her daughter went in for golf rather than tennis as long as it kept her off third base.

Glenna discovered that it took more than good coordination to play good golf. She chopped her score down from 150 to 130 but that was as low as she could get that first summer. It was all rather discouraging; the harder she concentrated on doing everything the pro told her, the worse she hit her shots. She was beginning to yearn to take-two-and-hit-to-right with Ned's gang when she went over to the Wannamoisett Club one afternoon to watch Alexa Stirling and Elaine Rosenthal team up with Jones and Adair in a Red Cross exhibition match. Elaine was in fine form that day, and Glenna stood silent and admiring as she shattered the woman's course record with an 80. Alexa impressed her even more strongly. Glenna had never seen anyone who hit an iron as crisply as the little Atlantan, and when it came to holing the crucial putts, Alexa stepped up to the ball as cool as a cantaloupe and plunked it in. The afternoon at Wannamoisett was just what the doctor ordered. The next day Glenna went out, and throwing off the encumbrance of a thousand *don'ts*, shot a 49 for nine holes.

SIX-TIME U.S. WOMEN'S CHAMPION GLENNA COLLETT, ABOVE, PLAYS A ROUND AT THE PEBBLE BEACH GOLF LINKS IN 1929. COLLETT BRIEFLY MADE CALIFORNIA'S MONTEREY PENINSULA HER HOME.

By 1927, when the photograph above was taken, Glenna Collett had won two of her six U.S. Women's titles and was the subject of a New Yorker magazine profile. "Most women who spend a lot of time playing in tournaments get a kind of baked look," wrote Niven Busch, Jr. "Well, Glenna Collett isn't like that. She is a very nice-looking girl."

The following summers Glenna worked diligently on the practice fairways, looked becoming in the red picture-hat she wore in tournament play, fell apart in competition, and retreated to the practice fairways. Her father had arranged for her to take two lessons a week from Alex Smith, then the pro at Shennecossett, and in the winters the Colletts followed Alex south to Belleair. Old Alex, the man who had made Jerry Travers, taught Glenna how to "miss 'em quick" on the greens with a compact putting stroke, cut down the backswing on her irons, squinted at her in mock anger until she learned to control her clubhead in her brassie and spoon play, and polished up her driving although Glenna had always looked like a 75-player off the tee.

MISS CECIL LEITCH.

At least once each season Alex's pupil would get going in a tournament, but, invariably, the day after she had looked like the most promising girl who had struck American golf in a decade, her game would fold like an Arab's tent and Glenna would silently steal away to brood over her chronic disappointments. There was the year— 1919—when Glenna was the only member of the Boston Griscom Cup team to win her match against the Philadelphia powerhouse, and then, in her next important test, she had been humiliated 9 and 8 in an eighteen-hole match by Mrs. Barlow, and

had barely been able to fight off her tears until she reached the clubhouse. And there was 1920, when she had astounded experts by defeating Elaine Rosenthal in the final of the Shennecossett tournament only to lose to Elaine when they met again in the second round of the U.S. Women's Championship. The same story in 1921—an 85 at Deal in the qualifying round of the national championship that was fast enough to tie for the medal and built her up to a painful letdown, a sound defeat in the first round by Edith Leitch, a sister of the English champion, Cecil.

Some of life's darkest moments come just before the floor-show goes on. Glenna followed the women's circuit from Deal to the Huntingdon Valley Country Club outside of Philadelphia to play in the Berthellyn Cup competition. When she found that she had drawn Cecil Leitch in the first round, Glenna prepared herself to accept another defeat. The safest means of carrying Cecil a respectable distance, Glenna decided, was to forget about winning holes with impossible shots and just go out and fight for a half on each hole. Cecil was a little off her game, and Glenna, sticking to her plan, halved one hole after another and was completely astonished when she found herself not only still in the match as they came to the eighteenth but actually protecting a 1-up lead. On the home green she had a 10-footer for a half, and the match.

The importance of this victory over Cecil Leitch cannot be overemphasized. Almost overnight Glenna became a different golfer, a confident golfer. She started to hit out, to strike her shots as forcefully as she did on the practice fairway. She carried off the Berthellyn Cup. And from that time on, Glenna was the woman to beat.

In 1922 the seasoned nineteen-year-old star captured the North and South, and then the Eastern, averaging 82 for her three rounds in the latter championship. She looked like the class of the field by several strokes. Golf writers composed psalms about her swing and told their readers that they could see no one else but Glenna winning the U.S. Women's Championship. It was all happening a little too rapidly for Glenna to be tranquil about her new eminence. Glenna was not dangerously close to that line where an athlete is too sensitive and too intelligent for his or her own good, but the superlatives frightened her. She was happy that at last she was playing winning golf, but she wasn't as good as all that. She realized how cardinally important it was to be confident about whatever she undertook, but super-confident people had never appealed to her, regardless of whether or not they were successful, and she found it vexing to adjust herself to the frame of mind she desired: to be able to think reasonably

well of herself and yet to stop many stations south of conceit. Fortunately, her sensibilities were somewhat dulled once she was on the course. Glenna wasn't an icebox like Helen Wills, but she cultivated a restraint that led many of her friends to accuse her of being a "cold woman" and in turn brought passionate protests from Glenna to the effect that it was just a pose designed to help her control the tautness and tension she always felt in competition.

In a warm-up round at the Greenbrier Club in White Sulphur Springs, West Virginia, two days before the 1922 Women's Championship, Glenna scored a 75. The evening previous to this round, she had eaten lamb chops, string beans, and creamed potatoes for dinner, and she continued with this menu while the tournament lasted, half laughing at herself for being so superstitious but hoping that somehow it would preserve her 75 form. For the same reason she stuck with the hat, sweater, and skirt she had worn on the hot round. It was silly, but it seemed to work. Glenna won the medal with an 81. She won her first three matches without extending herself. In the semi-final she met one of the most stunning girls who has ever graced American sports, cool, blonde Edith Cummings. "She has Marilyn Miller and Julia Sanderson beaten a mile for sheer beauty," raved one smitten writer. Edith could also play golf. In match play she was

IN 1922, 19-YEAR-OLD GLENNA COLLETT WON HER FIRST U.S. WOMEN'S CHAMPIONSHIP AT THE GREENBRIER CLUB. OPPOSITE, SHE PUTTS OUT ON THE 9TH HOLE OF HER SEMI-FINAL MATCH WITH EDITH CUMMINGS.

cocky and aggressive, and played hard to win. In her match with Glenna, Edith picked up three holes on the out-nine but had to give them back one by one as Glenna fought back. The two were all even coming to the seventeenth. Edith found the rough with her drive on that hole, and

dering her drives twenty-five to fifty yards farther than her opponent, built up a 6-hole lead at lunch. Mrs. Gavin played considerably better in the afternoon, but one hole was as much as she could win back, and the match was over on the fourteenth green. Glenna Collett, 5 and 4.

Glenna went 1 up. Glenna also won the short eighteenth when Edith was stymied, and was safely into the final.

The final against Mrs. W. A. Gavin was something of an anticlimax. Mrs. Gavin was an old-school woman golfer, a short-hitting control-player. Against Glenna, Mrs. Gavin couldn't find her groove, and Glenna, pow-

The new champion was undeniably attractive—a nice-looking brunette with an easy outdoor manner. Many of the women sports champions who had preceded Glenna had been fairly slim and feminine, but their charms had been successfully camouflaged by the apparel with which they were afflicted, and sports fans had chosen to remember the bulkier champions and to generalize that every woman athlete looked like Stanislaus Zbyszko. Glenna came along when a more liberal post-war attitude and the new emphasis on the country club had altered men's ideas about the place of women and women who played sports. If their wives and daughters turned out no worse than Glenna or the California tennis players — let them play. They would anyway.

The sports fans of the country began to follow Glenna. They liked a consistent winner, and Glenna was that. In 1923 she won the North and South and the Eastern again, and defeated her girlhood idol, Alexa Stirling, in adding the Canadian Championship. In 1924 she won fifty-nine out of sixty matches! She was a thrillingly long hitter for a woman; she once belted a tee shot 307 yards. And that manner! In a match she was businesslike and capable. She threw no tantrums and had no affectations. In addition, she possessed a good sense of humor and a superb social instinct. Mention Glenna Collett to any reporter who covered her matches and he smiles as he sighs, "Glenna. . . Now there was a real girl."

Through their interest in Glenna, Americans became acquainted with the other women who were playing tournament golf, and a very good group they were: Edith Cummings, from Lake Forest, Illinois, who provided the photographers with a field day when she won the national title in '23; Marion Hollins, champion in 1921, a course promoter, and a talented all-round sportswoman; Alexa Stirling, of course; Ada Mackenzie, a gritty competitor from Toronto; Bernice Wall, a pretty girl from Oshkosh who could putt; Edith Quier, the nicest sort of an aristocrat, from Philadelphia, like so many other top-ranking women golfers; Miriam Burns, who as Mrs. Horn became the first divorcée to win the title and was, by any name, the woman with the most sex appeal in the judgment of the galleries. In the later years of Glenna's rule, the ranks were augmented by many other good golfers — Helen Payson, Glenna's sidekick, a tall blonde from Maine; golf's hard-luck girl, Maureen Orcutt, who could win everything but the national championship; Mrs. Leona Pressler (later Cheney), from the West Coast, and Mrs. Opal Hill of Kansas City, who took up the game at thirty on the advice of her physician; Peggy Wattles, a child star from Buffalo, and petite Virginia Wilson, from Onwentsia, who was an expert horsewoman; long-hitting Helen Hicks, the first champion to turn pro; Glenna's successor as our top woman player, Virginia Van Wie, a fine-looking swinger who had been too sickly to attend school and was a walking advertisement for the wonders worked by the outdoor life.

ALEXA STIRLING, OPPOSITE, WON THREE CONSECUTIVE U.S. WOMEN'S TITLES BETWEEN 1916 AND 1920. IN 1923, WHEN THIS PHOTOGRAPH WAS TAKEN, SHE LOST IN THE FINALS TO EDITH CUMMINGS.

The public came to know the old champions who were still active, like Mrs. Clarence Vanderbeck, Mrs. Caleb Fox, over sixty and the grandmother of ten, and the great Dorothy Campbell Hurd, who had earlier dominated international golf as authoritatively as Glenna did American golf in the Twenties. A native of North Berwick, Scotland, Mrs. Hurd, as Dorothy Campbell, had extended her rule from Scottish golf to British golf and then to American golf as well. She had won the national championship for the first time in 1909 and repeated the following year when she also took the first of her several Canadian titles. After her marriage in 1913 to J. B. Hurd of Pittsburgh (and Oakmont), Mrs. Hurd went into semi-retirement. When she returned to the tournament whirl in the Twenties, she recognized that her old sweeping style, with the club held in the palms and the wrists stiff, was obsolete. She went to George Sayers, an old townie of hers from North Berwick, then a Philadelphia pro, and changed over to the Vardon grip and a semi-modern swing. In a very short time Mrs. Hurd was right up with the pacemakers again, mainly because she retained all the magic of her short game.

She chipped with "Thomas," a goose-neck mashie with a small face, and putted with "Stella" who had been with her since 1909. At the Augusta Country Club, in Georgia, thanks to Thomas (who chipped in twice) and Stella (who couldn't miss anything), Mrs. Hurd used only 19 putts on eighteen holes, lowering by two strokes Walter Travis' record for putts-in-one-round.

Glenna was the outstanding woman golfer during 1923 and 1924, but in neither year did she win the U.S. Women's Championship. In '23 Mrs. Vanderbeck eliminated her in the third round; Glenna played erratically over the first eleven holes, went 4 down, and the run of pars she finally unleashed did not worry an experienced campaigner like Mrs. Vanderbeck. (Edith Cummings beat Mrs. Vanderbeck in the semis and Alexa Stirling in the final.) In '24 Glenna was apparently on her way to the championship—she hadn't lost a match all year—when Mary K. Browne upset her in the semis. Mary was better known as a tennis player. She had won the United States Women's Singles Championship three times, and only two weeks before the 1924 national golf championship, Mary had made her way to the semi-finals at Forest Hills and given Helen Wills a real battle before going down 6–4, 4–6, 6–3. Mary had been one of Glenna's childhood idols,

and it was a big moment in that hero-worshipper's life when some friends had introduced her to Mary at Forest Hills after the Wills–Browne match. The knowledge that it was Mary K. Browne whom she had to beat bothered Glenna throughout their match. Glenna started slowly and found herself thinking more about Mary's game than her own. Down the stretch, though, Glenna did gain a one-hole lead, and that looked to be a safe margin when Mary's drive on the eighteenth rolled into a thick tangle of rough. Mary, however, was not conceding defeat. She went after the ball with her brassie and succeeded in slashing it to the vicinity of the green, where it caromed off the bough of an apple tree and bounced to within fifteen feet of the cup. Mary squared the match and forced it into extra holes. On the 19th, both women lay three on the edge of the green, Mary on the front, Glenna on the back, a few feet farther away. Glenna almost holed her fourth but it died on the edge of the cup. Mary stroked her fourth carefully. For a moment it seemed as though the putt had the perfect line but then it began to veer off the slightest bit, toward Glenna's ball. *Click!* It kissed off Glenna's ball and ricocheted into the cup.

Mary Kimball Browne lost to Mrs. Hurd the next day, but in reaching the semi-final round of the national tennis championship and the final round of the national golf championship *in the same year*

DURING THE SUMMER OF 1924, MARY K. BROWNE, OPPOSITE, MADE SPORTS HISTORY: SHE WENT TO THE SEMI-FINALS OF U.S. WOMEN'S CHAMPIONSHIPS IN TWO SPORTS — GOLF AND TENNIS.

she had displayed an athletic virtuosity that has never been equaled. Many other tennis stars—René Lacoste, Vincent Richards, Ellsworth Vines, Althea Gibson, to name just a few—have turned to golf and attempted to duplicate their success on the courts. Their splendid coordination and battle-born competitive temperaments helped them to become skillful golfers in one-fifth the time it took the average novice to become mediocre, and yet they never developed into cham- pion golfers. Striking a stationary ball with a club from a stationary stance calls for a different genius for timing than stroking a moving ball with a racket. Ellsworth Vines manufactured himself into one of the nation's

top fifteen pros and was capable of winning a major championship, but Vines' shots on the golf course somehow seemed to lack the authenticity with which he struck a tennis ball.

In 1925 Glenna fulfilled Walter Hagen's definition of a true champion: a person who is able to win a national championship more than once. Previous to reclaiming the U.S. Women's title at the St. Louis Country

Club in early October, Glenna campaigned in Europe, and rather successfully for the most part, since she won the French Championship at La Boulie and made Joyce Wethered play magnificent golf to oust her from the British Ladies' Champi- onship. Glenna and Joyce met in the third round at Troon. For nine holes Glenna managed to stay on even terms with the great English stylist. As a matter of fact,

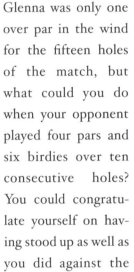

Glenna was only one over par in the wind for the fifteen holes of the match, but what could you do when your opponent played four pars and six birdies over ten consecutive holes? You could congratu- late yourself on hav- ing stood up as well as you did against the most correct and the loveliest swing golf had ever known, and thank your lucky stars that there was only one Joyce Wethered and that she lived in England.

Glenna had two close calls at St. Louis. After qualifying with a 78 (a stroke higher than Alexa Stirling Fraser) and having no trouble with Mrs. Caleb Fox in her first-round match, Glenna met the always-dangerous Canadian, Ada Mackenzie. A rain-storm saved Glenna. Ada had a two-hole lead on the fourteenth tee and was going well when the rain came. Glenna was wearing spikes, but Ada preferred rubber-soled shoes on a dry course and, not expecting a shower, had left her spikes in her locker. She sent someone to the clubhouse to fetch them but by the time he caught up with the players on

A review of the scoring at St. Louis helps to explain why women golfers were now viewed with respect, and occasionally with awe. The eighty-five entrants there played better golf than 99 percent of Amer-

the seventeenth, Ada, handicapped to some degree by the slippery footing, had lost three holes in a row and, as it turned out, the match. Glenna took Fritzi Stifel 3 and 2 in the third round, but in the semi-final against her favorite rival, Edith Cummings, Glenna had all she could do to pull out another 1-up victory. The final against Alexa Fraser saw Glenna in an invincible mood. She played a superb 77 in the morning and maintained that pace through the 28th green, when the holes ran out for Alexa—9 and 8. The girls decided to play out the bye holes, and Glenna finished the round in 75.

ican male golfers. They had come a long way since Mrs. C. S. Brown had won the first championship meeting at Meadow Brook in 1895 with 132 for eighteen holes, only twenty strokes less than Glenna had compiled over thirty-six in the final against Mrs. Fraser. Limiting the comparative figures to the previous decade underlined the women's improvement almost as effectively. In the 1915 championship, more than half of the qualifiers had failed to break 100, and Mrs. Vanderbeck had won the medal with an 85. Ten years later, nine qualifiers carded 85 or lower, Mrs. Fraser cracked all records with a 77, and three women who played 93s failed to get into the match play. After the qualifying round at St. Louis, the quality of play grew even better. There is nothing degrading about an 85, but if that was the best a player could score at St. Louis, she lost her match. Glenna, for example, was carried to the home green in two matches, and yet her average score for her seven completed rounds was 78. Her performance at St. Louis was the finest golf that had ever been played by an American woman. (It would not be irrelevant to bring out that the women frequently played much tougher and longer courses at this period than in later years, when the women's professional golf circuit sought to encourage low scoring by holding its tournaments on short, hazardless layouts.)

Again there was a two-year hiatus for Glenna between titles. Little Virginia Wilson ousted her in the semis at Merion in '26, the year Mrs. G. Henry Stetson, nervously followed by two daughters who towered above her, defeated another matron, Mrs. Wright D. Goss, in the final. In '27, Miriam Burns Horn's year, Alexa Fraser defeated Glenna 2 and 1 when they met in the second round. (Perhaps the seeding was faulty, but by 1927, with so many playing so well, placing thirty-two stars

with malice toward none had become a tough proposition.) Glenna won her third crown the next year on the Cascades course at Hot Springs, Virginia (13 and 12 over Gino Van Wie), repeated at Oakland Hills in '29 (4 and 3 over Leona Pressler), and in 1930 became the first modern golfer to win an American championship in three consecutive years when she beat Gino again, 6 and 5 this time, at the Los Angeles Country Club. Glenna took three more cracks at the British Ladies' crown. In 1927 Mabel Wragg defeated her in the fourth round. At St. Andrews in 1929 she bowed in the final to Joyce Wethered after a titanic seesaw struggle in which both champions shot sensational golf. Glenna played the first eleven holes in 41 strokes and at one time had a 5-up lead, but she could not hold it against Joyce's furious counter-charge. The following year, when Joyce did not defend, Glenna's chances appeared very favorable, and particularly so after she had edged by the formidable Enid Wilson in the semi-finals, but in the final she was upset by young Diana Fishwick. It remained for the phenomenal Babe Didrikson Zaharias to wrest this last championship away from the British some seventeen years later.

In 1931 Glenna married Edwin H. Vare, Jr., of Philadelphia. With her new responsibilities

In the 1928 U.S. Women's Championship at the Cascades course, Hot Springs, Virginia, Glenna Collett defeated a perennial rival, Virginia van Wie, by the lopsided match-play score of 13 and 12; in the photograph opposite, Collett putts on the 4th green.

demanding more of her attention, Glenna played less competitive golf than before, but she did make her way to the semi-finals one year and twice to the finals the three times she entered the championship. And then in 1935 at Interlachen, Glenna, now the mother of two children, came back to defeat the newest meteor, Patty Berg, and to win her sixth and last national title.

Glenna's popularity with her friends, her colleagues, and the public was achieved in an era when the art of public relations was in its comparative gutta-percha period. The

reasons why she cut ice with everyone, not just with one class or group or set or sex, were extremely simple ones: first, she was a beautifully consistent performer, a repeating champion; secondly, her attitude toward sport tallied exactly with the general conception of how an American girl should go about a career in sport. Glenna was popular with men, naturally. Any girl would have been, if she were good-looking and intelligent, able to smash a wood to the green like no other woman, and gifted with a conquering graciousness. She had a fine sense of humor at her own expense, she added verve to a party with her high spirits, and she was that very rare thing, a good winner.

STRIDING FROM THE 1ST TEE OF THE OLD COURSE, ST. ANDREWS, FOR THE 36-HOLE FINAL OF THE 1929 BRITISH LADIES' CHAMPIONSHIP ARE TWO IMMORTALS: AMERICAN GLENNA COLLET, SECOND FROM LEFT, AND, NEXT TO HER, BRITISH CHAMPION JOYCE WETHERED. THE TITANIC STRUGGLE, WHICH WETHERED WON ON THE 35TH HOLE, WAS CALLED THE GREATEST WOMEN'S MATCH OF ALL TIME.

They Also Played—Superbly

APART from the man who gave his name to the era, a score or more of unusually talented golfers flourished in the Age of Bobby Jones. Some, like Jock Hutchison and Jim Barnes, had seen their best days. Others, like Denny Shute and Johnny Goodman, were only starting out and would come into their own after Jones' retirement. Hagen and Sarazen and Ouimet, who had won championships before Bobby arrived, would win championships after Bobby had gone. There was also a considerable group of players whose peak years coincided too perfectly with Jones' to allow them to grab much more than the crumbs he left on the table, although they possessed the equipment to have become champions, and sometimes multiple champions, had there been no Jones in the Age of Bobby Jones.

Jones and the indomitable Walter Hagen did such a thorough job of dovetailing in the British Open that in only one year between 1924 and 1930 was another golfer able to break through their joint monopoly. That was Jim Barnes, the Cornishman who had moved to America years before; he won at

Prestwick in '25, a year neither Hagen nor Jones was entered. It was a curious victory all around. Jim was well past his prime when he won. His scoring was very high, even for a British Open; after an opening 70, he fell off to 77, 79, 74. What Jim actually did was slip in through the back door in a tournament that seemed like Macdonald Smith's from the second round on.

Old Mac had started off with a 76, but had vaulted into the van at the halfway mark with a beautifully played 69. It looked as if Mac's years of coming close were at long last to be terminated, and on the last day every Scot who could get there poured onto the course at Prestwick to watch the Old Carnoustie lad in his hour of triumph. Mac's 76 in the third round could have been several strokes lower with any luck on the greens, but it did give him a five-stroke lead on Barnes, the closest man, and that was, after all, what counted. Barnes had brought in a final 74 just as Smith was starting out on his last eighteen, and so Mac knew exactly what he needed: a 79 would tie, a 78 would win—and a 78 for a golfer like Mac Smith was as simple as stirring sugar.

That afternoon one of the most tragic chapters in the history of championship golf was written. Too intent on not being careless, Smith began to overstudy his shots and fussed away one stroke after another until he had used up 42 of them on the first nine. His enormous, all-too-devoted gallery, swarming over a course that was not made for galleries, pressed in closer on their hero, reassuring him that they knew he could play back in even 4s, completely forgetting their usually instinctive regard for a player's feeling because they wanted so much for Mac to win. They killed old Mac with their ardor. Whatever chance he might have had for coming home in 36 was smashed in the unruly rush of the unmanageable thousands, strangling the pace he wanted to play at, forcing him to wait ten minutes and more before playing a shot until they had filed across the narrow foot bridges and pounded through the bunkers ahead and grudgingly opened an avenue to the greens. Despairing but impotent, Macdonald Smith played out his nightmare of a round, posted his 82, and then, all too late, was finally left alone.

From 1910 to the mid-1930s, Scottish-born pro Macdonald Smith, seen above with his Scottie dog aboard a transatlantic Cunard liner in 1931, won 35 titles but never a major championship. In the 1925 British Open at Prestwick, Smith squandered a five-stroke lead on the final day to allow Jim Barnes, shown putting opposite, to steal the event.

The one other American victory in a British championship was Jess Sweetser's in the 1926 Amateur, a triumph that was notable not only in that Sweetser was the first American-born golfer to capture that reluctant title but also in the intense personal drama that accompanied the breakthrough.

Jess Sweetser may have been the best American amateur, Jones always excepted, in the early and middle Twenties. While an undergraduate at Yale—where he had run the quarter mile in a shade over fifty seconds—this broad-shouldered, powerful, frigidly aggressive young man from Siwanoy had taken the U.S. Amateur in 1922 at Brookline, defeating Jones and three ex-champions with the most dynamic golf ever exploded in the tournament. He was on the threshold of repeating his victory the next year when Max Marston, benefitting from the second of two stymies, ended a nerve-racking final on the 38th green. Jess was justly celebrated for his match-play temperament. When he opened up a lead on an opponent, he played with the unsocial determination that most players can capture only when they are behind. Splitting the fairways with his three-quarter-swing drives, punching his spade-mashie and his versatile 4-iron close to the pins, he never gave his opponents a chance to recover their balance. Even when he had a match all wrapped up, Jess would stride pugnaciously to his next shot tossing his jaw from one side to the other in an audible fight talk. In between fight talks he hummed popular songs to himself when he discovered by experimentation that this exercise took up

his mind and relaxed him and that he played well. Galleries admired rather than liked Sweetser. They attributed his great match-play record to his killer instinct, but Jess always believed that a considerable share of the credit for his temerity and his success rested on the warmup regimen arranged for him ten days or so before the big championships by Tommy Kerrigan, the pro at Siwanoy. Kerrigan would get two other New York area pros, say Sarazen and Farrell, to fill out the group, and Jess would play several matches against them at Quaker Ridge, Wykagyl, and other nearby courses. When he found that he could hold

his own with these stars, a tremendous confidence would come over Jess as he headed for the amateur tourneys. He knew that no one played better than these pros, and since he could stick with them, he could stick with any amateur. He was like the fighter who trains with extra-heavy gloves and weighted shoes before a bout and then goes into the fray feeling that his arms are as light as feathers in the regulation gloves, his legs full of drive in the lighter shoes.

The odd thing was that Jess, the strong boy, won his British Amateur crown when his body was wracked with flu, and incipient tuberculosis. No man has ever won a major athletic contest in poorer health. It was quite a saga of courage.

Jess had married in February of '26. Happiness and regular meals at home plus a modicum of golf had put some extra pounds on him. He planned to work them off by exercising in the gym aboard the ship that was carrying the Walker Cup team to Britain. Sweating pleasantly after one workout, Jess decided to take a dip in the pool . . . and his miseries began. His sinuses began to kick up, and he spent the rest of the passage stretched out on a deck chair, hoping that he would snap back once he was on land again. He didn't. In the raw air of early spring in England and Scotland, his cold was aggravated into an enervating flu. At Muirfield, where the American team was entered in the British Amateur previous to the Cup Match at St. Andrews, Jess got in only two practice rounds and stayed in his room the remainder of the time trying to nurse himself back into shape. He felt so rotten on the morning he was scheduled for his first-round match that, much as he wanted to play in the championship, he felt that there was no other course than to default. He stayed in the tournament only because his opponent chose to default before Jess did. After lunch—there were times during the tournament when Jess could hold hardly more than orange juice—he forced himself to go out and play his second-round match. He managed to win and staggered wearily into the clubhouse.

Day after day it was the same story. A masseur from Edinburgh, contacted by Henry Lapham of the American party, would work up Jess' circulation before he went out against his morning opponent. At lunch Jess would drink fruit juices and try a slice or two of beef, and push himself out to the tee for his afternoon match. He did no partying in the evening—took a hot bath and went straight to bed. His attitude was good. He wasn't expecting to win and he didn't worry when it took him six or seven holes to warm up. He kept hitting his shots, and eventually he caught and passed his opponents, although quite a few of Jess' matches went to the eighteenth hole. He defeated Ouimet on the eighteenth by pumping a beautiful second shot through the mist to the green. Against Robert Scott, he played another clinching approach on the home hole, toeing in his favorite 4-iron and punching it low and hard. Jess didn't have the energy at Muirfield to goad himself on with fight talks, but he hummed to himself as he went along, usually "Somebody Loves Me." He kept on winning.

In the semi-final round Jess came up against the Honorable W. G. Brownlow (later Lord Lurgan), a good golfer albeit a chap of weird sartorial tastes. Brownlow played in a small peaked cap, a long clerk's

A COURAGEOUS JESS SWEETSER OVERCAME SEVERE FLU AND THE HAZARDS HE ENCOUNTERED ON THE LINKS COURSE AT MUIRFIELD, SCOTLAND, OPPOSITE, TO WIN THE 1926 BRITISH AMATEUR TITLE.

coat, and black silk gloves. Jess, for once, started fast and picked up two holes on Brownlow early in the match, but he could make no further headway against his opponent's neat if not spectacular golf. On the seventeenth, however, this two-hole margin became dormie for Jess, and the match looked as good as over when he laid his third twelve feet from the pin with Brownlow forty-five rolling feet away in the same number of strokes. The game young Irish dandy had been putting, and putting well, with an orthodox blade putter. Now, as he eyed his long route to the cup, he switched to a wide-soled, wooden-headed Gassiat model and proceeded to hole his cross-country putt. Jess then missed his, but was still dormie one with the home hole coming cup. Once again Jess played the eighteenth perfectly. He was nicely inside Brownlow on the green, eighteen feet away to his opponent's thirty-five. His half seemed certain. And then the incredible Brownlow took his Gassiat in his black silk gloves and sent his ball trickling over the subtle rolls of the home green and into the very center of the cup. Jess made a courageous try for his putt but it slid by the rim of the cup.

By this time the match had taken on an unreal atmosphere, Jess exhausted by the sudden turn of events, Brownlow unnaturally serene, both of them perform-

J. SWEETSER

ing as if they were caught in the webbing of a dream. On the first extra hole, Brownlow had a big opening when Jess found a trap on his second, but Brownlow misfired with his Gassiat, taking three from twenty-five feet after slipping fifteen feet by on his first. On the 20th Jess went ten feet past the cup on his approach putt but Brownlow, timorous after his error on the 19th, fell nine feet short on his. Jess knocked in his 10-footer, and Brownlow stepped up and coolly holed his 9-footer. On the 21st tee the young Irishman finally cracked. He looked up badly on his drive. Jess smashed his two hundred and sixty yards down the fairway, and his faultless approach closed out the dramatic duel between two dead-game golfers.

The final between Jess and Archie Simpson, an East Coast Scotsman, was bound to be a letdown after the Sweetser-Brownlow match. Simpson didn't play nearly as well as he had against Andrew Jamieson in the semi-finals, and Jess won 7 and 6 after a dull match in which the outcome was never in doubt.

Jess' condition became worse after he was driven to St. Andrews on a very cold day. He asked to play and managed to win both his singles and foursome in the Walker Cup Match with a continuation of his impeccable golf, and then suffered a severe chest hemorrhage. Jess pleaded with the doctors to let him sail—he was frightened that he might not get home alive—and the doctors at length gave in. They shot him full of heroin and gave O. B. Keeler instructions on how to inject the drug if Jess suffered a relapse on board ship. Jess did have one more hemorrhage, but the heroin kept him going . . . . He reached home so utterly shattered that only after a full year of convalescence at Asheville did he begin to look and feel like the Jess Sweetser of old.

The one U.S. Open that Jones had nothing to say about was the 1927 event. Five good golfers came down the final nine at Oakmont with an equal opportunity to lead the field—Emmett French, Gene Sarazen, Bill Mehlhorn, Harry Cooper, and Tommy Armour. Oakmont licked three of them—French, Sarazen, and Mehlhorn. Harry Cooper licked one of them, Harry Cooper, when he three-putted the 71st from eight feet. One man licked Oakmont—Tommy Armour. After taking a 7 on the famous twelfth, the 66th hole of the tournament, Armour had to play the last six holes in 2 under par to tie with Cooper, and did this by cracking a 3-iron ten feet from the pin on the 72nd and holing his putt. In 1927 neither Harry nor Tommy Armour had earned the reputations by which we think of them today. It was the first time in the spotlight for both of them—Cooper, the brilliant consistent golfer who could never win a

major crown: Armour, the brilliant inconsistent golfer who at one time or another won the U.S. and British Opens and the P.G.A., the three big professional championships, as well as the Western, three Canadians, and his share of the non-prestige tourneys. Cooper was just a kid then, a twenty-three-year-old naturalized Texan of English descent who played his shots without a moment's hesitation and walked so rapidly between shots that he came into the sobriquet of "Light Horse Harry." As for Armour, he had turned professional after coming to the States in the early 1920s as an unheralded amateur. Tommy had lost the sight of one eye during World War I, and in his left shoulder he carried several mementos of his front-line service—eight pieces of shrapnel. Armour was reputed to have been the fastest man with a machine gun in the entire Tank Corps, and his fine, strong fingers and his superlative coordination of hand and eye were helping him to come to the forefront in his peacetime profession. The long irons he drilled to the pins at Oakmont nailed down once and for all the reputation Tommy had gradually been acquiring as one of the very best iron players in the business.

In the playoff Armour came from behind to win. He caught the Light Horse with a 50-foot putt for a 4 on the fifteenth and went in front by two strokes on the 226-yard sixteenth when Cooper shot boldly for the pin and caught a guarding bunker. Cooper stuck his approach to the seventeenth a foot and a half from the cup, and then the nerveless Armour showed his mettle by dropping his approach eight inches inside of Cooper's. That was the championship.

The 1927 U.S. Open probably decided more championships than just the 1927 U.S. Open. Had Harry Cooper not three-putted the 71st green, he would have galloped through to victory in his first real chance in a major championship and that might have been all that magnificent shot-maker need-ed to have become several-times-a-champi-on in name as well as in ability. Tommy Armour, on the other hand, would have probably broken through in some other year had he been repulsed at Oakmont. When-ever the Silver Scot played himself into a contending position, he always seemed to have that extra something that was the difference between barely losing and barely winning. He was singularly unaffected by the pressure of the last stretch. His hands were hot but his head was cool—one of the accidental rewards that only too rarely catch up with a war hero.

The one championship in which Jones could not play, the P.G.A., became Walter Hagen's personal tournament, the way the Amateur was Bobby's. Walter took the P.G.A. in 1921 and then in '24, '25, '26, and '27, winning twenty consecutive matches from the most talented players in the country. Some of Walter's victories were normally wrought: he outthought and outplayed his man. But an alarming number of Hagen's victories came in matches he should have lost and would have lost if that certain something in Walter's personality had not defeated his opponent for Walter. A few centuries before and he would have been burned as a disciple of the devil.

The manner in which Hagen won the 1927 P.G.A. was in character. He was 4 down to Johnny Farrell at lunch—Farrell could eat none—but won five of the first nine holes in the afternoon. Hagen, 3 and 2. Against Tony Manero, who had putted Bobby Cruickshank out of the tourna-ment, Walter put on an exhibition of green play that stampeded the young man. Hagen, 11 and 10. Armour was a different proposition. Walter played under wraps, just well enough to keep close to Tommy but giving the impression that he was far off-form that day and that no one would have to hurry to beat him. Then The Haig stuck his nose out in front and strategically poured on the pressure now that he had Armour down. Hagen, 4 and 3. Next it was Al Espinosa. Hagen played poorly and he wasn't fooling. He was 1 down with one to play, and all Espinosa had to do to win was

TOMMY ARMOUR, OPPOSITE, SANK THIS TEN-FOOT PUTT ON THE 72ND HOLE AT THE OAKMONT COURSE NEAR PITTSBURGH TO TIE HARRY COOPER, SEATED AT THE RIGHT EDGE OF THE GREEN, DURING THE 1927 U.S. OPEN. ARMOUR WON THE 18-HOLE PLAYOFF THE FOLLOWING DAY BY THREE STROKES.

sink a yard putt on the 36th green. Hagen, I up in extra holes. The opposing finalist was Joe Turnesa. Joe was 2 up at lunch, 3 up after the first hole in the afternoon, playing with confidence and smoothness. Hagen, I up.

The Twenties produced some remarkable bursts of scoring, though, like today, most of the sacrilegious sixties were fashioned in tournaments other than the major championships.

There were the brilliant rounds: Hagen's 62 at Belleair in the West Florida Championship . . . Virginia Van Wie's 74 at

Ormond Beach . . . Leo Diegel's 65 on a bitter cold day at Moortown in 1929 in the second Ryder Cup Match . . . The two 66s young Horton Smith, the Joplin Ghost, put together in winning the French Open that year . . . The 66 Mac Smith played in the *third* playoff for the Metropolitan in 1926 after he and Sarazen had matched 70s and 72s in the first overtime stretches . . . Watts Gunn's 71 at Oakmont, and that 69 by Watrous at Lytham . . . A 67 and a 68 by George Voigt in consecutive rounds on long, tree-lined Pinehurst #2 . . . Miriam Burns Horn's 74 at Pebble Beach . . . That final round of 63 which won the $15,000 LaGorce Open for Johnny Farrell . . . Hagen's 59 on a short resort course in

Switzerland . . . Harry Cooper's 60 on a course measuring 6,100 yards.

There were the torrid patches: Francis Ouimet's gallant finish at St. Andrews in his Walker Cup match in '23 with Roger Wethered, a 3-4-3 against a par of 4-5-4, which enabled Francis to halve with Roger after he had seemed hopelessly beaten standing on the 34th tee, 2 down and three to play . . . Watts Gunn at Oakmont in his first Amateur, taking one hole after another in his first-round match until he had made it fifteen holes in a row and could go on no farther since the match was over . . . The comeback by Roland MacKenzie, the teenage protégé of Freddy McLeod's, against George Von Elm in the Amateur of '24. Roland refused to quit when he was 8 down at the 23rd, kept plugging until he had cut away the last hole of Von Elm's lead on the 35th, and then had to go and lose the 37th . . . Al Espinosa's 22 for the last six in the 1929 Open when he had resigned himself to losing . . . Glenna against Mrs. Harley Higbie in the '29 Women's. Four down with four to go, Glenna swept the last four and then won on the 19th . . . Willie Macfarlane's 33 against Bobby on the last nine at Worcester, featuring two beautiful deuces . . . Diegel's informal 29 at Columbia when he was betting that he could break 30 . . .

ABE MITCHELL.

Willie Klein's out-of-this-world finish in the Shawnee Open of '25. The young assistant pro from Garden City needed a 29 on the last nine to tie for first place, and played in 3-4-2 4-4-3 3-4-2 — 29.

There were the bright flashes of form for the duration of a tournament: Armour's 273 at Ozaukee in the Western, and Diegel's 274 at Shreveport . . . Mac Smith's duplicate rounds of 35-35 — 70 over Charlie Macdonald's hazardous Lido course in a sectional qualifying round for the Open . . . Seventy-two easy, even holes by Billy Burke at Clearwater in '27, the first indication that the ex-iron molder from Naugatuck might have a champion's game . . . Old Abe Mitchell's victory in the Seminole Open (and the Englishman's relish for the sound of his new title) . . . Gene's 277 at Miami Beach and Walter's 275 at Wolf Hollow . . . Cooper's last-round 67 for a 279 in the Los Angeles Open . . . Leo's 65 for 274 in the Canadian, which he felt should have been lower.

And the streaks that carried through several tournaments: Walter's average of 70.5 for twenty-four rounds in the grapefruit belt in 1923 . . . The winter rush the next year by Joe Kirkwood when the Australian couldn't hit a crooked shot and carried off the Opens at San Antonio, Houston, Corpus Christi, and New Orleans . . . Mac Smith, elegant

Mac Smith, playing consecutive tournament rounds of 68, 70, 70, 73, 70, 70, 70, 70, 71, 69, 71, 70, 70, 68, 73 . . . Johnny Farrell's spring harvest in '27—the Met, the Shawnee, the Eastern, the Massachusetts, the Pennsylvania, the Philadelphia . . . Mehlhorn, not listed as potential Ryder Cup material for 1929, confounding the selectors by adding a 277 in the Texas Open to his 271 in the El Paso Open, piling up two 66s, two 67s, a 68, and a 69 in the course of eight rounds . . . Horton Smith's sensational debut in the bigtime on the winter circuit of '29. In winning seven tourneys and running-up in four, the handsome twenty-year-older cleaned up a record $14,000-plus.

And there were the great moments, the unforgettable pictures: Jimmy Johnston on the white sand at Pebble Beach, waiting for the waves to ebb so that he could play his recovery to the green . . . Chandler Egan at the same tournament, hitting the ball sharper than a quarter of a century before when he had twice won the Amateur . . . The heartbreaking collapse by Roland Hancock on the last two holes of the Open at Olympia. Young Hancock needed only to play a par and one-over-par, two 5s or a 4 and a 6, to edge out Jones and Farrell. He took two 6s, and never again came close . . . The passing of Walter J. Travis. In his last years the Old Man, the first great American champion, allowed his beard to grow again; no longer was it the black frame that went so well in 1900 with the Old Man's menacing eye; it was

white—as white as the dunes at Sandwich . . . That lesser oldtimer, Sandy Herd, was still going strong. At fifty-eight he captured the British equivalent of the P.G.A. . . . There was frail Cyril Walker playing the 72nd at Oakland Hills in a safe, smart 5 as Tet nodded her head . . . And Wiffy Cox, Brooklyn's leading pro, erupting on the greens with the choice epithets he had assimilated when he served as a fireman on the U.S.S. *Nevada* . . . Glenna buttonholing the experts and seriously asking them how she could get over being "social rather than savage" in her matches . . . Stewart Maiden rushing from Atlanta to Worcester in '25 on the eve of the Open, answering an urgent call for help from an out-of-the-groove Jones. Stewart watched Bobby hit out two batches of practice balls without saying a word, dourly sniffed, "Why don't you try hitting the ball with your backswing?," and walked away . . . Carl F. Kauffmann, "The Poor Man's Jones," who won three consecutive U.S.G.A.-sponsored Public Links Championships from '27 through '29 . . . The to-do in Texas when the unpredictable Mehlhorn, perched high in a tree by the eighteenth green, needled Bobby Cruickshank as the little Scot was about to stroke a thousand-dollar putt . . . Johnny Goodman, a stout-hearted kid from Omaha, traveling by cattle car to New York on a drover's pass to play in the Open at Winged Foot . . . The ridiculous hue and cry after the 1923 Amateur that Max Marston stymied his opponents on purpose. The

alacrity of the newspapermen, many of whom Marston had antagonized by his lofty manner, in pointing out to the public that any golfer with skill enough to stymie an opponent could hole out with far less trouble . . . Oscar Baun Keeler shepherding Jones at every tournament, recording the feats of his hero in such faithful detail that the golfing literati began to refer to Boswell as Sam Johnson's Keeler . . . Mrs. Hagen pouncing on Walter after his roaring finish in the 1924 British Open, and their big open-air kiss. The mellow scene when Walter filled the old cup and Vardon, Braid, Taylor, and the other old giants all came up and lifted it to their lips . . .

And there was always Jones.

WHEN WALTER HAGEN, ABOVE, WON THE SECOND OF HIS FOUR BRITISH OPEN CROWNS IN 1924, HE RECEIVED THE CLARET JUG TROPHY AND, FROM MRS. HAGEN, AN OUTDOOR KISS THAT COULD HAVE BEEN STAGED BY A FILM DIRECTOR.

The Grand Slam

IN 1930 Bobby Jones won the British Amateur, the British Open, the United States Open, and the United States Amateur Championships. Jones' clean sweep of the four major titles—what George Trevor neatly termed "the impregnable quadrilateral"—was, of course, the crowning achievement of his career, and, very probably, the greatest exhibition of skill and character by any individual athlete, bar none, since the beginning of recorded sports history.

In the winter of 1930 as he conditioned himself for his annual campaign, Bobby Jones had no presentiment that he was embarking on a historic year. His feelings about his potential in any one tournament season were about the same as they had been in 1927 when, in collaboration with O. B. Keeler, he had published his autobiography, *Down the Fairway*. The chapter on 1926, when Bobby had won two major crowns for the first time, was entitled "The Biggest Year." He was overjoyed with having trounced the percentages in 1926 "because I'll never have another chance to win both the British and American Open Championships in the same year."

Bobby, however, was looking forward to 1930 with more than his usual enthusiasm. It was a year when the Walker Cup Match was scheduled to be played in Great

Britain, and this meant that after two years of strictly domestic activity, Bob would have another shot at the British events, and particularly the British Amateur, the one major championship that had eluded him. During the winter Bobby, who put weight on rather quickly, kept in trim by playing "Doug," a combination of tennis and badminton evolved by Douglas Fairbanks, who had sent his friend the paraphernalia. From the first day that he began his light workouts on the golf course, it was evident to everyone who watched him that, for one reason or another, Bobby had something that he had never had before. Noteworthy, too, was the fact that, departing from his habit of tuning up informally, he entered two minor tournaments, the Savannah Open and the Southeastern Open, held at Augusta. At Savannah Jones finished second with 279, a stroke behind Horton Smith, the winter wonder. But at Augusta, Jones' 72, 72, 69, 71 for 284 was not only tops but thirteen full strokes ahead of Horton, the runner-up. After taking in Bobby's display at Augusta, Grantland Rice, who had studied the Georgian closely over a long period of years, expressed the opinion that Jones was playing discernibly better golf than ever before, and Bobby Cruickshank exploded with an indecently accurate prediction: "He's simply too good. He'll go to Britain and win the Amateur and the Open, and then he'll come back over here and win the Open and the Amateur. He is playing too well to be stopped this year."

Never one to enthuse about his own game, Jones confided to his intimate friends that he felt much more confident than in any previous year, that he was hitting every shot in the bag. Even those little pitches between 50 and 125 yards that had frequently displeased him were behaving properly. Psychologically, as well, Bobby was fit. His strong showing against Espinosa in the playoff for the Open the year before had not by any means erased from his mind the near-disgrace of kicking away a six-stroke lead on the last six holes and leaving himself a 12-footer to tie. The memory of Winged Foot would be a salutary spur. He was also rid of that mental block about eighteen-hole matches. At Pebble Beach he had lost the one he had been frightened of losing for years, and now he could go into the British Amateur free from any defensive phobia.

In Britain, before the stars of two continents convened at St. Andrews for the Amateur, Jones shot some of his best stuff in the Walker Cup Match at Sandwich. Partnered with Doc Willing, he won his foursome 8 and 7 and took his singles from Roger Wethered 9 and 8. As the captain of the American team, Jones could have placed himself in the number-one singles spot, for which his record logically qualified him. It was typical of Jones that he awarded the honor of playing number one to Jimmy Johnston, the Amateur Champion, and dropped himself to the second slot . . . And then on to St. Andrews and the one championship he had never been able to win—the British Amateur.

Right off the reel Bobby walked into a match he could have easily lost. Syd Roper, an ex-coal miner from Nottinghamshire without a clipping to his name, played one 5 and fifteen 4s over the sixteen holes of his match with Jones. On the very first tee Bobby seemed to divine what was coming on, for he got right down to business and knocked in a 20-footer for a birdie 3. He added a 4 and a 3, and on the fourth he holed out a 150-yard spade-mashie from Cottage Bunker for an eagle 2. Bobby's 5-under-par burst for the first five holes gave him only a three-hole lead, and this was the extent of the impression he was able to make against the amazing Mr. Roper.

In the fourth round Jones came up against Cyril Tolley, the defending champion, and a bitter battle ensued. Tolley's topped drive off the first tee was about the one mistake the long-hitting Englishman made for eighteen holes. At no time was either player able to edge ahead by more than one hole. They were all even as they came to the seventeenth, the famous Road Hole, a dogleg to the right that ordinarily required two good woods to reach unless

the player elected to risk cutting the corner over Auchterlonie's drying sheds and carrying the deep out-of-bounds elbow. Neither Tolley nor Jones thought this was the day for flirting with the straight-line route. Both drove out safely to the left, Jones far to the left. The shot Bobby elected to play for his second was a high spoon, cut just a fraction so that it would hold after landing

CYRIL J. H. TOLLEY.

on the back edge of the green. It didn't quite come off. The ball carried the vicious Road Bunker that guards the entrance to the middle of the green from the left, but instead of plopping itself down obediently, it kicked up like a colt and might have run on into trouble had it not struck a spectator standing on the back fringe. With this timely assist from Fortune, Jones was able to get his 4, and he needed it, for Tolley pitched two feet from the cup after playing short of the green with an iron on his second. They halved the eighteenth in 4. The match moved into extra holes. Both got off the 19th tee well but Tolley clubbed his approach off-line and it cost him the match. His chip was not stone-dead and Bobby, putting up on his third, laid Tolley a stymie he was unable to negotiate. (The entire population of St. Andrews seemed to stream from the town onto the links whenever Jones was playing, and on the day of

THE **FIRST STOP** ON BOBBY JONES' 1930 CONQUEST OF GOLF'S FOUR MAJOR CHAMPIONSHIPS WAS
THE BRITISH AMATEUR, THIS PAGE AND OPPOSITE, OVER THE OLD COURSE, ST. ANDREWS. IN AN
EARLY 18-HOLE MATCH, JONES ENCOUNTERED HIS MOST DANGEROUS OPPONENT, DEFENDING
CHAMPION CYRIL TOLLEY, SEEN LINING UP HIS PUTT ABOVE. PREFERRING 36-HOLE MATCHES,
JONES NEEDED ALL HIS SKILL TO DEFEAT TOLLEY ON THE FIRST PLAYOFF HOLE.

the Jones–Tolley match the town was so deserted the novelist Gerald Fairlie selected that afternoon as the time when the villain in one of his mysteries committed murder in downtown St. Andrews and, though marked with the stains of his crime, was able to make his way unnoticed down the empty streets.)

Had it been Jones who had been confronted with jumping a stymie on the 19th to keep the match alive, there is every reason to believe that he would have done it successfully. A confirmed fatalist in his attitude toward golf tournaments, at St. Andrews Bobby was visited by the strange and wonderful feeling that he simply could not lose, whatever he did. After the Tolley match, in which Jones had been outplayed but had gotten the breaks, O. B. Keeler was beginning to share this queer sense of fatality, and as the tournament moved on and Bobby escaped from two more ferocious matches that could have gone either way, Keeler was convinced that some large and intangible Providence simply would countenance no other person's winning the 1930 British Amateur. It was an odd way, a very odd way, to feel about a golf tournament, but for Keeler there was no other explanation for the things that were taking place at St. Andrews. In several of Jones' matches a single bad shot at numerous junctures could have changed the entire picture, but as O. B. remarked, Bobby stood up to the shot and performed what was needed with all the certainty of a natural phenomenon.

By the semi-final round, the feeling that Jones' triumph was mystically inevitable had communicated itself to many of the spectators. When Jones was I down to George Voigt with only three holes to play, Sir James Lieshman, a Scottish fan, declared, "His [Jones'] luck is as fixed as the orbit of a planet. He cannot be beaten here." On the very next tee Voigt drove into a bunker and lost the hole.

The struggle with Voigt followed a distressingly close scrape in the sixth round with Jimmy Johnston. Jones was 4 up on Jimmy with five to play, but Johnston won two of the next three holes and took the Road as well. A win for him on the eighteenth would have forced the match into extra holes, and Jimmy came within a hair of doing it. Both players took precautions to hit their approaches firmly enough to carry the Valley of Sin, and both ended up on the very back edge of that huge green, Johnston about ninety feet away from the pin, Jones not much closer. Playing the odd, Johnston putted up beautifully, inches from the cup, for a sure 4. It was up to Bobby to get down in 2 to save the match. His first putt began to slow down as it took the final dip toward the hole and died eight feet short, leaving Jones with a nasty sidehiller. He holed it precisely, just as Von Elm and Ouimet, watching from the balcony of the Grand Hotel, knew he would.

In the semi-final, Voigt, playing the finest golf of his life, sticking his irons inside of Jones' and putting very well indeed, had accumulated a two-hole advantage as he and Bobby prepared to play the fourteenth. There is an old golf fable that the man who is 2 up with five holes to play will lose the match. More often than not, the fable folds, but it holds up just often enough to perpetuate itself. Voigt, 2 up with five to play, cut across his tee shot, and the strong wind blowing from left to right tossed it out-of-bounds. Jones played safely down the left and won the hole. The fifteenth was halved. Up first on the next tee, Jones, who knew St. Andrews as well as he knew East Lake, played his drive fifty yards to the left of the center of the fairway to make certain he avoided the bunkers. Voigt, aiming for that patch of fairway to the left of the Principal's Nose, once again underestimated the force of the

ROGER H. WETHERED.

cross-wind and was blown into the bunker. Jones' hole. Hauled back to even now, Voigt made a brave counter-charge on the seventeenth. After two splendid shots had carried him to the front edge of the green, George all but holed his approach putt. To halve Voigt's 4, Jones had to hole an 18-footer. The weird sensation that someone was taking care of him was never stronger than when Bobby bent over his ball. He felt that no matter how he hit it, the putt would go in. It did. On the home green Voigt

failed to get down his 6-footer for a par and Bobby had won the match from an opponent who had been 2 up with five to play.

Roger Wethered was Jones' opponent in the final and faced the hopeless task of staying with Jones when Bobby was in one of his most determined moods. There was only one moment during the match when Jones was not patently in command. On the very first hole, after his drive had set him up with the easiest of pitches, Bobby looked up on his shot and missed it so badly that it didn't even make the burn cutting across the fairway twenty yards ahead. He chipped up close with his third, went down in one putt for his 4, and took nothing over a 4 until he squandered a miraculous recovery from the Road Bunker on the seventeenth by muffing a 2-footer. He finished the morning round 4 up.

Francis Ouimet, who walked back to the Grand Hotel with Bobby at lunchtime, could not figure it out when Jones began pacing his room, obviously burned up about something.

"What in the world has got into you, Bobby?" Ouimet finally asked. "You're four up."

"Did you hear what that official said on the first tee?" Jones asked.

Francis thought a moment and then

remembered that before Jones had teed off, an official had remarked that in all the years that the greatest golfers in the world had been playing the Old Course, no one had ever succeeded in going around with nothing higher than a 4 on his card.

"... And I," Bobby said in disgust, "I had to go and miss a two-foot putt to be the first man ever to play St. Andrews without taking a five."

Bobby had turned an innocent conversational sally into a personal challenge. He had been playing St. Andrews rather than Wethered.

In the afternoon, the scent of victory, that long-awaited victory, was sufficient to insure a continuation of Bobby's aggressive play. The strain began to tell on Roger and he began missing the 4-footers. Jones added one hole and then another to his lead, and the match ran itself out on the 30th green. Then, fifteen thousand mad Scots, who had been waiting all week for this moment no less anxiously than Jones, converged on their idol. In the wild stampede Henry Lapham was knocked into a bunker and converted into a trestle; the crowd attacked the policemen guarding Jones with the fury of bobby-soxers; and the band that was to play the victor in was scattered in the mêlée; and played not a note. Keeler finally made his way to the side of the young man whom he had followed

for fourteen years through twenty-four championships. "Honestly, I don't care what happens now," Bobby smiled at O. B. "I'd rather have won this tournament than anything else in golf. I'm satisfied."

There was no mysterious presence walking hand in hand with Bobby Jones at Hoylake. Jones won the British Open by the normal expedient of bringing in the lowest four-round total in the field. He did it the hard way, as he had at Lytham in '26, outscoring through sheer stick-to-itiveness a handful of fine golfers who were on their game when Bobby was not. He was neat around the greens. He was lucky in playing his bad shots when they hurt him least, and he managed to pull off the best shots in his repertoire at the critical moments. St. Andrews had been touched with destiny. Hoylake was manual labor.

The understandable contentment he derived from his victory in the British Amateur made it hard for Jones to buckle down to belligerency as the date of the British Open approached. He had twice before won the British Open. Furthermore, he had no Grand Slam on his mind. Bobby was taking things easy, and his indifference brought back to Keeler the similarly flat frame of mind Bobby had acquiesced to

At the Royal Liverpool Golf Club, Hoylake, opposite, Jones won his second 1930 Grand Slam event, the British Open, a four-round medal-play tournament. Jones' score of 70,72,74,75=291 was good enough to defeat Macdonald Smith and Leo Diegel by two strokes.

when he was preparing for the United States Open at Oakmont in '27. Then, he had never been able to rouse himself and had floundered into his worst showing in a major tournament since he had first become a champion. The English critics had no Oakmont as a touchstone, but they noticed the letdown in Jones' attitude and in his game. He looked stale.

Once the practice and qualifying rounds were over and the championship proper was underway, a change came over Jones. His desire to win reasserted itself. It drove him to an opening round of 70 and a second round of 72, although his game remained as imprecise as it had been when Bobby hadn't cared. "I simply don't know where the darn ball is going when I hit it," he said impatiently to O. B. "I guess I'm trying to steer it, and of course that's the worst thing in the world to do. But what can I do? This is a tight course. You can't get up there and slam away and trust to freedom of action to take care of the shot. You simply have got to exercise some control of the ball. And it's the most hopeless job I've ever tackled. I've never worked so hard before." Jones' 74 in the third round began with a par on the first when he escaped a bunker by inches. He went 1 over on the second, and instead of getting that stroke back on the 480-yard third, an easy birdie hole, Bobby took a 6 and lost another stroke. Then he settled down and fought. 3-4-4-3-4-4 gave him a 37 for the out-nine, and 3-3-4-3 braced him for the killing finish at Hoylake, five holes averaging

457 yards. 5-5-5-5-4 was not too sharp—another 37 for a 74, which dropped him from first to a stroke behind the pacemaker, Archie Compston. Compston had led off with a devastating rush of 4-3-4-2 and completed as fine a round as has ever been shot at Hoylake in 68.

Jones set out on his last round fifty minutes before Compston was called to the tee. Bobby began with a par 4, and then on the 369-yard second sliced his drive hectically to the right. The swerving ball bounced wildly off the head of a steward and careened a full forty yards forward into a bunker off the fourteenth fairway. Considering where the drive would have ended up without the intervention of the petrified steward, it was an incalculably lucky break; Bobby was fifty yards off-line but only 140 yards from the green and lying well in the bunker. He stroked a pitch onto the center of the green, holed his 20-footer, and had come out of the hole with a birdie 3 when he would have settled for a 5. A short while after this had happened, Compston was striding across the first green full of confidence. A putt of eighteen inches would give Archie his regulation 4, an adequate opening for the bright round the rawboned giant felt was coming on. Compston tapped his wee putt, and, in almost the same motion, bent over to pick the ball out of the cup. It wasn't in the cup. It was still on the lip. Compston straightened himself up and stood staring at the ball, bewildered and unbelieving. He was never the same afterwards. His confidence had been cut away before he reached the second tee, and lurching like an injured vessel, he needed fourteen strokes more than he had taken in the morning to get around the same course. Nothing could snap Archie out of it, not even the early report that on the eighth, a 482-yard 5 that Jones was expected to birdie, Bobby had blown himself to a big 7. Just off the green in 2 with a prosaic chip up a bank to the green, Jones stubbed his chip short, was ten feet away on his fourth, slid a foot by on his fifth, and missed that 12-inch kick-in. Bobby's 38 meant nothing to the broken Compston, but the reports of this wobbly first nine filtered back to Diegel and Mac Smith and pricked up the ears of those two great hard-luck golfers.

Bobby battled his way home. Two 4s on the short holes didn't help. Then into that backbreaking final five. A 4 and a 5. So far, so good. A 4 on the 532-yard 70th, thanks to a great out from a trap by the green with the 25-ounce niblick Horton Smith had got for him. Another 4 and a final 4. A 37. A 75. It could have been worse, a great deal worse, but would it be good enough to win? Bobby relieved his exhaustion with a good stiff drink. He sat nervously in the clubhouse, using two hands to steady his glass, as he sweated out the news on Leo and Mac.

Diegel, two strokes off Bobby's pace at the 63rd, turned it on. He picked up a stroke on Bobby on the first short hole coming in, picked up another on the second short hole. He came to the 70th, tied

JONES' PERFORMANCE AT THE 1930 BRITISH OPEN AT HOYLAKE OVERSHADOWED THE PLAY OF HIGHLY REGARDED BRITISH PRO HENRY COTTON, RIGHT, TOP, WHO PLAYED WELL DURING QUALIFYING ROUNDS BUT FINISHED WELL BEHIND THE LEADERS. ABOVE, JONES RECEIVES THE TROPHY AND A HANDSHAKE FROM THE CAPTAIN OF THE ROYAL LIVERPOOL GOLF CLUB; IT WAS JONES' THIRD BRITISH OPEN WIN.

WINNER OF THE TWO 1930 BRITISH CHAMPIONSHIPS, JONES, AN AMATEUR PLAYER, NEEDED A WIN IN THE U.S. OPEN AGAINST THE PROFESSIONALS TO CONTINUE HIS GRAND SLAM ASPIRATIONS. JONES GOT IT AT INTERLACHEN, MINNESOTA, DEFEATING MACDONALD SMITH, LEFT, ABOVE, BY TWO STROKES. EARLIER IN THE WEEK, JONES POSED WITH FORMER BRITISH OPEN WINNER JOCK HUTCHISON, OPPOSITE.

with Jones. Throwing every ounce of his power into his shot off that tee, Leo smashed out a long, hard drive. The direction might have been better. The kick might have been, too. The ball caught the corner of a trap. Leo did not give up, even after he had missed a short putt for his 4 on that hole, but it was no use. The Dieg couldn't do it.

Nor could Mac Smith. Starting six strokes behind Jones, the grim old bloodhound had made up four of those strokes but, to tie with Bobby, Mac had to play those last five holes in one-under-4s. It was an impossible task. Mac's chances for a tie at length simmered down to holing a pitch for an eagle 2 on the eighteenth. As that pitch danced past the pin, Bobby took one hand off the glass he was holding.

At Hoylake Bobby had won through patience and guts and philosophy and instinct.

The United States Open was played in early June at Interlachen in Minneapolis. A hot sun beat down on the parched fairways where $40,000 worth of perspiring fans — it wasn't so much the heat as the humanity — walked restively after Bobby Jones. There was no question about Bobby's goal, now that he had won the two British championships. He had his sights set on a Grand Slam now. This would be the tournament. If Bobby could get by the pros at Interlachen,

only the Amateur, the comparatively placid Amateur, would remain.

In many an Open Bobby had led off with fast rounds and had shaken off all but one or two of the pros before they could get going. At Interlachen Bobby started well with 71-73 for 144, but the big names were right along with him at the halfway mark— Horton Smith in front with 142, Cooper at 144, Mac Smith at 145, Armour at 146, and Hagen, Farrell, Golden, and others still close enough to pull out in front if they could get in a blazing third round.

It was Bobby who played the great third round. One of the earliest starters, he went out hard and handsomely, making no errors of commission or omission until he slipped one over par on the ninth. Even with that bogey, he had shot the first nine in 33 and was well on his way toward achieving the objective he had set for himself: to play so hot a round that he would demoralize the opposition and take a comfortable margin with him into the final eighteen. At Interlachen there are seven holes of the drive-and-pitch variety, and Jones was flicking his mashie-niblicks right at the pin. Three times he came within inches of holing 100-yard pitches, the ball, directly on line, pulling up less than a foot from the hole. Six strokes under par for sixteen holes, Jones could not maintain that pace over the last two, the 262-yard seventeenth and the 402-yard eighteenth. He went a stroke over par on each of these holes, but his 68 was sufficiently low to have the desired harassing effect on his rivals.

The news of Jones' 68 quickly reached Horton Smith, Tommy Armour, Mac Smith, and the other contenders. It sent them off on the hunt for birdies, forced them to go for everything. These tactics cost them more strokes than they saved. Mac Smith's 74 put him seven strokes behind Bobby; Horton's 76 put him six strokes behind. Jones started on his final eighteen with a five-stroke lead over his nearest rival, Harry Cooper, who had added a relatively low 73.

Nine to ten thousand well-meaning, annoying fans, the largest gallery that had ever hounded a golfer in an American championship, shrieked and groaned and some-

times applauded as Bobby went to the turn in 38, added three orthodox pars, and then played the last six holes in a bizarre blend of beautiful and bad golf. He went two over par on the 194-yard 67th, his second double-bogey of the round on a short hole. He rallied with a birdie 3 on the tough 444-yard 68th, parred the 69th, and got himself another birdie 3 on the 70th after a pin-splitting approach. Then, almost home, almost completely safe from the gallant last-round challenge of Mac Smith, who had picked up four strokes and was still coming, Bobby again messed up a short hole, the 262-yard 71st. He hit his tee shot on the heel of his club and the ball sliced off in a dipping parabola and skidded into the water hazard past the rough. A penalty stroke, a chip, two putts—his third 5 of the round on a par-3 hole. Now it was imperative that he play the last hole right.

Bobby pulled himself together. He took a nice full cut at his drive and sent it down the fairway toward the large home green 402 yards away. His iron was on nicely. He holed a 40-footer. 75.

That final birdie clinched it. Mac Smith, the only challenger who did not wilt, finished with a 70, one of those supremely elegant rounds Old Mac could always play when it was too late, but it still left him two strokes off Jones' mark of 287.

By nightfall the radio and newspapers had carried the good news to the fans in the countless Atlantas from Portland to Portland who had been fidgeting like first-time fathers. The wait was harder on the Jonesmen living in foreign countries who had to go until the next morning before learning of the outcome. Bernard Darwin's ordeal was characteristic of the plight of thousands. Bernard came down to breakfast, and his heart stopped beating when he caught sight of the morning newspaper lying on the table. He ripped it open as fast as he could to the sports section—for good or for bad, he would know soon. This would be the page . . . Phew! The old boy had done it . . . Bernard settled down to a slow, wonderful breakfast.

Two months after his burst in the third round had won the Open for him, Bobby Jones headed for the Merion Cricket Club and the Amateur. Merion—it looked like a good augury. Fourteen years before, when Bobby had been a pudgy club-heaving fourteen-year-older, he had played in his first national tournament at Merion and given the golfing world a startling preview of the shape of things to come. Six years before at Merion—Bobby had won so many titles between 1924 and 1930 that the Amateur of '24 seemed like paleolithic times—the Georgian had marched to his first Amateur Championship. It was historically right that Merion, which had twice served as a milestone in Jones' career, should be the battlefield for Bobby's climactic performance.

Three down and the Amateur to go!

What had appeared impossible five months before was now palpably achievable. Bobby could do it, the golfing world was sure . . . if he survived the qualifying round . . . and didn't run up against some unconscious stripling in the two rounds of eighteen-hole matches. . . and had the stamina to play Jonesworthy golf in his big matches. He was so close now on the eve of the tourney that these and other trepidations annexed themselves to the fervent hopefulness of golf fans, the way the lurking danger of a lucky hit tightens up a baseball crowd that has been in on a no-hitter for eight innings. Multiply the tension of the no-hitter by fifty. There have been many no-hitters. There had never been even the prospect of a Grand Slam before. No-hitters are spun in less than three hours. Jones had been working for four months on his Grand Slam, on two continents, in all sorts of weather, in all sorts of form.

Each evening Americans squirmed in their chairs by the radio waiting for the word from Merion.

Tuesday evening: Jones had qualified. More than that, he had won the medal with a record-equaling 69-73—142 and would have broken the record had he not overpitched the last green with his spade-mashie. Bobby was evidently in good form. Five former champions—Johnston, Guilford, Marston, Egan, and Herron—had failed to qualify, and this was strangely comforting news. One of them might have given Jones trouble.

To win the U.S. Amateur at Merion, Jones defeated Jess Sweetser, right, above, in the semi-finals of the match-play event. Opposite, Jones makes the last full swing of his competitive career, a perfect approach to the 11th hole, where he closed out his finals opponent, 8 and 7, to capture his fourth, and final, 1930 Grand Slam victory.

Wednesday evening: Bobby had got by his eighteen-hole matches safely. In the morning against the sound Canadian stylist, Ross Somerville, he had turned in 33 and had run out the match 5 and 4. That was the same count by which he had eliminated another Canadian, Fred Hoblitzel, in the afternoon. Bobby had played a wavering first nine of 41, but had started in 4-3-4-3-4. He seemed to be pacing himself intelligently, playing mediocre but winning golf when his opponent was playing downright poor stuff, stepping up his game when his opponent began to find himself. A bit of a relief, too, that some of the men who had the best chance of beating Bobby had run into some hot golf. Doc Willing, Phil Perkins, Francis Ouimet, and young Goodman had fallen in

the first round. Voigt had been stopped in the second, and so had George Von Elm, a real threat, after he and Maurice McCarthy Jr. had battled stubbornly and brilliantly for *ten extra holes*.

Thursday evening: Yes, Bobby had won his first 36-hole match, defeating Fay Coleman of California 6 and 5. He had the match securely under control all the way.

Friday evening: And he had got by the semi-final round. Jess Sweetser had been far off form, and Jones had coasted to a 9 and 8 victory without having to shoot his best golf. But he might have to in the final, for Gene Homans, the lean, ministerial-looking chap who would be opposing him, had played very well in defeating Lawson Little and Charley Seaver (Tom Seaver's father).

It was much cooler on Saturday morning than it had been all week, and a gusty wind blew over Merion. It was apparent from the outset that Gene Homans was nervous, decidedly uncomfortable that he now represented the one obstacle between Jones and the Grand Slam. Gene went six holes before he played his first par, and it was surprising that Jones, wind or no wind, had picked up only three holes. When Homans settled down, Jones, as he had in his previous matches, accelerated his own game. Bobby played the second nine in 33 and boosted his lead to seven holes. It was no longer a question of whether or not Bobby would win but how soon he would win. In the afternoon he climbed to 8 up, to 9 up, and then, believing that he had built up a formidable reservoir of holes, permitted the deep tiredness he felt to show through in his play. He three-putted the 25th and took two shots to get out of a trap on the 28th, but Homans could win back only one hole and Jones was dormie 8 as they came to the 29th tee. The thousands of spectators, sensing that the great moment could be postponed no longer, fought for positions of vantage around the 29th green. Both Bobby and Gene were on in two. Bobby laid his approach putt up close to the cup. To keep the match alive, Homans would have to hole his long one. He stroked it carefully but as soon as he saw it swerve off-line, Gene started over to be the first to congratulate Jones.

Before Homans reached Jones, the first standard shrieks and howls had crescendoed into a mighty, heartfelt roar. The cheers of the thousands were not for the Homans match. It had been a dull contest, an irritating, drawn-out anticlimax. And the cheers were for the Amateur Champion only inasmuch as the Amateur was the last quarter of the stupendous whole—the Grand Slam. The cheers were for May, June, July, and September, for St. Andrews, where the Grand Slam had several times hung by a thread, for Hoylake, where courage and perseverance had nurtured a faint possibility into a fair probability, for Interlachen, where Jones had risen to his full powers on his third round and scattered the field with his 68. And yes, dull match or no dull match, tame tournament or no tame tournament, the cheers were also for Merion, where Jones had not only completed the last leg of the impregnable quadrilateral but had done it with such concomitant authority that never once did he allow an opponent or a break or the strain of four months the smallest opening to destroy the chance of a lifetime.

Protected by a Marine bodyguard, which had dashed onto the green the second the match was over, the authentic hero walked thoughtfully to the clubhouse,

On his way to the Grand Slam in 1930, Bobby Jones was feted by New Yorkers during a parade up Broadway. By parade day, July 2, Jones had won the two British national championships; by the end of September he had added the two American titles.

acknowledging as best he could the respects his thousands of rejoicing subjects were paying him, unable to digest the fact that the Herculean task he had set himself was actually accomplished, tired, very tired after pushing himself all week, and happy, so very happy, that at last it was all behind him. The walk to the clubhouse seemed to take days, and it seemed weeks before the hordes of friends and admirers were finished shaking his hand and telling him how overjoyed they were, but at length, everyone had the good sense to clear out of the locker room and give Bob a few minutes alone with his dad, the old Colonel. The great friends let themselves go completely, and in the furious outpouring of heart and head, Bobby finally washed himself clean of the strain he had been carrying around for months.

There were no worlds left to conquer for Bobby Jones.

PART FOUR
THE CHANGING OF THE GUARD

THE BRIGHT LIGHTS OF THE DARK AGE

GENE SARAZEN'S YEAR

LAWSON LITTLE—THE MAN WHO COULD PLAY MATCHES

THE TRAGEDY OF HARRY COOPER

THE BIG MONEY AND THE BIG HITTERS

LOST: A WALKER CUP

ALL GOOD THINGS

The
Changing of
the Guard

1930-1941

The Bright Lights of
the Dark Age

S HORTLY after he had achieved his Grand Slam, Bobby Jones announced his retirement from tournament golf. The Emperor's abdication came as a colossal shock to the sports fans of the nation. Golf without Jones would be like France without Paris—leaderless, lightless, and lonely. But as they acclimated themselves to a Jonesless season, the fans could appreciate why Bobby had chosen to retire. He was still a very young man, twenty-eight years of age, but for fourteen full years, exactly one half of his life, he had been engaged in competitive golf; unreasonable as it may seem at first, there are few occupations that try a man's physical and mental stamina as harshly as year-in, year-out competitive golf. For years Bobby had felt his love of golf slowly eroding as the game came to mean to him the hyper-adulation of his exuberant fans, the bitter strain of tournaments, the violation of his private life. It was a vicious circle: the more often he won, the more often he was expect-ed to win, and the more he had to give of himself to win. Now that he had scaled the pinnacle that had loomed inaccessible, now while he was the quadruple champion and had more than satisfied his ambitions in golf,

Jones decided to get away from the pressure and the publicity and rediscover the joys of a game that had become joyless for him. It was an altogether sagacious decision. Few champions have the foresight to retire when they are at the top of the heap, but those who do live on as champions in the hearts of sports fans and not as ex-champions pitifully struggling against the laws of nature.

By retiring when he did, Jones was able to cash in with unprecedented success in the various entertainment media. For years the entrepreneurs of entertainment had been conscious of Jones' powerful hold on the American public, the non-golfing as well as the golfing public. Their offers had been fancy, but Bobby had not been interested; while he remained a competitive golfer, he chose to remain an amateur golfer. However, when he had made up his mind to retire, Jones did accept several handsome offers. He agreed to design Jones-model clubs for Spalding. Along with his alter ego, O.B., he went on the air with a weekly half-hour radio series, a flavorsome chat-and-dramat re-creation of the highlights of his career. He signed a contract with Warner Brothers and made two series of "shorts," among the very finest of the species ever produced. For the first series of twelve, Bobby received $120,000 with a share of the profits if the series grossed above $360,000, which it did. For the second series of six, Bobby received $60,000. Jones' haul was pretty hard on the pros whom he had beaten as an amateur and now again as a professional.

As Bobby rearranged his life, he was able to give his legal and business interests in Atlanta the time they demanded, but he never got very far away from golf. On Sunday mornings he was out with his old cronies at East Lake. He usually turned up for the national championships, walking unobtrusively among the galleries. At Augusta he began work with Alister MacKenzie on the Augusta National course, where in future years he would make his one annual appearance in tournament play. Jones never won the Masters or threatened to. Once he dropped out of regular competition, he discovered that he could not regain the super-concentration required of the tournament golfer.

Jones' departure hurt championship golf. There were other interesting personalities still operating, but without Jones the Open seemed colorless and the Amateur lost its stature. No longer did the country lean forward anxiously during the weeks of the championships to see if Bobby could do it again, and the galleries that turned out were comparatively sparse and almost entirely local. When Bobby was doing his stuff, both the Open and the Amateur regularly returned big profits; without its ace drawing card, the U.S.G.A. was now lucky if the take equaled the expense of staging the tournaments.

The sharp slump in gate receipts at the championships the next few years reflected not only the Joneslessness of the tournaments but also the depression that had rocked the country. By 1931 the full impact of non-prosperity had struck home. Golf, like all the appendages of basic living, was hit and hit hard. A number of the mammoth country clubs gave up after only a brief struggle. Expenses were as high as they had ever been, but club incomes had dropped as much as 65 percent. Men who had formerly belonged to two or three clubs now had to save up before blowing themselves to a round of miniature golf. Only a few Bubbling Bays had built up a healthy reserve through astute optioning and selling of new and old property, and a great many clubs, intent on maintaining the integrity of their holdings, found themselves saddled with a steadily rising tax base and heavy fixed maintenance charges. The banks came in and became the residuary legatees of a good percentage of the crippled clubs, and in some cases, although public golf had also declined, the salvation was to sell out to the city or the state. The better-managed, more resourceful private clubs succeeded in riding out the storm although the solutions varied with the individual problem and inclination of the club. One method was to take in more members, if you could find them, and if the board of governors did not mind fraternizing with the men they had blackballed in the good old days. Another method, if an increase in members seemed the way out, was to offer several types of less expensive memberships to the prospective joiners, golf memberships for those who were solely interested in golf, social mem-

berships for those who had no intention of playing golf but liked the environment. Some clubs discovered that they could keep going if they cut away the tennis courts, the polo field, the swimming pool—everything but the golf course; other clubs got back in the black by opening other sports facilities—bowling, squash, badminton, table tennis. Generally, however, retrenchment was the route. The valet and the masseur and the other janissaries of metropolitan-style service had to go. So did the money-losing dining room, or dining rooms, which a few years earlier had been cavalierly regarded as a necessary loss. Country clubs became golf clubs, and golf saw them through. When the gradual recovery, and Repeal, gave them the strength to restore some of the non-golfing attractions, the clubs wisely remembered to spend something more than thirty cents on the dollar, the old Bubbling Bay ratio, on the upkeep of the golf course.

With Jones no longer around to dominate and demoralize, the big tournaments regained their old unpredictable character. One year, for example, there were twelve co-favorites for the Amateur, and the Open was really open. The man who eventually won out was the man who had been solidly on his game during the vital week and additionally blessed with a hot putter and the breaks that decide championships when there are a number of equally equipped contenders. In the next few years the honors were divided among an amazing motley—veterans from the pre-Jones era striking again in stirring comebacks, moderately young men who had developed their games in the Twenties but whose light had been hidden beneath Jones' bushel, very young men, a horde of them, whose ambitions had been sparked by the deeds of the Georgian. In the spring of 1930, five Atlanta friends of Jones' had placed a wager with Lloyds of London that Bobby would carry off all four major crowns, a long-shot chance if there ever was one, but in the early Thirties a bet on the Grand Slam began to look as though it had been a sure thing, so bewilderingly form-less was the form. Anyone could win—the gray or the crewcut, the tortoise or the hare, even the favorite, just often enough to be disconcert-ing—everyone, that is, except Macdonald Smith and Leo Diegel, who had to do it then or never.

T. HENRY COTTON.

It is not easy to fix an arbitrary date as to when the patternless period of transition was terminated by the arrival of a new crop of consistent winners and form-abiding champions. Perhaps the closest one can come is the spring of 1934, when Lawson Little emerged as a great, not just a good, amateur, and when the monopoly of our pros in the British Open was broken after ten straight years by that excellent messiah, Henry Cotton. At home, after Cotton's tri-umph, our veteran pros continued to be influential on the circuit and in the Opens, but the newcomers, the Picards, the Run-yans, the Revoltas, were striding briskly into the limelight and laying the groundwork for the coming of Guldahl and Snead and a new age of professional golf.

Because of this very absence of predetermined winners, the tournaments of the early Thirties possessed an abundance of excitement, their own especial spontane-ity, and the charm, however accidental, of intimacy. They also produced some of the warmest human-interest stories in the entire chroni-cle of American golf.

The youngsters did fairly well in 1931. Twen-ty-year-old Helen Hicks took the U.S. Women's, Tom Creavy the P.G.A. But the veterans did better. Tommy Armour won the British Open, Billy Burke the U.S. Open, and a chap called Ouimet—the name brought back the rumble of the horse and buggy—captured his second Amateur after a brief hiatus of seventeen years.

Armour's victory was gained at Carnoustie, not far from the Braid Hills of

Edinburgh where Tommy had grown up. There was only one other golfer whom the Carnoustie gallery would have preferred to have won the championship, old Macdonald Smith, a native son returning to the course whose fame his and his brothers' exploits had helped spread throughout the New World. As the field entered the final eighteen holes at Carnoustie, Old Mac appeared to have the better chance of the two homegrown favorites; he was only two strokes off the pace set by the dapper little Argentinian, Jose Jurado, and Tommy was a full five strokes away. Tommy had the advantage of getting out early, and the 71 he carved with his great powerful hands gave the later starters a tough mark to shoot at in the high wind blustering over the long layout. Jurado came to Carnoustie's renowned finish, the last three holes, needing three pars, 3-4-5, to edge out Armour by a stroke. On the 71st—although it was learned afterwards that Jurado (who spoke only Spanish) did not know of Armour's score—the pressure caught up with the Argentinian and he plopped his tee shot into the Barry Burn, which coils like a serpent across the last two holes. He could still tie by birdieing the 72nd, but Jurado's unfortunate ignorance of what he had to shoot misled him into playing his second purposely short of the burn before the green, and his final 5 left him a stroke behind Armour. As if Jurado's finish

were not heart-rending enough, along came Mac Smith, needing 3-4-5 to tie with Armour, and failing once again, only failing a shade more pathetically this time, with a 6 and two 5s. It was a cruel and piteous spectacle, Old Mac's seemingly inevitable collapse in front of his hometown admirers.

Billy Burke, the 1931 Open winner, was actually a youngish man, in only his fifth season as a professional with a reputation; but there was a rather old look in Billy's kind, calm eyes, his movements were deliberate and plodding, and he gave the impression that he had been around for years. Born Burkauskus, of Lithuanian extraction, Billy had worked as a puddler in the iron mills of Naugatuck, Connecticut, before turning to golf. In a mill accident the fourth finger of his left hand had been clipped off at the second joint and the little finger damaged, and Billy took to inserting a sponge inside his glove in order to increase the pressure of the grip with his injured hand and so counteract the tendency of his right hand to overpower the left. After gaining minor prominence through his steady play in the South in 1927, Billy had settled into his pro job at Round Hill, Connecticut, and 1931 marked the first year he had done any campaigning to speak of.

In England to play against British professionals, the 1933 American Ryder Cup team included, left to right, Leo Diegel, Billy Burke, Horton Smith, Paul Runyan, Craig Wood, and Ed Dudley. Matches were played at the Southport and Ainsdale links course. The American team lost.

His consistent scoring in the Ryder Cup qualifications tests earned him a place on the American team, and he had borne out Hagen's confidence in him by winning both his foursome and singles matches. At Inverness in the Open, Burke played his four rounds in an average of 73, and unexciting as those figures were, only one other entry was able to match them.

George Von Elm, the man who had tied with Burke via a 10-footer on the last green, was also an easy person to root for. On the eve of the 1930 Amateur, the sleek Californian had announced that this would be his farewell appearance as an amateur. Amateur golf, he elaborated in a formal announcement at the close of the tournament, was too expensive a pursuit for him, and in the future he would play as a "busi-nessman golfer," depending on golf for his living and not for his hardware. He had exceeded his rosiest expectations in his first season as a professional, earning just short of $8,000 in January and February alone. Like Burke, George had won a sentimental hold on the public. It was difficult for most fans to align themselves against either Billy or George. They would have liked to have seen both of them win.

Von Elm had a proclivity for getting himself involved in marathon matches, with his match at Merion against Maurice McCarthy that went to the 28th green—ten extra holes—being the example that comes most readily to mind. The Von Elm–Burke playoff was set for thirty-six holes, but when both men totaled 149 over this distance, another thirty-six was decreed. Over the seventy-two holes of the playoff, Burke and Von Elm engaged in a terrific give-and-take. At one point, Von Elm, four strokes back, played four birdies in a row and turned his deficit into a two-stroke lead. Then Burke came churning back. That is how it went as the two battled on, Von Elm, the dashing swatter, outdriving his opponent by twenty to thirty yards but losing his advantage around the greens, Burke, the cigar-chewing plodder, sinking his head at the start of his swing, then bobbing it up as he seemed to lift the clubhead back with both hands, but, for all his transgressions of the copy book, keeping the ball very straight.

As they entered the fourth and final eighteen, Von Elm, who had added a 76 to his 75 and 74, led the tortoise by a stroke and tried to pull away. Burke, and Von Elm's own putting, wouldn't let him. On that last tour George required thirty-five putts. (In Bobby Jones' opinion, thirty-one putts approximate "par putting" for a tournament golfer.) Into the breach stepped Burke, with one superb iron after another. Billy came to the 72nd green with two putts for his par and a 70. With a two-stroke lead over George, however, Billy sensibly closed in on the cup with two approach putts and left himself an unmissable tap of one or two inches for the decisive stroke.

After playing 144 holes at Inverness, Burke and Von Elm had ended up only one stroke apart. During the five grueling days, Von Elm had lost nine pounds, and Burke, amazingly enough, had picked up two.

In 1931 the U.S.G.A. introduced the sectional-qualifying system, which had worked out well in the Open, into the operation of the national Amateur. In previous years a golfer with the requisite handicap status mailed in his entry blank and résumé to the U.S.G.A. and entered his first qualifying test at the scene of the tournament. Each year the same old faces, who could arrange to get away from business or local golf for the week, were on deck for the Amateur, and while there was nothing wrong with this annual convocation of the older hands, the system discouraged many promising young golfers from trekking to the championship when it was held in parts of the country remote from their homes. The new system didn't cut down travel expenses nor did it excuse the sectional qualifiers from the national qualifying rounds, but the young man who had succeeded in gaining a place in one of the twenty regional sections designated by the U.S.G.A. was able, more likely than not, to gain the active sympathy of his boss and/or the interest of his club members, now that he had given the definitive local proof of his ability.

In 1931 a stream of beardless youths, sectional qualifiers, converged on the Beverly Country Club in Chicago for the Amateur. Not only Jones and Von Elm were absent, but many others who always "made" the Amateur as regularly as their class reunions had been unable to hurdle the sectional tests. Of the thirty-two players who qualified at Beverly, seventeen were entering the match-play brackets for the first time. Chandler Harper from Virginia Beach and Billy Howell from Richmond, two who got in, were the first Virginians ever to qualify. It was a great thing for American golf, this fusion of the youngsters into the big leagues, although it was rather mystifying at first for the oldtimers like Ouimet to walk through the locker room and find so few of the old faces around.

Francis always came to the Amateur meaning business. Five times from 1921 through 1929 he had made his way into the semi-final round, but each year he had been ousted, and ousted usually by stern margins. Francis' friends used to kid him about being "just a semi-finalist," which he could appreciate, but he did not agree with their judgment that at his age he just didn't have the stamina to stand up to a full week of championship golf. Francis' own opinion was that he had simply been outplayed by his semi-final opponents and that whatever weariness he had shown was the weariness that always afflicts the golfer who is not doing well, whether he be seventeen or thirty-seven. It was a little hard to believe that Ouimet was only thirty-eight in 1931, since Taft had been in the White House when Francis had first tried to qualify in the Amateur. He had married the game when he was very young, but, still, thirty-eight years were in those days a heavy load for an athlete to cart around.

After qualifying adequately, the old campaigner came up against John K. Shields, a twenty-two-year-older from Seat-

tle. Francis outsteadied the young man 4 and 3, and moved on to Frank Connolly, a twenty-year-older from Mt. Clemens. Connolly had none of the fire he had shown in the morning when he had played a 71 against Gus Moreland, and Ouimet won 5 and 4. An older man, Paul Jackson, who had just turned twenty-one, was Ouimet's opponent in his first 36-hole match. Jackson was a pink-cheeked boy, no more than five-feet-five in height, and as he walked down the fairway with Ouimet, who was graying at the temples, the curious picture they made prompted one spectator to remark, "This looks like a father-and-son tournament." The father beat the son with plenty to spare, and once again Ouimet had reached the semi-finals.

His opponent was Billy Howell, a nineteen-year-old Virginian, a blue-eyed, sandy-haired boy, slim almost to the point of fragility, with a luxurious way of drawling "Yas, sah" that led the reporters to ask him more questions than they had really intended in order to get him to talk some more. The Howell-Ouimet match was the match of the tournament. There was nothing fragile about the golf that Billy shot that day. He was 1 up at lunch, and after he had given ground in the early part of the afternoon's play, he pulled off some courageous recoveries and evened the match on the 28th hole. On the 30th, Billy rolled in a putt for a birdie 2 and went one hole up. Francis got it back on the 31st. It is difficult to think of a better clutch-putter than Ouimet; the one

he dropped on the 31st was a good twenty feet. They halved the 32nd; still all even. On the 33rd Francis holed a 15-footer for a win. The next hole was halved, and Francis teed up on the 200-yard 35th 1 up and two to play. He hit the green with his midiron shot, the ball finishing twenty feet from the cup. Billy sliced his iron into a trap beside the green, but the Virginian was not conceding defeat. He took his time studying his lie in the trap and came up with a gorgeous explosion inches from the cup. The gallery began to hurry for places along the last hole, but it was unnecessary exertion. Francis gauged the skiddy surface perfectly and holed his 20-footer for the match. The old guy who

just didn't have the stamina had played the last ten holes in three under 4s.

Ouimet's opponent in the final was Jack Westland, who had accounted for Sam Parks, George Dunlap (the Intercollegiate champ), Ducky Yates (who had slimmed down to 270 pounds), and Junior McCarthy. Compared to the boys whom Ouimet had met in the earlier rounds, Westland was an out-and-out Methuselah, a doddering twenty-seven. Ouimet rushed off with a brace of birdies and stayed in front all the way. He was 4 up after nine, 5 up at lunch, dormie 6 after the 30th, and victorious on the 31st, 6 and 5. It was the identical margin by which Francis had beaten Jerry Travers in the final at Ekwanok seventeen years before to the day, almost to the minute.

1932 was Gene Sarazen's big year. Gene took the British Open and the United States Open to become, along with Jones, the only golfer to annex both titles in the same year. Bobby Cruickshank, who finished second to Gene at Fresh Meadow, had been hit much more directly by the Depression than any of the other name-golfers. The club at which Bobby had been the professional had gone under, and the courageous Scot had to win prize money in the Open. To a far lesser extent, Mac Smith, who finished second to Gene in Britain, also felt the pinch of the times. In winning his third Los Angeles Open, Mac's slice came from a pot that had been reduced from $10,000 to $7,500. Nearly all of the tournaments were cutting down, and a few of them had been suspended indefinitely.

Once again the Amateur, at Five Farms outside Baltimore, exceeded all expectations, except at the box office. The old tourney record of 31 for nine holes, created by Jerry Travers and equaled by Jones at Minikahda, was shattered by none other than Francis Ouimet. Francis went out in 30 in his match against George Voigt, and had par in, for a 64 when he closed out George on the four-teenth green. But Ouimet's friends were right this year; their man was just a semi-finalist.

Johnny Goodman, Ouimet's conqueror, was apparently on his way to the crown in the final against Sandy Somerville, but, standing 2 up on the 27th, Goodman missed four vital second shots and they cost him the championship, 2 and 1. For the first time since Harold Hilton had outlucked Freddy Her-reshoff at Apawamis away back in 1911, the Amateur had been carried off by a foreign threat. Somerville, who was twenty-nine and trying the Amateur for the fifth time, was a versatile games-player, not far behind Lionel Conacher as the finest all-round Canadian athlete. Sandy had been a regular on the Toronto rugby team, bowled for the all-star Canadian cricket team that toured Britain, and played center-ice for London in the Senior Ontario Hockey League. He was a very pretty golfer with a fine free swing off the tees and a dash of Armour in his irons. At Five Farms, Somerville hit the greens more often than anyone else, which is just another way of saying that the man who won the tour-nament deserved to win it.

Though Johnny Goodman had not won the Amateur, he had reached the final and on his way he had the warm satisfaction of beating Seaver, McCarthy, and Ouimet. This trio had been on the 1932 Walker Cup team, and for some reason, known only to the selectors, Goodman had not been included. The spokesman for the selectors answered the storm of protests that followed the slighting of Goodman with references to

IN 1931, AT THE AGE OF 38, FRANCIS OUIMET WON HIS SECOND U.S. AMATEUR TITLE AT THE BEVERLY COUNTRY CLUB IN CHICAGO. OUIMET IS SHOWN, OPPOSITE, DURING HIS FINALS MATCH.

his defeats in early rounds in the Amateur, but it wasn't good enough. It was a matter of record that Johnny had twice been a first-round casualty in the Amateur, but the books also showed that in the 1930 Open Jones had been the only amateur who had outscored Goodman, and in the 1932 Open Goodman had been the top amateur. The oversight by the Walker Cup selectors made Goodman's supporters wonder if it wasn't Johnny's lack of social qualifications that had kept him off the team.

Johnny was the fifth of ten children of a poor Polish-American family who lived in the packing-house district of Omaha. He had bumped into golf at the age of twelve. One morning he and his gang had walked down the railroad

tracks farther than they had ever gone before. Their hike took them by the Omaha Field Club. They stopped and watched the members playing by, and got a tremendous kick out of it. None of the kids had ever seen a golfer before. At home they dug up some poles and some balls, and simulated the motions of the men they had watched. Then they got the bright idea to walk down the tracks again to the Omaha Field Club and see if they could get jobs carrying those bags for the men.

Johnny caddied for four years. And then life, which had never been kind to the Goodmans, became very rough. Johnny's

mother died, and with her death the children were virtually orphaned. Their father had deserted the family and his whereabouts were unknown. Johnny's older brothers had troubles of their own, and the burden of supporting the five youngest children fell on Johnny. He quit school and went to work, but the seventeen-year-older couldn't swing it. The family was broken up.

Three of the youngest children were placed in an orphanage, and homes with families were found for the others. Johnny went to night school for one summer and was able to rejoin his class and achieve his ambition of graduating from high school.

The night of graduation, the minute after the ceremonies were concluded, Johnny and a couple of his friends jumped in a jalopy and headed for the Broadmoor course in Colorado Springs, where the twenty-seventh annual Trans-Mississippi Championship was being staged. Following the death of his mother, Johnny had been able to play golf only on odd weekends, but as a caddie he had developed a short, compact swing, the antithesis of the rhythmic but loose style most caddies come into, and it took him only two or three rounds to find his groove. Despite the infrequency of his play, the stocky boy had established himself as the best golfer in Omaha in the city tournaments. In 1927, when he had returned to high school, Johnny had the opportunity for the first time to devote his afternoons and evenings to working on his shots. He had come along rapidly. At Broadmoor he played with increasing finesse as the tournament progressed, and astonished the mid-Western golfing world by taking the Trans-Mississippi. Omahans were delighted. They were well acquainted with the story of Johnny Goodman. On the day the spunky eighteen-year-older returned from Colorado, the market center in South Omaha declared a half-holiday and greeted Johnny with a parade and a banquet. The next year a friend who worked for one of the packing houses arranged for Johnny to travel technically as a drover on a cattlecar when the young man signified his intention to go to the West Coast and try the Amateur at Pebble Beach. He catapulted himself to national fame in that tournament by outplaying and defeating the great Bobby Jones in the first round, and started on four years of campaigning, sectional and national, that convinced just about everyone but the Walker Cup selectors that he stood among the nation's top half-dozen amateurs.

Scarcely nine months after Somerville's rally on the last nine holes had denied him the 1932 Amateur, Johnny Goodman won an even more important championship, the Open. At North Shore, on the rim of Chicago, Johnny led off with a 75 and then left the pros far behind with a blistering 66 on which he used only twenty-five putts. He bolstered

his position with a 70 and carried so sturdy a lead into the final round that his 76 was not calamitous. Hagen, in one of his oldtime finishes, tore the course apart with a 66 (which included an out-of-bounds penalty) but Walter had started too far back. The one man who might have caught Goodman was a large, slope-shouldered, unexciting and unexcitable twenty-one-year-old graduate of a Texas public course, Ralph Guldahl. Six strokes behind Goodman when he began his last round, nine strokes behind after fifty-seven holes, the big Texan, playing pars and birdies where the tiring Goodman had played bogeys and pars, made up one stroke after another until he had wiped out eight of them, and loped onto the 72nd green needing to hole only a straight 4-footer to tie with Johnny. It slid by on the left.

Goodman's victory was the biggest upset in the Open since little Cyril Walker had won at Oakland Hills. The pros were furious with themselves for letting an amateur show them up once again, but when the first sense of outrage had worn off, they joined with the test of America in taking their hats off to a boy who had stood up to the hard blows of life like a man and had fought his way past one barrier after another to the top.

The Open champ was eliminated in the first round of the 1933 Amateur when he bumped

ONCE A CADDIE IN OMAHA, JOHNNY GOODMAN, OPPOSITE, BECAME A U.S. OPEN AND AMATEUR CHAMPION.

into a 70 by Chandler Egan. George Dunlap—who had to play off for his place at Kenwood, in Cincinnati—went on to defeat the rejuvenated Max Marston in the final. Virginia Van Wie, swinging more impressively every year, won her third consecutive Women's Championship and then decided that she had had enough of the strain. In the spring Denny Shute had won the British Open to become, as it turned out, the last invader who would twist the lion's tail for thirteen full years.

Denny was a well-schooled golfer but a hard person to warm up to off the links as well as on. He was about as loquacious as Calvin Coolidge, and there was also a similarity in their attitudes toward matters financial. A West Virginian of Scottish lineage, Denny could never forget that the people back in Scotland could join the local golf club for a full year by smacking five shillings on the counter. Had Denny not married a vivacious girl with a flair for conversation, the most that anyone might have learned about his views on life was his considered opinion that the soft turf of American courses made it more difficult for U.S. players to hold the shots they hit off the hard British fairways.

The most important shot in Denny's early career, unfortunately, was the 3-foot putt he missed that would have knotted the 1933 Ryder Cup Match. A week or so after the Ryder, the British Open got underway at St. Andrews. Nobody paid Shute much attention as he played his staid succession of 73s, but the men who seemed to be win-

ning the championship—Sarazen, Cotton, Kirkwood, Easterbrook, and, to be sure, Diegel—all ran into one form or another of disaster, with Diegel's, of course, the cruelest, and Craig Wood was the only one of the mid-tournament gallopers whose total matched Shute's 292. On the first hole of the playoff, Wood put his second into the Swilcan Burn and chose to remove his shoes and socks and play the ball from the water. The wisdom of resorting to such desperate measures with thirty-five holes to go was open to question, and particularly when Wood, for all his pains, was not able to do better than a 6. He dropped two strokes on that hole, two more on the second, and after that there was not much to choose between Wood and Shute. Denny did pick up one more stroke and won the playoff by five.

Shute's victory at St. Andrews made it a full decade since the British Open had been won by a resident Britisher. Following Havers' victory in 1923, Hagen had taken the old mug three times, Jones three times, Barnes, Sarazen, and Armour once apiece. Just when it looked to the despondent British fans as if a messiah would never come, Henry Cotton appeared on the scene. In 1934 at Sandwich, Cotton, who had taken a postgraduate course in the States on the inside-out swing, led off with a 67, added a great 65, and ultimately won by five strokes. The big parade was over.

Gene Sarazen's Year

E. SARAZEN

IN the spring of 1928 Walter Hagen and Gene Sarazen were stretched out sleepily on adjoining deck chairs watching the blue-gray Atlantic heave and duck, talking leisurely and frankly of their friends, their families, and their golf. The two friendly rivals were on their way to England to play in the British Open at Sandwich, and as the conversation turned to that tournament, Gene angled his head a bit more directly toward Walter and, in a tone appreciably more ardent than he had been using, confided that his ambition in golf was to win a British Open Championship.

There was nothing startling about this confession. Walter, and many other persons not as close to Gene, had known for five years that he would never be wholly happy until he had triumphed in a British Open. In 1923, on his first visit to Britain, Gene had received a colossal jolt to his self-esteem at Troon. Hailed by the British press as the brightest star in a decade to flash on the American horizon, lauded as the reigning United States Open and P.G.A. Champion and the victor over Hagen in a 72-hole duel, young Sarazen did not succeed in even qualifying for the British Open. He felt disgraced. He vowed he would be back again, even if he had to swim across, but he had never done anything to atone for his failure, and it weighed heavily on the mind of this young man who was not accustomed to being unsuccessful. Better than any other golfer, Hagen could understand Sarazen's humiliation at Troon. The same thing had happened to Walter in 1920 when he had arrived at Deal for *his* first British Open, press-agented as the golfer who would show the British a thing or two. Walter had showed them four rounds in the eighties and had finished a lurid fifty-fifth.

"All you need is one thing to win the British Open, Gene," said the man who had rebounded from his degradation at Deal to carry off the British Open in '22 and '24.

"What's that?" Gene was hoping Walter wouldn't come up with some bromide about patience or the breaks, not that Walter dealt in clichés, but from 1923 on, when Gene's golf had begun to go sour and he became understandably fretful about his continuing slump, hundreds of well-intentioned folks had chirped up with their free advice, and it always boiled down to something beautifully unhelpful, like "Slow down your hip action, Gene" or "You've just got to be patient."

"All you need to win the British Open," Walter continued, "is to have the right caddie."

"And who's that, Walter?"

"The old fellow I'm going to have caddie for me at Sandwich—that is, if you don't want him. Daniels's his name. He's an old fellow but he knows Royal St. George's like a book. I'd like to see you win one, Gene. It'll cost you two hundred bucks, but if you want him, you can have him."

"Okay, Walter, you're on," said Gene pressing his lips into that tight grin. "What did you say my man's name was?"

"Daniels."

Daniels turned out to be the article described by Hagen. He was well along in his sixties, old even for a British caddie, and British caddies are regarded as immature apprentices until they have passed forty. When Gene first saw his weather-beaten prize, he wondered if Old Dan would have the strength to carry his big bag. Dan could not only do that, which is the least important contribution a good caddie makes, but he got onto Gene's game quickly and could call the correct club without a moment's hesitation. He knew when to sympathize without uttering a word and when a compliment would perk up his man, and he buoyed Gene's confidence with his own honest confidence that "we" could win. It is always *we* for the professional British caddie.

Sarazen and Daniels played three good rounds in the Open but they played one relatively poor one, the second. They were purring along nicely on that round until they came to the fourteenth, the redoubtable Suez, a par 5, 520 yards long, where a fence along the right separates the hole (and the course) from the adjoining course, Prince's. On the fourteenth, playing away from the fence and out-of-bounds, Sarazen hooked his drive into the high rough. Dan counseled an iron—the important thing was to get out. Gene shook him off. Tough rough or not, he wanted to go for distance with a wood and be in a position to play his third from up close to the green. Daniels looked again at Gene standing in the alien corn and tapped the head of an iron. Gene thought for a moment, of Daniels' knowledge of the course, and then of Hagen striding down the fairways ahead of him, and took his spoon. The high grass snuffed out the shot before it got up, and the ball expired a short way ahead, still in the rough. Sarazen impetuously lashed at the ball again without changing clubs, and hit a second bad shot. He ended up with a 7. By not heeding Daniels' advice, Sarazen had thrown away the championship. He finished two strokes behind the winner, Hagen.

The galling disappointment of coming so close and then tossing it away on a bonehead play only redoubled Sarazen's determination to win the British Open. He tried it again at Muirfield in 1929, but the best he could do was a tie for eighth, eleven strokes behind the man who knew how to win that championship, Hagen. He tried it once more in 1931 at Carnoustie, finished third, two strokes behind Armour, might have won if the wind had not changed between the morning and afternoon rounds twice in three days, handicapping him and benefitting Armour on both occasions. Gene was not planning to go to Britain for the 1932 Open. Things were rough then,

what with the Depression, and much as he wanted that title, the two thousand dollars which his expedition would cost him seemed too high a sum to risk on three days' play. His wife Mary persuaded him to give it another try.

The 1932 British Open was scheduled for Prince's, a flat, wind-swept course measuring almost 7,000 yards, adjacent to Royal St. George's in Sandwich. Gene arrived at Prince's early. Daniels was waiting for him. Four years before, after they had failed so brilliantly at St. George's, Daniels had told the crestfallen runner-up, "I'm going to win this championship for you if it's the last thing I do before I die." He reminded Gene of that promise as they renewed their acquaintance, and it made what Gene had to tell Dan that much harder to say. Daniels was approaching seventy now and the past four years had exacted a heavy toll. His eyesight was almost completely gone. Friends of Sarazen's advised him against taking the old man. It would be folly, they had argued, to allow sentiment to interfere with his excellent chances of winning. Gene had decided they were right, but breaking the news to Dan was one of the hardest things he had ever had to do. He finally got it out, as delicately as he could, and walked away from the old caddie feeling like a heel.

Gene engaged a young caddie he had met at Stoke Poges. They did not get along at Prince's. Gene was in a frame of mind in which he could easily be irritated. He was training like a boxer for the Open, exercis-

ing to get rid of ten pounds he didn't want, practicing daily in weather that drove the less industrious challengers to the fireplace, swinging a 36-ounce driver an hour each day to strengthen his wrists. But this intensive preparation was doing Gene no good. He wasn't hitting the ball, he wasn't scoring. The young caddie was getting on his nerves, calling the wrong club, Gene thought, and then arguing that it wasn't his fault, that Sarazen had not hit the shot right. Old Dan had come around to the club nearly every day, shaking his head rather dolefully when he heard about Sarazen's poor form. Gene, of course, was expecting to snap out of the doldrums, but as the opening day of the championship grew closer and his game showed no signs of improving, he decided that something drastic had to be done. He fired the young caddie and told Daniels to grab his bag.

The old man straightened his celluloid collar and pulled his cap down lower over his old eyes, and Sarazen and Daniels went out to see what they could do about things. It was almost magical the way Gene reacted to his old partner's presence. He stopped fighting his caddie and himself, and before he knew it, he was on top of his game. Dan couldn't see very far, but when he called a club, much as Gene wondered how he could do it, it was always the right club. Daniels knew golf, he knew Sarazen's game, and he knew Prince's like Sinclair Lewis knew Sauk Center. After his practice rounds with Daniels, the odds on Sarazen went from 25–1 to 6–1 on the eve of the tournament.

It was a runaway for Sarazen and Daniels. They opened with a 70 on the par-74 course. They added a 69. On that crucial third round they didn't slip—they got another 70. They had a 35 out on the last round, faltered for a few holes in their tiredness, but roused themselves with two fine shots to the home green that gave them a par 74. They were five shots ahead of the second man, 13 under par for the seventy-two holes. Their record total of 283 was twice tied later but remained unbroken until Locke compiled his 279 at Troon in 1950.

Old Dan had given Gene everything he had. Early in the morning on the last day, long before the players went out, he had walked through a fifty-mile gale over Prince's noting the new positions of the flags, pacing out their distances from the edges of the greens so that his man would know just what alterations to make on his approaches. His stride had never flagged once in the entire tournament. He kept his promise. He won the championship for Gene. It was the last thing he did. For a few months he walked around happily in the polo coat Sarazen had given him, talking about how they had done it, and then Old Daniels died.

GENE SARAZEN AND HIS CADDIE DANIELS APPEAR ON THE PRECEDING AND OPPOSITE PAGES DURING SARAZEN'S 1932 BRITISH OPEN WIN. DANIELS' KNOWLEDGE OF HIS PLAYER AND OF THE PRINCE'S COURSE AT SANDWICH HELPED SARAZEN SET AN OPEN RECORD THAT WAS NOT BROKEN FOR ALMOST 20 YEARS.

292

There are many other chapters in the career of Gene Sarazen that read like fiction—his first win in the United States Open, his repeat performance ten years later, his triumph in the Masters, to name just a few. This patina of fiction was merely the residue of sweat. Few athletes have worked as strenuously as Gene Sarazen did to become a leader and to stay a leader in his chosen profession. Forthright, realistic, and as shrewd as David Harum, Sarazen enjoyed his success but did not let it rub out the hard facts he had learned when a boy and a hick pro. As he acquired money and polish and the opportunity to express his considerable charm, Sarazen did not change funda-

mentally. The hero of the Sarazen stories is a man who knows the way of the world.

The boy was born in Harrison, New York, in 1902, the son of Saraceni, an Italian carpenter-contractor. The Apawamis Golf Club was practically next door, and young Sarazen gravitated to the caddie ranks at an early age. He was caddie #99, a pleasant, knowledgeable kid, the personal caddie for Frank Presbrey, one of the founders of the U.S. Seniors Championship. Gene was adept at all sports and outstanding as a basketball forward. He was a squat youngster but in those days a basketball player didn't have to be seven feet tall.

Gene became a professional golfer

quite by accident. He had come down with pleurisy shortly after going to work in a factory in Bridgeport. His vitality was so low after the illness that he figured that the wisest move would be to find some outdoor work. His friend, Al Cuici, who had caddied with him at Apawamis, sent him over to see George Sparling, the pro at Brooklawn, a club on the edge of Bridgeport. Sparling took Sarazen on as an assistant clubmaker. The new assistant clubmaker had the privilege of playing once a week. In a short time he could outdrive, if not outscore, the pro, and Sparling helped him to improve his game. Gene was ambitious to get ahead, however, and he felt that as long as he remained close to home he would always be regarded as an ex-caddie and not as a golf professional. When he was offered the position of assistant professional at a club in Fort Wayne, Indiana, he lost no time in accepting it. One of the advantages of his new post was that he could get away periodically and test himself in competition against the ranking pros. He qualified for the Open in 1920, when he was eighteen, and again the following year when he had switched from Fort Wayne to a club in Titusville, Pennsylvania. His showings in the Open were creditable. He attracted some passing attention by defeating Jock Hutchison in an early round of the 1921 P.G.A. and by winning the New Orleans Open the following winter. That spring he took over as the pro at the Highland Country Club in Pittsburgh. Sarazen, neverthe-

less, was almost a complete unknown when he arrived at Skokie, near Chicago, for the 1922 Open. One of the big-name stars declined to practice with the young pro from Highland.

Gene had a premonition he might surprise the Open field and he practiced hour upon hour at Skokie during the week preceding the tournament. His first two rounds, a 72 and 73, put him up with the leaders, but a spotty 75, which included eight 5s, dropped him four strokes behind Jones and Mehlhorn with eighteen holes remaining to be played. No one was looking for any fireworks when Sarazen, paired with another unknown youngster, Johnny Farrell, started off on his last leg. Gene was shaky on the first hole and he choked badly on the second; he had no chance for a par 3 and was lucky to salvage a 4. He wasn't going to overhaul Jones and Mehlhorn by being timid— that was obvious. On the third green, after reaching that 450-yarder in two, he turned to Farrell and said, "I might as well go for everything now." He made sure he got his 40-footer up to the cup, and it went in. On the next hole, twenty-five feet from the pin after his drive and pitch, Gene looked the line over carefully. "I'll give this one a chance, too, Johnny," he said hopefully as he returned to his ball. He got that one, too. These two long putts restored Sarazen's confidence. He kept on hitting out, blocking his ears to the sirens' song of safety and going for everything. On the 72nd he smacked his second with a driver onto the green and earned a final birdie, which gave him a 68 for the round. He was rather pleased with himself, as he had a right to be. People would now know that Gene Sarazen was a damn good golfer, even if one of the players out on the course beat his 288. He felt fairly confident that his mark would stand up. When one of the clubhouse jockeys suffixed his congratulations with the reminder that Jones or Mehlhorn or Black or Hagen might come in with a 288, Gene took his big black cigar out of his mouth. "That's possible," the youngster nodded, "but I've already got mine."

Hagen took 291, Mehlhorn 290, Jones and Black 289. The fresh kid had been right. He had his 288 and it was the winning total. His 68 had stolen the championship right from under the noses of the big guns. The story was a natural—*Unknown Pro Wins Open*—and the press played it to the hilt.

The Open champ did not remain at Highland long. Everyone wanted to see this new fellow, this Sarazen, and he was deluged with invitations to play exhibition matches. When he was accorded the privilege of selecting his opponent from a list of several name-pros offered by the sponsoring club, he made it a point to select the golfer with the biggest reputation. He was out to show that he was no flash in the pan. He bolstered his standing by winning the P.G.A. and challenged Hagen to a special 72-hole match for the unofficial world championship. Not the least bit cowed by Walter's reputation as a killer in match play, the cocky kid trimmed

The Haig 3 and 2. In the space of a few months Gene Sarazen had shot from obscurity to nationwide fame.

The stringent circumstances of Sarazen's boyhood had taught him that money did not grow on trees. He had a chance to make money now and he intended to leave no angle uncalibrated. He endorsed clubs, balls, and cartridges. He established a golf correspondence school and made movie shorts. He played countless exhibitions. He turned down lucrative contracts from seven clubs in the metropolitan area of New York and waited until Briarcliff Lodge offered him a record sum to become its professional. Gene was making hay while his star shone, but within a year his star was definitely on the wane. He perceived it himself early in 1923, when he had attempted to add the British Open to his list of conquests. At Troon he had followed a 75 with an 85 played in a fierce gale, and had failed to qualify. He did succeed in holding his P.G.A. crown at Pelham, but that was the one tournament in which he hit the ball with the flaming confidence he had exhibited the year before.

After his second P.G.A. victory, Sarazen did not go into total eclipse. He won respectable chunks of the purse money on the tournament circuit, bobbing up occasionally in first place. But his golf, which had been so consistently topnotch in 1922, was now hot, cold, and in-between. There were mornings when the tidy, olive-skinned campaigner was putting for birdies on fifteen or more of the eighteen greens, but it was not unlike him to follow such a round with a highly exasperating struggle to keep his drives straight and his approaches out of the hazards. Gene had lost his groove. When he had won his first important tournaments, he hadn't been bothered by how he got his pars as long as he got them. He was a natural swinger. When he was hitting the ball, he was hitting the ball, and that was that. When he was off, well, he kept practicing until the feel and the timing came back. But after his banner season in '22, Gene had been visited by the idea that he could improve his game if he took the time to study it. He had run into the usual troubles that beset a person who tears down something he has been doing naturally, almost instinctively. Horton Smith, for another, was not content to leave well enough alone after his record-breaking campaign in 1929. Bill Mehlhorn had a few shots he didn't have, Horton thought. In trying to acquire these strokes, Horton had lost that first flawless groove and never entirely recaptured it. Dissection can be a very dangerous process. Sometimes the dissector comes out of it more skilled than before. Sometimes he doesn't.

Gene Sarazen was in midstream and changing horses every week. He couldn't put his old swing back together again and he couldn't manufacture a swing that would give him equally sound results. One week he would think he had himself all straightened out—why hadn't he thought of taking the club back with the *right* hand before?—and then, wham! he would run into a 78 on which it seemed a physical impossibility to put the ball within forty feet of his target. The next week it was the grip—the change from the interlocking to the Vardon—but that wasn't it either. He became involved in other men's theories. Jock Hutchison had played many exhibitions with Gene, and Jock, who prided himself on his exhaustive knowledge of theory, enthusiastically mixed Gene up a little more. Other fine shot-makers, long-armed and almost a foot taller than Gene, made sincere efforts to help the appealing, impatient young man, but in their zeal to be the doctor, they overlooked the fact that the patient was of a quite dissimilar physique and that the cure did not necessarily lie in imitating their style of play. It was a slow, tedious crawl, and it led down many blind alleys on the way, but Sarazen, after four years of worry, at length made his way out of his slump. There was a conscious casualness to the swing he settled for. Gene held his hands in close to his body, brought the club back a little flatter than taller men with a longer hitting arc, threw his right side furiously into the shot, and let himself take a step forward or a step to the side if he felt like it at the finish. The informality of this finish, plus the calculated abandon with which Gene stepped up to his shot once he had made up his mind how he was going to play it, was a striking contrast to the super-deliberate, super-refined methods most of the pros were striving to master. Gene's wasn't the better style. But it was better for him. Then he began to work on his grip—making sure that it did not slip or become unglued at the top of the backswing—and that really helped.

By the late Twenties, Sarazen was again a factor in the major tournaments as well as in the subsidiary outings. In the 1930 U.S. Open, he was back in the ruck, tied for 28th, but with that single exception, he was a steady contender in both the U.S. and British Opens. He hadn't won, though, and now that he was striking the ball with conviction again, Gene began to speculate on the idea that there might be some other ingredient in that curious amalgam, the winning golfer, he might have overlooked. Sarazen had always felt that his size had militated against him, and this led him to investigate the possibilities of counteracting his physical limitations by experimenting with the *equipment* a golfer used. In 1931 he discovered the reminder-grip on some clubs he saw lying around a Wilson storehouse. Wilson had never used the grip. Gene tried it, liked it, and adopted it for his own sticks. The next year he struck on a far

more valuable idea. Gene had never thoroughly conquered his fear of traps, and trap shots in many tournaments are the difference between first and second place. No niblick would ever be disaster-proof, but wasn't it feasible to evolve some variation on the conventional niblick that would cut down the percentage of error? During the winter of 1932, he worked out his idea in a machine-shop in Florida and fashioned the club that later became known as the sand-iron or the dynamiter or blaster or sand-wedge. Using this new heavy-soled, flanged sand-iron, Gene became the most proficient trap-player in the game almost overnight. To demonstrate to his fellow pros the wizardry he could wield with his new club, he used to invite them to place a batch of balls anywhere in a trap and bet that he could blast them all within ten feet of the pin—including the balls the pros always buried in the sloping back edge of the trap. The faithful Daniels, of course, made the chief contribution to Gene's victory in the British Open a few months later, but it should be noted that when Gene's years of drought were at last ended, he was carrying a sand-iron in his bag.

In the last week of June, a short time after he had returned to the States after his glorious gallop at Prince's, Gene took himself to Long Island to tune up on the Fresh Meadow course, the site of the Open. Fresh

Meadow was a "second-shot course"—plenty of room to clout a drive but plenty of trouble around the greens. Gene had at one time been the pro at Fresh Meadow, and in the hundreds of informal rounds he had played over it, he had never been able to break 67. He had a wholesome respect for its pits and pitfalls; it was his contention that a topflight golfer could, with no trouble at all, drop five strokes to par over the course of nine holes. Perhaps Gene had too much respect for Fresh Meadow. Warming up in practice rounds with Bobby Jones on the Monday and Wednesday before the Open, he revealed to Bobby that he planned to play cautiously to the greens, to shoot for the openings rather than for the pins, to be a little short, if anything. Gene's set strategy surprised Bobby. Gene was best when he banged, Bobby felt, but if Gene wanted to play this one close to his vest, it was his business. Had the information been generally circulated that Gene was going to forsake his old give-it-everything tactics, a great many other golf enthusiasts would have shared Jones' surprise. Gene had admitted several times that he was temperamentally unsuited to playing cute golf, and on top of this he had intimated that now that he had built up a new confidence in his bunker play, there was one less reason for him to play conservatively. Why be frightened about getting into traps when you knew you could

get out of them? Three years later in the Open at Oakmont, Sam Parks, Jr., using the same tactics that Sarazen had adumbrated to Jones, walked off with the championship, but Oakmont was a much different physical problem than Fresh Meadow, to begin with, and Parks was no Sarazen.

Gene's first cautious round gave him a 74, his second, a 76. Tidiness around the greens was the only thing that saved him from soaring higher. Nevertheless, he persisted with his plan on the third round until he found he had a 3 on the ninth for a 38 out. That was enough of that. He played his 7-iron boldly for the pin, rolled in his 12- foot putt for a 2, and threw caution to the winds. He began to lash his woods with his normal fury. He hit his irons extra hard, punching a 6-iron, for example, where a 5-iron looked like the shot, or even a 4. On the greens he maintained that nice easy stroke that had kept him alive during his first two rounds. The result was a 32 on the second nine, which gave Gene a 70 for the round and put him back in the running. The leaders had been finding Fresh Meadow obstinate. Bobby Cruickshank was the only contender who beat 70 on the third round, and most of the scores were high. Philip Perkins, the former English amateur who had become an American pro, had used up 74 strokes on his third round, and his 219, the low total at the three-quarter

WHEN GENE SARAZEN WON HIS SECOND NATIONAL CHAMPIONSHIP OF 1932, THE U.S. OPEN AT FRESH MEADOW, LONG ISLAND, HE PLAYED THE FINAL 28 HOLES IN 100 STROKES, AN AVERAGE OF 3.57 STROKES PER HOLE. IN THE PHOTOGRAPH OPPOSITE, SARAZEN IS SEEN IN THE MIDDLE OF THAT REMARKABLE STREAK.

mark, was only one better than Sarazen's. Cruickshank was another stroke behind.

Perkins played a 70 on his last round—289. Cruickshank added a 68 to his morning 69—289. Many holes before he knew the exact score he needed to win—a 68—Sarazen realized that he would have to clip several strokes off par. Attacking on every shot, he went out in 32—4-5-3 2-5-3 4-4-2. He kept pushing himself—4-4-3 4-3-3. Going to the 70th he was 7 under even 4s. Three stiff holes lay ahead—a 5 that was not a birdie hole, a tricky 4, and a long 4. One error he was determined he would avoid: he wasn't going to try to outsmart the topography. He kept hitting the ball hard and was rewarded with three firm pars and a wonderful 66.

Ten years after he had first astonished the golfing world at Skokie, Gene Sarazen had come back to win his second U.S. Open with the most inspired charge ever unleashed in the championship: He had played the last twenty-eight holes in an even 100 strokes.

Gene Sarazen had won two national championships in 1932. He was not destined to win another. Three times he came painfully close, once in Britain, twice at home.

The year that Shute and Wood tied at St. Andrews—1933—Sarazen was only a stroke behind. He played far and away the best golf in the field. Ironically, the great bunker-player kicked it away in the bunkers—in two, to be specific, Hill and Hell. Gene had made no mistakes of consequence on his second round until he buried his tee shot on the short eleventh in the sidewall of Hill, a deep pit to the left of the green. He clambered into Hill and braced himself for an explosion shot. He took a terrific cut at the sand behind the ball and succeeded only in dislodging it. He shoveled his feet into a firm stance, snapped his clubhead into the sand again, and semi-topped the ball; it rolled up the face of the bunker and then back to its original position. Looking up at the lip of the bunker, he shook his club belligerently at it. Gene hadn't bargained for this trouble. His fourth shot was on, sixty feet from the cup. Two putts and a 6. As if it wasn't upsetting enough to report a 6 on a par 3, Gene's count was challenged by the official in charge of marshaling the gallery. The marshal, who had been standing near the green in such a position that he had seen Sarazen take seven shots on the hole. Gene counted them again. He was certain it was 6 and he turned for corroboration to the person whose job it was to know, the official scorer.

She happened to be a former Scottish Ladies Champion. She had counted 6. The marshal, who was technically outside his province now, insisted it was 7. He had seen Sarazen take four to get out of the bunker: the first shot from the buried lie, the second shot up the face and down again, that swing with his club, and . . . That was no wild swing, Sarazen interrupted. He had simply shaken his club at the lip in that conventional threatening gesture, the way a woman shakes a rolling pin at her husband. The marshal was sorry, but he had counted 7, and advised Sarazen that he would so report to the Championship Committee. Even with this black cloud weighing on his spirits, and a 6 (but not a 7) on his card, Sarazen kept control of his concentration and finished the round in a par 73. He would be in the thick of the battle on the last day if he was not disqualified. He was instructed that a decision would be made that night.

That evening Sarazen was summoned to the clubhouse of the Royal and Ancient Golf Club of St. Andrews, the *sanctum sanctorum* of golf. He was shown into a small room where twelve men sat expressionless around a table. Gene was nervous and depressed. The tournament was not what he was worried about. He had won enough of them. But should these men—the Championship Committee—see fit to accept the report of the marshal who had questioned Sarazen's word and disqualify him from the tournament, they would be placing a black mark beside the name of

Sarazen, and Gene valued his good name above everything. He was asked to give his side of the story. He was brief. He had taken six shots. The official scorer had counted six shots. That was the story. He asked to be excused, if that was all they wanted of him.

The marshal's protest was thrown out by the committee, but after his ordeal that night, it was an unstrung golfer who started out on the final thirty-six of the Open. Once on the course, warming to the task at hand, Sarazen was able to keep the unpleasant incident far enough at the back of his mind so that it did not interfere with his playing. He had a 73 on his morning round and was percolating along in fine fashion in the afternoon until he came to the 68th hole, the Long Hole. His drive was out there nicely. He decided to go for his birdie, to take the direct line toward the green over Hell Bunker and put himself in position for a little pitch and a putt for his birdie. Considering the closeness of the championship and the penalty if the gamble did not come off, it was perhaps an error in judgment. It did seem so, of course, when Sarazen's brassie failed to carry Hell Bunker and the ball thudded into the hazard. It took him two to get out, and when he reached the green, he three-putted. It was an 8. He pulled himself together once again and dashed down the last four holes, but the damage had been done.

It was a tough championship to lose by one stroke.

Gene lost by one stroke to Olin Dutra in the 1934 Open at Merion. One bad hole cost him the title, the 65th. On this hole, the eleventh, the Baffling Brook cuts across the fairway from right to left and then twists sharply back to the right and almost encircles the green. Both the drive and the approach take some figuring out. On the third round Sarazen had played an iron off the tee safely down the fast fairway and punched his approach safely onto the promontory green. He decided to play the hole the same way on his final round. Something went drastically wrong with his tee shot. The ball curved far to the left in a roundhouse hook and bounded into the Baffling Brook. He lifted and then played his third into a bunker to the left of the green. His fourth skidded over the green, and it took him another three to get down. Sarazen's 7 on that short par 4 simply left him too much to do.

Sarazen provided a great thrill on the last round of the Open six years later when he roared down the last nine at Canterbury in 34 to tie with Lawson Little. But in the playoff the young man shot a 70, and this was too good for Gene, three strokes too good.

The veteran's greatest victory in his later years came in the second Masters tournament at the Augusta National in 1935. That week Gene played some of the best golf of his career. Over the testing layout designed by Jones and MacKenzie, Gene totaled 271 for his four warmup rounds. He had not taken a 6 during this streak, and he didn't take a 6 for the four rounds of the tournament, yet, with four holes to go, despite a 68, a 71, a 73, and fourteen adequate holes on his last round, Gene seemed fated to be second. Craig Wood had also been on his game, very much on his game, and his final round of 73, after 69-72-68, had given him a total of 282. Wood's score was relayed to Sarazen as Gene stood on the fifteenth tee. He figured it out. To tie, he would have to play birdies on three of the last four holes.

The fifteenth at Augusta—then 485 yards long, now 525—is not a hard hole to birdie, and it is also pretty easy to wind up with a 6 on it. It all depends on the second shot. Unless the wind is unfavorable, the golfer who belts a long drive can reach the green

with his second, and the green will hold a wood. But the golfer who is going for his birdie must make sure to be up or else he is in the soup—the pond Jones and MacKenzie created by widening the brook before the green. Gene was out 250 yards on his drive, on the right-hand side of the fairway. He inspected his close lie and selected a 4-wood. He took a quick look over the hill to the distant green, and then rode into the ball. It shot up like a streak and fled for the green. The spectators, grouped in a crescent around the back edge of the green, saw the ball coming. It was a good-looking shot. It would carry the water hazard with yards to spare and give Gene a very useful birdie. They saw the ball alight on the front section of the green and pop off the turf on a line for the pin. Say, Gene would have a crack for an eagle! And then they watched the ball slow down to a walk and roll dead for the hole, as if the cup were a magnet. The ball rolled straight into the cup. Gene had holed that 235-yard spoon shot for a deuce, a double-eagle! With a single shot—one of the most sensational ever played in tournament golf, if not the most sensational—Gene had, in effect, made the three birdies he needed on one hole. He still had to play the last three holes in par to tie with Wood, but after the double-eagle, he felt he was in. It had been a well-played shot, but well-played shots don't drop in the cup unless a golfer is playing in luck, and Gene interpreted this as a sign that he was meant to win. Whenever Sarazen got the idea in his head that he was the chosen man, he could usually do what had to be done. He played three sound pars for his 282. The next day he went out and put together a 71 and a 73 to win the playoff from Wood by five strokes.

Whether he was winning or losing, coming close or straggling back in the pack, Gene Sarazen has always been an enchanting player to watch and one of sport's most attractive personalities. After his victory at Fresh Meadow, although he was only thirty at the time, in the mind of the golfing public Sarazen was an oldtimer, along with Hagen a glorious survival of the Happy Twenties. Until Walter began to slip badly after the '36 Open and his tournament appearances became increasingly rare and decreasingly serious, Gene and Walter, with the occasional addition of cryptic Tommy Armour, formed the romantic old guard. The men who had watched them scale the heights in the Twenties found that they could not get as excited about the newer stars. They pointed out their heroes to their sons, told them to watch how Walter cut that one out of the rough and how Tommy played that spoon from the trap. They took an intense pride in Gene's scoring—"See, Gene's still right up there with the boys." The sons, while not as blind to the merits of the new champions, discovered that the old men knew what they were talking about for once. There was no getting away from it—the old boys executed their shots with an *éclat* few of the new scoring machines could approach; the old boys had golf in them right down to their fingertips.

For their part, the veterans relished the roles in which they were cast. When they were on their game, and putting, they could still give the young pups a lesson or two. When they were out of the running, there was nothing to fret about and a lot of fun to be had. Gene, who was about ten years younger than Walter, used to give him the grand-old-man treatment, and Walter retaliated with some amusing gags, like sending a rocking chair out to Sarazen as he staggered down the final nine holes of the 1933 Open. In many ways the two great professionals were as unlike as Asia and Europe, but they shared an equally realistic philosophy about the twentieth century, and they had a genuine affection and respect for each other.

And then it was only Gene. Until the advent of Bobby Locke, he was the only one of the crowd who regularly wore knickers. You could spot him two fairways away—the slicked dark-brown hair, the olive complexion so deeply tanned that there seemed to be some purple in it, the knickers, usually some off-shade of brown, the complementary sweater and socks, the quick step away from his ball almost before he had slapped himself into his followthrough. And he could still play golf. The new champions were longer off the tees and could out-putt him, but when it came to hitting one shot and then another shot and another shot, there was not much to choose between Sarazen and the Sneads and the Nelsons and the Hogans.

Sarazen had ordered his life wisely. When he had set out to be a golfer, the boy from Harrison, New York, was thinking in terms of a lifetime career. Golf was a game, but it was always for Gene a full profession and a continuous business. Success, he appreciated, depended on being a winner, and from the beginning he believed implicitly in his ability to win. After Skokie one person summed up Sarazen's credo like this: "All men are created free and equal, and I am one shot better than the rest." He made winning golf do for him what a smash hit does for an actor or a specialized process does for a shoe manufacturer. He cashed in when his irons were hot, and adroitly kept himself a leader in the eyes of the public even in the periods when he was not winning. Gene had an understanding of publicity superior to that of any of his colleagues. There was always some innovation in the Sarazen-model clubs—the reminder-grip, the sand-iron, the 4-wood that he popularized with his double-eagle. He knew the value of dissenting. He once plumped for an 8-inch cup; he criticized the selection of the Ridgewood course for the 1935 Ryder Cup Match; he had qualifying clauses whenever he discussed the heroes of the

day. His tours were theatrically sound. His partners were always drawing cards in their own right—Kirkwood, the trick-shot artist; Babe Didrikson, when that colorful all-round phenomenon first turned to golf in 1935; Ed Oliver, immediately after Oliver had been disqualified from tying with Little and Gene in the 1940 Open because he had started out on his last round before it was officially his starting time.

From the people he met through his golf, Sarazen, who absorbs like a Cronkite, picked up a solid education that he has supplemented by extensive travel. He is still going strong today. During the winter he is the golf director at Marco Island, in Florida. The rest of the year he lives with his wife at a farm in New London, New Hampshire, near their married daughter and her family. He likes the life of the country squire. It is what he has always worked for: the strong sense of security, the privilege of picking his friends and associates. He is a remarkably honest person. His manner is as direct as a left jab. In conversation he is lively and very entertaining. He is a voracious acquirer. If he hears a phrase or an idea he likes, he adopts it instantly. His natural intelligence makes him at home in all strata of society.

Gene Sarazen has come a long, long way. Golf has given him a very great deal, but it works both ways. Gene has also given golf a very great deal.

Lawson Little— The Man Who Could Play Matches

LAWSON LITTLE

A S the United States Open Champion, Johnny Goodman could not very well have been left off the Walker Cup team that was selected to oppose the British at St. Andrews in May 1934. Goodman was not only on the team, but it was almost a fore-gone conclusion that, barring a complete reversal of form, he would be accorded the number-one post. Johnny was playing gleaming good golf, and compared to some earlier Walker Cup personnel, his team mates were not a distinguished group. They were competent amateurs, each of whom had done one or two things in the previous eighteen months, or earlier, which had lifted him a rank higher perhaps than the host of other competent amateurs. Max Marston's place on the 1934 team depended almost solely on his play at Kenwood in the 1933 Amateur, when Max briefly flashed his old form and reached the final. George Dunlap, the perennial Pinehurst paragon who had won at Kenwood, was, of course, on the club. In addition to Dunlap, there were three other holdovers from 1932: Francis Ouimet, returning as captain; Jack West-land; and Gus Moreland, the lean, graceful Texan who continued to play amazing golf in the sectional tournaments and to flop annually in the Amateur. The side was rounded out by one oldtimer, Chandler Egan, and two youngsters, Johnny Fischer and Lawson Little. The choice of Egan, then a full fifty years old, was largely sentimental and conditioned by the fact that a comparable graybeard, the Honorable Michael Scott, had automatically earned himself a place on the British side by his extraordinary triumph in the British Amateur at the age of fifty-five. Fischer, a Michigan law student, had lasted only one round at Kenwood, but his qualifying mark of 141 had broken the old record of 142, which he had equaled the year before at Five Farms. Little was a bull-necked slugger from Stanford University who had looked like a golfer of promise when he was eighteen and, in the minds of not a few authorities, would probably continue to look like a golfer of promise until he was eighty.

Of all the Walker Cuppers, Little unquestionably had the least impressive over-all record. He had appeared in the Amateur on five occasions. At Pebble Beach in '29, he had beaten Goodman in the second round, 2 and 1, in the afternoon following Johnny's stunning upset victory over the great Bobby. He had played a lot of golf in his third-round match against Ouimet, and while he eventually lost on the 36th green, he had made old Francis drop a 35-footer for a birdie to keep out of extra holes. At Merion in '30, Little had given a further demonstration of his staying pow-

ers by beating Doc Willing in twenty holes, but Gene Homans took him into camp in the second round, 4 and 2. The next year at Beverly, he failed to qualify. In '32 at Five Farms, he was defeated quite roundly by Fischer in his very first match. Just when most golf critics were ready to give up on him, Lawson finally came to life at Kenwood and showed that he could do something more than hit a golf ball a country mile. He made his way into the third round for the first time in four years and there outgeneraled Sandy Somerville in a thriller that went to the 35th green. Dunlap ended his march in the semis, 4 and 3. It was the resourcefulness of his play against Somerville that had won Lawson his place on the Walker Cup squad, plus the dearth of outstanding amateurs in a decade when most of the talented young men were turning professional for the right good reason that they could not afford to play non-profit-making golf. Lawson was not a bad golfer, mind you, but he certainly had given no forenotice of the wonders he would perform once he reached Scotland in the spring of '34.

In the practice rounds at St. Andrews before the international match, Lawson turned in one good score after another, and what was more important, he was not slugging and scrambling but playing a succession of fine golf shots. At Kenwood his iron-play, though effective from the standpoint of results, had been anything but a delight to watch. When he had a 5-iron to play, for example, he habitually took one or two clubs less and pressed his shot with the exaggerated inside-outside swing young golfers were in the habit of adopting to gain that vain distinction, extra distance. He played his irons off his right foot, a style that can produce shots of beeline accuracy and also some frightening errors when a player's timing slips the merest fraction. After Kenwood, Little had taken a series of lessons in iron-play from Tommy Armour, and for the first time began to look like a first-class golfer once he had an iron in his hands. Lawson's woods had always been tremendous, but at St. Andrews he appeared to have absolute control over where they were going. He was not only hitting them long and straight but he was dropping them on the particular patch of the fairway he had selected as the best spot from which to play his second. Ouimet was properly delighted with the young man's form. He placed him with Goodman in the leadoff foursome and in second position, the notch below Goodman, for the singles. Goodman and Little won their foursome from Wethered and Tolley 8 and 6, and Little crushed Tolley 6 and 5 in their singles match. Lawson was immense against Tolley, outdriving the famous long-hitter by ten to twenty yards and outplaying him in every department. As they shook hands after the match, one Scottish admirer of Little's turned to a friend and winked, "Tolley's thanking the lad for the lesson."

Lawson's golf had such a convincing air about it that when the bookmakers offered him at 14 to 1 in the Amateur at Prestwick, many Scots and Englishmen who had watched the Walker Match could not resist buying a little of Lawson. It proved to be just about the best investment many of them would ever make in their lives. In his seven 18-hole matches on his way to the final, Lawson was in danger only once. In the semi-finals, Leslie Garnett stood firm all the way, and 1 down to the pulverizer on the 18th proceeded to hole a lengthy putt for a win. Lawson, showing no signs of discomfiture, finished Garnett on the 19th. Meanwhile, as Lawson was winning his one scrap with Garnett and coasting in his other matches, in the other half of the draw great fratricide was going on, Americans against Americans, Scots against Scots. Moreland, for illustration, put out Ouimet. Then Fischer put out Moreland. Jock McLean, a Scottish star who would later meet Fischer in the final of the 1936 U.S. Amateur, then stopped Johnny's bid by playing seventeen holes in 2 under 4s. In the sixth round McLean met his countryman, thirty-year-old James Wallace, and became the fourth Walker Cupper—Egan, Tolley, and Eric Fiddian had preceded him—to fall before the straight shooting of the unimposing and unheralded carpenter from Troon. In the semis, Wallace accounted for his fifth Walker Cupper, George Dunlap, 3 and 1. Little was favored over Wallace in the final but he was expected to have no walkover. Wallace had been steady as sin in going through by far the sterner half of the draw, and in his match with Dunlap he had been 3 under 4s for the seventeen holes of the match.

A half hour before he and Wallace were scheduled to begin the 36-hole final, Lawson spread out his equipment on the practice area. The shafts of his clubs felt light in his hands and the clubheads seemed to be loaded with power. He was hitting his shots exactly the way he wanted to, and began to watch anxiously for the signal to proceed to the first tee so that he could get to work on Wallace while he was in that mood where hitting a golf ball seems the simplest thing in the world. He chafed at the momentary delay on the first tee as the formalities were taken care of. He walloped his opening drive far down the fairway and walked after it with, for Lawson, unusual speed.

Lawson's par was good for a win on the first hole when Wallace nervously three-putted. After they had halved the second in 3's, Lawson tied together two terrific woods on the long Cardinal and dropped a 34-foot putt for an eagle. The unlucky Wallace had played a birdie. Now 2 up, the burly Californian moved quickly to the fourth tee. He was in a hurry. There was no knowing how long this hot streak would last, and he wanted to play each shot as fast as he could and win as many holes as possible before he cooled off. He won the fourth, the fifth, and the sixth, this last with another breathtaking putt. He walked a little slower after this but he didn't cool off. He followed his 33 out

with a 33 in for a 66. (Since Little's 66 was made in match and not in stroke play, Mac Smith's 71 still stood as the official record for Prestwick.) In the face of this ruthless golf—Little had plucked one eagle, four birdies, and had barely missed a half-dozen other birdies—poor Wallace never had a chance to get back into the match. The wrinkled Scot walked in to lunch bewildered and *12 down*.

When play was resumed, Little continued his brutal attack. On the first hole he dropped a 36-foot putt for a 3, added still another hole with still another birdie on the fourth, and wound up the slaughter on the fifth—*14 and 13*.

Hundreds of Scottish fans arriving at Prestwick to take in the afternoon portion of the final were astonished to find that all the golf that was going to be played that day had already been played. Their astonishment mounted when they were informed of what Little had done—played the 23 holes in ten under 4s with twelve 3s on a card that read like this:

	OUT	IN
PAR (Approximated)	435 434 445—36	535 544 444—38—74
LITTLE	433 433 544—33	435 434 343—33—66

PAR (Approximated)	435 43
LITTLE	334 33

If Little had given Wallace half a stroke a hole, he would still have been 3 up!

In recent American history there have been frequent examples of young men and women of talent, theatrical or athletic for the most part, who first became known to their countrymen by their successes in Europe—on Wimbledon's center court, in Olympic competition, in tiny night clubs of Paris, in the opera houses of Germany and Italy, and on the waters of the Thames at Henley. American authorities who scarcely knew-them-when cannot wait to pass judgment on the young men and women returning home with European reputations. In 1934 American golf critics wanted to see this Lawson Little and find out for themselves if he had played way over his head in Scotland or if he was really the amateur of the decade who had suddenly discovered the full range of his powers. In the 1934 Amateur, at The Country Club in Brookline, Little provided the skeptics with a very definite answer.

The face of the Amateur was lifted once again in 1934. The sectional qualifying tests had made the Amateur seem thoroughly *national*, and in 1934 the U.S.G.A. decided to grant even more importance to these sectional preliminaries. The 188 golfers who succeeded in gaining one of the varying number of positions allotted to the twenty-four districts from New England to Hawaii would *not* have to qualify for the match-play rounds once they unpacked at the championship proper. All 188 of these sectional qualifiers would enter directly into the match play. Six rounds of eighteen-hole matches plus two rounds of thirty-six—it was bound to be a battle-royal and it would not be in the least surprising if by the time the quarter-finals were reached, the survivors would be golfers whose names would ring no bells even for the enthusiasts who could reel off the middle initial of every golfer who had ever succeeded in winning a first-round match in the Amateur.

The new Amateur was not the kind of a tournament that favors the favorites. The big names were ousted early. In the first round Ouimet fell before an eighteen-year-old boy from Detroit with the vaguely familiar name of Bobby Jones. Goodman drew a bye in the first round, but in his first match he was eliminated on the 19th by Bobby Jacobson, a sixteen-year-older. The defending champion, George Dunlap, met his downfall in the third round at the hands of Willie Turnesa, the youngest member of that prolific golfing tribe. In the quarter-finals the last of the ex-champions, Chick Evans, who had started his Amateur campaigning a full quarter of a century before, was put out by Don Armstrong of Illinois.

All of the favorites had found the going too hard—all of the favorites but

PERFORMING UNDER A DRAMATIC BRITISH SKY AND BEFORE A GALLERY THAT INCLUDES A FUTURE KING OF ENGLAND, AMERICAN LAWSON LITTLE, NEXT TWO PAGES, FOLLOWS ONE OF THE TITANIC DRIVES THAT HELPED HIM WIN FOUR NATIONAL AMATEUR CHAMPIONSHIPS IN 1934 AND 1935. KING GEORGE VI, STANDS AT FAR RIGHT, JUST BEHIND THE ROPE, HOLDING A CAP AND WALKING STICK.

Lawson Little. Round by round the burly one advanced. His scores were not spectacular but there was a rock-bound quality to his golf. His opponents could find no crevices, and Little wore them down, one by one, by the fifteenth or sixteenth green. In the quarter-finals against Willie Turnesa, Lawson was called on to play sub-par golf to wrest the advantage away from a young man who had been striking the ball as well as anyone at Brookline. Lawson was equal to it. A 34 out gave him a three-hole lead, and he protected it by sticking even with par on the in-nine until the holes ran out for Willie on the sixteenth. He had a 73 in the morning against his semi-final opponent, Don Armstrong, and staved off Armstrong's rush in the afternoon by staying one shot under par until he had the match won 4 and 3. Lawson's physique was proving itself to be an invaluable asset. He was scoring better and better as the killing tournament progressed, and would probably carry a good reserve with him into the final.

While Lawson was taking care of Armstrong, two young friends from Texas, Dave "Spec" Goldman and Reynolds Smith, were battling it out in the other semi to determine which of them would have the honor of facing the British Amateur Champion in the final. Goldman, a metal-lathe worker, and Smith, a clerk for an oil company, had qualified together at Dallas. They had traveled to the Amateur together, hooking a free plane ride as far as Cleveland and then hitchhiking the rest of the way. In Boston they had found quarters in a rooming house on Beacon Street and had spent their evenings wondering if their joint fund, forty dollars, would take care of their expenses if they kept winning their matches. Of the two, Smith looked to be the crisper golfer. A pleasant fellow with a face like Mickey Cochrane's, Smith had established a record for winning extra-hole matches on his pull toward the semi-final. In the second round he beat Billy Howell on the 19th with a birdie. He won his next match from Ernest Caldwell on the 20th, also with a birdie. In the fourth round against Somerville, Reynolds drilled a 3-iron three feet from the pin on the 19th to win that one. Winfield Day then took him to the 20th before Smith came up with yet another bird. Right after this he went into overtime against Ernest Pieper, and on the twenty-third hole the bantam-sized Texan won his *fifth consecutive extra-hole match*. When the two roommates, Smith and Goldman, met in the semis, Smith's energy was about spent. Neither of them played particularly bright golf, and Goldman, the steadier golfer that day, accounted for his more colorful sidekick, 4 and 2.

Spec Goldman played better in the final but it made little difference. Lawson was in one of those not-to-be-trifled-with moods of his, as he had been against Wallace at Prestwick. Goldman was 5 down at noon to Little's 69, and did very well to carry the match to the 29th green. Over that distance Lawson was 3 below par, bagged six birdies, was in only one bunker, and did not three-putt a green.

The double Amateur Champion had shown himself to be a golfer with great confidence in his ability to perform and with great ability to perform. Off the tees he was overpoweringly long, this barrel-chested, broad-shouldered young man, this "Andalusian yearling bull," as Bob Davis described him. Little's was a deceptive build. Until you actually stood beside him and discovered that Lawson was only of average height, you would have wagered that he stood at least two inches over six feet. He was a shut-faced hitter, but his control of his length was something that Craig Wood or Jimmy Thomson and the other bombers of the professional brigade had reason to envy. His iron-play was strong and steady now, and he had developed, for a man who had once built his game on distance, a wonderful touch around and on the greens. Jones, who had looked Lawson over at Brookline, thought that he was the equal of Hagen when it came to canning the 12-footers for birdies.

Beyond this, Lawson Little was blessed with a majestic competitive temperament, a fine fusion of phlegm and fire. The fire burned at all times and his opponents felt the heat, but at no time in a match did Lawson allow the fire to show through. He took an inordinate amount of time over his shots, and acted as if there were no one on the course but Lawson Little. If you were a fan of Lawson's, you called him a painstaking craftsman who wanted to leave nothing to chance; if his personality nettled you, you called him a maddeningly slow player. He walked down the fairways swinging his arms emphatically, with his large head thrust forward, concentrating fiercely, his forehead serrated in a scowl, a brooding dullness in his eyes, no expression whatsoever around his tight mouth. A gallery to Lawson was an enemy, not a friend—a collection of people who might get in his way and mar his concentration and, if he wasn't careful, influence the progress of the match. Lawson wasn't trying to make friends, he was trying to win, and when a spectator or group of spectators bothered him, he could be as surly as a New York waiter. Much as they respected the new champion's ability, most golf fans found it impossible to take him into their hearts.

Lawson's background went a long way in explaining his attitude and his manner. The son of a colonel in the Medical Corps of the Army, he had grown up in a military environment at bases in the States and in China and had acquired some of the less attractive characteristics of that way of life: a humorless seriousness about himself, an inability to relax with "outsiders," a bearing that was at all times rigid and could be quite condescending on occasion. (Later, when Lawson turned professional, he became a much more regular fellow, though he never could be accused of geniality. The verdict of his colleagues was that he was a nice enough guy, and after his fourth martini a very nice guy.)

His boyhood environment undoubtedly assisted Little in developing many of his praiseworthy traits: an unshakable self-reliance, a furious will to combat, physical and mental endurance. Lawson thought of a golf course as a battlefield, or, rather, as eighteen battlefields. Before opening fire, he surveyed each of these battlefields with infinite attention to detail. In his mind he marked the position on each hole where each shot should be played. He recorded the facts about each green, with special emphasis on the greens of the one-shotters. He reviewed his eighteen battlefields, and selecting five or six holes where the risk was at a minimum and the possibility at the maximum, charted these holes for birdies. The secret of good golf, he believed, was good brains. "It's all mental," he once remarked. "The man who doesn't plan out every shot to the very top of his capacity for thought can't attain championship form. I say this without any reservations whatsoever. It is impossible to outplay an opponent you can't outthink."

In the spring of 1935 Little went to Britain to defend his title at Lytham St. Annes. A course that rewards long drives and forcing iron-play, Lytham should have been ideal for Little, but the fact of the matter is that Lawson never quite got going in the steamroller style he had evinced at Prestwick the year before. He was lucky not to get beaten in his first-round match. Lawson played a ragged

80, but his opponent, T. H. Parker, conveniently played a slightly worse round, and Lawson won out on the eighteenth green. After that scare, Little began to control his matches with more of the authority one had come to expect of him. While he played some very beatable golf en route to the final, none of his opponents was able to take full advantage of his lapses, and Little could always summon a timely shot to break the back of their belated rallies. Despite the lackluster quality of his play, he was an odds-on favorite to take the final from Dr. William Tweddell and to take it by 7 and 6, 8 and 7, or some similarly secure margin.

Dr. Tweddell had won the British Amateur in 1927. He was a consistent low-70s shooter although, at first glance, he looked like a golfer who would have his work cut out to break 85. His arm action was stiff, and on his irons especially he aimed far to the right of his target and allowed for lots of draw. In 1935 he was playing hardly any tournament golf and might not have entered the Amateur had the week of the championship not coincided with the vacation the doctor's doctor had ordered him to take. Tweddell lost to Little, but it is difficult not to think of him as the hero of their exciting match.

Little started off as if he were going to make even shorter work of the doctor than he had of Wallace. He carried off three of the first four holes by dint of some remarkable iron shots into the wind, and would have taken the fifth hole had he gotten the breaks on a short putt. And then Tweddell turned around and made it a match. He refused to let the Californian go more than 4 up on him and started hacking away at Little's lead with his old wooden putter. At lunch, though he had scored an excellent 73 in the gusty morning, Little had only his original margin of three holes. In the afternoon Tweddell won the first two holes on Little's errors and was on the verge of making it three in a row when he failed for the first time to sink a holeable putt. With his margin reduced to one hole, Little's expression changed not the slightest whit, but he dug in with increased determination and by the 26th hole (the eighth of the afternoon) he had regained his three-hole margin. Tweddell then launched a brilliant counter-attack. He carried off the 27th with a birdie 2, and after halving the 28th, took the 29th with another birdie and squared the match on the 30th, a difficult short hole, with a fighting 3. On the 31st, Tweddell had a 12-footer for a win and 1 up, but his putt died on the edge of the cup. Still outwardly unconcerned by the surprising fight Tweddell was putting up, Little called on himself for everything he had. He won the 32nd and the 33rd to go 2 up with three holes to play, and once again set himself up in what seemed an invulnerable position.

However, he had to hole from eighteen feet to get a half on the 34th, and he lost the 35th when Tweddell exploded from a bunker and sank a long one for a 4. Tweddell could square the match if he took the 36th.

The doctor made a brave attempt. He had his par 4 all the way, but when Lawson played a courageous recovery onto the green after pushing his drive into the high rough, Tweddell's chances narrowed down to holing an 18-footer for a 3, and this was something that valor could not do all by itself. Tweddell made a game try, but the putt was wide, and Lawson Little had successfully defended his British crown.

Little arrived at the Cleveland Country Club in early September in fighting trim for the United States Amateur. Behind him was a string of twenty-one consecutive victories in championship matches, and in front, another battle-royal. Two years later the U.S.G.A. reverted to a national qualifying test with the 64 lowest scorers entering match play, but in 1935 the tournament was patterned after 1934, and the 201 sectional qualifiers constituted the largest field ever to start out in match play in the Amateur. The odds were against Little's going all the way again.

IN 1934, LITTLE POSES WITH THE BRITISH AMATEUR TROPHY, ABOVE. HE WON IT AGAIN THE FOLLOWING YEAR.

Nineteen-year-old Rufus King, Little's first-round opponent, had won the Grand American Handicap at trap-shooting as a boy of fourteen, but he had attained comparatively little distinction in the few years he had been concentrating on golf. Against the defending champion, young Rufus started off sedately with a par for a half. His birdie halved the second. He won the third with a birdie, the fourth with a birdie, and the fifth with a birdie. A golfer of less mental stamina than Little might have thrown up his hands then and there and comforted himself with the rationalization that no one could blame him for losing an 18-hole match to a kid who was 4 under for the first five. Little placidly went about his business, and at the tenth tee he had drawn level with King. Little went ahead for the first time and, in retrospect, won the match with his birdie on the 580-yard twelfth. The twelfth was as birdie-proof as a par 5 can be. It is a dogleg, but the break to the right occurs about 500 yards down the fairway, and the longest hitters are forced to use three shots to reach the green—two woods down the fairway to the opening and then the tight approach almost at a right angle. Lawson had not charted the twelfth as a birdie hole, but the closeness of the match called for extreme measures and the 330-yard drive he crashed out was all the immediate encouragement he needed to go for his 4. He squared away on the pin with his 4-wood, and imparting a slight cut to the ball, banged it high and

hard over the tops of the elms in the angle of the dogleg. The ball came down on the bank a few yards short of the green and kicked back into a trap. Unfazed by this harsh punishment, Little recovered neatly from the trap and holed a fair-sized putt for the birdie he wanted. King continued to play impressively, but Lawson, 2 up on the sixteenth tee, produced another spectacular birdie to win that hole and the match.

After getting by King, Little's pilgrimage to the final was without serious incident until he met up in the semis with his old Walker Cup partner, Johnny Goodman. The Goodman–Little duel was a humdinger. Both men were distinctly on their games. After the morning eighteen, Little held a slight lead, but Goodman cut loose with a dazzling 32, 4 under, over the first nine holes in the afternoon, and the two stalwarts were all square as they walked to the 28th tee. Johnny had made a bold bid for the lead on the 27th, a 148-yarder. He had planted his tee shot close to the cup, but Little had followed with a three-quarter 5-iron to the green and holed for his birdie, and for the second time the rivals had halved the ninth in 2. It was Lawson, however, who came up with the irresistible rush down the stretch. He threw four birdies at Johnny in winning four of the next six holes, and the match, 4 and 3.

Another tough competitor lay ahead of Lawson in the person of Walter Emery, a law student from Oklahoma. Emery won the first three holes of the final and made

Lawson fight a hard rear-guard action to gain them back by lunchtime. Taking his time, mapping his shots with massive deliberation, Lawson struck back in the afternoon. By the 28th he had built up a three-hole lead, and only eight remained to be played. Emery wasn't through, though. He took the 29th, the 30th. Only 1 down now, his confidence repaired, Emery meant to keep going. Little would not allow it. He played a 4, a 3, and another 3 to win back the two holes he had lost. On the 520-yard 34th, he smashed a long drive into the teeth of the wind, smashed a spoon all the way to the green, and holed an 11-foot putt for an eagle 3...4 and 2. He was still the champion.

No other golfer has ever done what Lawson Little did in 1934 and 1935: sweep both the British and United States Amateur Championships in two consecutive years. No one else, as a matter of fact, has even come close to this historic double double. From Prestwick to Cleveland, William Lawson Little won *31 consecutive matches* under the rigors of championship play, 25 of them over the eighteen-hole route in which upsets are not uncommon. Thirty-one consecutive match-play victories, and 32 if you count his triumph at St. Andrews against Tolley when the rugged Californian first came into his own. It is one of the few golf records that approaches the Grand Slam in its invulnerability.

Lawson Little had everything a great match-player needed: golf, guts, stamina, a contempt for the breaks, an unquestioning belief in his ability to beat any other amateur golfer. There was something of the strong adaptability of Joe Louis in Lawson Little. He could cope with all types of challengers, all turns of events. He could come from behind and wear down an opponent who had rushed off to an almost forbidding lead. He could be merciless when in front, as poor Jimmy Wallace knew. He could win when he was off-form through fortitude of spirit and a champion's extra-something, that unique capacity for hitting and not missing the blow on which the outcome of a match depended. There was no one like him for counter-punching, taking three birdies on the jaw and losing a lead, shaking it off and sailing right back with three birdies of his own and an eagle for good measure. He had, as he demonstrated most forcibly against Goodman and Emery, a last-ditch reserve that few golfers could begin to match. He was always the aggressor, tirelessly stalking his opponent, measuring him, hitting him where it hurt the most, and finally putting him away.

In 1936 it was time to select another Walker Cup team. Johnny Goodman was on it, and Johnny again played number one, for Lawson Little, the man who could play matches, had turned professional.

The Tragedy of Harry Cooper

WHENEVER there are winners, there must be losers. In golf the winner is the man who brings in the lowest score, in stroke play, or who scores lower on more holes than his opponent, in match play. Nine times out of ten, scores are very just bases on which to judge the respective merits of golfers. The sharpshooter who lips five cups one day often finds all the side doors open the next day or the day afterwards. The stroke that is lost when a perfectly played approach kicks into a bunker invariably comes back through the hooked drive that ricochets back onto the fairway, the bellied iron that rolls through a trap, or some other undeserved chunk of luck. The unpredictability of the game is one of its bittersweet charms, and in the end the breaks even up fairly well.

Three of the greatest scorers in the full course of American golf were Macdonald Smith, Leo Diegel, and Harry Cooper. Their scores won them tournaments galore and huge percentages of the prize money. But above and beyond their aptitude for sub-par scoring was the method by which they got their pars and birdies. They were superb shot-makers. Smith and Cooper, according to many critics, deserve to be ranked among the top dozen·tee-to-green golfers of all times. Diegel could put his second shots closer to the pins than any other golfer in his day, and he played in an age of giants. They were golfers' golfers, Smith, Diegel, and

Cooper, and among them they probably hit as many exquisite shots as any other trio that might be named.

For all his skill, Macdonald Smith never won a national Open championship. Neither did Diegel, nor Cooper. Season after season one of the three was on the brink of victory in a national championship, but they always found a way to lose. In the long run their victorious deeds in the other tournaments have been forgotten and they are remembered by their failures in the Opens. When their names are mentioned, which is all too infrequently, there is almost invariably a shade of sadness in the speaker's voice, the sadness that accompanies names of men who are remembered not as winners but as losers.

There is no knowing the heights Mac Smith might have scaled in major championship play if he had seized his first golden opportunity in 1910. A par on either the 71st or the 72nd would have won the Open for the gauche twenty-year-old boy, but he went one over on each hole and landed in a tie

HARRY COOPER, SHOWN ABOVE AT THE OAKMONT COURSE NEAR PITTSBURGH, SITE OF THE 1927 U.S. OPEN, HAD THE TOURNAMENT WON UNTIL THE 71ST HOLE WHEN A DISASTROUS 3-PUTT FROM 8 FEET LED TO A LOSS TO TOMMY ARMOUR. SIMILAR MISFORTUNE PLAGUED COOPER AT THE OPEN IN 1936.

with his big brother Alex and Johnny McDermott. In the playoff young Mac finished six strokes behind Alex, who had a 71, and two behind Johnny. No one went in for elaborate condolences. Macdonald was just a kid. He had plenty of time. Before he was through he would probably win more national titles than the rest of the Smiths rolled together. Harry Vardon thought so too. Harry had a look at the young man in 1913—another year when Macdonald came close—and pronounced him the best golfer he had seen in America.

Macdonald continued to win his share of the prizes until he went to work in a shipbuilding plant in 1918. After the war was over, he stayed away from golf for a few seasons, but in 1922 or so he drifted back to the game and in no time at all was right back where he had left off—winning the small ones but letting the big ones get away. *Nine times* in all Mac finished within three strokes of the man who won the United States or British Open, yet there was always something that prevented him from winning, a ghastly round early in the tournament that he couldn't make up, an inspired finish by an opponent, or—this is where the heartbreak enters—a tendency to fall utterly to pieces when he was within sight of the promised land.

Why was it that a golfer of Mac Smith's caliber cracked wide open with an 82 on his last round at Prestwick in 1925 when even a 79 would have seen him through? What lay behind that other stupendous collapse, his 6-5-5 finish at Carnoustie in '31, when he was going after pars of 3-4-5? Why was it an impossibility for him to play his best golf in an Open Championship? Was it his nerves? No, not exactly. Mac was less prey to pressure than many players who won major championships with heroic finishes. Was it temperament? No, not that either. Tommy Armour spoke for many when he declared that Mac had "the most ideal golfing temperament Providence ever put in a man's bosom." Could it have been lack of guts in the clinches? The records say otherwise.

IN THE MID-1920S, WHEN THE PHOTOGRAPH ABOVE WAS TAKEN, MACDONALD SMITH HAD ALREADY COME CLOSE TO WINNING BOTH THE 1910 U.S. AND 1925 BRITISH OPEN TITLES. HE CAME CLOSE AGAIN AT CARNOUSTIE IN 1931 BUT ENDED HIS CAREER WITHOUT WINNING A MAJOR CHAMPIONSHIP.

Mac was a very strong finisher who time after time in the lesser championships uncorked his sub-par streaks precisely when he had to. When he won the Los Angeles Open in '34, to give but one example, he started with a 73 and a 70 and then raced hard with a 69 and a final 68. Was it his personal habits? Mac was a pretty heavy drinker, but it would be as false to construe his fondness for whisky as the reason for his downfalls in the Opens as it would be to claim that his drinking explained why he was off the fairway or green only twice over the seventy-two holes of the 1933 Western. Was he a bad putter? No, he was a good putter and at times a beautiful putter. Then, why did he fail in the Opens year after year? Perhaps the best explanation is that Mac was harried in these events by some psychic injury sustained in his first mishaps that, fed by his subsequent failures to produce in the Opens, grew into a complex of such obstinate proportions that the harder he fought to defeat it, the more viciously it defeated him. John Kieran summed it up lucidly with his comment that achieving and not achieving certain things, for Mac Smith and for others, resolves itself into a basic personal equation.

Whereas Mac Smith was the nearest thing to a male counterpart of Joyce Wethered when it came to style, Leo Diegel was not a particularly graceful golfer. Leo hit from a rather flat-footed stance, and there was a sudden lurch to his backswing. But his arms, wrists, and fingers were powerful and sensitive, so beautifully attuned to the close timing of striking a golf ball that Leo could stand on one leg and regularly break 75 for eighteen holes. His contemporaries were sold on The Dieg. When he was on his game, they felt, no one, not Jones or Hagen or Sarazen or anyone else, could hit shots that could compare with Leo's. Willie Macfarlane believed that Leo, if given a week's time, could break the record on any course in the country. Leo struck Bernard Darwin, a sterling judge of golfers, as being "in a way the greatest golfing genius I have ever seen."

Like Mac Smith, Leo labored under a defeatist complex in national championships that prevented him from playing the golf he demonstrated he could play in all other tournaments. He never got over his experience at Inverness in 1920 in the first Open in which he played. With a victory in the Michigan State Open as his top reference, the keen-eyed, nervous, affable young man played three lovely rounds and lay only a stroke behind Vardon, the leader. When Vardon faltered in the gale and the other front-runners also ran into varying degrees of trouble, the gates were open wide for Leo. He had a 37 for his first nine. If he could have played a 39 back, he would have tied with Ray, and a 38, of course, would have won. And then on the fourteenth, with only five more holes to go, the keyed-up youngster succumbed to two upsetting incidents. He missed his drive, though not harmfully, when a spectator coughed as he was starting down from the top of his back-swing. Right on top of this, when he was lining up his second and concentrating on hitting a brassie that would make up for what he had lost on his drive, a well-meaning brother professional fought his way through the gallery to tell Leo of some minor misfortune that had befallen Ted Ray. Under the circumstances, Leo could be excused for dashing his brassie to the ground and pleading to be left alone to play his own game, but after that untimely interruption, the young man was done for. He blew to 40 for his last nine, and this was a stroke too many.

With several hardening campaigns behind him in 1925, Diegel was not expected to collapse the way he did as he neared the tape in the Open at Worcester. Leo was 3 under 4s for the first twelve holes of his final round. Even par on the last six holes would have given him a 69 and a total of 287, which would have beaten the field by four full strokes. Ordinarily, Leo could have played six pars standing on one leg, literally. But over those last six holes, and they are not terrors, Leo lost no less than nine strokes to par. He lost four of them on the last hole through an awful 8. (This 8 on the 72nd hole of an Open naturally brings to mind Sam Snead's similar calamity in the 1939 event. The wonder is not so much that Sam took an 8 but that, after this disaster, he was able to come

back and win a national championship, the 1946 British Open. Sam deserves a great deal of credit for doing what the other great hard-luck golfers could not do.)

All in all, Diegel came close eight times in the Open in the United States and in Britain. His last, and without a doubt his most pathetic, failure came at St. Andrews in 1933. He had only to play 1-over-par golf on the last five holes and the crown was his for the taking. Leo looked as though he was going to do it this time, for on the 68th he successfully atoned for an error that might have got him down; after leaving himself five feet short with a timid approach putt, he holed that worrisome 5-footer. He should have been all set after that, but on the 69th Leo needed three shots to get down from the edge of the large green. He got by the 70th all right, but on the 71st he three-putted from forty feet. On the last hole he had two putts for a tie with Shute and Wood. He rolled his tricky approach putt nicely up to the hole . . . and missed the short one.

Leo's weakness was his temperament. He was the high-strung, worrying type of player. On a golf course he could never stand still. He wanted to race, race, race. He couldn't wait to hit his next shot, and there are stories about his climbing tee boxes so that he could see the lie from which he would be playing his second. Usu-

LEO DIEGEL COULD WIN MATCHES AND TOURNAMENTS—HE WON TWO P.G.A. TITLES, FOUR CANADIAN OPEN TITLES, AND PLAYED ON THE WINNING U.S. RYDER CUP TEAM IN 1927, OPPOSITE—BUT THROUGHOUT HIS CAREER, MAJOR CHAMPIONSHIPS ELUDED HIM.

ally, though, he limited himself to jumping in the air to get his preview. There were days, too, when Leo could talk himself out of winning by persuading himself that he was not in the proper frame of mind. On the other hand, he could talk himself into unbeatable moods. He felt that he was invincible in any tournament staged in Maryland, and since he was, it was entirely inconsiderate of the U.S.G.A. not to have selected some Maryland course as the Open battleground during Leo's heyday.

No one was more aware of Diegel's too-mercurial disposition than Leo himself. After he had lost two Opens he should have won, he set about eradicating the physical and psychic jitters that had brought on his fiasco. He made himself walk slower, and won a number of tournaments . . . but not the Open. He had himself psychoanalyzed and played like a new and freer man for a spell, trouncing his old nemesis, Hagen, in a series of matches ... but he tied up in the Open. Another and undoubtedly the best known of his experiments was the contorted putting style he adopted. Under pressure Leo had been stabbing the 4-footers from the normal putting stance and, theorizing that the elbow nerves should be steadier than the wrist nerves, he switched to that singularly uncomfortable-looking style in which his chin rested almost on top of the shaft of his putter and his elbows were extended straight out like the wings of a plane. For a while he got improved results with this out-elbows push, but it wasn't too long before he began missing those all-important 4-footers with his old consistency . . . especially in the Opens. He was sold on his theory, however, and could never be persuaded to change back to the orthodox method. Like Mac Smith, Diegel regularly confounded the critics who accused him of lack of guts with his Hagenesque sprints down the stretch in the lesser tournaments in which he overtook and passed the same golfers whom he let beat him in the Opens. He could be immense in match play. It was Diegel who finally stopped Hagen in the P.G.A. after Walter had run off twenty-two consecutive victories. He did it by rifling a mashie to the 34th green and holing a 42-foot putt for a birdie 2. Yet in 1928 and '29, the years in which he ousted Hagen and carried off the P.G.A., only one of the eight rounds Diegel played in the U.S. Open was under 74.

In the end Leo Diegel had to settle for two P.G.A. titles and a slew of Canadians, much more meager honors than his exceptional talents warranted.

Harry Cooper didn't come close and then lose as often as Smith and Diegel, but, in a way, his experiences in the U.S. Open—Cooper never played in the British—were of an even more tragic character. Smith and Diegel were at least spared the anguish of believing that they had won. Harry Cooper twice thought that he had become the Open Champion.

Harry was a curious cross, an Englishman who grew up in Texas. His father, Sid, was a golf professional who, at the time young Harry started to win, was affiliated with Tenison Park, a municipal course in Dallas. In 1926 Harry culminated a year of coming up by leading the field in the rich Los Angeles Open. His total was an eye-catching 279, and best of all he had finished with a 67. He looked like a fine under-pressure golfer. On the greens he reminded one California sportswriter of a perky robin. Light Horse Harry, as they called the twenty-two-year-old pro because of the speed with which he played his shots and chased after them, was a happy extrovert. He bubbled with confident conversation. He loved galleries.

In 1939, Harry Cooper, opposite, hoists The Goodall Trophy he won by defeating Craig Wood in the Palm Beach Match Play Tournament at Fresh Meadow, Long Island, New York.

Twelve feet of turf at Oakmont changed Harry into a much more sober young man. He had the Open of 1927 as good as won when he placed his approach eight feet from the cup on the 71st green. He had been putting well up to then, and it was a better than even bet that Cooper would drop that downhiller for his bird. He went for it aggressively, missed the corner of the cup, and ran four feet by. An expression of worry and regret invaded Cooper's face. It was stupid to have been that bold, he was musing. He should have been up, of course, but he should have left himself no more than a tap of a foot coming back if he missed. There was nothing of the perky robin about Harry as he sighted the line on his 4-footer and checked it from all angles. Satisfied with his survey, Harry crouched over the ball and tapped it. The line was fine, but in his preoccupation with direction, Harry had babied his putt. The ball stopped an inch or two short of the hole. Harry had taken a 5 when he had had a grand chance for a 3 and a simple, sure 4.

This misadventure on the 71st eventually meant the championship. For a while, though, Harry's 301 seemed safe, and with only Armour to come in, Harry was instructed to change into his best clothes and be ready for the cup presentation. The new champion went about dressing gaily, and finished just in time to watch Armour sink a 10-footer on the home green for the birdie that earned him a tie with Cooper. In the playoff, Tommy defeated Harry decisively.

It was a stinging disappointment, reminiscent of Smith's and Diegel's in their first Opens, but Harry got over it. He worked hard on his game, practicing on the average of two or three hours a day. He cut down the length of his swing, and was the steadier for

it. He kept himself in the best physical shape. Although he was never as carefree after Oakmont, the confident dash slowly came back to his game, and in the Thirties he was year in and year out among the top professionals in stroke-average and purse totals. His record in the Open was irregular, but he was fourth in 1930, tied for seventh in

'32, and tied for third in '34. For no good rea-son, Cooper seemed to do better in the even years, but numerology had little or no con-nection with Cooper's being made the out-standing favorite for the 1936 Open. Harry Cooper was simply the best golfer in Amer-ica, and he was overdue.

The 1936 Open was held on the Upper Course of the Baltusrol Golf Club, in Springfield, New Jersey. The course was playing very fast during the three days of the tournament, and the long-hitting stars made it seem decidedly shorter than its measurement of 6,866 yards. Taking advan-tage of the added distance they were gaining off the tees and the trueness of the greens, the pack opened up with the hottest pace in the history of the tournament.

Three men broke 70 on the first day, and Cooper could easily have been a fourth had he not been unlucky on the thirteenth. A spectator darted out of the crowd just as Harry was swinging into his drive. Harry flinched slightly and hooked his shot into the side of a ditch. He elected to play it rather than lift and incur a penalty stroke. His recovery was a good one, long and not too much off-line, but the ball ended up snuggled against the trunk of a low fir tree whose function was intended to be purely ornamental. Harry again elected to play the ball where it lay in preference to lifting for a two-stroke penalty. Twisting himself under

the low branches, he flailed at the ball with the back of his club, and missed it clean. He tried it again, and this time he banged it clear. In an admirable display of self-control, he lofted a 7-iron two yards from the cup, sank his putt, and had escaped with only a 6. He finished with a 71.

At the halfway mark, Ray Mangrum and big Vic Ghezzi were out in front with 140. Cooper was a stroke behind. His 70 was Harry at his best. He was splitting the fair-ways with his drives, and his straight, arch-ing approaches were leaving him little to worry about on the greens. He went over par on only one hole, the 213-yard seventh, and filled out his round with three birdies and fourteen pars.

The Light Horse stuck his nose out in front on the third round when he added another beautifully played 70 for 211, a new record for the 54-hole mark. He threw a scare into his supporters on the sixteenth hole of this round, however. Lying two in the clumpy grass in the fringe of a bunker by the green, he had to chop at his ball and succeeded only in knocking it into the bunker. But he played his fourth with great poise, and holed it. The ball was rolling for Harry. When he followed with a 45-footer for his bird on the seventeenth, there was a quiet understanding among the spectators at Baltusrol that this was Harry Cooper's tournament. The uncrowned champion was going to win himself a crown, and it was pleasant to be in on it.

Harry's 211 gave him a lead of two

strokes on Ghezzi, three on Denny Shute, and four on Clarence Clark, Tony Manero, Henry Picard, and Ky Laffoon. Between rounds Harry ate only a sandwich. He stretched himself out on a bench in the locker room and tried to relax, but he felt fidgety. He was anxious to get going again.

At thirty-two Harry Cooper looked years older than his age. His light-brown hair had thinned, he had taken to wearing glasses, and there was a drawn, pinched look to his face. During a tournament his pulse leaped twenty beats above its normal rhythm, and as he started on his final round, the fans who followed him could almost feel the terrific nervous strain under which Cooper was playing. On the first nine of his last round, he made nearly as many errors as he had on the three rounds previous when he had hit 49 of the 54 greens, but he managed to produce enough of those lovely shots of his to turn the nine in 35. His eagle on the first cushioned the three putts he required on the second. He missed the green on three par 4s in a row with his second shots, but each time he got down in two, playing a particularly brilliant cut-shot from a trap on the sixth. He went one over on the tough seventh but got it back by birdieing the eighth. He was holding up gallantly. Apart from a few conversations with his trainer, Harry was keeping pretty much to himself and his task.

On the 340-yard twelfth, Harry hit another one of his fine drives and dumped his short iron about four feet from the hole. There was a feeling among the gallery that if Harry seized this opportunity, the title would be his. Bobby Jones, leaning on a spectator-sports-stick behind the green, studied the Light Horse closely, as if he, too, thought that the 4-footer was Cooper's test. Harry seemed almost too painstaking about his putt, but he stroked the ball firmly into the cup, and that appeared to be it. Practically all the other contenders had faltered on their last round—Ghezzi had an 81—and Cooper now had a safe margin for error. He did peter out discernibly after that birdie, going one over on the fourteenth and fifteenth, and he went over once more on the eighteenth when he took three to get down from the apron. But it was a 73 and Harry was to be congratulated for bearing up so nobly to the strain. This 73 gave him a total of 284, two strokes lower than the previous Open record of 286, held jointly by Evans and Sarazen. As Harry headed off the last green, the gallery around the clubhouse, as jubilant over Cooper's apparent victory as he was, broke out in the resounding volley of applause that greets the champion.

As Harry made his way to the locker room, well-wishers slapped him on the back and yelled that wonderful phrase, "Hi ya, champ." The reporters and photographers and radio men were waiting for him. The reporters asked a few questions, and then began pounding out their stories about Cooper's victory. The photographers scurried around looking for the cup so that they could photograph the new champion smiling at his trophy. The radio men led him to the microphone and asked him to tell the world how it felt to be the champion. "I haven't won this thing yet," Cooper said cautiously. "There are several men out there on the course who may catch me. Better wait a while." Cooper was fairly certain that his 284 could not be beat, but he hadn't forgotten Oakmont.

Harry Cooper had not been in very long when the word came over the grapevine that Tony Manero was 4 under par at the twelfth. There was some confusion as to who was 4 under. What was that name? Manero? Well, if this Manero had a chance, the only thing to do was to go out and watch him come in. The spectators plodded back onto the course, forcing themselves to dogtrot, asking each other questions about Manero as they headed for the fourteenth fairway. Someone knew that Manero had started only four strokes behind Cooper. Somebody else wasn't sure but thought Manero came from the same neighborhood in Westchester that had produced Sarazen, Joe Turnesa, and the other fine golfers of Italian lineage. No one could recall any important tournament this Manero had ever won. Panting heavily as they converged on the fourteenth fairway, they saw a small, slight, dark man with a neat little mustache walking briskly down the fairway with Sarazen, his playing partner. Charter members of the gallery

brought the newcomers up to date. Sarazen had gone out in 33, and this had given Tony something tangible to beat. He had shot a 33 himself. Gene had started back poorly, but he was out of it anyway. Tony had kept right on going with two pars and a birdie on the twelfth. He had knocked in another birdie on the thirteenth to put himself 5 under par. On the fourteenth the swelling gallery watched the diminutive pro play a safe iron to the green and hole out in two safe putts that gave him a 4 and the exact figure Cooper had totaled for 68 holes. One over par for the last four—Cooper had missed his pars on the 69th and 72nd—would win the Open for Tony Manero.

On the deceptive, downhill 140-yard fifteenth, Tony failed to gauge the distance correctly and his tee shot voomed into a trap before the green. He blasted out and two-putted for a 4, which wasn't costly since Cooper had also missed his 3 on that hole. Sarazen three-putted after being on with his tee shot, and the gallery began to wonder if he had purposely passed up his 3 so that Tony, a short driver, would retain the honor and not be tempted to press. (Sarazen has often received credit for "bringing Tony in," but Gene disclaims any credit for doing more than setting a hot pace going out and being as helpful as he could to a fellow he liked who had a chance to win. He did not purposely three-putt.) Tony teed up nervously on the sixteenth (70th) hole, a straightaway 439-yard par 4. Addressing the ball off the heel of his club, as was his odd and unattractive method with his woods, he hit a drive that was not long but useful. An iron twelve feet from the hole gave him a crack for his birdie. He sank it. Now he was one stroke ahead of Cooper.

On the 563-yard 71st Tony played three careful strokes to the green and would have had another birdie if he had holed a 7-footer. It was just about the only putt he missed all afternoon. Cooper had taken a 5 on the 71st, so Manero was still one stroke to the good with the home hole to be played. On the last tee Tony had a trying ten-minute wait. Sarazen filled in with conversation until the twosome ahead was out of the way and the officials had finally cleared the excited spectators from the route to the green on this long two-shotter. Tony kept his drive straight, which was the important thing, and played a cautious iron to the front edge of the green. (The spectators immediately encircled the green and Sarazen was forced to play his second over their heads.) As Tony came walking with quick steps down the fairway, the largest gallery since the days of Jones saluted him with a long round of applause. Tony had the presence of mind to acknowledge the ovation by tipping his flat white cap toward the spectators sandwiched on the steps and verandas of the clubhouse. It was a very winning gesture. A way was made for him to the green, and he saw for the first time exactly where his approach had ended up. He was about forty feet short.

Tony's up-putt could have been stronger. It finished about five feet below the hole. Cooper had taken a 5 on the 72nd, so Tony could take two from five feet and still win. He could have been excused if he had elected to take two cautious putts, but Manero finished like a champion by dropping his 5-footer. His 67 gave him a total of 282, two shots better than Cooper's and four under the old tournament record.

And what about Cooper? A few weeks later Harry competed in the St. Paul Open, which he had previously won three times. A 63 on his third round helped him to tie with Dick Metz, and a 66 and a 69 won the playoff handily for Harry. He finished the year among the top money-winners, as usual, and compiled the second lowest strokes-per-round average. The next season, 1937, was Cooper's best. He had the lowest strokes-per-round average, and his earnings, $13,573.69, were almost $4,000 more than his closest rival's. His 1937 campaign featured his second triumph in the Canadian and a 274 in the Los Angeles Open, in which the Light Horse cantered home in 66. There was no question about it: he was a superb golfer with all the requisites for winning the Open. But like Mac Smith and Diegel, of whom he was a compound, Harry Cooper was a champion whose name is not inscribed among America's national champions.

The Big Money and
the Big Hitters

IN 1936, the year Cooper made his bid for the Open, Americans were on their way out of the Depression and looking for sports heroes with whom they could fall head over heels in love. Baseball would soon offer them a suitable idol in Joe DiMaggio, and football with a number of qualified candidates, Larry Kelley and Whizzer White, to name two. In boxing there was Joe Louis, in tennis Don Budge, in track Jesse Owens, in basketball Hank Luisetti. While most of the new heroes could compare favorably in ability and spectator appeal with their precursors in the Golden Age of Sport, golf was not quite so fortunate in the personalities who had taken the places of Jones, Hagen, Farrell, Diegel, Armour, and the other attractive figures who had made golf a major sport. There was no denying the skill of the young men who had become the leaders in professional golf, but when it came to color and the ignition of personal ardor, the new stars couldn't hold a mashie to the old boys.

Early in 1937, the P.G.A. released the figures on the division of spoils among the professional pack during the year extending from January 1, 1936, through December 31, 1936. The top twelve money-winners were the following:

Horton Smith	$7,884.75
Ralph Guldahl	$7,682.41
Henry Picard	$7,681.00
Harry Cooper	$7,443.00
Ray Mangrum	$5,995.00
Jimmy Thomson	$5,927.00
Jimmy Hines	$5,599.00
Gene Sarazen	$5,480.00
Byron Nelson	$5,429.00
Johnny Revolta	$4,317.00
Tony Manero	$3,929.00
Ky Laffoon	$3,592.00

This is not, to be sure, a ranking of the professionals. If it were, several changes in the lineup would have to be made. Room near the top would have to be found for Denny Shute, for example, the winner of the P.G.A., whose name does not appear since he participated in few winter and regional tournaments. Moreover, many golf fans and authorities would have argued for the inclusion in the top twelve of Craig Wood and Paul Runyan, maybe Ed Dudley or Jug McSpaden or Dick Metz, all of whom had experienced lean seasons in 1936 but who ordinarily were in the thick of the competition. The list merely tabulates the leading money-winners of 1936 and how much they won. Beyond this, it serves as a fair introduction to the post-Depression pro pack with its four new faces for every one old face surviving from the Age of Jones.

Apart from Sarazen and Cooper, the one veteran professional with a place among the top dozen money-winners of '36 was

Horton Smith. At twenty-seven Horton was the same wholesome, overlogical, studious, finicky, and handsome young man who seven years earlier had come out of Missouri to dominate the winter season as no debutant had ever done before him. In that first fine careless rapture, the Joplin Ghost had won seven tournaments and finished second in four others. With the coming of summer his game had slumped, not disturbingly but appreciably nonetheless, and he had not been the factor in the big tournaments that his winter record had implied he would be. In the years that followed, Horton continued to capture a heavy share of the winter loot and to lose his scoring touch when the prestige tournaments came along in June and July. As assiduously as he worked on it, his swing was not the simplified and correct thing it had been in 1929. In attempting to add several new shots to his repertoire, Horton had lost that first compact groove. He had to battle a tall man's tendency to overswing, and even when he periodically cut down the length of his arc, it did not always follow that he corrected a certain looseness in his swing. He compensated for his increased number of tee and fairway errors by improving a short game that had always been remarkable. In the long gamut from Travis to Trevino, there have been few golfers in the same class with Horton as a consistently great putter. On the practice green he did not try to see how many putts he could hole. He would select a stretch of cupless grass and concentrate on stroking the ball correctly, checking his grip, his backswing, the position of the blade, the followthrough, the way the ball rolled. Horton was a brilliant exponent of the theory that the man who strokes the ball correctly is bound to hole more than his share of putts. In 1936, when he won his second Masters—he had taken the maiden Masters in 1934—he holed a 43-footer on the 68th, an 8-footer on the 69th, and a 16-footer on the 71st on greens drenched by a torrential rain. Horton Smith continued to campaign for many more years, but his two victories in the Masters remained the zenith for this "unseasonal" golfer whose birdies flew away when the warm weather came.

Horton Smith, the precocious veteran, was extremely popular with the galleries because of his splendid appearance and polished golf and, additionally, because he was a reminder of the glamorous giants of the Twenties. The Great American Golf Fan found that as much as he wanted to identify himself heart and soul with the more recently arrived stars, he couldn't. They were lacking in those qualities of charm and magnetism that transform a golfer into a personality with easy access to an enthusiast's emotions. The Great American Golf Fan who had died a thousand deaths with Hagen and shared in Jones' moments of exaltation and dejection could not immerse himself in the tides of fortune that washed for and against the new stars. From a technical point of view, of course, the newcomers were magnificent. As scorers, they were

incredible. They lowered one record after another until a score in the 70s seemed like a nightmare. Into golf reporting came those distracting phrases: "He blew to a 71" and "He soared to a disastrous 73." But for

all their sabotage, the new stars failed to make contact with the sympathies of the sideliners, and golf began to take on a flat, mathematical flavor.

The Great American Golf Fan knew a few facts about each of the newcomers to the pro pack. These were the set squibs, repeated with little variation in all the reports of the tournaments, adhering to the individual whether he lost, won, scrambled, rebounded, or floundered to a dismal 72: Ray

Mangrum was The Human One-Iron. He lacked stamina. . . . Ky Laffoon liked to wear bright yellow socks and canary-colored sweaters with his knickers. He was of Irish-French-Cherokee ancestry, and had traveled from Kansas to Oklahoma in a covered wagon at the age of six. . . . Ed Dudley was a slow Southerner with a languid swing. . . . Johnny Revolta was a gnarled-faced young man with an obdurate marcel who had been encouraged to take his fling at the circuit when he had beaten the best-ball of Sarazen and Armour during their tour of the North Woods country. He and Picard made a redoubtable combination and seemed to win the Miami Four-ball every year. . . . Henry Picard was a tall, clean-cut Yankee from Plymouth, about as gregarious as Greta Garbo. He took fewer chances than any of his brethren when it came to shooting the works for birdies. His first important victories were scored when he was playing out of Hershey, and he was called The Chocolate Soldier. . . . Ralph Guldahl was sensationally dull to watch, but steady as a rock. He had been an automobile salesman. . . . Paul Runyan was the shortest hitter of the pack, but what he lacked in distance off the tees, he made up in the accuracy of his long approaches. He could sweep a spoon shot closer to the pin than his opponent's 5-iron, and on the greens he could be murderous. He was a dapper dresser, and it took some believing when you heard he was only a few years away from milking cows on his father's farm in Arkansas. . . . Dick Metz came from Arkansas too. He was always "handsome Dick Metz." Wavy black hair and a cowboy's complexion. Liked deep-sea fishing. . . . Byron Nelson, one of the newest faces, was a Texan whom George Jacobus had taken on as assistant pro at Ridgewood in New Jersey. Nelson was winning more tournaments and more money each year. . . . Harold "Jug" McSpaden, from Kansas City, was "brilliant but erratic." Dangerous in match play. . . . Jimmy Hines was also brilliant but erratic. Probably the best of the pros situated on Long Island. A long hitter. . . . Craig Wood's golf was like the little girl who had a little curl right in the middle of her forehead. He was very handsome. Called The Blond Bomber. . . . Jimmy Thomson was the longest hitter in the pack, longer than Wood, Hines, Little. (With the exception of winning the Canadian Open with four rounds in the 60s, Lawson was finding the going rough among the pros.) Thomson, golf's Babe Ruth, averaged about 275 yards from the tees, and had thrilled the galleries at Oakmont by reaching the green in two on the 621-yard twelfth. That was in the 1935 Open, when he had finished second. Jimmy was married to Viola Dana, the actress. . . .

Every man in the pack was an accomplished shot-maker. Over the long run, three of them emerged as distinguished golfers—Byron Nelson and Ralph Guldahl,

HORTON SMITH, SHOWN OPPOSITE AT PEBBLE BEACH, WAS A SHORT-GAME AND PUTTING SPECIALIST, WHO WON THE FIRST MASTERS AT AUGUSTA NATIONAL IN 1934 AND REPEATED TWO YEARS LATER.

of course, and Henry Picard, whom many of the best golfing minds esteem one of the really fine swingers of all time. As 1937 got underway, though, only one of the newcomers had attained a hold on the public's fancy of sufficient strength to have made him a successful attraction had he chosen to set out on an exhibition tour. This was Jimmy Thomson. The Great American Golf Fan would have traveled a good many miles to see whether Jimmy hit them as long as they said he did.

The members of the pro pack had their individual fortes and weaknesses, but they shared a large number of things in common. With the exception of Runyan, they were wickedly long off the tees. Hypodermic injections, stepping up the internal pressure of the golf ball to the neighborhood of 800 pounds per square inch, gave the ball lots of carry when it was properly struck. The steel shaft—steel had been approved in 1924 by the U.S.G.A., but the Royal and Ancient withheld its sanction until 1930—had been perfected, and was also a major factor in the added yardage the golfers were getting. With steel-shafted clubs eliminating the torque and torsion of the hickory, a strong-wristed golfer could put everything he had into a

shot, for a slight departure from the perfect coordination of hands and clubhead resulted in errors far less acute than with the wooden shafts. With this wider zone for an error in timing, the advantages of the swinger over the hitter were considerably reduced. Walter Hagen, who was regarded by his contemporaries as a hitter, was a rippling swinger compared with the stars of the new generation. Some of the newer crop were out-and-out sluggers; they tore into the ball almost exclusively with their hands. Few of them were caressers of the Mac Smith school. The best golfers lay halfway between the two poles. They had grooved swings that made provision for an accentuated hitting action.

Once they were off the tee and down the fairway, the golfers of the Thirties had a generous range of perfectly matched clubs from which to choose. In the earlier periods golfers built up their sets by discarding clubs whose weight or balance was not precisely to their feel, and gradually assembled sets that were interbalanced from the driving-iron to the niblick. This experimentation was now passé with the coming of age of the scientifically wrought and pretested steel shaft. (To their matched sets the pros added a liberal number of pet clubs, in-between clubs, trouble clubs, and clubs that were useful for only one extreme and exotic type of shot, until some of them were carrying around close to thirty weapons. From this vast armory, the pro, and the professional amateur, could select the club that would give him just the distance he needed if he hit a full shot. Those delightful half-shots and three-quarter shots, by which you could distinguish a true golfer from the men who played golf, were fast disappearing and might have vanished entirely had the U.S.G.A. not invoked in the winter of 1937 a regulation limiting to fourteen the number of clubs a golfer could carry in his bag. Some of the real oldtimers, remembering that Vardon had six times broken 70 playing with only six clubs, lobbied for a further reduction of armaments, but the adoption of fourteen as the maximum was generally hailed as a sage and sound compromise.)

Around the greens the new pro pack displayed astonishing skill. In the eyes of the reactionaries—who were reluctant to admit that the newcomers could do anything better than Jones or Hagen—the improved quality of the professionals' bunker play could be explained by the new agents of excavation, the sand-iron or the blaster or the dynamiter, depending on the trade name stamped on the super-niblick by the various sporting-goods manufacturers.

In the previous decade the golfer who got down in 2 from a trap by the green believed that he had saved himself a stroke. By the middle Thirties, the pro who failed to put his recovery from a trap ten feet or less from the cup felt that he had tossed away a stroke. The new clubs greatly simplified the problem of getting out and getting up close, but it still took nerve and decision to execute the shot correctly under pressure.

On the greens the pros, as a group, were definitely ahead of the earlier performers. The equipment for putting hadn't changed. Indirectly, though, the improved irons and wooden clubs were more germane to the superior standards of putting. With the greater length they had gained, the pack turned all but the longest layouts into drive-and-pitch courses. A hole measuring 410 yards, for instance, which formerly demanded a drive and a 4-iron or so, could now be reached with a drive and a 6-iron or even a 7. Everyone was getting on in 2, and the premium on tee-to-green play, consequently, was not as high as it once had been. More than ever before, putting was the department of the game that separated the winners from the losers. The pro who finished tenth or fifteenth in a tournament might have used no more shots to reach the seventy-two greens than the pro who finished first. The knowledge that the gulf between $1,000 and $50 could be bridged

JIMMY THOMSON, LEFT, OPPOSITE, AND CRAIG WOOD, SHOWN AT BALTUSROL FOR THE 1936 U.S. OPEN, WERE MEMBERS OF A NEW GENERATION OF PLAYERS WHO DRESSED LIKE MOVIE STARS, USED MATCHED STEEL-SHAFTED CLUBS, AND HIT AN IMPROVED GOLF BALL FARTHER THAN EVER.

only by putting better than the other fellow drove the professionals on to acquiring their phenomenal skill on the greens. In time, after the players had created for themselves higher and higher criteria, a putt of five feet came to be regarded as a short putt that a golfer had to hole if he had financial aspirations. Because the pros were so uncanny on the greens, particularly on the flat tables of the courses over which many of the winter tournaments were played, any fan who had watched their performances could almost sympathize with the lobby who wanted putts to be counted half a stroke and thus re-establish the value of the other shots in golf.

Intrinsic as were the peppier ball, the steel shaft, and the sand-wedge to the new assaults on the old marks, in the opinion of many students of the game the rash of record-breaking performances resulted not so much from the refined equipment as from the changes that came over the golf courses themselves. Golfers may say that they don't care how well they score as long as they hit the ball well, but the fact of the matter is that every golfer is concerned with his score. At almost every club in the Thirties, as now, pressure was brought to bear on the green committee to fill in traps, thin the rough, and, all in all, muzzle the terrors that transformed possible 89s into actual 97s. The cry was answered. Architects were called in to remodel the sterner holes and the greenkeepers were informed of the new standard of maintenance required. In the Thirties for

the first time the greenkeepers at the wealthy clubs had at their disposal machines like the seven-gang mower which could domesticate a course and keep it scoreable. The clubs that could not afford the new machinery manicured their courses as best they could. American golfers got what they asked for: easier courses and lower scores. The average golfer cut four to seven strokes off his score now that bunkers were scaled down and their lips removed, fairways groomed to resemble a hairbrush, and roughs reduced to such a state of obedience that women could play a brassie from them.

The professional golfer as well as the average golfer benefitted from the New Look of the nation's golf courses. He, too, received better lies in the fairway. More important, he did not have to sacrifice a shot when he found the rough. In fact, he could play almost the same shot from the rough as he did from the fairway; a soft green might still hold a shot even if it carried no backspin. In time, as the soft, watered green became the rule and not the exception, the pitch-and-run approach practically vanished from professional golf in America. Just as instrumental as the new construction of greens in the lower scoring, if not more instrumental, were the new grass strains introduced for the putting surfaces. Quite a number of golf authorities, architects predominantly, give the improved texture and uniformity of the greens 100 per cent of the credit for the advanced standards of putting and 65 per cent of the credit for the reduction in scores.

One reason why it is important to talk about the changes that made lower scoring possible for the professionals of the Thirties and afterwards is that too many fans today dismiss the champions of the first three decades of the century with a flip comparison of scores. Jones and Hagen, they state categorically, couldn't have been particularly good golfers. They were rarely in the 60s and often in the middle and high 70s. They won with totals that would not even place them in the money today. They just happened to be around when the competition was seedy. That isn't quite right. Golf was a different game in the Twenties than it is today, a much harder game, just how much harder it is impossible to gauge.

On the other hand, by explaining the less arduous conditions under which the new stars performed, one runs the danger of detracting, inadvertently, from the abilities of these later champions. To begin with, the record-breakers of the Thirties and Forties were golfers of very high talent. On top of this, the ever-surging competition forced them to discover new peaks of efficiency and new styles of play. In the Twenties, for example, a tournament golfer was content to get his drive out by the 225-yard marker except on the extremely long holes. Since the rough was rougher and the penalty for an off-line drive much stiffer, the earlier golfers placed high value on straightness. The idea was to keep the ball in play off the

tee and to postpone any thoughts about a birdie until the birdie shot presented itself. These tactics rapidly became obsolete in the Thirties. The hunt for the birdie began with the drive—the longer the drive, the shorter the approach; the shorter the approach, the easier the putt. A golfer attacked with every shot.

If some of the old masters appeared to have "more golf in them" than their heirs, it can be argued that it only seemed that way since the new stars made the game look like a science rather than an art.

During the Depression and the years of slow recovery, some of the winter tournaments had been forced to give up, and there was, naturally, a halt in the race between tournament sponsors to see who could offer the highest prize money. But, all things taken into account, the winning pros were still well paid for their efforts. For example, statisticians computed that Paul Runyan received $1.61 per stroke played during his sixty-one tournament rounds in the winter season of 1934 when Paul picked up checks totaling $7,026. The leaders usually made between $5,000 and $7,000 with the rest of the tour checking in between $2,500 and $5,000. When a top pro's salary at his home club was added to this figure, plus his gleanings from instruction, endorsements, and his fee from the manufacturer whom he "advised," his yearly take was quite respectable. Fighters, of course, outearned him, as did a few of the outstanding baseball players and newly turned-professional tennis stars, but compared with most professional athletes who flourished in the bad times, the winning golfer received a generous compensation for his skill.

With things brightening up somewhat by the end of 1936, both the well-heeled stars and the penniless "dew sweepers" who slept in autos were hoping that some of the new money would blow their way. As things turned out, due to a number of circumstances more or less beyond their control, the pros were entering upon a period far more lucrative than they had dreamed it could be. For, beginning in 1937, professional golf graduated into Big Business.

An energetic, imaginative Irishman from Boston, Fred Corcoran, was one of the "circumstances" behind golf's big boom. Corcoran had been around golf all his life. He began as a caddie at the Belmont Country Club. In 1918, when he was thirteen, he became the caddie-master. He moved on to the position of handicapper with the Massachusetts Golf Association, where his amiability and his progressive ideas about such items as scoreboards and publicity brought him to the attention of the U.S.G.A. and other organizations that ran golf tournaments. Richard Tufts, the head of Pinehurst, asked Fred to take charge of press

relations when that North Carolina resort was host to the P.G.A. Championship in the late fall of 1936. Fred's systematic methods at Pinehurst sold George Jacobus, the P.G.A. president, on the advantages of having in his organization a young man who could transform "dirty work" into bright columns on the sporting pages of the country. After a three-month tryout, Corcoran became what amounted to tournament director of the P.G.A., succeeding Bob Harlow, who had been shepherding the pros wisely and well for almost a score of years.

Well stocked with sincerity and figures, thoroughly sold on his product, Corcoran invaded the offices of organizations he thought he could interest in sponsoring tournaments, concentrating on the Chambers of Commerce of ambitious cities and the publicity bureaus of resorts. How well Corcoran succeeded in imposing his factual enthusiasm on his customers is best illustrated by figures: In 1936, the year before Corcoran took over, the touring professionals played about twenty-two tournaments a year; ten years later they were lined up for tournaments during *forty-five* weeks of the year. Where tournament purses had totaled $100,000 in 1936, the pros in 1947 were shooting at prize money exceeding $600,000. During the ten years that Corcoran had been promoting the pros, the size of the galleries had increased 300 per cent.

SAILING ON THE S.S. MANHATTAN, OPPOSITE, IS THE 1937 U.S. RYDER CUP TEAM OF AMERICAN PROFESSIONALS EN ROUTE TO ENGLAND TO DEFEND THEIR TROPHY. AT FAR RIGHT IS FRED CORCORAN, THE P.G.A. EXECUTIVE WHO HELPED TURN THE PRO GAME INTO BIG BUSINESS.

Corcoran is the first to admit that it was the times and not the tournament director that was responsible for the boom. However, Fred is deserving of copious praise for the shrewdness with which he diagnosed his problem and the drive with which he followed it through. Fred's work did not end with selling prospective sponsors the idea that a golf tournament would not lose money and would insure them more publicity per dollar invested than any other means of attracting attention to their fair city or spa. He won the cooperation, and space, of the newspapermen covering golf by obligingly reeling off the statistics, color, and anecdotes that columns are made of, rescuing the boys from blank sheets of paper on many rainy days. Realizing that it was not so much the competitive angle of a tournament as the in-person stars that brought in the customers, Corcoran watched carefully over his troupe of golfers, a restless combination of Barnum, Mrs. Wiggs, and Pygmalion. There were times when he oversucceeded and experienced the qualms of a Frankenstein, for every so often one or two of the professional stars, taking their write-ups too seriously, would demand special courtesies that Louis B. Mayer would have been reluctant to grant Lana Turner. By the time Fred

left his P.G.A. post in 1948 to turn to newer promotions in golf and other sports, he had made the American public extremely circuit-conscious.

A great many of the golfers Corcoran trumpeted into pseudo-personalities were as drab as a comedian in his own home. But hardly had Corcoran stepped into his job when there arrived on the scene, with no advance notice, a golfer who exuded color from every pore and who, far more than any other professional, was responsible for the tremendous resurgence of interest in tournament golf. This newcomer was a lean, supple, fluidly coordinated twenty-four-year-old pro from the mountain resort town of Hot Springs, Virginia, making his first tour on the winter circuit. His golfing background was not exceptional. During his school vacations he had caddied to get away from plowing and milking on his father's farm. He was no great shakes as a golfer when he was in high school. He won a driving contest held in conjunction with a high school golf tournament but finished no better than eighth in the tournament. His sports were baseball, football, and basketball, and he played them well enough to receive scholarship bids from

SAM SNEAD, AT LEFT, EXPLODED ON THE NATIONAL GOLF SCENE IN 1937 BY WINNING FIVE TOURNAMENTS IN HIS ROOKIE YEAR. HERE, HE DISPLAYS HIS SWEET SWING ON THE TENTH TEE AT AUGUSTA DURING THE 1937 MASTERS.

two West Virginia colleges. What turned out to be his big break was the broken left hand he suffered in a football game during his senior year in high school. Golf, it seemed to him, helped him in recovering the use of the hand, and for the first time he devoted the bulk of his free time to the game. After graduation in 1933, he landed himself a job in the pro shop at the Homestead course as assistant caddie-master and handyman. He found himself a better job shortly afterwards at the Cascades course down the road. Three weeks after his switch, he played a record-breaking 68 over that hilly 6,800-yard layout. He returned to the Homestead course a year later as assistant to Freddie Gleim, but stayed only one season. His play in a local tourney had caught the eye of Fred Martin, the manager of the Greenbrier Golf Club in White Sulphur Springs, and the young man, now twenty-two, spent the next two years attached to that rival spa in West Virginia. In 1936 he won the West Virginia Open and P.G.A., scoring a 61 in the latter tourney, and gained further confidence by outplaying Lawson Little, Billy Burke, and Johnny Goodman in an exhibition four-ball match at White Sulphur Springs. (He had filled in at the last minute when Jack Davison could not make it.) He tried the Hershey Open, and when he succeeded in finishing a good sixth, thought himself ready to battle for the big money. His club felt that he deserved the chance and backed him for a swing around the circuit in the winter of 1937.

The smooth-swinging mountaineer's first start was the $10,000 Miami-Biltmore tournament. He finished in tenth place, which was not as noteworthy as it might appear at first glance, since most of the name-players had been lured away from Florida to compete in the California tournaments. He joined the pack on the West Coast in January, still such a total unknown that when he finished sixth in the Los Angeles Open the newspapers misspelled the name "Sneed." They learned to spell the name right when Samuel Jackson Snead caught fire during the Oakland Open, shooting 69-65-67-69 for a winning total of 270.

Many of the golf writers knew more about James K. Polk than they did about Samuel J. Snead. Fred Corcoran filled them in on Snead's background as best he could, and the writers who had been energetic enough to leave the press tent and follow the young man for a few holes could supplement the hillbilly angle with enthusiastic reports on this fellow Snead's fine swing and his extraordinary length. Sam was bewildered by his overnight fame. When Corcoran showed him the photo *The New York Times* had run along with its account of the Oakland Open, Sam cocked his head to one side and said in his worried Appalachian drawl, "How'd they ever get my picture? I ain't never been to New York."

Following his breakthrough at Oakland, Sam Snead built up his bio by winning the Rancho Santa Fe Open (sponsored by

Bing Crosby) and carrying off his share of the spoils as the caravan swung cross-country to Florida and up the Atlantic coast. A suitable name was coined for him—"Slamming Sammy." All the world loves a long-hitter, and Snead could really powder that apple. In the driving contest held at the P.G.A. Championship, Sam averaged 307 yards on his three tries and won in a walk. Perhaps Jimmy Thomson hit them a bit farther when he really caught hold of the ball, but Jimmy could not compare with Sam in consistency. Or method. The marvelous thing about Snead was that he hit his tee shots with one of the sweetest, soundest swings golf has ever known. For many discerning students of the game, Sam Snead was simply in a class by himself when it came to the mechanics of hitting a golf shot. In the excitement over Snead's proficiency with his woods, his iron-play received less attention than it merited. Like most golfers who strike the ball decisively on the downswing, Sam could run into error on his irons when his timing was off, but he played them with the same smooth compactness that characterized his woods. Without pressing, relying on the perfect coordination of his pivot and his hitting action, Snead could drill a 4-iron to tight greens over two hundred yards away. (On par 5s he had room to use a 4-iron.) If there was a weakness in Snead's game—although it was not so apparent at the time—it was his putting. He was a fair birdie-holer, but by professional standards he was erratic on his short putts. The 2-foot-

ers bothered him even when he made them.

Wherever Sam Snead played, he made a fan of every person in the gallery who subconsciously was waiting for another Jones. In personality and manner, Sam and Bobby were miles apart, but when it came to that indefinable quality called magnetism, the shambling mountaineer had it. Spectators ignored the proven stars to give the newcomer the once-over, and after they had seen him hit one or two shots, they found it was impossible to leave. Snead's shots were far more beautiful than the raving sportswriters had claimed they were. Watching him, like watching Jones, provided an aesthetic delight. Here was that rarity, the long-hitter who combined power with the delicate nuances of shot-making, this slow-speaking, somewhat timid, somewhat cocky young man from the mountains.

Sam Snead did not cool off. In the 1937 Open, his first big test, he finished second. A strong finish by Ralph Guldahl was all that kept Snead from winning the crown in his first crack. The sensational freshman made the Ryder Cup team, and won his match from Dick Burton 5 and 4. He finished the year in fourth place among the money-winners with a take of $8,801. His sophomore season was even more successful. Included in his list of victories were the Nassau Open, the Miami Open (via a spectacular 30 on the last nine), Bing Crosby's 36-hole tourney at Del Mar (72-67—139), the Canadian, the first Goodall, and the Westchester 108-hole tourney. His total winnings between the first of

January and the fifteenth of October climbed to $17,572.83.

Two or three bad tournament days did disclose, much to the chagrin of Snead and his most ardent supporters, certain chinks in Slamming Sammy's armor. In the Pasadena Open, after a first-round 76 had made him cantankerous, Sam threw down his clubs after batting one out-of-bounds on the twelfth hole of his second round, and walked into the clubhouse. His subsequent apology for this childish petulance helped a bit. In the 1938 Open at Cherry Hills, he finished far back; after a ragged start, he had no comeback. In the final of the 1938 P.G.A. he was routed 8 and 7 by Paul Runyan, whom he was outdriving by fifty yards, and outputting by several yards as well. It was the widest margin ever run up in a P.G.A. final. When he was off his game, Sam was prone to sulk rather than hang in there like a Travers or a Hagen and think his way out of the wilderness. But Snead was mostly on and was regarded as the coming golfer, the next great champion. 1939 would undoubtedly be his year. Ralph Guldahl could not go on winning the Open indefinitely.

While Slamming Sammy Snead was setting the golfing world agog in 1937 and 1938, an immeasurably less attractive golfer, Ralph Guldahl, was colorlessly going about the job of doing something that only three men before him had been able to do—win two consecutive United States Open Championships.

Guldahl had reentered the professional picture in 1936, two and a half years after he had blown a chance for quick fame by missing the 4-footer that would have tied Johnny Goodman in the 1933 Open. The big, tousled Texan was a much improved golfer. Olin Dutra had helped him to change from a palm grip to finger control in 1935. Through long hours of practice he had corrected his principal bad habits, picking the clubhead up too early and cutting across the ball from the outside in. On his last two rounds of the 1933 Open, Ralph had taken 35 and 36 putts, but he had remedied this defect of his game as well. In that unexciting but important department of putting, rolling the long ones close to the hole, Ralph was now unsurpassed. The new Guldahl, however, was no more electric in action than the old Guldahl. In 1936, the year in which he won the first of three consecutive Westerns, the Radix trophy for low average, and $7,682.41, he was paired on the final day of the Open with Paul Runyan. For the gallery, Runyan was the attraction. The heavy slouching fellow in the sloppy white cap and rumpled trousers was merely the golfer who was playing along with Paul. When the spectators studied the final

standings on the board, they discovered that Guldahl had compiled the same total score as Runyan, 290, and a tie for eighth. This puzzled them elaborately. The big fellow seemed to have been playing about 77 golf. They could think of ten or twenty stylish shots that Runyan had played, but try as they would, they could not remember one brilliant shot by Guldahl.

A year later, 1937, Guldahl won his first Open, at Oakland Hills. Even in winning, Guldahl was partially overshadowed by the runner-up, Snead. Ralph was regarded more or less as "the other man," the fellow who beat Snead. It was grossly unfair to Ralph, since he won at Oakland Hills by playing a 69 on his final round, holding up sturdily under the pressure of knowing that he would lose unless he could match the 71 Snead had brought in on his last round. For seven holes Ralph was even 4s. On the eighth he chipped in from sixty-five yards for an eagle 3. On the ninth, a rugged par 3, he was on with a 2-iron and holed from twenty-five feet for his 2. These two sharp thrusts carried Ralph to the turn in 33. With nine holes to go, he was two or three strokes lower than he had figured he would be. He could drop one stroke to par on the last nine, a par 36, and still nose out Snead. This was not asking too much of a man who would be champion, and Ralph felt exactly that way about it. "If I can't play this last nine in thirty-seven strokes," he said on

DURING THE FINAL MATCH OF THE 1938 P.G.A. CHAMPIONSHIP, DIMINUTIVE PAUL RUNYAN, SHOWN PUTTING OPPOSITE, WAS INVARIABLY OUTDRIVEN BY THE LONG-HITTING SNEAD. RUNYAN'S ACCURACY AND SUPERB SHORT GAME, HOWEVER, GAVE HIM A LOPSIDED VICTORY OVER SNEAD.

the tenth tee, "I'm just a bum and don't deserve to win the Open."

He dropped a stroke to par on the tenth. He dropped another on the eleventh. The spectators began to speak in whispers, the way they always do when a crack-up seems imminent. Ralph brought them to life again with a birdie on the twelfth. On the thirteenth he all but holed his tee shot for an ace, and his easy birdie brought him back to even par on the back-nine. The fourteenth was routine, but on the next hole the pressure of the Open began to tell on Ralph. He hit his second shot very poorly, but was lucky. As it was about to bounce into the heavy rough, the ball struck the foot of a spectator and was diverted into a smooth trap by the green. Ralph played his wedge just right, and dropped his short putt. Harry Cooper, Guldahl's playing partner, nursed him along with skillful conversation as the bulky Texan managed his par on the sixteenth. Still even with par coming in. A stroke to spare on the last two holes. On the short seventeenth Ralph belted a low iron ten feet from the cup but nervously jabbed his putt. He holed his second putt for his 3 and was all for racing to the eighteenth tee when Cooper slowed him down by making him take his 10-footer over three times. It helped to relieve the tension. Going to the last hole, a par 5, Guldahl still carried his safety stroke, but he was comfortably on with his third shot, fifteen feet from the cup, safely home. He got down in 2 for his par. He had played the last nine in 36. He was not a bum and deserved to win the Open.

At Oakland Hills, Ralph Guldahl had put together rounds of 71-69-72-69 for a record-breaking 281. Thereafter he was profoundly respected as the magnificent stroke-play virtuoso he was, but he did not catch hold of the affections of the public. He went about his golf most of the time in a solemn, sluggish way that was utterly lacking in showmanship. When he felt sullen, he made no effort to conceal it, and even his grouchiness lacked the theatricality that would have turned him into a character whom Fred Corcoran could have billed as "The Scrooge of the Fairways." He had no idea what the galleries wanted in a champion. Where Tony Manero had won hearts by doffing his cap as he walked to the 72nd green, Ralph had paused a moment before his final 15-footer at Oakland Hills and combed his hair.

In 1938 Snead, Picard, and the other boys gobbled up the lesser tourneys, and the publicity, but when it came to the Open, the unglamorous champion again ran away from them. At Cherry Hills, in Denver, Guldahl won as he had at Oakland Hills, by playing a 69 on his last round to overtake the leader. Apart from Guldahl, only Dick Metz had completed his first three rounds without one score in the high 70s. Metz's 73-68-70 put him four strokes ahead of the defending champion, and only a fifty-foot chip by Guldahl smack into the cup on the 54th had prevented Metz from assuming a more commanding lead. Playing just in front of Guldahl, Metz ran headlong into a series of mistakes on his last round. Guldahl stalked his man with four deliberate 4s, all pars. On the fifth Ralph ran down another 4 for a birdie. At this point he caught Metz. On the sixth he went out in front by two strokes, picking up a birdie 2 where Metz had taken a 4. Metz was unable to get going, and the big unemotional man behind him pulled farther and farther away to win by six strokes, the widest margin that had separated an Open winner from the runner-up since Barnes had spread-eagled the field at Columbia in 1921. Ralph made only two errors on his machinelike 69, one on the eighth and the other on the eighteenth, where his spoon-shot ran over the green.

In joining Jones, McDermott, and Willie Anderson in that exclusive fraternity, winners of two consecutive Opens, Ralph had played his eight rounds in eleven under 4s—281 at Oakland Hills, 284 at Cherry Hills.

RALPH GULDAHL WAS A LARGE MAN WITH AN AWKWARD SWING WHO WON BACK-TO-BACK U.S. OPEN TITLES IN 1937 AND 1938. IN THE 1937 PHOTOGRAPH OPPOSITE, GULDAHL, IN THE DARK HAT, STANDS WITH SAM SNEAD, A MAN WITH A SMOOTH SWING WHO NEVER WON A U.S. OPEN TITLE AT ALL.

Lost: A Walker Cup

THE WALKER CUP.
(GOLF)

THE primary purpose of the Olympic Games is, of course, to promote international understanding. Whether or not the past Olympics have created more friction than friendship is a highly debatable topic. But sidestepping the moral issues involved, or not involved, and focusing on the contests themselves, the Olympic Games and other international rivalries have provided many of the most dramatic moments in sports, for the very good and obvious reason that whenever the representatives of different nations meet in competition, the air is supercharged with a tingle and electricity that strictly domestic rivalries cannot engender. Players and fans alike who pride themselves on being blasé about such things find a sense of patriotism—or simply a sense of involvement—tightening the throat and heightening the pulse beat. Track and field sports would be immeasurably poorer were there no Olympic Games, as tennis would be without the Davis Cup matches, soccer without the World Cup, and so on. Where international sports are concerned, there are few isolationists.

In golf through the years a keen though friendly rivalry has flourished

between the Americans and the British. They have invaded and carried off our championships. We have retaliated. The international aspect, as goes without the saying, was what made the feats of Travis, Ouimet, Hagen, and Jones seem so momentous to us, and made the British, for their part, so unanimously relieved when Henry Cotton (and, later, Tony Jacklin) revived the oriflamme of Vardon and Ray.

In addition to the personal sorties of Americans and Britishers, the players of the two countries have contended against one another in three sets of team matches, the amateurs battling for the Walker Cup, the pros for the Ryder Cup, the women for the Curtis Cup. The first of these competitions

to get underway was the Walker. Shortly after World War I, America developed able golfers in numbers for the first time, and a victory by a side of American amateurs over a British side in an informal match in 1921 dispelled any doubts among the Britishers that they still held a superiority that would make an international team match uninteresting and one-sided. In 1922 the top British and American amateurs met in the first official competition for the cup donated by George H. Walker, a past president of the U.S.G.A. Four years after the Walker Cup Matches were inaugurated, the groundwork for a similar transatlantic rivalry between American and British professionals was laid during an informal match at Wentworth in

England in which, incidentally, the Americans took a terrific lacing. Samuel Ryder of St. Albans, a wealthy English seed merchant, provided a trophy, and in 1927 a British squad journeyed to America for the first official Ryder Cup Match. In 1932, five years after the Ryder had gotten started at the Worcester Country Club, the top women golfers of the two countries met at Wentworth, outside London, in the maiden match for the cup donated by the Curtis sisters, Margaret and Harriot, two early champions. All three competitions were held biennially, in alternate countries, the Curtis and Walker in the even years, the Ryder in the odd. Taking their cue from the Walker Cup pattern, the Ryder Cup Matches consisted of four foursomes followed by eight singles; the Curtis modified it to three foursomes and six singles.

Before World War II canceled their outings, the women had met in four Curtis Cup competitions. Three times the Americans were victorious after hard-fought battles, and once, in 1936, at Gleneagles, they were held to a 4 1/2–4 1/2 tie when Wee Jessie Anderson won the vital singles by holing a 60-footer all the way across the home green. The standard of play in the Curtis Cup has been exceedingly high, and the atmosphere surrounding the matches has been ideal — serious, but not overserious, pleasantly warm but not gushy.

The Ryder Cup competitions, considering the wealth of colorful golfers who have been participants, have never been the events they should have been. The P.G.A. has shown less savvy than the U.S.G.A. (which supervises the Curtis and the Walker) in mounting the matches held in America; and in handling their end of the deal, the British professionals' organization has not upheld the reputed British genius for administration. To insure large galleries and healthy gate receipts, the British P.G.A., after selecting Moortown for the first match played in Britain, fastened on the mediocre course at Southport as the Ryder Cup stamping grounds. Southport became a stamping grounds in a most literal sense, for the seaside vacationers who formed the huge galleries carried their Coney Island *joie de vivre* with them onto the links. The marshals and the bamboo bearers were swept helplessly aside, concessionaires blatantly hawked their wares, while, amidst this confusion, the golfers did their best to bear up under the distracting carnival. Until 1937, when the Americans triumphed 8 points to 4 at Southport, neither side had been able to win a match on a foreign course. An odd sidelight was that a British victory in the Ryder Cup Match was invariably followed by an American victory in the British Open.

American teams, through 1974, won twenty-one of the twenty-four Walker Cup Matches, tying in 1965 and bowing only in 1938 and 1971. Though a bit more one-sided than the Ryder feud, the Walker, paradoxically enough, has been the more successful series — more tastefully presented, played on better courses, altogether higher-pitched. An amateur is less apt to "lose" his nationality than a professional, and even when the Matches were farcical from the standpoint of team totals, the Walker retained its aura of a serious but civilized international rivalry. The series has abounded in colorful incident. The "hero" of the first Match was none other than Bernard Darwin. Bernard, the great and the lovable, accompanied the British team to Charlie Macdonald's National in 1922 in the capacity of a reporter for the *Times* of London. When Robert Harris, the British captain, fell ill on the eve of the Match, Bernard stepped coolly into the breach, played creditably in his foursome, and won his singles from Bill Fownes 3 and 1. Jones was unfailingly superb in Walker Cup play. Bobby won all five of his singles by wide margins and four of his five foursomes, his one defeat coming in 1924, when he and Fownes were beaten on the last hole. Foursomes being a peculiarly British addiction, the Americans' aptitude in winning a type of match they play only during the Cup series came as a distinct surprise. Except for the 1923 and 1938 Matches, up to the outbreak of World War II the Americans were never outscored in the foursomes.

That meeting in 1923 at St. Andrews—until 1925 the Match was held annually—was won by the American team 6 points to 5 (with one singles halved) after one of the most thrilling team finishes on record. Trailing by two points after the foursomes, with two singles irretrievably lost and only one

singles definitely going their way, the Americans seemed hopelessly beaten, and then, at the last moment, one courageous rally after another snatched the victory away from the British. George Rotan swept eleven out of twelve holes and won easily. The other matches were closer. Standing 2 down with three to go against Wethered, Ouimet played birdies on the 34th and 35th, and earned a split in his match by holing from eighteen feet for a third birdie when he was partially stymied on the 36th green. Bob Gardner capped his comeback by sinking a 5-footer on the 36th for the hole and the match. Fred Wright, 2 down with three to go, evened his match by carrying the 34th and 35th, and won it with a birdie on the 36th. The winning or the losing of the cup eventually hung on the match between Willie Murray and Doc Willing, and Willing struck the decisive blow on the 35th by holing a 10-footer for a birdie.

The American team won the 1926 Match at St. Andrews by that identical score, 6–5, but thereafter the Matches were runaways for the Americans. The new and unseasoned players who replaced Jones and his crowd were as dependable as the veterans when it came to rising to the occasion. Don Moe, for example, shot the finest golf of his career in his first international competition, the 1930 Match. Out in 32 at Sandwich, the young Oregonian found himself 1 down to James Stout, who had collected six 3s. At lunch Moe was 4 down, and after the first three holes of the afternoon, 7 down.

Stout continued to play well and his card for the afternoon round was 72, but Moe beat him. All square coming to the 441-yard 36th, Moe played his second shot from a tough sidehill stance to within a yard of the cup and took the crucial hole. His 3 gave him a 67, a magnificent performance.

But while the American newcomers were turning the Walker Cup Matches into a springboard to fame, the Britishers who took over for the aging were far weaker competitors than the Tolley–Wethered generation. Only Tony Torrance had the stuff that wins singles matches. Torrance's 1-up victory over Chick Evans saved his side from the ignominy of a shutout in the '28 Match at the Chicago Golf Club. In 1930 he accounted for half of the British points by submerging Ouimet 7 and 6 at Sandwich. Tony received the symptoms of support in 1932, when he halved with Ouimet, for Stout and John Burke also halved their matches and Leonard Crawley actually won his. But in 1934 it was the same sad story, Torrance alone rising above the inferiority complex that now gripped the British side and winning his singles once again in his last appearance as Walker Cupper.

In their efforts to assemble a team that would at least lose by a respectable score, the British selectors resurrected veterans, dug up more Scots, gave youth a chance, and became a little less blinded by the social

stripes of the Old School Tie. When their teams continued to lose by vast margins, the selectors resorted to even more desperate measures and included in their 1936 squad a teenage schoolboy champion (John Langley), a left-hander (Laddie Lucas), and an Irishman (Cecil Ewing). The 1936 British team at length succeeded in gaining the distinction the four previous teams had been flirting with, a coat of whitewash.

The 9–0 humiliation at Pine Valley in the 1936 Match shocked the British into cleaning house from the cellar up. The old selectors were excused, and a new board installed. In studying the form of the players who looked to be Cup timber for the 1938 Match, the new selectors covered the geographical areas in more detail than their predecessors. They gave proof that they meant business when they invited a large number of candidates to come to St. Andrews in late May and play in tryout tests on which the final selection of the team would be based. Jettisoning all social distinctions, they named to their squad Charley Stowe, a hulking ex-coal miner, one of the unprettiest technicians on the island but a golfer who got results. A major problem the selectors and the team captain, John Beck, knew they faced was ridding their players' minds of the myth that the Americans were supermen. At the tryouts at St. Andrews, Jimmy Bruen, an eighteen-

year-old boy from Ireland, accomplished this invaluable service for the selectors and Beck. Aggressive, strong, and with a brilliant flair for the game, young Bruen reeled off a succession of sub-par rounds. Bruen's scoring bred a feeling among the British players that for once their side had a leader who could match any American star, and this confidence in Bruen kept on enlarging until the British players came to believe that as a side they were just as good as the Americans. In addition to Bruen and Stowe, the British team was made up of Hector Thomson, the 1936 British Amateur Champion, an amateur with a professional's poise; Gordon Peters and Alex Kyle, like Thomson, from Scotland; Cecil Ewing from Ireland, the runner-up to Charley

Yates in the 1938 British Amateur; Frank Pennink, a steady Oxfordian; Leonard Crawley, a pupil of Cotton's, ex-schoolmaster and cricketer, a natural competitor, and the proud possessor of a ginger mustache and an antique mustard-colored sweater; and Harry Bentley, a merry Lancashireman, the comedian of the team. Bentley, who had won the French Amateur and always played well in France, got a great boot out of referring to France as "my country" and in muttering phrases like "*C'est difficile*" to relieve the seriousness of a match.

The American team that Francis Ouimet shepherded to Britain was a fairly well-balanced young team composed of four Walker Cup veterans and four novitiates. The man expected to play number one was

Johnny Goodman, now an insurance sales-man and at twenty-eight the oldest man on the squad. Goodman had finally won the Amateur at Alderwood in Portland, Oregon, in 1937. The one other veteran of two Walker Cup Matches was Johnny Fischer. After helping to apply the whitewash at Pine Valley in 1936, Fischer had taken the Amateur, at Garden City Golf Club, by coming from behind in the final to overhaul Jock McLean with a birdie on the 36th green and to win out with a birdie on the first extra hole. Reynolds Smith and Charley Yates, who had won their matches handily in 1936, were back again. The four freshmen had the following credentials: Freddy Haas, from New Orleans, had captured the Intercollegiate and the Southern; Charley Kocsis, from Detroit, had a sound all-round record in sectional, collegiate, and national tournaments; Ray Billows, the kingpin in the New York area, had reached the final of the 1937 Amateur; Marvin "Bud" Ward, from Tacoma, had an adequate sectional record and in the 1936 Amateur had fought a fine semi-final with Goodman before losing. (Ward's credentials were not too formidable, and the followers of Frank Strafaci, Harry Givan, and Wilfred Wehrle let it be known that they thought their men had been done dirt.) The 1938 team was certainly not up to the standards of the 1922 team, for instance—every member of the '22 team won at least one national championship—

but the American golfing public had become so accustomed to lopsided victories over the British that the possibility of losing the tenth Walker Cup Match scarcely entered their minds.

Ouimet was able to get a line on his boys during the British Amateur, which was held at Troon just before the Cup Matches. On the strength of what they showed at Troon, Ouimet was led to make several changes in his batting order. Goodman, far off his best form (and displeased with himself for losing to Kocsis in an early round), was dropped to the second spot, and Charley Yates was promoted to number one. Yates had hit the ball wonderfully well in winning the British Amateur. Everything was coming into his strenuous swing at the right time, and several Scots who had witnessed Charley's impressive march were almost convinced that what was holding back British golfers was that they didn't dip their knees as Yates did when he hurled his right side viciously into his shots. The Scots cottoned on to Yates as soon as they heard he was a fellow-townsman of Bobby Jones', and Charley's forcing golf and rich sense of humor made him the most popular man in Scotland.

The third of June, the first day of the two-day meeting at St. Andrews, brought good weather for golf. A light breeze off the bay was stirring the whins and the air was agreeably cool as the rival captains,

DURING THE 1938 WALKER CUP MATCHES AT ST. ANDREWS, IRISH PLAYER JIMMY BRUEN, OPPOSITE, DRIVES FROM THE RAILWAY-FLANKED 17TH TEE OF THE TREACHEROUS ROAD HOLE.

Ouimet and Beck, watched their charges tee off in the four 36-hole foursome matches. Seven hours later, for the first time in fifteen years, a British team was out in front after the first day's play—2 points to 1. Pennink and Crawley, in the fourth foursome, defeated Smith and Haas 3 and 1 in a match that was not as close as the score implies. The British team was always in command, and Crawley's irons and Pennink's putting abruptly halted the periodic attempts of the Americans to get back into the match. Peters and Thomson, the Scottish combo, raced off to a lead against Goodman and Ward in the second foursome and were never seriously threatened as they went on to a 4 and 2 victory. Goodman, still off his game, was conspicuously irritated by his own errors and Ward's, and his attitude did not make it any easier for

his less experienced partner to settle down. Because of the many criticisms of his selection for the team, Ward had felt that he was on the spot before he sailed for Scotland, and his poor play at Troon, where he was fighting a quick hook, gave the anti-Ward society further fuel for its second-guessing. Ward was handicapped by being overdetermined to "show them," it seemed, and Goodman was certainly not the steadying influence he might have been. The American victory was racked up by the team of Yates and Billows, who had their match against the third British pair, Kyle and Stowe, under control at all times. The feature foursome, which pitted Fischer and Kocsis against Bruen and Bentley, was definitely the hardest-fought and best-played match. At the close of the morning round, in which they had dovetailed for a

72, 1 under St. Andrews' par, Fischer and Kocsis were 3 up on the British pair. Though not playing badly, Bruen was not up to the brilliance of his practice rounds, and it had been Bentley who had prevented the Americans from gaining a larger lead. The British did not win a hole all morning, and while they were the aggressors in the afternoon, not until the 27th did they break through with a win. Had the British wanted to be technical, however, they could have claimed the 21st. On this hole, after Bentley and Bruen had made their 4, Fischer lined up the 10-footer for a birdie 3 that Kocsis' approach had set up. Johnny babied the putt. It stopped a foot or so short of the cup. It would have been a routine half in 4s if Johnny, momentarily upset by being unforgivably short on the birdie putt, had not walked up to the ball and tapped it into the hole. By tapping the ball, Fischer had played out of turn. It had been Kocsis' shot. Bruen, impatient to get going, was all for demanding the hole on Fischer's infraction of foursome rules. Bentley was just as eager as his young partner to win a hole, but the cool Lancashireman did not choose to win one this way. He finally calmed young Bruen with his explanation that he had conceded the Americans their foot putt before Fischer had tapped it, and waiving any claim to the hole, assured his partner that he thought they were playing good enough golf to win the match if they stuck to their knitting. On the 27th, still 3 down, Bruen and Bent-

ley won their first hole of the day when the Irish boy holed for a birdie from eighteen feet. On the 29th they won another with a birdie 2, Bruen once more dropping a sizable putt. Fischer and Kocsis stopped this rally when they took the 30th, and the Americans' lead of two holes loomed larger and larger as the 31st, 32nd, and 33rd were halved. Then the British pair struck back with a gallant last-ditch drive. On the 34th Bentley put his chip inside of Kocsis', and Bruen holed for a win that cut the Americans' margin to one hole. On the 35th, Bentley squared the match by knocking a 45-footer into the can for an eagle 3. Bentley's sharp approach to the 36th gave Bruen a crack for a birdie that would have beaten the Americans, but the young man's putt was wide of the mark, and the hole and the match were halved. It was probably a fortunate thing for the Americans that Walker Cup Matches do not go into extra holes, for Bentley and Bruen, who had used only 68 strokes on their afternoon comeback, were getting hotter and hotter whereas Fischer and Kocsis were fading fast.

In Walker Cup Matches at this time, no points or fractions thereof were given for a halved match, hence the 2–1 lead the British carried into the second day of play. Insignificant as the British margin seems on paper, that one-point difference backed the Americans against the wall. A split in the eight singles matches would result in a British victory. To hold the Cup, Ouimet's boys could afford to lose no more than three of the eight singles.

At noon things didn't look too rosy for the Americans. Johnny Goodman had been thoroughly outclassed by Hector Thomson's 69, and stood 6 down. Fischer was 4 down to Crawley's 71. These two matches seemed as good as lost, and that wasn't all. The outcome of four matches—Smith versus Peters, Haas versus Kyle, Billows versus Ewing, Kocsis versus Stowe—was still undetermined after the first eighteen, but any of them could go to the Britisher as easily as to the American, and the loss of just one would be disastrous. Only two matches were going the way of the Americans. Charley Yates had a slight lead in his scrap with Bruen, and there was a feeling that he would be able to match anything the Irish whiz threw at him; Charley was playing confidently. Ironically, the much-maligned Ward was the one American who had his match virtually won after the morning round. In an exhibition of very great shot-making, the grim tax accountant from Tacoma had whirled around St. Andrews in 67 strokes and was 9 *up* on the hapless Pennink.

In the afternoon the tide of battle seemed to be turning. Once more the Americans appeared to be off on one of those team rallies that had so often overcome the British challenges in the past. Charley Yates successfully protected his thin lead over Bruen and registered his victory on the 35th. Bud Ward, piling it on, took three of the first seven holes from Pennink to win 12 and

11, and here was another point for the Americans. Kocsis, the report came in, was getting the upper hand over Stowe, and, most heartening of all, a match that had been chalked off as lost was won. Standing 4 down to the man with the ginger mustache, Johnny Fischer had turned his battle with Crawley inside out by shooting six consecutive 3s from the 25th through the 30th, and closed Leonard out on the 34th green.

Most of the spectators had been following the exciting Fischer–Crawley match. When it was over, they lingered around the sixteenth green exchanging information on the matches that were "in" and rumors on the matches that were still in progress. Thomson had finished Goodman, Peters had trounced Smith, and some hasty addition disclosed that each side had now garnered four points (including the foursomes) with three matches yet to be decided. Fischer's remarkable recovery had raised the hopes of the handful of American spectators and sobered the spirits of the British. By taking two of the three matches still out, the Americans could win.

And then the tide of battle swung back to the British, suddenly and dramatically. Kocsis and Stowe were coming into sight on the sixteenth tee, the 34th hole of their match. The last definite word on this pair was that Kocsis was 1 up on the ex-coal miner as they left the 29th green. But Kocsis carried no lead as he and Stowe walked set-faced down the 34th. Kocsis was 2 down. Stowe had taken the 30th, the 31st, and the

32nd. The spectators picked up this match and followed it to the 35th green, where Stowe tucked it away 2 and 1. His victory put the British team in front by a point. Haas would have to beat Kyle, Billows would have to beat Ewing, or else the British were in.

Nobody seemed to know how Haas and Kyle, the last starters, were coming along. They would be somewhere around the thirteenth, and rather than chase after them, the majority of the spectators back-tracked a hole to pick up Ewing and Billows on the sixteenth. Beyond the fact that these two fighters were locked in an extremely tight give-and-take, nothing more was known for certain. Billows was seen to be driving first off the 34th, and it was soon discovered that he had won the honor by birdieing the 33rd. But it was also discovered that he was 1 down to Ewing. Ewing batted one out-of-bounds on the 34th, and Billows squared the match. They moved on to the Road Hole, both men patently worn from their furious duel. Billows put his second into the deep bunker by the green and would have to fight hard for his half ... and then, as the thousands tensely watched Billows enter the bunker, over the hill came Kyle and Haas preceded by the small gallery who had watched their match. It was good news for the British and it spread across the fairway like wildfire. Kyle had defeated Haas on the 32nd.

That was it. Great Britain had won the Walker Cup. For the first time!

The Billows–Ewing match didn't matter now. Ewing did win the 35th, guarded his one-hole advantage on the 36th, and this made the final count Great Britain 7, United States 4.

The British had been the better team at St. Andrews. When the better team wins, it is not so hard to lose. The Americans quickly got over the sting of losing a cup they had held without interruption since 1922, and joined with the overjoyed Britons in celebrating the successful conclusion of their sixteen-year vigil. On the steps of the Royal and Ancient, the cup changed hands as thousands smiled. The Scottish majority in the crowd began calling for Yates, their favorite, who had gone undefeated in eleven matches in Scotland, and with very little coaxing the uninhibited Georgian sauntered onto the "stage" wearing that cockeyed grin of his. Completely at home with his friends, Yates passed up speech-making in favor of leading the crowd in an old Scottish song: With Gordon Peters helping him out, Charley bellowed his way through "A Wee Deoch and Doris." The high-spirited community-sung chorus ended on a happy note, and so did The Walker Cup Matches of 1938. It would have been grand to have won, but if you had to lose, where else would circumstances have made defeat so sweet?

All Good Things

A FTER he had won his Walker Cup match 12 and 11, Bud Ward stayed out on the course to see how his team mates were faring. An American fan, spotting Ward on the fringe of the gallery following the Fischer–Crawley match, walked over to Bud and congratulated him on his splendid victory. How much had he won by, the fan asked. "Twelve and eleven," was the stern-voiced answer. The American went on to say that he had watched Ward on his morning round and knew about the marvelous 67, but how well had he scored in the afternoon? "I had four-four-three-three-six-four-four," Ward answered. When Ward had come to the 6, the American had smiled one of those smiles

meant to imply that he understood—sooner or later a bad hole must creep onto the card of every golfer, even if he be the man who has just taken St. Andrews apart like no amateur before him. The smile offended Ward. "I would have had my par on the fifth if I hadn't three-putted," he said testily. "I hit three good shots. I three-putted, that's all."

In his attitude toward the game's camp followers, Bud Ward bore the marks of the severe beating he had taken before his crashing victory over Pennink had silenced his detractors. He brushed off compliments and declined to cultivate the little courtesies that would have made him popular with the galleries, for he had

learned the painful way of the fickleness of sports fans. Win and you're a great guy, lose and you're a monkey. On the golf course Ward tended strictly to winning. The social amenities could wait until later when he was among his friends.

But if Ward's experiences in the spring of 1938 had put acid in his attitude, they had also put iron in his self-confidence. In vindicating himself so gloriously against Pennink, Ward had acquired an unshakable belief in himself that changed him from a fair golfer

into the outstanding amateur in the four-season stretch between the last prewar Walker Cup Match and Pearl Harbor.

In the qualifying round for the 1938 Amateur, at Oakmont, Ward tied for second place with Willie Turnesa and Dick Chapman, two strokes behind the medalist, Gus Moreland. Some very hot golf by Art Doering, however, was too much for Bud and he went out in the first round, 3 and 1. (Turnesa, the quiet, smooth swinger, took the title by defeating Pat Abbott 8 and 7. In the final Willie gave an amazing demonstration of blaster-play from Oakmont's furrowed bunkers and one-putted no less than fourteen of the twenty-nine greens.) The next year, 1939, Ward crashed through. In the Open he matched the best professionals stroke for stroke. *Ifs* do not count, of course, but if Ward had not hooked a tee shot on a short hole on the last nine and ended up with a 5, he might have won the Open. As it was, his 285 (69-73-71-72) was one stroke above the winning mark shared by Nelson, Wood, and Shute. Ward's showing in the Open made him a heavy favorite to take the Amateur at the North Shore Country Club, near Chicago, some three months later. In the semi-finals he got his revenge on Doering, 2 and 1. Against Ray Billows in the final, played in a twisting, gusty wind, Ward was 1 under par for the thirty-one holes he required to win the match.

The hard-boiled champion took it on the chin when he attempted to defend his title at Winged Foot a year later. Bud appeared to be on his game as he took care of Ellis Knowles, Freddy Haas, and Pat Abbott on his way to the quarter-finals, but there he ran into a wild streak, and Ray Bil-

lows defeated him with no more trouble than the 4 and 3 count suggests. (Ward's successor was Dick Champman, the son of a wealthy man who had raised his boy to be a golf champion. It was curious that Champman, who had sat before the most celebrated instructors in golf, and Joe Ezar as well, won the Amateur when he was employing a swing so awkward and unrhythmic that it looked as if he had never taken a lesson in his life. But at Winged Foot—which, incidentally, was one of Dick's home courses— he was getting results, and was an unpressed and deserving winner.)

Ward regained his crown in 1941, and in doing so defeated not only some capable opponents but also some of the most hostile galleries a golfer had faced since Travis at Sandwich. The Omaha Field Club, where the Amateur was held, was not in the best of shape—the fairways scorched by the summer heat, several of the greens mottled with bare spots. Many of the competitors were unhappy about the conditions, and Ward, according to the hometown newspapers, had called the Omaha Field Club "a cow pasture." Ward denied having made this statement, but some of the proud people of Omaha, affronted by the general slurs against their leading golf course (and additionally upset by the elimination in the first

Bud Ward, opposite, was the top American amateur player in the post-Lawson Little era. Ward proved himself by winning the U.S. Amateur title in 1939 and 1941, and by playing a flawless Walker Cup round at St. Andrews in 1938. On the following pages, Sam Snead faced heartbreak on the 72nd hole of the 1939 U.S. Open at the Philadelphia Country Club. Needing only a par five to win the Open, Snead's two shots out of this bunker and three putts yielded an 8 on the final hole and a devastating loss.

round of their favorite son, Johnny Good-man), decided, under the influence of the dogstar, to square accounts with Ward. If he had lost, all would have been forgiven, most likely, but the man they wanted to see lose, this sour, unrepentant, businesslike competitor from Spokane, was too good for his opponents. He reached the final, where he was opposed by Pat Abbott, who had been a finalist against Turnesa three years before.

In the morning round the gallery of three thousand Omahans looked on with displeasure as the genial Abbott, an actor by profession, fell farther and farther behind the man they wanted him to beat. In the afternoon Abbott revived their hopes when he struck a streak of chipping and putting that reduced Ward's lead from five holes to two. Ward was on his way to winning or halving the 24th hole, or rather, Abbott had apparently halted his own surge when his iron approach, played from a downhill lie in the coarse rough, hit the green with no stop on it and was heading for the steep bank behind the green. It was at this moment that some members of the raucous anti-Ward gallery, as Bill Richardson of *The New York Times* reported it, decided that the time had come for more demonstrative partici-pation. As Abbott's ball was running fast over the green, six spectators on the far apron moved in front of the ball and stopped it short. It may have been an acci-dent. Then, as the partisan gallery unwound itself from Abbott's ball, a marshal kicked

the ball nearer the pin as accidentally as the six spectators had stopped it. At this junc-ture, Harold Pierce, the president of the U.S.G.A., walked to the center of the green and addressed the gallery. "We all know what is happening here today," Mr. Pierce began slowly, and he went on to request an immediate cessation of the conduct that was making a travesty of a national champi-onship. After this censure, the spectators did not touch Abbott's ball again, but in spirit they remained unchastised. On the 31st hole, for instance, Ward hit an approach that was much too strong. "Let her through. Let her through," yelled some members of the gallery who were fearful lest their col-leagues clustered behind the green inadver-tently prevent Ward's shot from carrying over the green into trouble. Despite the gallery and competent golf by Abbott, Ward built up his lead again and ended the match on the 33rd green. The gallery then swooped in on the loser and hoisted him triumphant-ly to their shoulders.

It was not one of the shining chapters in American sportsmanship.

As close as Bud Ward came to winning the 1939 Open, Sam Snead came closer, much closer. With only two more of the seventy-two hells of the grind to endure, the popular man from the mountains had the title in the bag. Pars on the 71st and 72nd would give Sam 282, two strokes better than the total at which Nelson, Wood, and Shute had tied. Sam looked shaky, very shaky, in dropping a stroke to par on the 71st, when he fell a full foot shy on his putt from six feet, yet there was no cause for alarm. Hitting a golf ball under pressure, the spectators knew from their own experience, takes it out on a man's nerves more vehemently than any other effort in sports. Nearly every member of the gallery at one time or another in his life had stood on the eighteenth tee with a chance to win the Saturday tournament and had found that his vertebrae shivered like a marimba and kept on shivering when he tried to relax and laugh at himself for becoming so keyed up at the prospect of getting his name in the paper and winning an electric clock. The 90s-golfers and the 107-golfers watching Snead knew that nearly every other athlete has an incalculable advantage over the golfer under tournament pressure. The football or the hockey player can get rid of his nervousness by bodily contact, the old releaser, and even the ping-pong player can *move*, and the act of moving does wonders for the athlete under tension. But the golfer, stationary before a stationary ball, is helpless. No one jars him out of his introspection with a left to the jaw. He cannot run three steps to the left and by that physical motion assuage the rat-tat-tat of his nerves and banish that indigo foreboding that he will be fifty yards off-line if his hands fail by a fraction of a second to do the right thing at the right time. What other sport punishes a minuscule error by the *fingers* so savagely? What other sport

gives a player less chance to wipe out an error? Double-fault in tennis; you have lost only a point in a game of a set of a match; win a point and you're often as well off as you were before your error. Miss a lay-up in basketball; you have a dozen other opportunities to atone, and scoring is merely part of a player's efficiency anyhow. Throw wild to first base, and it may not hurt at all, but if it does, you can play the next ball hit to you as if nothing had happened. Compared to golf, other sports are lenient with the transgressor. But golf—roll your wrist before your swing is ready for it and the ball flies madly into the rough . . . and you don't tee up again and say to yourself that that was a bad one and you'll make up for it by hitting a good one now. Golf does not revert to a set situation. There is no fresh restart. Each thing you do you are stuck with. When the ball flies wildly into the rough, on your next shot you pay the immediate penalty for your error, and error breeds error. More than the terror of knowing you must beat forty players and not a single player, more than the always-varying, ever-unpredictable character of the terrain on which the game is played, more than the unreasonable proportion with which a small error in muscular control is often punished, it is the knowledge that there is no recourse from a bad shot plus the unrelenting accumulativeness of shot on shot that makes tournament golfers old before their time and that made a seasoned golfer like Sam Snead shiver like a marimba as he teed up his ball on the 72nd hole of the

Spring Mill course of the Philadelphia Country Club in the United States Open Championship of 1939.

There was no cause for alarm, however. All Sam Snead had to do to win was to play the 558-yard eighteenth in five strokes, par. An expert like Sam would not take a 6 on a fairly easy par 5, but in the event that he did, he would still tie for first.

Snead hit his drive squarely, but his right hand apparently turned over too quickly, for the ball hooked into the trampled rough. Snead elected to play a wood from the rough. Maybe it would have been smarter to have taken an iron. Anyhow, Sam played a brassie in an effort to eat up as much distance as possible, and he pushed it off into a bunker about a hundred yards before the green. He was worried now, and his face and his walk showed it. He failed to get the ball out of the bunker on his third shot, and now he was lost. He played his fourth before he had thought the shot out, and barely extricated the ball from the bunker. He made the green with his fifth. He putted once, to three feet. He putted again. He putted once more.

Sam Snead walked like a man hypnotized through the stunned, muttering crowd. He sat silently in the clubhouse trying to adjust himself to the unreal fact that he had taken an 8 and blown the championship. He didn't want to speak to anyone, least of all to the reporters.

Outside the crowd was still muttering. Few of them had seen Diegel take his 8 at Worcester or Hancock his two 6s at Olympia Fields. Most of the spectators had never before witnessed a crackup of this dimension. They talked it over and tried to puzzle it out, as if it had been caused by something occult and mysterious. And one well-known professional, recalling the transfixed look in Sam Snead's eyes as he had walked away from his nightmare, shook his head and said, neither cruelly nor sentimentally, simply said, "Snead will never be able to get over this. He will never be able to win an important championship after this. He'll never be the same."

Had the sympathies of the sports fans of America not been drained dry by Sam Snead's tragic collapse, they might have been more affected than they were when Craig Wood, after tieing for first place with Byron Nelson and Denny Shute, lost still another championship playoff in the 1939 Open.

Wood had made the playoff through a courageous finish. On the last hole he had busted his second shot all the way to the green and got the birdie he realized he had to get. In the extra round to decide the first triple tie in the Open since the historic Ouimet–Ray–Vardon playoff in 1913, Shute fell by the wayside early. Nelson and Wood

BY THE END OF 1940, BEN HOGAN, A YOUNG TEXAS PRO, OPPOSITE, HAD WON A FEW TOURNAMENTS AND HAD BEGUN TO WIN SERIOUS MONEY ON TOUR. HOGAN EVENTUALLY MADE GOLF HISTORY.

fought it out tooth and nail to the eighteenth green, and there Wood could have ended it had he holed an 8-footer. He missed, so Craig and Byron went into a second playoff, and this time Byron had it and Craig didn't—70 strokes for Byron, 73 for Craig.

By losing the Open playoff Craig Wood ran to three the championships he had lost after tieing for the top. In 1933 Shute had beaten him in the playoff for the British Open. In 1935 Sarazen had snatched the Masters away from him by holing that double-eagle and then outplaying him over the extra thirty-six. The only one of the four big professional championships that Wood had not lost in a playoff was the P.G.A., and in 1934 Wood had been defeated by Runyan in the final of that tourney. Considering the gall and wormwood he had swallowed, the manner in which Wood took his latest and most bitter disappointment was thoroughly to be admired. He was not downcast. He would have liked to have won, but he salvaged some satisfaction in knowing that at Spring Mill he had played the finest golf of his life.

Craig wasn't getting any younger. He was thirty-seven when he lost to Nelson, and after they have reached thirty-five, most golfers have passed their peak and are on the way down. In the 1940 Open, however, Wood came through with another excellent performance. He totaled 289 for his four rounds over the stiff Canterbury course

and finished fourth, two strokes behind Little and Sarazen, a stroke behind Horton Smith (making his last strong bid for a national championship), a stroke ahead of Nelson, Guldahl, Ray Mangrum's brother Lloyd, and the sensational Ben Hogan, who had cleaned up on the circuit and was starting out on a prolonged streak of superlative golf that would carry him into the money in fifty-six consecutive tournaments. (Snead, by the way, the-man-who-had-taken-an-8-on-the-72nd-hole-of-the-Open, had an 81 on his fourth round when a 72 would have won for him. It was rather pitiable.)

Craig Wood philosophically readied himself for another campaign in 1941. It proved to be the year that amply rewarded his gameness and his patience.

In the spring Wood won the Masters. The situation at Augusta was tense from the moment Wood posted his first-round score, a 66. Here was the best chance he had ever had. No gallery ever pulled harder than the gallery at Augusta was pulling for Craig. A brace of 71s gave him a three-stroke edge on the field with a round to go. So far in the tournament, Craig had not suffered any of his usual bad breaks, and when his caddie caught a rabbit that had been scooting across the fairway, Craig instructed the young man to carry the good-luck omen the rest of that final round. Despite the four rabbit's feet, Craig lost his lead by the 63rd.

Craig Wood, a hard-luck golfer, finally won big in 1941. In April, he won the Masters. In June, he captured the U.S. Open at the Colonial course in Ft. Worth where a local newspaper diagrammed his winning putt, opposite—an 18-footer he sank for a birdie on the 72nd hole.

He had needed 38 strokes going out, and Byron Nelson had burned up the nine in 33. With nine holes to go, Nelson and Wood were exactly even. But Wood did not buckle. He came home in 34, and when Nelson slipped to a 37, Wood had scored the most notable triumph in a career that went back to the Kentucky Open of 1925.

Wood's dreams of going on to take the U.S. Open received a rude jolt two weeks before the big event. On the morning of May 22, Craig was preparing to shave. As he was reaching in the cabinet for his razor, he suffered an excruciating muscle spasm in his back, in the lumbo-sacral region near the fifth vertebra, as a specialist later informed the worried veteran. To enable Wood to walk and hit his shots without pain—Craig had his heart set on playing the Open—the specialist prescribed a heavy and involved corset belt. Working out in his harness on the course of the Colonial Golf Club in Fort Worth, the Open site, Wood felt uncomfortably restricted, but when he removed the belt, the pain was intense and he could not concentrate on his shots. He put the belt on again.

Colonial was not then a course worthy of the Open. It was too young a course, barely six years old. Two holes were being played for the first time. Under perfect conditions, Colonial would have been somewhat of a trial; in the weather that prevailed during the Open, Colonial was a quagmire. The ground was not porous enough to drain the many inches of rain that electric storms and a steady downpour cast on the course. Fairways and greens were puddled with water. Traps were almost unplayable. The most impervious stretches of Colonial were turned into muck and mud as the golfers sloshed toward the greens. Wood, oddly enough, profited from the inundation. His strong legs and Mehlhornesque shoulders made him a consistently good mudder, and even with a corset restricting his swing, he met the conditions at Colonial more successfully than the younger, haler pros. A 73 and a 71 placed Craig in a tie for the lead at the halfway mark. His woods were straight, as they had to be in the narrow fairways, and he was fading his irons elegantly into the pin. A 70 put him in the van by two strokes after fifty-four holes. Another 70 made it conclusive. There was no challenge. Wood's was a striking, clear-cut, three-stroke triumph.

Thirty-nine when he won in the marshes of Fort Worth, Craig Wood was the oldest American to win our most important championship. (In later years Ben Hogan took the 1953 Open at forty and Julius Boros the 1963 Open at forty-three.) The gamester in the corset had finished like a colt. On the 72nd he had slammed out his best drive of the tournament. He had faded a 7-iron eighteen feet from the cup. Then he had rammed in his putt for a birdie.

What had happened to Guldahl? This was the question that golf fans were asking more and more insistently. When Wood won at Colonial, Guldahl was not even among the first twenty. It was not a momentary slump, not one of those bad weeks that punctuate the good ones. In 1941 Ralph Guldahl, the masterful medalist, did not have one week in which he performed like the golfer who had swept three successive Westerns, two successive Opens, and the 1939 Masters. What had happened to Guldahl?

Ralph Guldahl didn't know. He was still trying to hit the ball the same way he had in '37, '38, '39. He hadn't monkeyed around with his swing. It wasn't his personal habits, for Ralph was a clean liver, didn't drink or smoke. He was baffled when he found that he could not shake off his slump. He asked his friends among the pros for their suggestions. None of them knew for sure what had happened to Guldahl. They stood by as Ralph hit hundreds of balls off the practice tees, checking each position of his hands, his clubhead, and his body, but they could not spot what he was doing wrong. Ralph had slow-motion pictures taken of his "slump swing" and studied them along with the pictures shot at Augusta when he had triumphed in 1939. As far as he or any of his friends could make out, the two swings were identical, fundamental for fundamental, detail for detail. But, obviously, they weren't. If they were, Ralph still would have been playing winning golf and not struggling to break 76. His shots would have had that sharp click and not sounded as though Ralph were hitting a soggy pudding-bag.

Although no one could point out what had happened to Ralph Guldahl, there was no dearth of theories. A popular one was that the invisible, infinitesimal error in Ralph's timing was caused by his breathing. Another well-supported theory blamed it on the hands; an upright swinger, Ralph, who used the merest suspicion of a pivot, might have thrown too heavy a burden on his arms and hands; his was, therefore, the easiest kind of a groove to lose and the hardest to rediscover. Sam Snead, as close to Guldahl as anyone, didn't claim to know what Ralph's trouble was but Sam thought he knew when it had begun—in the tail end of the winter of 1940. Partnered with Snead in the annual Miami Four-ball, in one match Ralph had hit only three greens in eighteen holes. Sam's views on the Guldahl mystery synthesized the opinions of most of Ralph's colleagues. "When Ralph was winning," Sam once commented, "he had some peculiar habits, like all of us. His left elbow used to be stuck out a bit. He used to toe in his irons. He drew the ball a little. But those small things didn't amount to anything. When Ralph was at his peak, his clubhead came back on the line and went through on the line as near perfect as anyone I've seen. I don't know what happened to Ralph."

Nor does anyone, even now.

The outbreak of World War II in September 1939, as this survey of the highlights of the 1938-41 stretch may imply, did not put a damper on sports schedules and sports enthusiasm in the United States. However, the Ryder Cup Match, planned for Ponte Vedra, Florida, in November 1939, had to be called off, as did the other Anglo-American competitions. Johnny Bulla, the clouter who played the drugstore ball, could not try to better the runner-up position he had gained in the 1939 British Open. There was no French Championship for Dick Chapman to recapture. International golf, what there was of it, was inter-American. (The winner of the Argentine Open of 1941 was Jimmy Demaret, a Texan who had jumped to the forefront by taking the 1940 Masters.) But in the United States, since it was life-as-usual, it was golf-as-usual, making minor allowances for the increase in griping among the Scotch-drinking clique in the locker room, the threadbare look coming over the tweeds of the tweedy, and the unflinching despotism of club pros as they doled out their shrinking supply of good balls. But after December 7, 1941, the United States was in it, and there were some changes made.

U.S. AND INTERNATIONAL GOLF RECORDS

Winners of United States Golf Championships

Year	U.S. Open	U.S. Amateur	U.S. Women's Amateur
1895	Horace Rawlins	Charles B. Macdonald	Mrs. C.S. Brown
1896	James Foulis	H.J. Whigham	Miss Beatrix Hoyt
1897	Joe Lloyd	H.J. Whigham	Miss Beatrix Hoyt
1898	Fred Herd	Findlay S. Douglas	Miss Beatrix Hoyt
1899	Willie Smith	H.M. Harriman	Miss Ruth Underhill
1900	Harry Vardon	Walter J. Travis	Miss Frances C. Griscom
1901	Willie Anderson	Walter J. Travis	Miss Genevieve Hecker
1902	Lawrence Auchterlonie	Louis N. James	Miss Genevieve Hecker
1903	Willie Anderson	Walter J. Travis	Miss Bessie Anthony
1904	Willie Anderson	H. Chandler Egan	Miss Georgiana M. Bishop
1905	Willie Anderson	H. Chandler Egan	Miss Pauline Mackay
1906	Alex Smith	Eben M. Byers	Miss Harriot S. Curtis
1907	Alex Ross	Jerome D. Travers	Miss Margaret Curtis
1908	Fred McLeod	Jerome D. Travers	Miss Katherine C. Harley
1909	George Sargent	Robert A. Gardner	Miss Dorothy I. Campbell
1910	Alex Smith	William C. Fownes, Jr.	Miss Dorothy I. Campbell
1911	John J. McDermott	Harold H. Hilton	Miss Margaret Curtis
1912	John J. McDermott	Jerome D. Travers	Miss Margaret Curtis

Year	U.S. Open	U.S. Amateur	U.S. Women's Amateur
1913	Francis Ouimet	Jerome D. Travers	Miss Gladys Ravenscroft
1914	Walter Hagen	Francis Ouimet	Mrs. H. Arnold Jackson
1915	Jerome D. Travers	Robert A. Gardner	Mrs. C. H. Vanderbeck
1916	Charles Evans, Jr.	Charles Evans, Jr.	Miss Alexa Stirling
1917	*No tournament held*	*No tournament held*	*No tournament held*
1918	*No tournament held*	*No tournament held*	*No tournament held*
1919	Walter Hagen	S. Davidson Herron	Miss Alexa Stirling
1920	Edward Ray	Charles Evans, Jr.	Miss Alexa Stirling
1921	James M. Barnes	Jesse P. Guilford	Miss Marion Hollins
1922	Gene Sarazen	Jess W. Sweetser	Miss Glenna Collett
1923	Robert T. Jones, Jr.	Max R. Marston	Miss Edith Cummings
1924	Cyril Walker	Robert T. Jones, Jr.	Mrs. Dorothy Campbell Hurd
1925	Willie Macfarlane	Robert T. Jones, Jr.	Miss Glenna Collett
1926	Robert T. Jones, Jr.	George Von Elm	Mrs. G. Henry Stetson
1927	Thomas D. Armour	Robert T. Jones, Jr.	Mrs. Miriam Burns Horn
1928	Johnny Farrell	Robert T. Jones, Jr.	Miss Glenna Collett
1929	Robert T. Jones, Jr.	Harrison R. Johnston	Miss Glenna Collett
1930	Robert T. Jones, Jr.	Robert T. Jones, Jr.	Miss Glenna Collett
1931	Billy Burke	Francis Ouimet	Miss Helen Hicks
1932	Gene Sarazen	C. Ross Somerville	Miss Virginia Van Wie
1933	John G. Goodman	George T. Dunlap, Jr.	Miss Virginia Van Wie
1934	Olin Dutra	W. Lawson Little, Jr.	Miss Virginia Van Wie
1935	Sam Parks, Jr.	W. Lawson Little, Jr.	Mrs. Edwin Vare, Jr.
1936	Tony Manero	John W. Fischer	Miss Pamela Barton
1937	Ralph Guldahl	John G. Goodman	Mrs. Julius A. Page, Jr.
1938	Ralph Guldahl	William P. Turnesa	Miss Patty Berg
1939	Byron Nelson	Marvin H. Ward	Miss Betty Jameson
1940	W. Lawson Little, Jr.	Richard D. Chapman	Miss Betty Jameson
1941	Craig Wood	Marvin H. Ward	Mrs. Frank Newell

Winners of the P.G.A. Championship

1916	JAMES M. BARNES	1929	LEO DIEGEL
1917	*No tournament held*	1930	THOMAS D. ARMOUR
1918	*No tournament held*	1931	TOM CREAVY
1919	JAMES M. BARNES	1932	OLIN DUTRA
1920	JOCK HUTCHISON	1933	GENE SARAZEN
1921	WALTER HAGEN	1934	PAUL RUNYAN
1922	GENE SARAZEN	1935	JOHNNY REVOLTA
1923	GENE SARAZEN	1936	DENNY SHUTE
1924	WALTER HAGEN	1937	DENNY SHUTE
1925	WALTER HAGEN	1938	PAUL RUNYAN
1926	WALTER HAGEN	1939	HENRY PICARD
1927	WALTER HAGEN	1940	BYRON NELSON
1928	LEO DIEGEL	1941	VIC GHEZZI

Winners of the Masters

1934	HORTON SMITH
1935	GENE SARAZEN
1936	HORTON SMITH
1937	BYRON NELSON
1938	HENRY PICARD
1939	RALPH GULDAHL
1940	JIMMY DEMARET
1941	CRAIG WOOD

American Winners of the British Open Championship

1921	JOCK HUTCHISON
1922	WALTER HAGEN
1924	WALTER HAGEN
1925	JAMES M. BARNES
1926	ROBERT T. JONES, JR.
1927	ROBERT T. JONES, JR.
1928	WALTER HAGEN
1929	WALTER HAGEN
1930	ROBERT T. JONES, JR.
1931	THOMAS D. ARMOUR
1932	GENE SARAZEN
1933	DENNY SHUTE

American Winners of the British Amateur Championship

1904	WALTER J. TRAVIS
1926	JESS SWEETSER
1930	ROBERT T. JONES, JR.
1934	W. LAWSON LITTLE, JR.
1935	W. LAWSON LITTLE, JR.
1937	ROBERT SWEENY
1938	CHARLES YATES

The Walker Cup

1922	U.S. 8, G.B. 4
1923	U.S. 6, G.B. 5
1924	U.S. 9, G.B. 3
1926	U.S. 6, G.B. 5
1928	U.S. 11, G.B. 1
1930	U.S. 10, G.B. 2
1932	U.S. 8, G.B. 1
1934	U.S. 9, G.B. 2
1936	U.S. 9, G.B. 0
1938	G.B. 7, U.S. 4

The Ryder Cup

1927	U.S. 9 ½, G.B. 2 ½
1929	G.B. 7, U.S. 5
1931	U.S. 9, G.B. 3
1933	G.B. 6 ½, U.S. 5 ½
1935	U.S. 9, G.B. 3
1937	U.S. 8, G.B. 4

The Curtis Cup

1932	U.S. 5 ½, G.B. 3 ½
1934	U.S. 6 ½, G.B. 2 ½
1936	U.S. 4 ½, G.B. 4 ½
1938	U.S. 5 ½, G.B. 3 ½

PICTURE CREDITS

The sources for the illustrations are listed below. Credits from right to left are separated by semicolons; from top to bottom by dashes.

Front cover: Bobby Jones 1928 portrait, ©Bettman/CORBIS.
Back cover: Glenna Collett and Joyce Wethered, courtesy of Ned Vare, Guilford, CT.
12: Phil Sheldon.
16: Phil Sheldon.
17: from *The Badminton Library*: *Golf* by Horace Hutchinson, published by Longmans, Green, and Co., London, 1893.
22: Courtesy USGA. All Rights Reserved.
24: The Scottish National Portrait Gallery.
25: from *The Badminton Library*: *Golf* by Horace Hutchinson, published by Longmans, Green, and Co., London, 1893.
26: Hobbs Golf Collection.
28: The Scottish National Portrait Gallery.
29: Courtesy USGA. All Rights Reserved.
30: Hobbs Golf Collection.
34: Courtesy USGA. All Rights Reserved.
36: from *The Badminton Library*: *Golf* by Horace Hutchinson, published by Longmans, Green, and Co., London, 1893.
38: Chicago Golf Club, Chicago, IL.
39: Phil Sheldon.
40: The Scottish National Portrait Gallery.
42: from *The Badminton Library*: *Golf* by Horace Hutchinson, published by Longmans, Green, and Co., London, 1893.
46: from *The American Golfer*, January 1936, published by Condé Nast Publications, Inc.
49: Hobbs Golf Collection.
52: Library of Congress, Prints and Photographs Division [LC-USZC2-515].
53: H.P. Harrington, courtesy of the Ralph W. Miller Golf Library.
54: Courtesy USGA. All Rights Reserved.
55: Hobbs Golf Collection; Courtesy USGA. All Rights Reserved—Archive Photos.
57: both, Tufts Archives of the Given Memorial Library.
58: Tufts Archives of the Given Memorial Library.

61: Courtesy of Dr. William G. Anderson.
63: from *The Badminton Library*: *Golf* by Horace Hutchinson, published by Longmans, Green, and Co., London, 1893.
65: from *Golf Courses of the British Isles* by Bernard Darwin with illustrations by Harry Rountree, published by Duckworth & Co., Convent Garden, 1910.
71: Patent Number 723, 534. Golf-Club. Arthur F. Knight, Schenectady, NY.
74: Phil Sheldon.
76: Brown Brothers.
78: Corbis/Bettman-UPI.
81: Phil Sheldon.
84: Phil Sheldon.
86: Hobbs Golf Collection.
89: Library of Congress, Prints and Photographs Division [LC-USZ62-102326].
93: Allsport Hulton Deutsch/ALLSPORT.
96: Library of Congress, Prints and Photographs Division; Allsport Hulton Deutsch/ALLSPORT—Courtesy of Michael J. Hurdzan—Courtesy of Dr. William G. Anderson.
100: both, Phil Sheldon.
101: Phil Sheldon; Library of Congress, Prints and Photographs Division [LC-USZ62-100345]—Library of Congress, Prints and Photographs Division [LC-USZ62-102329].
106: Courtesy USGA. All Rights Reserved.
115: ©Bettman/CORBIS.
117: Hobbs Golf Collection.
119: from *Golf: Scotland's Game* by David Hamilton, published by The Partwick Press, Kilmacolm, 1998.
121: from *The American Golfer*, March 1935, published by Condé Nast Publications, Inc.
125: ©Bettman/CORBIS.
126: ©Bettman/CORBIS.
129: J.P. Graham, courtesy of the Ralph W. Miller Golf Library.
132: ©Bettman/CORBIS.
135: Phil Sheldon.
138: Corbis/Bettman-UPI.
140: ©Bettman/CORBIS.
141: Courtesy of Western Golf Association.

146: ©Bettman/CORBIS.

148: Courtesy USGA. All Rights Reserved.

151: ©Bettman/CORBIS.

152: Courtesy of the Ralph W. Miller Golf Library.

153: ©Underwood & Underwood/CORBIS.

154: Corbis/Bettman-UPI.

156: D. Scott Chisholm, courtesy of the Ralph W. Miller Golf Library.

158: ©Bettman/CORBIS.

162: Corbis/Bettman.

168: Courtesy of the Ralph W. Miller Golf Library.

171: Phil Sheldon.

173: Corbis/Bettman-UPI.

174: Courtesy USGA. All Rights Reserved.

181: AP/Wide World Photos.

182: from *The Encyclopedia of Golf* by Nevin H. Gibson, published by A.S. Barnes and Company, New York, 1958.

187: AP/Wide World Photos.

188: Courtesy of the Ralph W. Miller Golf Library.

191: from *Bobby Jones Flicker Book*, published by The American Golfer, 135 East Putnam Avenue, Greenwich, CT 06830.

195: Ray Fardy, courtesy of the Ralph W. Miller Golf Library.

199: Phil Sheldon.

206: Special Collections Department, R.W. Woodruft Library, Emory University.

209: Pebble Beach Archives.

210: Sidney L. Matthew Golf Collection.

214: from *The World of Golf* by Charles Price, published by Random House, New York, 1962.

216: from *Golf Illustrated*, November 1929, published by Golf Illustrated, Inc.

217: from *The Fairway*, June 1929, published by Fairway Publishing Company, Inc.

218: D. Scott Chisholm, courtesy of the Ralph W. Miller Golf Library.

219: The Pat Hathaway Collection.

220: Hobbs Golf Collection.

223: Courtesy of the Ralph W. Miller Golf Library.

225: from *The American Golfer*, November 1929, published by Condé Nast Publications, Inc.

226: from *Golf Illustrated*, December 1929, published by Golf Illustrated, Inc.

229: J.P. Graham, courtesy of the Ralph W. Miller Golf Library.

230: ©Bettman/CORBIS.

233: Courtesy of Ned Vare, Guilford, CT.

235: Ray Fardy, courtesy of the Ralph W. Miller Golf Library.

237: Courtesy of Ned Vare, Guilford, CT.

238: ©Bettman/CORBIS.

240: Courtesy of Ned Vare, Guilford, CT.

242: ©Bettman/CORBIS.

243: Hobbs Golf Collection.

244: ©Bettman/CORBIS.

249: ©Bettman/CORBIS.

252: Phil Sheldon.

256: AP/Wide World Photos; Phil Sheldon—AP/Wide World Photos.

257: Corbis/Bettman-UPI— from *The World of Golf* by Charles Price, published by Random House, New York, 1962.

261: ©Bettman/CORBIS—Courtesy of the Ralph W. Miller Golf Library.

263: The Illustrated London News Picture Library—AP/Wide World Photos.

264: Corbis/Bettman-UPI.

265: Corbis/Bettman-UPI.

268: AP/Wide World Photos.

269: ©Underwood & Underwood/CORBIS.

271: ©Bettman/CORBIS.

274: Phil Sheldon.

279: Corbis/Bettman-UPI.

282: Courtesy of the Ralph W. Miller Golf Library.

284: Courtesy USGA. All Rights Reserved.

290: ©Bettman/CORBIS.

293: The Illustrated London News Picture Library.

297: Courtesy USGA. All Rights Reserved.

299: ©Bettman/CORBIS.

310: AP/Wide World Photos.

319: ©Bettman/CORBIS.

320: ©Bettman/CORBIS.

323: Corbis/Bettman-UPI.

325: AP/Wide World Photos.

332: Courtesy of the Ralph W. Miller Golf Library.

334: ©Bettman/CORBIS.

339: ©Bettman/CORBIS.

340: AP/Wide World Photos.

344: Corbis/Bettman-UPI.

346: Lester Nehamkin, courtesy of the Ralph W. Miller Golf Library.

349: Courtesy of Ned Vare, Guilford, CT.

353: AP/Wide World Photos.

355: The Illustrated London News Picture Library.

360: AP/Wide World Photos.

362: Corbis/Bettman-UPI.

366: ©Bettman/CORBIS.

369: Courtesy, Fort Worth Star-Telegram Photograph Collection, The University of Texas at Arlington Libraries, Arlington, Texas.

INDEX

ABOUT THE AUTHOR

Herbert Warren Wind, America's foremost golf writer, was on the staff of *The New Yorker* magazine from 1947 to 1991, with the exception of several years in the 1950s when he left to help launch a new weekly, *Sports Illustrated.* He is the author of numerous books, many of which are derived from his articles. In addition, Wind collaborated with golfing great Ben Hogan to produce the perennially best-selling instruction book, *The Modern Fundamentals of Golf.*

In 1995, Wind received the Bob Jones Award, given by the United States Golf Association, for distinguished contributions to the game of golf; he is the only writer to receive the award.

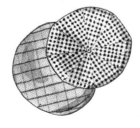